THE FIFA WOMEN'S
WORLD CUP
1991-2019
– *a statistical record*

Dirk Karsdorp

British Library Cataloguing in Publication Data
A catalogue record for this book is available from the British Library

ISBN: 978-1-86223-411-6

Copyright © 2019, SOCCER BOOKS LIMITED (01472 696226)
72 St. Peter's Avenue, Cleethorpes, N.E. Lincolnshire, DN35 8HU, England
Web site   www.soccer-books.co.uk
e-mail   info@soccer-books.co.uk

Printed in the UK by 4edge Ltd.

AN INTRODUCTION TO
THE FIFA WOMEN'S WORLD CUP

Although the first World Cup for men was organised by FIFA in 1930, the creation of a similar competition for women wasn't considered for many years. This is not perhaps surprising in view of the attitude to women's football in many countries for much of the 20th Century. In the present, it is hard to believe that the English Football Association only lifted a 50-year ban on women's teams playing on their members' pitches as late as 1971!

Taking this into account, it is perhaps understandable that, although women's football had become very popular in many countries over the years, it wasn't until June 1988 that FIFA organised an invitational tournament in China as a test to see if a Women's World Cup competition would be viable. Twelve national teams took part in this invitational competition – four from UEFA, three from AFC, two from CONCACAF and one each from CONMEBOL, CAF and OFC. The matches were played between 1st and 12th June and, such was the success of the tournament, FIFA approved the establishment of an official Women's World Cup a little over two weeks later, on 30th June 1988! It was decided that the inaugural Women's World Cup was to take place in 1991, with China once again hosting the finals tournament. Twelve teams competed in the 1991 finals (following a qualification process which whittled down the 48 countries to enter the competition), and the United States beat Norway 2-1 in the Final to be crowned the first Women's World Champions. Since then, the scope of the competition has continued to grow with 16 teams competing in the 1999 finals tournament (with 67 countries in the qualifiers) and 24 finalists in 2019 (with 143 countries in the qualifiers).

This book covers the matches played in each of the seven Women's FIFA World Cup competitions held between 1991 and 2019. Complete and comprehensive statistics are included for each of the 286 finals games played during this period. Additionally, the date and result of all qualification games are also included in this book, with the scorers included where known. It should be noted that the six confederations (UEFA, CONMEBOL, CONCACAF, AFC, CAF and the OFC) have generally doubled up to use their continental championships as the qualifiers for the Women's World Cup. Unfortunately, it has only proved possible to locate the results for the 1991 and 1995 CAF African Women's Championship from the quarter-final stages onwards but subsequent years and those for the other continental confederations are complete.

A series of sister publications containing complete statistics for the men's FIFA World Cup competitions from 1930 through to 2018 is also published by Soccer Books. These include all qualification matches in addition to the finals matches.

Details of all of our World Cup titles as well as many other statistical books can be found on the back cover of this publication.

FIRST EDITION FIFA WOMEN'S WORLD CUP 1991

QUALIFYING TOURNAMENTS

CAF AFRICAN WOMEN'S CHAMPIONSHIP 1991

Only the winner of the CAF African Women's Championship 1991 tournament will qualify for the FIFA Women's World Cup 1991

QUARTER-FINALS

16.02.1991   National Stadium, Lagos: Nigeria – Ghana 5-1
Goals: Uche, ... / ...
03.03.1991   Accra Sports Stadium: Ghana – Nigeria 1-2

Senegal withdrew, **Guinea** advanced.
Zimbabwe withdrew, **Zambia** advanced.
Congo withdrew, **Cameroon** advanced.

SEMI-FINALS

04.05.1991   National Stadium, Lagos: Nigeria – Guinea 3-0
19.05.1991   Stade du 28 Septembre, Conakry: Guinea – Nigeria 0-4

Zambia withdrew, **Cameroon** advanced.

FINALS

15.06.1991   National Stadium, Lagos: Nigeria – Cameroon 2-0
30.06.1991   Stade Ahmadou Ahidjo, Yaoundé: Cameroon – Nigeria 0-4

Nigeria qualified for the FIFA Women's World Cup 1991.

AFC ASIAN WOMEN'S CHAMPIONSHIP 1991

The winner, runners-up and third place of the AFC Asian Women's Championship 1991 tournament will qualify for the FIFA Women's World Cup 1991. The tournament was held in Fukuoka, Japan from 26 May to 8 June 1991.

GROUP STAGE
GROUP A

29.05.1991   China PR – Chinese Taipei 3-0 (2-0)
Goals: Shui Qingxia (13), Sun Qingmei (40), Niu Lijie (67)
29.05.1991   Thailand – South Korea 3-0 (2-0)
Goals: Sunee Kridsanachandee (32), Prapa Bourthong (42), Anchalee Khaolaung (66)

5

31.05.1991   Chinese Taipei – South Korea 9-0
Goals: Huang Yu-Chung (3, 32, 49), …
31.05.1991   China PR – Thailand 10-1
Goals: Niu Lijie (27, 28, 41, 76), … / …
02.06.1991   Chinese Taipei – Thailand 0-0
02.06.1991   China PR – South Korea 10-0

Team	Pld	W	D	L	GF	GA	GD	Pts
China PR	3	3	0	0	23	1	+22	6
Chinese Taipei	3	1	1	1	9	3	+6	3
Thailand	3	1	1	1	4	10	-6	3
South Korea	3	0	0	3	0	22	-22	0

GROUP B

26.05.1991   Hong Kong – Singapore 2-0 (1-0)
Goals: Chan Shuk-Chi (16, 51)
26.05.1991   Japan – North Korea 1-0 (0-0)
Goal: Kaori Nagamine (66)
28.05.1991   Japan – Hong Kong 4-1
Goals: Takako Tezuka, Kaori Nagamine, Asako Takakura / Law Ka-Lai (17)
28.05.1991   North Korea – Malaysia 12-0
Goals: Yang Mi-sun, …
30.05.1991   North Korea – Hong Kong 5-0
30.05.1991   Malaysia – Singapore 1-0
01.06.1991   North Korea – Singapore 8-0
Goals: Yang Mi-sun, …
01.06.1991   Japan – Malaysia 12-0
Goals: Takako Tezuka, Etsuko Handa, Kaori Nagamine, Akemi Noda,
Yuriko Mizuma, …
03.06.1991   Japan – Singapore 10-0
Goals: Riko Matsuda, Takako Tezuka, Akemi Noda, Asako Takakura,
Sayuri Yamaguchi, Tamaki Uchiyama, …
03.06.1991   Jong Kong – Malaysia 0-0

Team	Pld	W	D	L	GF	GA	GD	Pts
Japan	4	4	4	4	27	1	+26	8
North Korea	4	3	0	1	25	1	+24	6
Hong Kong	4	1	1	2	3	9	-6	3
Malaysia	4	1	1	2	1	24	-23	3
Singapore	4	0	0	4	0	21	-21	0

SEMI-FINALS

06.06.1991   China PR – North Korea 1-0 (1-0)
Goal: Zhang Yan (16)
06.06.1991   Japan – Chinese Taipei 0-0
Japan won after extra time on penalties (5:4).

6

THIRD PLACE PLAY-OFF

08.06.1991   Chinese Taipei – North Korea 0-0
Chinese Taipei won after extra time on penalties (5:4).

FINAL

08.06.1991   China PR – Japan 5-0

China PR, Japan and **Chinese Taipei** qualified for the FIFA Women's World Cup 1991.

UEFA EUROPEAN WOMEN'S CHAMPIONSHIP 1991

The qualification was held between 9 September 1989 and 12 December 1990.
Quarter finals winners will qualify for the FIFA Women's World Cup 1991.

GROUP STAGE
GROUP 1

18.11.1989   Hoornseveld, Koog aan de Zaan:
             Netherlands – Republic of Ireland 2-0 (1-0)
Goals: Vestjens (33 pen, 78 pen)
09.12.1989   Clandeboye Park, Bangor:
             Northern Ireland – Republic of Ireland 1-2 (1-1)
Goals: O'Neill (42) / Reynolds (43, 78)
19.03.1990   Solitude, Belfast: Northern Ireland – Netherlands 0-6 (0-5)
Goals: de Bakker (5, 13), Pauw (26), Limbeek (26), Timisela (29, 72)
29.04.1990   Dalymount Park, Dublin: Republic of Ireland – Netherlands 0-0
22.09.1990   Eikendijk, Kaatsheuvel: Netherlands – Norhtern Ireland 9-0 (3-0)
Goals: de Bakker (1, 2, 46, 49), Geeris (3), Limbeek (47), van Waarden (48),
Baal (50), Vestjens (51)
07.10.1990   Belfield Park, Dublin: Republic of Ireland – Northern Ireland 4-0 (4-0)
Goals: Scanlan (2, 43), Cross (5), Williams (45)

Team	Pld	W	D	L	GF	GA	GD	Pts
Netherlands	*4*	*3*	*1*	*0*	*17*	*0*	*+17*	*7*
Republic of Ireland	4	2	1	1	6	3	+3	5
Northern Ireland	4	0	0	4	1	21	-20	0

GROUP 2

15.10.1989   Knurów: Poland – France 1-3 (0-2)
Goals: Makowska (59 pen) / Musset (19), Jézéquel (38), Mismacq (49)
22.10.1989   Olympia, Helsingborg: Sweden – Poland 4-1
Goals: Fahlström, Karlsson, Carlsson, Videkull / Gospodazyk
13.05.1990   Stade Municipal, Melun: France – Sweden 0-2 (0-0)
Goals: Sundhage (60 pen, 67)

7

19.06.1990   Stadium OSiR, Gorzów: Poland – Sweden 0-2
Goals: Vikedull, Sundhage
29.09.1990   Creutzwald, Metz: France – Poland 2-0 (2-0)
Goals: Le Boulch (16), Mismacq (19)
14.10.1990   Lekevi IP, Mariestad: Sweden – France 4-1 (2-0)
Goals: Stålklint (19), Vikedull (38), Fahlström (48), Sundhage (79) / Jézéquel (75)

Team	Pld	W	D	L	GF	GA	GD	Pts
Sweden	4	4	0	0	12	2	+10	8
France	4	2	0	2	6	7	-1	4
Poland	4	0	0	4	2	11	-9	0

GROUP 3

09.09.1989   Varkauden Keskuskanttä, Varkaus: Finland – Norway 0-1 (0-1)
Goal: Grude (27 pen)
01.10.1989   Griffin Park, Brentford: England – Finland 0-0
15.10.1989   Gjemselund Stadion, Kongsvinger: Norway – Belgium 4-0 (3-0)
Goals: Haugen (32), Strædet (43, 76), Støre (45)
17.03.1990   Het Minneplein, Ypres: Belgium – England 0-3 (0-2)
Goals: Powell (32, 39), Sempare (66)
07.04.1990   Hillsborough Stadium, Sheffield: England – Belgium 1-0 (0-0)
Goal: Coultard (63)
12.05.1990   Taplolan Urheilupuisto, Espoo: Finland – Belgium 3-0 (2-0)
Goal: Toikka (8), Rautiainen (20 pen), Ojala (69)
27.05.1990   Klepp Stadion, Klepp: Norway – England 2-0 (0-0)
Goals: Medalen (51), Haugen (76)
13.06.1990   Kjølnes Stadion, Porsgrunn: Norway – Finland 4-0 (1-0)
Goals: Hegstad (1), Carlsen (60), Støre (61, 75)
02.09.1990   Old Trafford, Manchester: England – Norway 0-0
27.09.1990   Stadion Jos Van Wellen, Kapellen: Belgium – Norway 0-1 (0-1)
Goal: Zaborowski (34)
29.09.1990   Ratina Stadion Tampere: Finland – England 0-0
13.10.1990   Stade Joseph Marien, Brussels: Belgium – Finland 1-0 (0-0)
Goal: van Laethem (52)

Team	Pld	W	D	L	GF	GA	GD	Pts
Norway	6	5	1	0	12	0	+12	11
England	6	2	3	1	4	2	+2	7
Finland	6	1	2	3	3	6	-3	4
Belgium	6	1	0	5	1	12	-11	2

GROUP 4

01.10.1989   Straubing Stadium, Straubing: Germany – Hungary 0-0
14.10.1989   Czechoslovakia – Bulgaria 2-0
28.10.1989   Bulgaria – Hungary 0-3

8

22.11.1989   Georg-Gaßmann-Stadion, Marburg:
Germany – Czechoslovakia 5-0 (3-0)
Goals: Unsleber (14), Mohr (34, 75), Bindl (35), Neid (46)
11.04.1990   Georgi Asparuhov Stadium, Sofia: Bulgaria – Germany 1-4 0-2)
Goals: Georgieva (69) / Lohn (9), Mohr (39), Damm (67), Unsleber (88)
29.04.1990   Stovky, Frydek-Mistek: Czechoslovakia – Germany 0-1 (0-0)
Goal: Nardenbach (46)
26.05.1990   Hungary – Czechoslovakia 2-0
09.06.1990   Hungary – Bulgaria 2-0
26.09.1990   Rheinstadion, Düseldorf: Germany – Bulgaria 4-0 (1-0)
Goals: Unsleber (18), Neid (46, 52), Mohr (76)
29.09.1990   Czechoslovakia – Hungary 3-0
14.10.1990   Sopron Stadion, Sopron: Hungary – Germany 0-4 (0-4)
Goals: Unsleber (4), Voss (27), Lohn (32), Wiegmann (44 pen)
14.10.1990   Bulgaria – Czechoslovakia 2-3

Team	Pld	W	D	L	GF	GA	GD	Pts
Germany	6	5	1	0	18	1	+17	11
Hungary	6	3	1	2	7	7	0	7
Czechoslovakia	6	3	0	3	8	10	-2	6
Bulgaria	6	0	0	6	3	18	-15	0

GROUP 5

14.10.1989   Wankdorfstadion, Bern: Switzerland – Denmark 0-4 (0-1)
Goals: H.Jensen (25, 63), Obel (71), Nissen (73)
04.11.1989   Campo Municipal Torre San Vicente, Benicàssim:
Spain – Switzerland 0-0
25.11.1989   Estadio El Maulí, Antequera: Spain – Denmark 1-3
Goals: … / H.Jensen, Rotbøll, J.Hansen
02.12.1989   Stadio Mirabello, Reggio Emilia: Italy – Switzerland 4-1 (3-0)
Goals: Morace (20), Carta (37), Mariotti (41), Baldelli (50) / Spinner (78)
10.02.1990   Stadio San Ciro, Portici: Italy – Spain 3-1 (1-0)
Goals: Ferraguzzi (32), Morace (53, 73) / Artola (81)
07.04.1990   Stadio Cornaredo, Lugano: Switzerland – Italy 0-4 (0-3)
Goals: Morace (23, 35), Marsiletti (43), Saldi (64)
28.04.1990   Vejle Stadion, Vejle: Denmark – Italy 1-0 (1-0)
Goal: H.Jensen (40)
02.05.1990   Spiegelfeld, Binningen: Switzerland – Spain 2-1 (2-0)
Goals: L.Käser (26), Gubler (44) / Á.Jiménez (75)
23.05.1990   Vejle Stadion, Vejle: Denmark – Switzerland 4-0 (2-0)
Goals: H.Jensen (4, 11), Rotbøll (67), Thychosen (79)
13.06.1990   Vejle Stadion, Vejle: Denmark – Spain 5-0 (2-0)
Goals: H.Jensen (12, 50), Rotbøll (15), Gam-Pedersen (74), Kolding (80)
06.10.1990   Stadio Comunale di Oristano, Oristano: Italy – Denmark 1-1 (0-1)
Goals: Ferraguzzi (51 pen) / Bagge (12)
21.10.1990   Estadio Cartagonova, Cartagena: Spain – Italy 0-0

Team	Pld	W	D	L	GF	GA	GD	Pts
Denmark	*6*	*5*	*1*	*0*	*18*	*2*	*+16*	*11*
Italy	*6*	*3*	*2*	*1*	*12*	*4*	*+8*	*8*
Switzerland	6	1	1	4	3	17	-14	3
Spain	6	0	2	4	3	13	-10	2

QUARTER FINALS

14.11.1990   Kristiansand Stadion, Kristiansand: Norway – Hungary 2-1
Goals: Stenberg, Riise / ...
18.11.1990   Malmö Stadion, Malmö: Sweden – Italy 1-1 (1-1)
Goals: Sundhage (19) / Carta (43)
24.11.1990   Vejle Stadion, Vejle: Denamrk – Netherlands 0-0
25.11.1990   Adams Park, Wycombe: England – Germany 1-4 (1-3)
Goals: K.Walker (28) / Mohr (18, 37, 54), Lohn (34)
25.11.1990   Promontor utcai Stadion, Budapest: Hungary – Norway 0-2
Goals: Bakken, Haugen
08.12.1990   Stadio Romeo Mente, Castellammare di Stabia: Italy – Sweden 0-0
08-12.1990   Sportpark De Molendijk, Denekamp:
             Netherlands – Denmark 0-1 (0-0, 0-0) (a.e.t.)
Goal: Rotbøll (95)
16.12.1990   Ruhrstadion, Bochum: Germany – England 2-0 (1-0)
Goals: Unsleber (34, 80)

SEMI-FINALS

10.07.1991   Hjørring Stadium, Hjørring: Norway – Denmark 0-0
Norway won after extra time on penalties (8:7).
11.07.1991   Frederikshavn Stadion, Frederikshavn: Germany – Italy 3-0 (1-0)
Goals: Mohr (30, 58), Raith (60)

THIRD PLACE PLAY-OFF

14.07.1991   Aalborg Stadion, Aalborg: Denmark – Italy 2-1 (1-0, 1-1) (a.e.t.)
Goals: H.Jensen (22), Furlotti (85 og) / Fiorini (68)

FINAL

14.07.1991   Aalborg Stadion, Aalborg: Germany – Norway 3-1 (0-0, 1-1) (a.e.t.)
Goals: Mohr (62, 100), Neid (110) / Hegstad (54)

Germany, **Norway**, **Denmark**, **Italy** and **Sweden** (best quarter final loser) qualified
for the FIFA Women's World Cup 1991.

10

CONCACAF WOMEN'S CHAMPIONSHIP 1991

The North, Central America & Caribbean (CONCACAF) tournament took place in Port-au-Prince, Haiti in April 1991. Only the winner of the tournament will qualify for the FIFA Women's World Cup 1991.

GROUP STAGE
GROUP A

18.04.1991   Stade Sylvio Cator, Port-au-Prince: United States – Mexico 12-0 (7-0)
Goals: Hamm (8), Akers (10, 25), Heinrichs (21, 36), Foudy (28), Chastain (40, 43, 47, 66, 74), Jennings (77)
18.04.1991   Stade Sylvio Cator, Port-au-Prince:
      Martinique – Trinidad and Tobago 1-1
20.04.1991   Stade Sylvio Cator, Port-au-Prince: Trinidad and Tobago – Mexico 3-1
20.04.1991   Stade Sylvio Cator, Port-au-Prince: United States – Martinique 12-0
Goals: Heinrichs (3x), Akers (2x), Hamm (2x), Biefeld (2x), Foudy, Gebauer, Chastain
22.04.1991   Stade Sylvio Cator, Port-au-Prince: Martinique – Mexico 1-8
22.04.1991   Stade Sylvio Cator, Port-au-Prince:
      United States – Trinidad and Tobago 10-0
Goals: Hamm (2x), Jennings (2x), Gebauer (2x), Akers (2x), Bates, Chastain

Team	Pld	W	D	L	GF	GA	GD	Pts
United States	3	3	0	0	34	0	+34	6
Trinidad and Tobago	3	1	1	1	4	12	-8	3
Mexico	3	1	0	2	9	16	-7	2
Martinique	3	0	1	2	2	21	-19	1

GROUP B

16.04.1991   Stade Sylvio Cator, Port-au-Prince: Canada – Costa Rica 6-0
Goals: Hooper (2x), McEachern, Vamos, Gareau, Caron
17.04.1991   Stade Sylvio Cator, Port-au-Prince: Jamaica – Haiti 0-1
19.04.1991   Stade Sylvio Cator, Port-au-Prince: Canada – Jamaica 9-0
Goals: Hooper (4x), Gareau (3x), Mairs, ????? (og)
19.04.1991   Stade Sylvio Cator, Port-au-Prince: Haiti – Costa Rica 4-0
21.04.1991   Stade Sylvio Cator, Port-au-Prince: Jamaica – Costa Rica 1-2
Goals: ... / Alemán, Álvarez
21.04.1991   Stade Sylvio Cator, Port-au-Prince: Haiti – Canada 0-2
Goals: Hooper, Vamos

Team	Pld	W	D	L	GF	GA	GD	Pts
Canada	3	3	0	0	17	0	+17	6
Haiti	3	2	0	1	5	2	+3	4
Costa Rica	3	1	0	2	2	11	-9	2
Jamaica	3	0	0	3	1	12	-11	0

SEMI-FINALS

24.04.1991   Stade Sylvio Cator, Port-au-Prince: Canada – Trinidad and Tobago 6-0
Goals: Caron (3x), Vamos (2x), Cant
25.04.1991   Stade Sylvio Cator, Port-au-Prince: United States – Haiti 10-0
Goals: Heinrichs (2x), Akers (2x), Jennings (2x), Bates (2x), Lilly, Biefeld

THIRD PLACE PLAY-OFF

27.04.1991   Stade Sylvio Cator, Port-au-Prince: Trinidad and Tobago – Haiti 4-2

FINAL

28.04.1991   Stade Sylvio Cator, Port-au-Prince: Canada – United States 0-5 (0-3)
Goals: Akers (3, 13, 70), Lilly (15), Heinrichs (66)

United States qualified for the FIFA Women's World Cup 1991.

OFC WOMEN'S CHAMPIONSHIP 1991

The Oceania (OFC) tournament took place in Sydney, Australia in May 1991. Only the winner of the tournament will qualify for the FIFA Women's World Cup 1991.

xx.05.1991   Sydney: New Zealand – Papua New Guinea 16-0
17.05.1991   Sydney: New Zealand – Australia 1-0
19.05.1991   Sydney: Papua New Guinea – Australia 0-12
Goals: Hughes (4x), Iannotta (2x), Wass (2x), Gegenhuber, Tann, Barlett, ?????
xx.05.1991   Sydney: Papua New Guinea – New Zealand 0-11
23.05.1991   Sydney: Australia – New Zealand 1-0
Goal: Dodd
25.05.1991   Sydney: Papua New Guinea – Australia 0-8
Goals: Hughes (6x), Vinson (2x)

Team	Pld	W	D	L	GF	GA	GD	Pts
New Zealand	*4*	*3*	*0*	*1*	*28*	*1*	*+27*	*6*
Australia	4	3	0	1	21	1	+20	6
Papua New Guinea	4	0	0	4	0	47	-47	0

New Zealand qualified (by goal-difference) for the FIFA Women's World Cup 1991.

CONMEBOL SUDAMERICANO FEMENINO 1991

The South America (CONMEBOL) Sudamericano Femenino 1991 tournament was held in Maringá, Brazil between 28 April and 5 May 1991. Only the winner will qualify for the FIFA Women's World Cup 1991.

RESULTS

28.04.1991 Estádio Willie Davids, Maringá: Brazil – Chile 6-1
Goals: Roseli, Adriana (2x), Márcia Taffarel, Elane, Marisa / Ada Cruz
01.05.1991 Estádio Willie Davids, Maringá: Chile – Venezuela 1-0
05.05.1991 Estádio Willie Davids, Maringá: Brazil – Venezuela 6-1
Goals: Adriana (2x), ... / Infante
(To some sources the result was 5-1)

Team	Pld	W	D	L	GF	GA	GD	Pts
Brazil	*2*	*2*	*0*	*0*	*12*	*2*	*+10*	*4*
Chile	2	1	0	1	2	6	-4	2
Venezuela	2	0	0	2	1	7	-6	0

Brazil qualified for the FIFA Women's World Cup 1991.

FIFA WOMEN'S WORLD CUP FINAL TOURNAMENT IN CHINA PR 1991

GROUP STAGE
GROUP A

16.11.1991 Tianhe Stadium, Guangzhou: China PR – Norway 4-0 (1-0)
China PR: ZHONG Honglian, WEN Lirong, NIU Lijie, MA Li, LIU Ailing, ZHOU Yang, ZHOU Hua, SUN Qingmei, LI Xiufu, SUN Wen (70 ZHU Tao), WU Weiying (47 SHUI Qingxia). (Coach: SHANG Ruihua).
Norway: Reidun SETH, Linda MEDALEN, Tina SVENSSON, Gro ESPESETH (62 Anette IGLAND), Agnete CARLSEN, Gunn Lisbeth NYBORG, Hege RIISE, Tone HAUGEN, Heidi STØRE, Catherine ZABOROWSKI, Birthe HEGSTAD (59 Ellen SCHEEL). (Coach: Even PELLERUD).
Goals: MA Li (22), LIU Ailing (45, 50), SUN Qingmei (75)
Referee: Salvador IMPERATORE MARCONE (Chile)   Attendance: 65,000

17.11.1991 Tianhe Stadium, Guangzhou; Denmark – New Zealand 3-0 (2-0)
Denmark: Helle BJERREGAARD, Karina SEFRON, Jannie HANSEN, Bonny
MADSEN, Lisbet KOLDING (64 Lotte BAGGE), Susan MACKENSIE, Irene
STELLING, Marianne JENSEN, Helle JENSEN, Annie GAM-PEDERSEN, Hanne
NISSEN (54 Annette THYCHOSEN). (Coach: Keld GANTZHORN).
New Zealand: Leslie Catherine KING Moore, Jocelyn Edna PARR, Cinnamon June
CHANEY (41 Teresa Ann (Terry) McCAHILL), Kim Barbara NYE, Deborah Anne
PULLEN Kok, Maureen Dale JACOBSON, Monique Annette VAN DE ELZEN,
Donna Marie BAKER (54 Lorraine Robin TAYLOR), Julia Petryce CAMPBELL,
Wendi Judith HENDERSON, Amanda Anne CRAWFORD.
(Coach: Dave BOARDMAN).
Goals: Helle JENSEN (15, 40), Susan MACKENSIE (42)
Referee: Omer YENGO (Congo)   Attendance: 14,000

18.11.1991 Guangdong Provincial People's Stadium, Guangzhou:
          Norway – New Zealand 4-0 (3-0)
Norway: Reidun SETH, Linda MEDALEN (YC34), Tina SVENSSON, Agnete
CARLSEN, Gunn Lisbeth NYBORG, Hege RIISE, Tone HAUGEN (76 Margunn
HUMLESTØL Haugenes), Heidi STØRE, Catherine ZABOROWSKI, Liv
STRÆDET, Birthe HEGSTAD (59 Ellen SCHEEL). (Coach: Even PELLERUD).
New Zealand: Leslie Catherine KING Moore, Cinnamon June CHANEY (28 Lynley
Joy PEDRUCO Lucas), Kim Barbara NYE, Teresa Ann (Terry) McCAHILL,
Deborah Anne PULLEN Kok, Lorraine Robin TAYLOR, Maureen Dale JACOBSON,
Donna Marie BAKER, Julia Petryce CAMPBELL, Wendi Judith HENDERSON,
Amanda Anne CRAWFORD (45 Monique Annette VAN DE ELZEN).
(Coach: Dave BOARDMAN).
Goals: Teresa Ann (Terry) McCAHILL (30 og), Linda MEDALEN (32, 38),
Hege RIISE (49)
Referee: Salvador Imperatore MARCONE (Chile)   Attendance: 12,000

19.11.1991 Guangdong Provincial People's Stadium, Guangzhou:
          China PR – Denmark 2-2 (1-1)
China PR: ZHONG Honglian, WEN Lirong, NIU Lijie (71 WEI Haiying), MA Li,
LIU Ailing, ZHOU Yang, ZHOU Hua, SUN Qingmei, LI Xiufu (YC50), SUN Wen,
WU Weiying (59 ZHANG Yan). (Coach: SHANG Ruihua).
Denmark: Helle BJERREGAARD, Karina SEFRON, Jannie HANSEN, Bonny
MADSEN, Mette NIELSEN, Lisbet KOLDING, Susan MACKENSIE, Irene
STELLING, Helle JENSEN, Annie GAM-PEDERSEN, Hanne NISSEN (71 Lotte
BAGGE). (Coach: Keld GANTZHORN).
Goals: SUN Wen (37), WEI Haiying (76) / Lisbet KOLDING (24),
Hanne NISSEN (55)
Referee: Vassilios NIKKAKIS (Greece)   Attendance: 27,000

14

21.11.1991 New Plaza Stadium, Foshan: China PR – New Zealand 4-1 (3-0)
China PR: ZHONG Honglian, WEN Lirong, NIU Lijie, MA Li, LIU Ailing, ZHOU
Yang, ZHOU Hua, SUN Qingmei, LI Xiufu (28 SHUI Qingxia), SUN Wen, WU
Weiying (63 WEI Haiying). (Coach: SHANG Ruihua).
New Zealand: Leslie Catherine KING Moore, Lynley Joy PEDRUCO Lucas, Kim
Barbara NYE, Teresa Ann (Terry) McCAHILL, Deborah Anne PULLEN Kok,
Lorraine Robin TAYLOR, Maureen Dale JACOBSON, Monique Annette VAN DE
ELZEN, Donna Marie BAKER (26 Amanda Anne CRAWFORD), Lynne WARRING
(65 Julia Petryce CAMPBELL), Wendi Judith HENDERSON.
(Coach: Dave BOARDMAN).
Goals: ZHOU Yang (20), LIU Ailing (22, 60), WU Weiying (24) /
Kim Barbara NYE (65)
Referee: Gyanu Raja SHRESTA (Nepal) Attendance: 14,000

21.11.1991 Ying Dong Stadium, Panyu: Norway – Denmark 2-1 (1-0)
Norway: Reidun SETH, Linda MEDALEN (YC30) (62 Ellen SCHEEL), Tina
SVENSSON, Agnete CARLSEN, Gunn Lisbeth NYBORG (YC33), Hege RIISE,
Tone HAUGEN, Heidi STØRE, Catherine ZABOROWSKI, Liv STRÆDET (29 Gro
ESPESETH), Birthe HEGSTAD. (Coach: Even PELLERUD).
Denmark: Helle BJERREGAARD, Karina SEFRON, Jannie HANSEN, Bonny
MADSEN, Mette NIELSEN (41 Annette THYCHOSEN), Lisbet KOLDING, Susan
MACKENSIE, Irene STELLING, Helle JENSEN, Annie GAM-PEDERSEN, Hanne
NISSEN (50 Marianne JENSEN). (Coach: Keld GANTZHORN).
Goals: Tina SVENSSON (14 pen), Linda MEDALEN (56) / Annette THYCHOSEN
(54 pen)
Referee: Vadim ZHUK (USSR) Attendance: 15,500

Team	Pld	W	D	L	GF	GA	GD	Pts
China PR	3	2	1	0	10	3	+7	5
Norway	3	2	0	1	6	5	+1	4
Denmark	3	1	1	1	6	4	+2	3
New Zealand	3	0	0	3	1	11	-10	0

GROUP B

17.11.1991 New Plaza Stadium, Foshan: Japan – Brazil 0-1 (0-1)
Japan: Masae SUZUKI, Midori HONDA, Mayumi KAJI, Sayuri YAMAGUCHI,
Kyoko KURODA, Asako Takemoto TAKAKURA (52 Yuriko MIZUMA), Futaba
KIOKA, Kaori NAGAMINE, Michiko MATSUDA, Akemi NODA, Takako
TEZUKA. (Coach: Tamotsu SUZUKI).
Brazil: Margarete Maria Pioresan "MEG", ELANE dos Santos Rêgo (YC67), Rosilane
Camargo Mota "FANTA", MARISA Pires Nogueira (15 DORALICE Santos),
SOLANGE Santos Bastos, Maria Gomes de "ROSA" LIMA, MÁRCIA Honório da
SILVA, ROSÂNGELA ROCHA (YC79), MARIA Lúcia da Silva LIMA (YC58),
ROSELI de Belo, ADRIANA "VIOLA" Burke (70 CENIRA Sampaio Pereira do
Prado). (Coach: FERNANDO Luís Brederodes PIRES).
Goal: ELANE Rego dos Santos (4)
Referee: LU Jun (China PR) Attendance: 14,000

15

17.11.1991   Ying Dong Stadium, Panyu: Sweden – United States 2-3 (0-1)
Sweden: Elisabeth LEIDINGE, Malin LUNDGREN, Anette HANSSON, Camilla
FORS (54 Ingrid JOHANSSON), Lena VIDEKULL, Eva ZEIKFALVY, Malin
SWEDBERG, Marie KARLSSON (64 Helen NILSSON), Pia Mariane SUNDHAGE,
Anneli ANDELÉN, Helen JOHANSSON *(YC64)*. (Coach: Gunilla PAIJKULL).
United States: Mary HARVEY, Joy Lynn FAWCETT Biefeld, Carla Werden
OVERBECK, Debbie Belkin RADEMACHER, Kristine Marie LILLY Heavey (33
Linda HAMILTON), Julie Maurine FOUDY, Michelle Anne AKERS Stahl, Shannon
Danise HIGGINS Cirovski, Mariel Margaret (Mia) HAMM *(YC24)*, Carin
JENNINGS Gabarra, April HEINRICHS. (Coach: Anson DORRANCE).
Goals: Lena VIDEKULL (65), Ingrid JOHANSSON (71) / Carin JENNINGS Gabarra
(40, 49), Mariel Margaret (Mia) HAMM (62)
Referee: John TORO RENDÓN (Colombia)   Attendance: 14,000

19.11.1991   New Plaza Stadium, Foshan: Japan – Sweden 0-8 (0-6)
Japan: Masae SUZUKI, Midori HONDA, Mayumi KAJI, Sayuri YAMAGUCHI
(YC55), Kyoto KURODA, Asako Takemoto TAKAKURA, Futaba KIOKA, Kaori
NAGAMINE (67 Yuriko MIZUMA), Michiko MATSUDA, Akemi NODA, Takako
TEZUKA. (Coach: Tamotsu SUZUKI).
Sweden: Elisabeth LEIDINGE, Malin LUNDGREN, Anette HANSSON, Lena
VIDEKULL (41 Susanne HEDBERG), Eva ZEIKFALVY, Ingrid JOHANSSON,
Marie KARLSSON, Pia Mariane SUNDHAGE, Anneli ANDELÉN, Helen
NILSSON, Helen JOHANSSON (35 Camilla SVENSSON Gustafsson).
(Coach: Gunilla PAIJKULL).
Goals: Lena VIDEKULL (1, 11), Anneli ANDELÉN (15, 60), Malin LUNDGREN
(25), Helen NILSSON (27), Pia Mariane SUNDHAGE (35), Sayuri YAMAGUCHI
(70 og)
Referee: Gyanu Raja SHRESTA (Nepal)   Attendance: 14,000

19.11.1991   Ying Dong Stadium, Panyu: Brazil – United States 0-5 (0-4)
Brazil: Margarete Maria Pioresan "MEG", ELANE dos Santos Rêgo, Rosilane
Camargo Mota "FANTA", MARISA Pires Nogueira, SOLANGE Santos Bastos (39
DORALICE Santos), Maria Gomes de "ROSA" LIMA, CENIRA Sampaio Pereira do
Prado, MÁRCIA Honório da SILVA, MARILZA Martins da SILVA (46 Delma
Gonçalves "PRETINHA"), ROSELI de Belo *(YC70)*, Lunalva Torres de Almeida
"NALVINHA". (Coach: FERNANDO Luís Brederodes PIRES).
United States: Mary HARVEY, Joy Lynn FAWCETT Biefeld, Carla Werden
OVERBECK, Linda HAMILTON, Kristine Marie LILLY Heavey (67 Debbie Belkin
RADEMACHER), Julie Maurine FOUDY, Michelle Anne AKERS Stahl, Shannon
Danise HIGGINS Cirovski, Mariel Margaret (Mia) HAMM, Carin JENNINGS
Gabarra, April HEINRICHS (41 Brandi Denise CHASTAIN).
(Coach: Anson DORRANCE).
Goals: April HEINRICHS (23, 35), Carin JENNINGS Gabarra (38), Michelle Anne
AKERS Stahl (39), Mariel Margaret (Mia) HAMM (63)
Referee: Vadim ZHUK (Belarus)   Attendance: 15,500

16

21.11.1991 New Plaza Stadium, Foshan: Japan – United States 0-3 (0-3)
Japan: Masae SUZUKI, Midori HONDA, Mayumi KAJI, Sayuri YAMAGUCHI, Kyoto KURODA, Asako Takemoto TAKAKURA (60 Etsuko HANDA), Futaba KIOKA, Kaori NAGAMINE, Michiko MATSUDA, Akemi NODA, Takako TEZUKA. (Coach: Tamotsu SUZUKI).
United States: Mary HARVEY, Carla Werden OVERBECK *(YC31)*, Linda HAMILTON, Lori Ann HENRY, Debbie Belkin RADEMACHER, Brandi Denise CHASTAIN, Julie Maurine FOUDY, Michelle Anne AKERS Stahl (41 Mariel Margaret (Mia) HAMM), Tracey LEONE Bates, Carin JENNINGS Gabarra (41 Kristine Marie LILLY Heavey), Wendy GEBAUER Palladino.
(Coach: Anson DORRANCE).
Goals: Michelle Anne AKERS Stahl (20, 37), Wendy GEBAUER Palladino (39)
Referee: John Jairo TORO RENDÓN (Colombia) Attendance: 14,000

21.11.1991 Ying Dong Stadium, Panyu: Brazil – Sweden 0-2 (0-1)
Brazil: Margarete Maria Pioresan "MEG", ELANE dos Santos Rêgo, Rosilane Camargo Mota "FANTA", MARISA Pires Nogueira, Maria Gomes de "ROSA" LIMA, DORALICE Santos, CENIRA Sampaio Pereira do Prado, MÁRCIA TAFFAREL, MÁRCIA Honório da SILVA (60 Delma Gonçalves "PRETINHA"), ROSELI de Belo, ADRIANA "VIOLA" Burke (62 Lunalva Torres de Almeida "NALVINHA"). (Coach: FERNANDO Luís Brederodes PIRES).
Sweden: Ing-Marie OLSSON, Camila FORS, Marie EWRELIUS, Camilla SVENSSON Gustafsson, Susanne HEDBERG, Malin SWEDBERG, Marie KARLSSON (41 Ingrid JOHANSSON), Pernilla LARSSON, Pia Mariane SUNDHAGE, Anneli ANDELÉN, Helen NILSSON. (Coach: Gunilla PAIJKULL).
Goals: Pia Mariane SUNDHAGE (42 pen), Susanne HEDBERG (56)
Referee: LU Jun (China PR) Attendance: 12,000

Team	Pld	W	D	L	GF	GA	GD	Pts
United States	*3*	*3*	*0*	*0*	*11*	*2*	*+9*	*6*
Sweden	*3*	*2*	*0*	*1*	*12*	*3*	*+9*	*4*
Brazil	3	1	0	2	1	7	-6	2
Japan	3	0	0	3	0	12	-12	0

GROUP C

17.11.1991 Jiangmen Stadium, Jiangmen: Germany – Nigeria 4-0 (3-0)
Germany: Marion ISBERT, Doris FITSCHEN, Birgitt AUSTERMÜHL, Jutta NARDENBACH, Silvia NEID (36 Roswitha BINDL), Martina VOSS-TECKLENBURG, Bettina WIEGMANN, Britta UNSLEBER (35 Frauke KUHLMANN), Petra DAMM, Heidi MOHR, Gudrun GOTTSCHLICH. (Coach: Gero BISANZ).
Nigeria: Ann CHIEJINE, Florence OMAGBEMI, Mavis OGUN, Omo-Love BRANCH, Phoebe EBIMIEKUMO, Diana NWAIWU, Nkiru OKOSIEME, Ann MUKORO, Ngozi UCHE (41 Chioma AJUNWA), Rita NWADIKE, Adaku OKOROAFOR (34 Gift SHOWEMIMO). (Coach: Johannes (Jo) BONFRERE).
Goals: Silvia NEID (16), Heidi MOHR (32, 34), Gudrun GOTTSCHLICH (57)
Referee: Rafael RODRÍGUEZ Medina (El Salvador) Attendance: 14,000

17

17.11.1991 Jiangmen Stadium, Jiangmen: Chinese Taipei – Italy 0-5 (0-3)
Chinese Taipei: HONG Li-Chyn, CHEN Shwu Ju, LO Chu-Yin, HSU Chia Cheng,
LAN Lan Fen, CHOU Tai Ying, SHIEH Su Jean, WU Su-Ching, LIN Mei Jih (49
WU Min Hsun), HUANG Yu Chuan (62 LIN Mei Chun), KO Chiao Lin.
(Coach: CHING Tsu-Pin).
Italy: Stefania ANTONINI, Marina CORDENONS, Rafaella SAIMASO, Muara
FURLOTTI (48 Emma IOZZELLI), Maria MARIOTTI, Federica D'ASTOLFO,
Feriana FERRAGUZZI, Adele MARSILETTI, Fabiana CORRERA (59 Nausica
PEDERSOLI), Silvia FIORINI (YC59), Carolina MORACE.
(Coach: Sergio GUENZA).
Goals: Feriana FERRAGUZZI (15), Adele MARSILETTI (29), Carolina MORACE
(37, 52, 66)
Referee: Fathi BOUCETTA (Tunisia)   Attendance: 11,000

19.11.1991 Zhongshan Sports Center Stadium, Zhongshan: Italy – Nigeria 1-0 (0-0)
Italy: Stefania ANTONINI, Paola BONATO (63 Anna Maria MEGA), Marina
CORDENONS, Muara FURLOTTI, Elisabeth BAVAGNOLI (36 Maria MARIOTTI),
Federica D'ASTOLFO, Feriana FERRAGUZZI, Adele MARSILETTI, Fabiana
CORRERA, Silvia FIORINI, Carolina MORACE. (Coach: Sergio GUENZA).
Nigeria: Ann CHIEJINE, Florence OMAGBEMI, Mavis OGUN, Ngozi EZEOCHA,
Omo-Love BRANCH, Diana NWAIWU (78 Nkechi MBILITAM), Edith ELUMA
(YC75), Nkiru OKOSIEME, Ngozi UCHE (73 Rachael YAMALA), Rita NWADIKE,
Chioma AJUNWA. (Coach: Johannes (Jo) BONFRERE).
Goal: Carolina MORACE (68)
Referee: James McCLUSKEY (Scotland)   Attendance: 12,000

19.11.1991 Zhongshan Sports Center Stadium, Zhongshan:
            Chinese Taipei – Germany 0-3 (0-2)
Chinese Taipei: LIN Hui Fang, CHEN Shwu Ju, LO Chu-Yin, HSU Chia Cheng,
LAN Lan Fen, WU Min Hsun, CHOU Tai Ying, SHIEH Su Jean, WU Su-Ching,
HUANG Yu Chuan (66 LIU Hsiu Mei), KO Chiao Lin (46 LIN Mei Chun).
(Coach: CHING Tsu-Pin).
Germany: Marion ISBERT, Doris FITSCHEN, Birgitt AUSTERMÜHL (61 Beate
WENDT), Jutta NARDENBACH (41 Frauke KUHLMANN), Christine PAUL,
Martina VOSS-TECKLENBURG, Bettina WIEGMANN, Roswitha BINDL, Petra
DAMM, Heidi MOHR, Gudrun GOTTSCHLICH. (Coach: Gero BISANZ).
Goals: Bettina WIEGMANN (10 pen), Heidi MOHR (21, 50)
Referee: Fathi BOUCETTA (Tunisia)   Attendance: 10,000

21.11.1991   Jiangmen Stadium, Jiangmen: Chinese Taipei – Nigeria 2-0 (1-0)
Chinese Taipei: LIN Hui Fang, CHEN Shwu Ju, LO Chu-Yin, HSU Chia Cheng,
LAN Lan Fen, WU Min Hsun, LIU Hsiu Mei (6 HONG Li-Chyn *goalkeeper*), CHOU
Tai Ying, SHIEH Su Jean, WU Su-Ching (78 LIN Mei Jih), LIN Mei Chun.
(Coach: CHING Tsu-Pin).
Nigeria: Ann CHIEJINE, Florence OMAGBEMI (60 Ann MUKORO), Mavis OGUN,
Ngozi EZEOCHA (41 Rachael YAMALA), Omo-Love BRANCH, Diana NWAIWU,
Edith ELUMA, Nkiru OKOSIEME, Ngozi UCHE *(YC46)*, Rita NWADIKE, Chioma
AJUNWA. (Coach: Johannes (Jo) BONFRERE).
Goals: LIN Mei Chun (38), CHOU Tai Ying (55)
Referee: Rafael RODRIGUEZ Medina (El Salvador)   Attendance: 14,000

Sent-off: 6' LIN Hui Fang.

21.11.1991   Zhongshan Sports Center Stadium, Zhongshan:
Italy – Germany 0-2 (0-0)
Italy: Stefania ANTONINI, Marina CORDENONS, Rafaella SAIMASO, Emma
IOZZELLI, Elisabeth BAVAGNOLI, Maria MARIOTTI, Federica D'ASTOLFO,
Feriana FERRAGUZZI *(YC50)*, Adele MARSILETTI, Silvia FIORINI (34 Anna
Maria MEGA, 64 Fabiana CORRERA), Carolina MORACE.
(Coach: Sergio GUENZA).
Germany: Marion ISBERT, Doris FITSCHEN, Birgitt AUSTERMÜHL, Christine
PAUL, Martina VOSS-TECKLENBURG, Bettina WIEGMANN, Britta UNSLEBER
(YC50), Roswitha BINDL, Sandra HENGST (41 Frauke KUHLMANN), Heidi
MOHR, Gudrun GOTTSCHLICH (68 Beate WENDT). (Coach: Gero BISANZ).
Goals: Heidi MOHR (67), Britta UNSLEBER (79)
Referee: James McCluskey (Scotland)   Attendance: 12,000

Team	Pld	W	D	L	GF	GA	GD	Pts
Germany	3	3	0	0	9	0	+9	6
Italy	3	2	0	1	6	2	+4	4
Chinese Taipei	3	1	0	2	2	8	-6	2
Nigeria	3	0	0	3	0	7	-7	0

QUARTER FINALS

24.11.1991   Zhongshan Sports Center Stadium, Zhongshan:
Denmark – Germany 1-2 (1-1,1-1)
Denmark: Helle BJERREGAARD, Karina SEFRON *(YC17)*, Bonny MADSEN,
Mette NIELSEN, Lisbet KOLDING, Susan MACKENSIE, Irene STELLING, Helle
JENSEN (73 Janne RASMUSSEN), Annie GAM-PEDERSEN *(YC70)*, Hanne
NISSEN (47 Lotte BAGGE), Annette THYCHOSEN. (Coach: Keld GANTZHORN).
Germany: Marion ISBERT, Doris FITSCHEN, Birgitt AUSTERMÜHL *(YC37)*,
Frauke KUHLMANN, Christine PAUL, Martina VOSS-TECKLENBURG, Bettina
WIEGMANN, Roswitha BINDL (89 Beate WENDT), Petra DAMM, Heidi MOHR,
Gudrun GOTTSCHLICH (51 Britta UNSLEBER). (Coach: Gero BISANZ).
Goals: Bettina WIEGMANN (17 pen), Susan MACKENSIE (25 pen), Heidi MOHR
(98)
Referee: Vassilios NIKAKIS (Greece)   Attendance: 12,000

Germany qualified after extra time.

24.11.1991   Tianhe Stadium, Guangzhou: China PR – Sweden 0-1 (0-1)
China PR: ZHONG Honglian, WEN Lirong, MA Li *(YC66)*, LIU Ailing, ZHOU
Yang, ZHOU Hua, SUN Qingmei, LI Xiufu, SUN Wen, WU Weiying (75 NIU Lijie),
ZHANG Yan (46 WEI Haiying). (Coach: SHANG Ruihua).
Sweden: Elisabeth LEIDINGE, Malin LUNDGREN *(YC39)*, Anette HANSSON,
Lena VIDEKULL, Eva ZEIKFALVY, Ingrid JOHANSSON, Marie KARLSSON, Pia
Mariane SUNDHAGE, Anneli ANDELÉN *(YC58)*, Helen NILSSON (67 Susanne
HEDBERG), Helen JOHANSSON *(YC57)* (65 Marie EWRELIUS).
(Coach: Gunilla PAIJKULL).
Goal: Pia Mariane SUNDHAGE (3)
Referee: John Jairo TORO Rendón (Colombia)   Attendance: 55,000

24.11.1991   Jiangmen Stadium, Jiangmen: Norway – Italy 3-2 (1-1,2-2)
Norway: Reidun SETH, Tina SVENSSON, Agnete CARLSEN, Gunn Lisbeth
NYBORG, Margunn Humlestøl HAUGENES (79 Anette IGLAND), Hege RIISE
(YC37), Tone HAUGEN, Heidi STØRE, Catherine ZABOROWSKI, Birthe
HEGSTAD, Ellen SCHEEL. (Coach: Even PELLERUD).
Italy: Stefania ANTONINI, Marina CORDENONS *(YC20)*, Rafaella SAIMASO (36
Paola BONATO), Emma IOZZELLI, Elisabeth BAVAGNOLI, Maria MARIOTTI
(68 Rita GUARINO), Federica D'ASTOLFO, Feriana FERRAGUZZI, Adele
MARSILETTI, Silvia FIORINI, Carolina MORACE. (Coach: Sergio GUENZA).
Goals: Birthe HEGSTAD (22), Agnete CARLSEN (67), Tina SVENSSON (96 pen) /
Rafaella SAIMASO (31), Rita GUARINO (80),
Referee: Rafael RODRIGUEZ Medina (El Salvador)   Attendance: 13,000

Norway qualified after extra time.

24.11.1991　New Plaza Stadium, Foshan: United States – Chinese Taipei 7-0 (4-0)
United States: Mary HARVEY, Joy Lynn FAWCETT Biefeld, Carla Werden
OVERBECK (57 Lori Ann HENRY), Linda HAMILTON, Kristine Marie LILLY
Heavey, Julie Maurine FOUDY, Michelle Anne AKERS Stahl, Shannon Danise
HIGGINS Cirovski, Mariel Margaret (Mia) HAMM), Carin JENNINGS Gabarra,
April HEINRICHS (41 Debbie Belkin RADEMACHER).
(Coach: Anson DORRANCE).
Chinese Taipei: HONG Li-Chyn, CHEN Shwu Ju *(YC23)*, LO Chu-Yin, HSU Chia
Cheng, LAN Lan Fen, WU Min Hsun, CHOU Tai Ying, SHIEH Su Jean, WU Su-
Ching (74 LIU Hsiu Mei), CHEN Shu Chin, LIN Mei Chun.
(Coach: CHING Tsu-Pin).
Goals: Michelle Anne AKERS Stahl (8, 29, 33, 44 pen, 48), Julie Maurine FOUDY
(38), Joy Lynn FAWCETT Biefeld (79)
Referee: Omer YENGO (Congo)　Attendance: 12,000

SEMI-FINALS

27.11.1991　Ying Dong Stadium, Guanghzhou: Sweden – Norway 1-4 (1-1)
Sweden: Elisabeth LEIDINGE, Malin LUNDGREN, Anette HANSSON (51 Helen
NILSSON), Marie EWRELIUS, Lena VIDEKULL, Susanne HEDBERG (63 Malin
SWEDBERG), Eva ZEIKFALVY, Ingrid JOHANSSON, Marie KARLSSON, Pia
Mariane SUNDHAGE, Anneli ANDELÉN. (Coach: Gunilla PAIJKULL).
Norway: Reidun SETH, Linda MEDALEN, Tina SVENSSON (61 Anette IGLAND),
Gro ESPESETH, Agnete CARLSEN, Gunn Lisbeth NYBORG, Hege RIISE, Tone
HAUGEN, Heidi STØRE, Catherine ZABOROWSKI, Birthe HEGSTAD.
(Coach: Even PELLERUD).
Goals: Lena VIDEKULL (6) / Tina SVENSSON (39 pen), Linda MEDALEN (41,
77), Agnete CARLSEN (67)
Referee: James McCLUSKEY (Scotland)　Attendance: 16,000

27.11.1991　Guangdong Provincial People's Stadium, Guangzhou:
　　　　　　Germany – United States 2-5 (1-3)
Germany: Marion ISBERT, Doris FITSCHEN *(YC59)*, Birgitt AUSTERMÜHL (60
Britta UNSLEBER), Jutta NARDENBACH, Frauke KUHLMANN, Christine PAUL,
Martina VOSS-TECKLENBURG, Bettina WIEGMANN, Roswitha BINDL, Heidi
MOHR, Gudrun GOTTSCHLICH (50 Beate WENDT). (Coach: Gero BISANZ).
United States: Mary HARVEY, Joy Lynn FAWCETT Biefeld, Carla Werden
OVERBECK, Linda HAMILTON, Kristine Marie LILLY Heavey, Julie Maurine
FOUDY, Michelle Anne AKERS Stahl *(YC67)*, Shannon Danise HIGGINS Cirovski,
Mariel Margaret (Mia) HAMM), Carin JENNINGS Gabarra, April HEINRICHS.
(Coach: Anson DORRANCE).
Goals: Heidi MOHR (34), Bettina WIEGMANN (63) / Carin JENNINGS Gabarra
(10, 22, 33), April HEINRICHS (54, 75)
Referee: Salvador IMPERATORE Marcone (Chile)　Attendance: 15,000

21

THIRD PLACE PLAY-OFF

29.11.1991   Guangdong Provincial People's Stadium, Guangdong:
Sweden – Germany 4-0 (4-0)
Sweden: Elisabeth LEIDINGE, Malin LUNDGREN, Marie EWRELIUS, Lena
VIDEKULL, Eva ZEIKFALVY, Malin SWEDBERG, Marie KARLSSON, Pia
Mariane SUNDHAGE, Anneli ANDELÉN (YC60), Helen NILSSON (YC53), Ingrid
JOHANSSON. (Coach: Gunilla PAIJKULL).
Germany: Marion ISBERT (38 Michaela KUBAT), Doris FITSCHEN, Jutta
NARDENBACH, Martina VOSS-TECKLENBURG, Bettina WIEGMANN, Britta
UNSLEBER, Roswitha BINDL (60 Elke WALTHER), Petra DAMM, Heidi MOHR,
Beate WENDT, Gudrun GOTTSCHLICH. (Coach: Gero BISANZ).
Goals: Anneli ANDELÉN (7), Pia Mariane SUNDHAGE (11), Lena VIDEKULL
(29), Helen NILSSON (43)
Referee: CLAUDIA VASCONCELOS Guedes (Brazil)   Attendance: 20,000

FINAL

30.11.1991   Tianhe Stadium, Guangzhou: Norway – United States 1-2 (1-1)
Norway: Reidun SETH, Linda MEDALEN, Tina SVENSSON, Gro ESPESETH,
Agnete CARLSEN, Gunn Lisbeth NYBORG, Hege RIISE, Tone HAUGEN, Heidi
STØRE, Catherine ZABOROWSKI (79 Liv STRÆDET), Birthe HEGSTAD.
(Coach: Even PELLERUD).
United States: Mary HARVEY, Joy Lynn FAWCETT Biefeld, Carla Werden
OVERBECK, Linda HAMILTON, Kristine Marie LILLY Heavey, Julie Maurine
FOUDY, Michelle Anne AKERS Stahl (YC54), Shannon Danise HIGGINS Cirovski,
Mariel Margaret (Mia) HAMM), Carin JENNINGS Gabarra, April HEINRICHS.
(Coach: Anson DORRANCE).
Goals: Linda MEDALEN (29) / Michelle Anne AKERS Stahl (20, 78)
Referee: Vadim ZHUK (Belarus)   Attendance: 63,000

UNITED STATES BECAME WORLD CHAMPIONS

22

SECOND EDITION FIFA WOMEN'S WORLD CUP 1995

QUALIFYING TOURNAMENTS

CAF AFRICAN WOMEN'S CHAMPIONSHIP 1995

Only the winner of this tournament will qualify for the FIFA Women's World Cup 1995.

QUARTER-FINALS

05.11.1994 South Africa – Zambia 5-3
06.11.1994 Lagos: Nigeria – Sierra Leone 9-0
20.11.1994 Freetown: Sierra Leone – Nigeria 0-2
20.11.1994 Zambia – South Africa 2-6

Cameroon withdrew, **Angola** advanced.
Guinea withdrew, **Ghana** advanced.

SEMI-FINALS

07.01.1995 South Africa – Angola 3-1
09.01.1995 Ghana – Nigeria 0-3
21.01.1995 Luanda: Angola – South Africa 3-3
23.01.1995 Lagos: Nigeria – Ghana 2-0

FINALS

04.03.1995 Ibadan: Nigeria – South Africa 4-1
18.03.1995 Johannesburg: South Africa – Nigeria 1-7

Nigeria qualified for the FIFA Women's World Cup 1995.

AFC ASIAN GAMES 1994

The winner and the runner-up of this tournament will qualify for the FIFA Women's World Cup 1995. The tournament was held in Fukuyama, Japan between 3 & 12 October 1994. It was combined with the men's tournament.

RESULTS

03.10.1994 Takegahana Stadium, Fukuyama: Chinese Taipei – China PR 0-5
04.10.1994 Takegahana Stadium, Fukuyama: Japan – South Korea 5-0
06.10.1994 Takegahana Stadium, Fukuyama: Chinese Taipei – Japan 0-3
07.10.1994 Takegahana Stadium, Fukuyama: China PR – South Korea 2-0
09.10.1994 Takegahana Stadium, Fukuyama: Chinese Taipei – South Korea 2-0
10.10.1994 Takegahana Stadium, Fukuyama: China PR – Japan 1-1

Team	Pld	W	D	L	GF	GA	GD	Pts
Japan	*3*	*2*	*1*	*0*	*9*	*1*	*+8*	*7*
China PR	*3*	*2*	*1*	*0*	*8*	*1*	*+7*	*7*
Chinese Taipei	3	1	0	2	2	8	-6	3
South Korea	3	0	0	3	0	9	-9	0

GOLD MEDAL MATCH

12.10.1994   Takegahana Stadium, Fukuyama: Japan – China PR 0-2 (0-1)
Goals: Chen Yufeng (21), Sun wen (47)

China PR and **Japan** both qualified for the FIFA Women's World Cup 1995.

UEFA WOMEN'S EURO 1995

The qualification for UEFA Women's Euro 1995 was held between 15 August 1993 & 30 October 1994.

GROUP STAGE

GROUP 1

04.09.1993   Gvarv Stadion, Gvarv: Norway – Czech Republic 6-1 (2-1)
Goals: Aarønes (3, 60, 76), Leinan (25), Hegstad (81), Sandberg (84) / Hekelová (5)
26.09.1993   Finland – Hungary 1-1
16.10.1993   Varden Amfi, Bergen: Norway – Hungary 8-0 (6-0)
Goals: Leinan (1, 3, 30), Carlsen (8, 39), Hegstad (43), Aarønes (63), Medalen (90)
23.04.1994   Stadion Pod Lipou, Roudnice nad Labem: Czech Republic – Finland 0-0
14.05.1994   Stadion Siruch, Staré Mesto: Czech Republic – Hungary 0-0
21.05.1994   ISS Stadion, Vantaa: Finland – Norway 2-2
Goals: ??, ?? / Aarønes (52), Carlsen (80)
04.06.1994   Hidegkuti Nándor Stadion, Budapest: Hungary – Norway 0-4 (0-2)
Goals: Zaborowski (22), Aarønes (43), Myklebust (51), Risse (68)
19.06.1994   ISS Stadion, Vantaa: Finland – Czech Republik 4-0 (2-0)
Goals: ?? (16), ?? (33), ?? (48), ?? (79)
04.09.1994   Bislett Stadion, Oslo: Norway – Finland 4-0 (1-0)
Goals: Støre (29), Leinan (48), Aarønes (60), Medalen (82)
10.09.1994   Széktói Stadion, Kecskemét: Hungary – Czech Republic 4-4 (1-2)
Goals: ?? (31), ?? (65), ?? (66), ?? (73) / Chlumecká (15, 77), Smeralová (40, 60)
24.09.1994   Strahov Stadium, Prague: Czech Republic – Norway 0-9 (0-4)
Goals: Sandberg (3, 44, 58, 64), Aarønes (6), Medalen (13, 55), Tangeraas (90), ?? (og)
24.09.1994   Hungary – Finland 0-1

Team	Pld	W	D	L	GF	GA	GD	Pts
Norway	*6*	*5*	*1*	*0*	*33*	*3*	*+30*	*11*
Finland	6	2	3	1	8	7	+1	7
Hungary	6	0	3	3	5	18	-13	3
Czech Republic	6	0	3	3	5	23	-18	3

GROUP 2

29.08.1993 FFU Training Complex, Kiev: Ukraine – Russia 0-2 (0-2)
Goals: Egorova (35), Svetlitskaya (44)
18.09.1993 Ukraine – Romania 2-2
10.10.1993 Poland – Ukraine 1-3
16.10.1993 Stadionul Poiana, Câmpina: Romania – Russia 2-2 (1-2)
Goals: Apostol (35), Simion (68) / Savina (5, 17)
07.11.1993 Poland – Romania 0-4
15.05.1994 Stroitel Stadium, Selyatino: Russia – Poland 0-0
14.06.1994 Stroitel Stadium, Selyatino: Russia – Romania 1-0 (1-0)
Goals: Grigorieva (6)
21.08.1994 Ukraine – Poland 3-0
03.09.1994 Romania – Poland 3-0
18.09.1994 Tsentralnyi Stadion, Voronezh: Russia – Ukraine 2-1 (1-1)
Goals: Grigorieva (41), Bosikova (86) / Gusakova (42)
25.09.1994 Stadion Amica, Wronki: Poland – Russia 1-2 (1-1)
Goals: Szondermajer (16) / Bosikova (11, 57)
28.09.1994 Romania – Ukraine 5-0

Team	Pld	W	D	L	GF	GA	GD	Pts
Russia	*6*	*4*	*2*	*9*	*9*	*4*	*+5*	*10*
Romania	6	3	2	1	16	5	+11	8
Ukraine	6	2	1	3	9	12	-3	5
Poland	6	0	1	5	2	15	-13	1

GROUP 3

15.08.1993 S.Dariaus ir S.Giréno Stadium, Kaunas: Lithuania – Denmark 0-11 (0-3)
Goals: H.Jensen (9, 89), Rasmussen (17, 67 pen), Bagge (21 pen), Nissen (48),
Petersen (54), Eggers Nielsen (70), M.Jensen (76, 87), Stelling (84)
10.09.1993 S.Dariaus ir S.Giréno Stadium, Kaunas: Lithuania – Bulgaria 0-1 (0-1)
Goal: Kovatscheva (10)
29.09.1993 Hjørring Stadion, Hjørring: Denmark – Bulgaria 6-1 (4-1)
Goals: Thychosen (5, 87), H.Jensen (15, 18), M.Jensen (37), Brink (52) / Manova (45)
13.10.1993 Hristo Botev Stadium, Blagoevgrad: Bulgaria – Lithuania 1-1 (1-0)
Goals: Manova (19) / Vashtchilko (88)
25.05.1994 Osogovo Stadium, Kiustendil: Bulgaria – Denmark 0-4 (0-3)
Goals: ?? (7 og), C.Nielsen (30, 77), A.Larsen (37)

15.06.1994   Stadium Ikke Angivet, Idestrup: Denmark – Lithuania 11-0 (7-0)
Goals: H.Jensen (3, 6, 26, 44), B.Madsen (7), Thychosen (11), Rasmussen (45, 83),
Kolding (53), Brink (64), Petersen (72)

Team	Pld	W	D	L	GF	GA	GD	Pts
Denmark	*4*	*4*	*0*	*0*	*32*	*1*	*+31*	*8*
Bulgaria	4	1	1	2	3	11	-8	3
Lithuania	4	0	1	3	1	24	-23	1
Yugoslavia	0	0	0	0	0	0	0	0

Yugoslavia withdrew.

GROUP 4

18.08.1993   Kvarnängens IP, Nynäshamn: Sweden – Latvia 9-0
Goals: Kalte, Videkull (3x), Lundgren (2x), H.Johansson, P.Larsson, Wällersten
22.09.1993   Latvia – Slovakia 0-1
13.10.1993   Stadión Pasienky, Bratislava: Slovakia – Sweden 0-2
Goals: H.Johansson, Andelén
22.05.1994   Ozolnieki Stadion, Ozolnieki: Latvia – Sweden 0-5
Goals: Lovén, Kalte (2x), Videkull, Andelén
15.06.1994   Strömvallen, Gävle: Sweden – Slovakia 6-0
Goals: Nessvold, Lundgren, Andelén (2x), S.Johansson, P.Larsson
21.09.1994   Slovakia – Latvia 3-1

Team	Pld	W	D	L	GF	GA	GD	Pts
Sweden	*4*	*4*	*0*	*0*	*22*	*0*	*+22*	*8*
Slovakia	4	2	0	2	4	9	-5	4
Latvia	4	0	0	4	1	18	-17	0

GROUP 5

09.09.1993   Wales – Switzerland 2-3
24.10.1993   Stadion Niedermatten, Wohlen: Switzerland – Germany 0-5 (0-2)
Goals: Brocker (14, 53, 61), Mohr (43, 72)
10.11.1993   Stadion Wchützenwisse, Winterthur: Switzerland – Croatia 1-2
Goals: ?? / Drijaca (8, 32)
31.03.1994   Schüco Arena, Bielefeld: Germany – Wales 12-0 (5-0)
Goals: Mohr (1), Wiegmann (6, 38, 87), Meinert (26, 54, 80), Neid (43, 70),
Voss (57, 67), Jones (72)
02.04.1994   Switzerland – Wales 4-2
05.04.1994   Stadion Kranjceviceva, Zagreb: Croatia – Wales 3-0
04.05.1994   Stadion Kranjceviceva, Zagreb: Croatia – Switzerland 1-1
Goals: Focic (7) / ??
05.05.1994   Vetch Field, Swansea: Wales – Germany 0-12 (0-4)
Goals: Neid (7), Minnert (16, 31), Brocker (35, 59, 61, 77), Meinert (48, 80),
Austermühl (83), Wiegmann (85), Voss (87)
22.05.1994   Deeside Stadium, Deeside: Wales – Croatia 1-2

02.06.1994   Stadion Kranjceviceva, Zagreb: Croatia – Germany 0-7 (0-1)
Goals: Mohr (32, 72), Brocker (67, 77, 80), Meinert (74), Neid (87)
21.09.1994   Floschenstadion, Sindelfingen: Germany – Croatia 8-0 (3-0)
Goals: Brocker (9, 58, 84), Voss (20), Neid (43), Prinz (80, 90), Meinert (89)
25.09.1994   Arena Weingarten, Weingarten: Germany – Switzerland 11-0 (6-0)
Goals: Brocker (14, 19, 48), Mohr (23, 73), Wiegmann (36), Voss (43),
Meinert (45, 62), Tschöke (64), Neid (76)

Team	Pld	W	D	L	GF	GA	GD	Pts
Germany	*6*	*6*	*0*	*0*	*55*	*0*	*+55*	*12*
Croatia	6	3	1	2	8	18	-10	7
Switzerland	6	2	1	3	9	23	-14	5
Wales	6	0	0	6	5	36	-31	0

GROUP 6

16.10.1993   Stadio Comunale, Senigallia: Italy – Scotland 4-0 (3-0)
Goals: Fiorini (17), Salmaso (30), Baldelli (33), Marsiletti (54)
20.11.1993   Stadio San Vito, Cosenza: Italy – France 2-0 (1-0)
Goals: Ciardi (38 pen), Marsiletti (79)
11.12.1993   Estádio de São Luis, Faro: Portugal – France 0-1 (0-0)
Goal: Gout (48)
26.02.1994   Stade des Trois Sapins, Ozoir-la-Ferrière: France – Scotland 1-0 (1-0)
Goal: Mugneret-Béghé (24)
05.03.1994   Estádio do Bilhão, Fiães: Portugal – Italy 1-3 (0-3)
Goals: Bé (78) / Costanzo (33), Morace (35, 41)
26.03.1994   Stade Lebon, Angoulême: France – Portugal 3-0 (1-0)
Goals: Sykora (19, 88), Richoux (56)
03.04.1994   Forthbank Stadium, Stirling: Scotland – Italy 0-4 (0-2)
Goals: Costanzo (33, 53), Fiorini (43), Morace (83)
24.04.1994   Forthbank Stadium, Stirling: Scotland – Portugal 1-2 (0-0)
Goals: Brown (52) / Anabela (47), Adilia (68)
14.05.1994   Stade de l'Aar, Schiltigheim: France – Italy 1-1 (1-0)
Goals: Sykora (22) / Carta (68)
29.05.1994   Estádio Dr.Manuel de Mello, Barreiro: Portugal – Scotland 8-2 (4-1)
Goals: Anabela (16, 57, 66), Bé (25), Carla Couto (28, 71), Paula Freitas (32),
Patricia Sequeira (55) / Winchester (12), Mitchell (68)
11.06.1994   Stadio Dei Marmi, Carrara: Italy – Portugal 1-2 (1-1)
Goals: Ulivi (25') / Carla Couto (16), Tesse (71 og)
25.09.1994   Allan Park, Aberdeen: Scotland – France 0-3 (0-0)
Goals: Guitti (48), Guillemin (49), Pichon (86)

Team	Pld	W	D	L	GF	GA	GD	Pts
Italy	*6*	*4*	*1*	*1*	*15*	*4*	*+11*	*9*
France	6	4	1	1	9	3	+6	9
Portugal	6	3	0	3	13	11	+2	6
Scotland	6	0	0	6	3	22	-19	0

27

GROUP 7

25.09.1993 Bezigrad Stadium, Ljubljana: Slovenia – England 0-10 (0-5)
Goals: Taylor (20), Spacey (22, 36, 72, 87), Borman (30), Walker (39, 48, 82),
K.Davis (88)
06.10.1993 Soevereinstadion, Lommel: Belgium – Slovenia 7-0 (5-0)
Goals: Maus (8), Vanslembrouck (18, 43, 77), Yde (31), Demeester (44),
Vanstraelen (84)
30.10.1993 Heysel Stadion, Brussels: Belgium – Spain 0-0
06.11.1993 Henri Houtseagerstadion, Koksijde: Belgium – England 0-3 (0-1)
Goals: Walker (26, 87), Taylor (83)
19.12.1993 Reyno de Navarra, Pamplona: Spain – England 0-0
20.02.1994 Valley Parade, Bradford: England – Spain 0-0
13.03.1994 City Ground, Nottingham: England – Belgium 6-0 (3-0)
Goals: Spacey (13, 22), Walker (19, 63), K.Davis (58), Coultard (86)
20.03.1994 Spain – Slovenia 17-0
Goals: Mar Prieto (7x), Bakero (3x), García (2x), González (2x), Castillo (2x), ?? (og)
17.04.1994 Griffin Park, Brentford: England – Slovenia 10-0 (2-0)
Goals: Taylor (1, 58), Walker (14, 62), Britton (60), Coultard (65, 81), Powell (71),
Borman (74), Spacey (87)
24.04.1994 Estadio Municipal, Tortosa: Spain – Belgium 4-0
Goals: Pascual (2x), Bakero, Deudorede (og)
14.05.1994 Bezigrad Stadium, Ljubljana: Slovenia – Belgium 0-8 (0-4)
Goals: Maus (7, 38), Vanstraelen (10), Van Laethem (12, 47), Dermul (30),
Kimpe (58, 66)
29.05.1994 Slovenia – Spain 0-8

Team	Pld	W	D	L	GF	GA	GD	Pts
England	*6*	*4*	*2*	*0*	*29*	*0*	*+29*	*10*
Spain	6	3	3	0	29	0	+29	9
Belgium	6	2	1	3	15	13	+2	5
Slovenia	6	0	0	6	0	60	-60	0

GROUP 8

26.09.1993 Laugardalsvöllur, Reykjavik: Iceland – Netherlands 2-1 (1-0)
Goals: Sæmundsdóttir (11), Gunnlaugsdóttir (86) / Leemans (46)
19.03.1994 Fortuna Wormerveer, Wormerveer: Netherlands – Greece 2-0 (1-0)
Goals: Keereweer (42), Roos (75)
16.04.1994 Xanthi Ground, Xanthi: Greece – Netherlands 0-4 (0-2)
Goals: van Dam (1, 2), Limbeek (46), Noom (47)
29.05.1994 Valsvöllur, Reykjavik: Iceland – Greece 3-0 (0-0)
Goals: Gunnlaugsdóttir (49), Ólafsdóttir (56), Kristjánsdóttir (77)
24.09.1994 Sportpark De Vaan, Rotterdam: Netherlands – Iceland 0-1 (0-0)
Goal: Færseth (60)
28.09.1994 Katerini Stadium, Katerini: Greece – Iceland 1-6
Goals: ?? / Helgadóttir (17, 25, 66, 71), Sæmundsdóttir (49), Færseth (80)

Team	Pld	W	D	L	GF	GA	GD	Pts
Iceland	*4*	*4*	*0*	*0*	*12*	*2*	*+10*	*8*
Netherlands	4	2	0	0	7	3	+4	4
Greece	4	0	0	4	1	15	-14	0

QUARTER FINALS

08.10.1994   Laugardalsvöllur, Reykjavik: Iceland – England 1-2 (1-1)
Goals: Ólafsdóttir (31) / Coultard (5), K.Davis (61)
09.10.1994   Stroitel Stadium, Selyatino: Russia – Germany 0-1 (0-0)
Goal: Mohr (70 pen)
15.10.1994   Hjørring Stadion, Hjørring: Denmark – Sweden 2-0 (0-0)
Goals: Eggers Nielsen (84), Krogh (87)
15.10.1994   Stadio Danilo Martelli, Mantova: Italy – Norway 1-3 (1-2)
Goals: Salmaso (14) / Medalen (10), A.Nymark Andersen (28), Sandberg (85)
27.10.1994   Stadion an der Bremer Brücke, Osnabrück: Germany – Russia 4-0 (4-0)
Goals: Mohr (5, 45), Brocker (23), Neid (29)
29.10.1994   Bislett Stadion, Oslo: Norway – Italy 4-2 (2-1)
Goals: Sandberg (1), A.Nymark Andersen (30, 62), Pettersen (84) / Morace (34),
Guarino (87)
29.10.1994   Malmö Stadion, Malmö: Sweden – Denmark 3-0 (3-0)
Goals: Andelén (7, 45), H.Johansson (32)
30.10.1994   Goldstone Ground, Brighton: England – Iceland 2-1 (1-1)
Goals: Coultard (13), Spacey (65) / Gunnlaugsdóttir (36)

SEMI-FINALS

11.12.1994   Vicarage Road, Watford: England – Germany 1-4 (1-1)
Goals: Farley (7) / Mohr (32, 80), Brocker (68), Wiegmann (87 pen)
23.02.1995   Ruhrstadion, Bochum: Germany – England 2-1 (1-1)
Goals: Waller (34 og), Prinz (79) / Farley (1)
26.02.1995   Sørlandshallen, Kristiansand: Norway – Sweden 4-3 (1-1)
Goals: Aarønes (44, 64), Sandberg (60), Waage (89) / Kalte (15), Andelén (55'),
H.Johansson (61)
04.03.1995   Tipshallen, Jönköping: Sweden – Norway 4-1 (0-1)
Goals: Kalte (53), Videkull (59, 61, 76) / Medalen (28)

FINAL

26.03.1995   Fritz-Walter-Stadion, Kaiserslautern: Germany – Sweden 3-2 (1-1)
Goals: Meinert (33), Prinz (64), Weigmann (85) / Andersson (6), Andelén (89)

Sweden (qualified as host of the World Cup), **England, Germany**, **Norway** and
Denmark (best quarter-final loser) qualified for the FIFA Women's World Cup 1995.

29

CONCACAF WOMEN'S CHAMPIONSHIP 1994

The North, Central America & Caribbean CONCACAF was held in Montreal, Quebec, Canada between 13 & 21 August 1994. The winner and runner-up will qualify for the FIFA Women's World Cup 1995.

RESULTS

13.08.1994   Canada – Jamaica 7-0
13.08.1994   United States – Mexico 9-0
15.08.1994   Trinidad and Tobago – Jamaica 2-1
15.08.1994   Canada – Mexico 6-0
17.08.1994   Mexico – Jamaica 3-1
17.08.1994   United States – Trinidad and Tobago 11-1
19.08.1994   United States – Jamaica 10-0
19.08.1994   Canada – Trinidad and Tobago 5-0
21.08.1994   Mexico – Trinidad and Tobago 3-3
21.08.1994   Canada – United States 0-6

Team	Pld	W	D	L	GF	GA	GD	Pts
United States	*4*	*4*	*0*	*0*	*36*	*1*	*+35*	*12*
Canada	*4*	*3*	*0*	*1*	*18*	*6*	*+12*	*9*
Mexico	4	1	1	2	6	19	-13	4
Trinidad and Tobago	4	1	1	2	6	20	-14	4
Jamaica	4	0	0	4	2	22	-20	0

United States and runner-up **Canada** qualified for the FIFA Women's World Cup 1995.

OFC WOMEN'S CHAMPIONSHIP 1994

The OFC (Oceania) was the only one of the six FIFA confederations to hold a specified qualifying competition. Only three teams participated in the tournament which was held in Papua New Guinea between 14 & 20 October 1994. Only the winner will qualify for the FIFA Women's World Cup 1995.

RESULTS

14.10.1994   Port Moresby: New Zealand – Australia 2-1
Goals: Sharpe (2x) / Forman
15.10.1994   Port Moresby: New Zealand – Papua New Guinea 2-0
Goals: Baker (2x)
16.10.1994   Port Moresby: Australia – Papua New Guinea 7-0
Goals: Pumpa (2x), Salisbury (2x), Casagrande, Hughes, Forman
18.10.1994   Port Moresby: Australia – New Zealand 1-0
Goal: Murray

19.10.1994   Port Moresby: Papua New Guinea – Australia 0-4
Goals: Salisbury, Casagrande, Hughes, ?? (og)
20.10.1994   Port Moresby: Papua New Guinea – New Zealand 0-6
Goals: Dermott (2x), Henderson, Crawford, Jacobson, Sharpe

Team	Pld	W	D	L	GF	GA	GD	Pts
Australia	*4*	*3*	*0*	*1*	*13*	*2*	*+11*	*9*
New Zealand	4	3	0	1	10	2	+8	9
Papua New Guinea	4	0	0	4	0	19	-19	0

Australia qualified for the FIFA Women's World Cup 1995.

CONMEBOL SUDAMERICANO FEMENINO 1995

The South America (CONMEBOL) Sudamericano Femenino 1995 tournament was held in Uberlândia, Brazil between 1 & 22 January 1995. Only the winner will qualify for the FIFA Women's World Cup 1995.

GROUP STAGE

08.01.1995   Estádio Parque do Sabiá, Uberlândia: Brazil – Ecuador 13-0
Goals: Pretinha (4x), Cenira, Roseli, Michael Jackson (2x), Sissi (2x), Russa (3x)
08.01.1995   Estádio Parque do Sabiá, Uberlândia: Chile – Bolivia 11-0
Goals: Flores (4x), Sánchez (2x), Astudillo, Cruz, Acevedo, Bravo, Ayala
10.01.1995   Estádio Parque do Sabiá, Uberlândia: Chile – Ecuador 6-1
Goals: Sissi (2x), Roseli, Cenira, Michael Jackson (2x) / Bravo
10.01.1995   Estádio Parque do Sabiá, Uberlândia: Argentina – Ecuador 5-1
Goals: Ochotorena (2x), Morales (2x), Arce / Carmen
12.01.1995   Estádio Parque do Sabiá, Uberlândia: Argentina – Bolivia 12-0
Goals: Ochotorena (4x), Villanueva (3x), Morales (2x), Cardoso (2x), Asperes
12.01.1995   Estádio Parque do Sabiá, Uberlândia: Chile – Ecuador 2-2
Goals: Bravo, Flores / Mercedes, Fabiola (og)
14.01.1995   Estádio Parque do Sabiá, Uberlândia: Brazil – Argentina 8-0 (3-0)
Goals: Sissi (16, 31, 57 pen, 83 pen), Roseli (43), Pretinha (47, 84), Elane (64)
14.01.1995   Estádio Parque do Sabiá, Uberlândia: Ecuador – Bolivia 6-1
Goals: Ramírez (2x), Vera (3x), Carmen / Duran
18.01.1995   Estádio Parque do Sabiá, Uberlândia: Brazil – Bolivia 15-0
Goals: Roseli (3x), Márcia Taffarel, Michael Jackson (2x), Sissi (4x), Elane, Duda, Bel, Cenira (2x)
18.01.1995   Estádio Parque do Sabiá, Uberlândia: Argentina – Chile 1-0
Goal: Ochotorena

Team	Pld	W	D	L	GF	GA	GD	Pts
Brazil	*4*	*4*	*0*	*0*	*42*	*1*	*+41*	*12*
Argentina	*4*	*3*	*0*	*1*	*18*	*9*	*+9*	*9*
Chile	4	1	1	2	14	9	+5	4
Ecuador	4	1	1	2	9	21	-12	4
Bolivia	4	0	0	4	1	44	-43	0

FINAL

18.01.1995 Estádio Parque do Sabiá, Uberlândia: Brazil – Argentina 2-0 (1-0)
Goals: Michael Jackson (4), Roseli (50)

Brazil qualified for the FIFA Women's World Cup 1995.

FIFA WOMEN'S WORLD CUP FINAL
TOURNAMENT IN SWEDEN 1995

GROUP STAGE

GROUP A

05.06.1995 Tingvalla IP, Karlstad: Germany – Japan 1-0 (1-0)
Germany: Manuela GOLLER, Anouschka BERNHARD, Birgitt AUSTERMÜHL, Ursula LOHN, Silva NEID, Maren MEINERT, Martina VOSS-TECKLENBURG (65 Birgit PRINZ), Bettina WIEGMANN, Dagmar POHLMANN, Heidi MOHR, Patricia BROCKER Grigoli (82 Melanie HOFFMANN). (Coach: Gero BISANZ).
Japan: Junko OZAWA, Yumi OBE, Rie YAMAKI, Kae NISHINA, Yumi TOMEI, Maki HANETA, Homare SAWA, Asako Takemoto TAKAKURA, Futaba KIOKA (80 Etsuko HANDA), Tamaki UCHIYAMA (73 Kaori NAGAMINE), Akemi NODA. (Coach: Tamotsu SUZUKI).
Goal: Silva NEID (23)
Referee: Petros MATHABELA (South Africa) Attendance: 3,824

05.06.1995 Olympia, Helsingborg: Sweden – Brazil 0-1 (0-1)
Sweden: Elisabeth LEIDINGE *(YC75)*, Gärd Kristin BENTSSON, Malin LUNDGREN (43 Anna POHJANEN), Åsa JAKOBSSON (83 Sofia JOHANSSON), Malin Elisabeth ANDERSSON, Lena VIDEKULL, Anneli OLSSON (61 Susanne HEDBERG), Eva ZEIKFALVY, Pia Mariane SUNDHAGE, Anneli ANDELÉN, Ulrika KALTE. (Coach: Bengt SIMONSSON).
Brazil: Margarete Maria Pioresan "MEG", ELANE dos Santos Rêgo, Rosilane Camargo Mota "FANTA", SUZY Bitencourt de Oliveira, Sisleide do Amor Lima "SISSI", VALERIA Aparecida Bonifacio, LEDA MARIA Cozer Abreu (16 SOLANGE Santos Bastos, 83 TÂNIA Maria Pereira Ribeiro), CENIRA Sampaio do Prado, Delma Gonçalves "PRETINHA" *(YC21)*, Mariléia dos Santos "MICHAEL JACKSON" *(YC57)*, ROSELI de Belo. (Coach: ADEMAR FONSECA Júnior).
Goal: ROSELI de Belo (37)
Referee: Sonia DENONCOURT (Canada) Attendance: 14,500

07.06.1995   Olympia, Helsingborg: Sweden – Germany 3-2 (0-2)
Sweden: Elisabeth LEIDINGE, Gärd Kristin BENGTSSON (35 Åsa LÖNNQVIST), Åsa JAKOBSSON, Malin Elisabeth ANDERSSON, Anna POHJANEN (51 Malin FLINK), Lena VIDEKULL, Eva ZEIKFALVY (84 Anneli OLSSON), Pia Mariane SUNDHAGE, Anneli ANDELÉN, Ulrika KALTE, Helen NILSSON.
(Coach: Bengt SIMONSSON).
Germany: Manuela GOLLER, Anouschka BERNHARD, Birgitt AUSTERMÜHL (YC61), Ursula LOHN, Silva NEID (YC14), Maren MEINERT, Martina VOSS-TECKLENBURG (84 Sandra MINNERT), Bettina WIEGMANN, Dagmar POHLMANN, Heidi MOHR, Patricia BROCKER Grigoli (57 Birgit PRINZ).
(Coach: Gero BISANZ).
Goals: Malin Elisabeth ANDERSSON (65 pen, 86), Pia Mariane SUNDHAGE (80) / Bettina WIEGMANN (9 pen), Ursula LOHN (42)
Referee: Linda May BLACK (New Zealand)   Attendance: 5,855

07.06.1995   Tingvalla IP, Karlstad: Brazil – Japan 1-2 (1-2)
Brazil: Margarete Maria Pioresan "MEG", ELANE dos Santos Rêgo (YC26), Rosilane Camargo Mota "FANTA", SOLANGE Santos Bastos (72 Miraildes Maciel Mota "FORMIGA"), SUZY Bitencourt de Oliveira, Sisleide do Amor Lima "SISSI", VALERIA Aparecida Bonifacio, CENIRA Sampaio do Prado, Delma Gonçalves "PRETINHA", Mariléia dos Santos "MICHAEL JACKSON" (YC10) (83 Lunalva Torres de Almeida "NALVINHA"), ROSELI de Belo.
(Coach: ADEMAR FONSECA Júnior).
Japan: Junko OZAWA, Yumi OBE (YC48), Rie YAMAKI, Kae NISHINA, Maki HANETA, Homare SAWA, Asako Takemoto TAKAKURA, Futaba KIOKA, Tamaki UCHIYAMA, Nami OTAKE, Akemi NODA. (Coach: Tamotsu SUZUKI).
Goals: Delma Gonçalves "PRETINHA" (7) / Akemi NODA (13, 45)
Referee: Catherine Leann HEPBURN (United States)   Attendance: 2,286

09.06.1995   Arosvallen, Västerås: Sweden – Japan 2-0 (0-0)
Sweden: Elisabeth LEIDINGE, Gärd Kristin BENGTSSON, Åsa JAKOBSSON (46 Anneli OLSSON), Malin Elisabeth ANDERSSON, Anna POHJANEN (90 Malin FLINK), Lena VIDEKULL, Eva ZEIKFALVY (58 Åsa LÖNNQVIST), Pia Mariane SUNDHAGE, Anneli ANDELÉN, Ulrika KALTE, Helen NILSSON.
(Coach: Bengt SIMONSSON).
Japan: Junko OZAWA, Yumi OBE, Rie YAMAKI (YC15), Kae NISHINA, Maki HANETA, Homare SAWA (76 Etsuko HANDA), Asako Takemoto TAKAKURA, Futaba KIOKA, Tamaki UCHIYAMA, Nami OTAKE (46 Kaori NAGAMINE), Akemi NODA. (Coach: Tamotsu SUZUKI).
Goals: Lena VIDEKULL (66), Anneli ANDELÉN (88)
Referee: Petros MATHABELA (South Africa)   Attendance: 7,811

33

09.06.1995 Tingvalla IP, Karlstad: Brazil – Germany 1-6 (1-3)
Brazil: Margarete Maria Pioresan "MEG", ELANE dos Santos Rêgo, Rosilane
Camargo Mota "FANTA", SOLANGE Santos Bastos *(YC30)*, SUZY Bitencourt de
Oliveira, Sisleide do Amor Lima "SISSI", VALERIA Aparecida Bonifacio (80
Miraildes Maciel Mota "FORMIGA"), LEDA MARIA Cozer Abreu *(YC62)* (90
MARCIA TAFFAREL), CENIRA Sampaio do Prado *(YC25)*, Delma Gonçalves
"PRETINHA" (66 TÂNIA Maria Pereira Ribeiro), ROSELI de Belo.
(Coach: ADEMAR FONSECA Júnior).
Germany: Manuela GOLLER, Anouschka BERNHARD, Birgitt AUSTERMÜHL
(YC35) (46 Tina WUNDERLICH *(YC65)*), Ursula LOHN, Silva NEID, Maren
MEINERT (74 Patricia BROCKER Grigoli), Martina VOSS-TECKLENBURG,
Bettina WIEGMANN (83 Pia WUNDERLICH), Dagmar POHLMANN, Birgit
PRINZ *(YC59)*, Heidi MOHR. (Coach: Gero BISANZ).
Goals: ROSELI de Belo (19) / Birgit PRINZ (5), Maren MEINERT (22), Bettina
WIEGMANN (42 pen), Heidi MOHR (78, 89), Anouschka BERNHARD (90)
Referee: Alain HAMER (Luxembourg) Attendance: 3,203

Sent-off: 63' SUZY Bitencourt de Oliveira.

Team	Pld	W	D	L	GF	GA	GD	Pts
Germany	*3*	*2*	*0*	*1*	*9*	*4*	*+5*	*6*
Sweden	*3*	*2*	*0*	*1*	*5*	*3*	*+2*	*6*
Japan	*3*	*1*	*0*	*2*	*2*	*4*	*-2*	*3*
Brazil	3	1	0	2	3	8	-5	3

GROUP B

06.06.1995 Tingvalla IP, Karlstad: Norway – Nigeria 8-0 (2-0)
Norway: Bente NORDBY, Linda MEDALEN, Anne NYMARK ANDERSEN (77
Nina NYMARK ANDERSEN Jakobsen), Tina SVENSSON, Gro ESPESETH, Merete
MYKLEBUST, Hege RIISE (69 Tone Gunn FRUSTØL), Ann Kristin AARØNES,
Tone HAUGEN, Heidi STØRE (55 Marianne PETTERSEN), Kristin SANDBERG.
(Coach: Even Jostein PELLERUD).
Nigeria: Ann CHIEJINE, Florence OMAGBEMI, Mavis OGUN, Ngozi EZEOCHA
(YC69) (71 Prisca EMEAFU), Omo-Love BRANCH (73 Nkechi MBILITAM
(YC86)), Phoebe EBIMIEKUMO, Nkiru OKOSIEME, Ann MUKORO, Mercy
AKIDE (46 Patience AVRE), Rita NWADIKE, Adaku OKOROAFOR.
(Coach: Paul Ebiye HAMILTON).
Goals: Kristin SANDBERG (30, 44, 82), Hege RIISE (49), Ann Kristin AARØNES
(60, 90), Linda MEDALEN (67), Tina SVENSSON (76 pen)
Referee: Alain HAMER (Luxembourg) Attendance: 4,344

06.06.1995 Olympia, Helsingborg: England – Canada 3-2 (0-0)
England: Pauline COPE Boanas, Tina Ann MAPES (70 Hope Patricia POWELL),
Samantha BRITTON, Clare Elizabeth TAYLOR, Brenda SEMPARE, Karen BURKE,
Gillian COULTARD, Marieanne SPACEY, Deborah (Debbie) BAMPTON, Karen
FARLEY (YC77), Karen WALKER (75 Kerry DAVIS). (Coach: Ted COPELAND).
Canada: Carla CHIN, Charmaine HOOPER, Janine HELLAND Wood, Michelle
RING, Cathy ROSS (78 Suzanne MUIR), Andrea NEIL, Geraldine DONNELLY
(YC44), Veronica O'BRIEN, Angela KELLY, Silvana BURTINI, Helen STOUMBOS
(YC17). (Coach: Sylvie BÉLIVEAU).
Goals: Gillian COULTARD 1-0 (51 pen, 85), Marieanne SPACEY (76 pen) / Helen
STOUMBOS (87), Geraldine DONNELLY (90+1)
Referee: Eva ÖDLUND (Sweden) Attendance: 655

08.06.1995 Olympia, Helsingborg: Nigeria – Canada 3-3 (1-2)
Nigeria: Ann CHIEJINE, Yinka KUDAISI, Florence OMAGBEMI, Mavis OGUN,
Prisca EMEAFU, Omo-Love BRANCH (41 Nkechi MBILITAM (YC83)), Phoebe
EBIMIEKUMO, Maureen MMADU (60 Ann MUKORO), Patience AVRE (YC14),
Rita NWADIKE, Adaku OKOROAFOR. (Coach: Paul Ebiye HAMILTON).
Canada: Carla CHIN, Charmaine HOOPER, Janine HELLAND Wood, Michelle
RING, Luce MONGRAIN (YC44), Andrea NEIL, Geraldine DONNELLY, Veronica
O'BRIEN (61 Suzanne GERRIOR), Annie CARON (77 Helen STOUMBOS), Angela
KELLY, Silvana BURTINI. (Coach: Sylvie BÉLIVEAU).
Goals: Rita NWADIKE (26), Patience AVRE (60), Adaku OKOROAFOR (77) /
Silvana BURTINI (12, 55), Geraldine DONNELLY (20)
Referee: Pirom UN PRASERT (Thailand) Attendance: 250

08.06.1995 Tingvalla IP, Karlstad: Norway – England 2-0 (2-0)
Norway: Bente NORDBY, Linda MEDALEN (73 Randi LEINAN), Anne NYMARK
ANDERSEN (YC34), Nina NYMARK ANDERSEN Jakobsen, Tina SVENSSON,
Gro ESPESETH, Merete MYKLEBUST, Hege RIISE (85 Hege GUNNERØD), Ann
Kristin AARØNES, Tone HAUGEN, Kristin SANDBERG (66 Marianne
PETTERSEN). (Coach: Even Jostein PELLERUD).
England: Pauline COPE Boanas, Tina Ann MAPES, Samantha BRITTON (65 Kerry
DAVIS), Clare Elizabeth TAYLOR, Brenda SEMPARE (YC54), Karen BURKE,
Gillian COULTARD (82 Rebecca EASTON), Marieanne SPACEY (36 Hope Patricia
POWELL), Deborah (Debbie) BAMPTON, Karen FARLEY, Karen WALKER.
(Coach: Ted COPELAND).
Goals: Tone HAUGEN (7), Hege RIISE (37)
Referee: Eduardo GAMBOA Martinez (Chile) Attendance: 5,520

35

10.06.1995 Tingvalla IP, Karlstad: Nigeria – England 2-3 (1-3)
Nigeria: Ann CHIEJINE, Yinka KUDAISI *(YC68)*, Florence OMAGBEMI, Mavis
OGUN, Prisca EMEAFU, Ngozi EZEOCHA (44 Maureen MMADU *(YC90)*), Phoebe
EBIMIEKUMO *(YC5)*, Patience AVRE (47 Nkiru OKOSIEME), Ann MUKORO,
Rita NWADIKE, Adaku OKOROAFOR. (Coach: Paul Ebiye HAMILTON).
England: Lesley HIGGS Shipp, Tina Ann MAPES, Clare Elizabeth TAYLOR (81
Samantha BRITTON), Brenda SEMPARE (58 Rebecca EASTON), Karen BURKE,
Gillian COULTARD, Marieanne SPACEY (70 Hope Patricia POWELL), Deborah
(Debbie) BAMPTON, Kerry DAVIS, Karen FARLEY, Karen WALKER.
(Coach: Ted COPELAND).
Goals: Adaku OKOROAFOR (13), Rita NWADIKE (74) / Karen FARLEY (10, 38),
Karen WALKER (27)
Referee: Ingrid Jonsson (Sweden) Attendance: 1,843

10.06.1995 Strömvallen, Gävle: Norway – Canada 7-0 (3-0)
Norway: Bente NORDBY, Linda MEDALEN (46 Randi LEINAN), Anne NYMARK
ANDERSEN, Tina SVENSSON, Gro ESPESETH, Merete MYKLEBUST, Hege
RIISE (46 Kristin SANDBERG), Ann Kristin AARØNES, Tone HAUGEN (69
Agnete CARLSEN), Heidi STØRE, Marianne PETTERSEN.
(Coach: Even Jostein PELLERUD).
Canada: Carla CHIN, Charmaine HOOPER *(YC36)*, Janine HELLAND Wood,
Suzanne MUIR (85 Andrea NEIL), Michelle RING *(YC88)*, Cathy ROSS, Geraldine
DONNELLY *(YC80)*, Annie CARON *(YC26)*, Angela KELLY, Silvana BURTINI,
Helen STOUMBOS. (Coach: Sylvie BÉLIVEAU).
Goals: Ann Kristin AARØNES (4, 21, 90+3), Hege RIISE (12), Marianne
PETTERSEN (71, 89), Randi NEINAN (84)
Referee: MARIA Edilene SIQUEIRA (Brazil) Attendance: 2,715

Team	Pld	W	D	L	GF	GA	GD	Pts
Norway	*3*	*3*	*0*	*0*	*17*	*0*	*+17*	*9*
England	*3*	*2*	*0*	*1*	*6*	*6*	*0*	*6*
Canada	3	0	1	2	5	13	-8	1
Nigeria	3	0	1	2	5	14	-9	1

GROUP C

06.06.1995   Strömvallen, Gävle: United States – China PR 3-3 (2-1)
United States: Briana Collette SCURRY, Joy Lynn FAWCETT Biefeld, Carla Werden
OVERBECK, Linda HAMILTON, Kristine Marie LILLY Heavey, Tiffany Marie
ROBERTS Sahaydak, Julie Maurine FOUDY, Michelle Anne AKERS (18 Tiffeny
Carleen MILBRETT, 76 Holly Jean MANTHEI), Tisha Lea VENTURINI Hoch,
Mariel Margaret (Mia) HAMM, Carin Jennings GABARRA.
(Coach: Tony DiCICCO).
China PR: ZHONG Honglian, FAN Yunjie, WANG Liping *(YC3)*, WEN Lirong, NIU
Lijie, ZHAO Lihong, ZHOU Yang, SUN Qingmei (84 SHUI Qingxia), CHEN Yufeng
(47 LIU Ailing), SUN Wen, SHI Guihong (35 WEI Haiying).
(Coach: YUANAN Ma).
Goals: Tisha Lea VENTURINI Hoch (22), Tiffeny Carleen MILBRETT (34), Mariel
Margaret (Mia) HAMM (51) / WANG Liping (38), WEI Haiying (74), SUN Wen (79)
Referee: Ingrid JONSSON (Sweden)   Attendance: 4,635

06.06.1995   Arosvallen, Västerås: Denmark – Australia 5-0 (3-0)
Denmark: Dorthe LARSEN Nielsen, Lene TERP, Rikke BRINK Holm, Kamma
FLÆNG, Anne DOT EGGERS NIELSEN, Katrine Søndergaard PEDERSEN (78
Jeanne AXELSEN), Birgit CHRISTENSEN, Anette LAURSEN *(YC28)* (65 Christina
BONDE), Gitte KROGH, Lene MADSEN (63 Christina HANSEN), Helle JENSEN.
(Coach: Keld GANTZHORN).
Australia: Tracey WHEELER, Cheryl SALISBURY *(YC37)* (57 Angela
IANNOTTA), Sarah COOPER, Anissa TANN DARBY, Jane OAKLEY, Sonia
GEGENHUBER, Lisa CASAGRANDE (79 Lizzy CLAYDON), Alison FORMAN
(YC25), Julie MURRAY, Sunni HUGHES (57 Kim LEMBRYK), Michelle
WATSON *(YC45)*. (Coach: Tom SERMANNI).
Goals: Gitte KROGH (12, 48), Anne DOT EGGERS NIELSEN (25), Helle JENSEN
(37), Christina HANSEN (86)
Referee: Bente Ovedie SKOGVANG (Norway)   Attendance: 1,500

Sent-off: 30' Sonia GEGENHUBER.

08.06.1995   Arosvallen, Västerås: China PR – Australia 4-2 (1-1)
China PR: ZHONG Honglian, FAN Yunjie, WANG Liping, XIE Huilin, ZHAO
Lihong, LIU Ailing, ZHOU Yang *(YC79)*, SHUI Qingxia (27 WEI Haiying), CHEN
Yufeng (69 WEN Lirong), SUN Wen, SHI Guihong. (Coach: YUANAN Ma).
Australia: Tracey WHEELER, Cheryl SALISBURY *(YC73)* (77 Lizzy CLAYDON),
Sarah COOPER, Anissa TANN DARBY, Jane OAKLEY, Angela IANNOTTA,
Alison FORMAN, Kim LEMBRYK *(YC62)* (62 Lisa CASAGRANDE), Julie
MURRAY (81 Denie PENTECOST), Sunni HUGHES, Michelle WATSON *(YC45)*.
(Coach: Tom SERMANNI).
Goals: ZHOU Yang (23), SHI Guihong (54, 78), LIU Ailing (90+3) / Angela
IANNOTTA (25), Sunni HUGHES (89)
Referee: MARIA Edilene SIQUEIRA (Brazil)   Attendance: 1,500

37

08.06.1995 Strömvallen, Gävle: United States – Denmark 2-0 (1-0)
United States: Briana Collette SCURRY, Joy Lynn FAWCETT Biefeld, Carla Werden
OVERBECK, Linda HAMILTON (53 Thori Yvette STAPLES BRYAN), Kristine
Marie LILLY Heavey, Tiffany Marie ROBERTS Sahaydak, Julie Maurine FOUDY
(YC38), Tisha Lea VENTURINI Hoch, Tiffeny Carleen MILBRETT (61 Debbie
KELLER), Mariel Margaret (Mia) HAMM, Carin Jennings GABARRA (85 Sarah
RAFANELLI). (Coach: Tony DiCICCO).
Denmark: Dorthe LARSEN Nielsen *(YC55)*, Lene TERP, Rikke BRINK Holm,
Kamma FLÆNG, Anne DOT EGGERS NIELSEN, Katrine Søndergaard
PEDERSEN, Birgit CHRISTENSEN, Anette LAURSEN (46 Jeanne AXELSEN),
Gitte KROGH (53 Christina HANSEN), Lene MADSEN (61 Christina PETERSEN
(YC89)), Helle JENSEN. (Coach: Keld GANTZHORN).
Goals: Kristine Marie LILLY Heavey (9), Tiffeny Carleen MILBRETT (49)
Referee: Mamadou Engage CAMARA (Guinea)   Attendance: 2,704

Sent-off: 88' Briana Collette SCURRY.

10.06.1995 Arosvallen, Västerås: China PR – Denmark 3-1 (1-1)
China PR: GAO Hong, FAN Yunjie, WANG Liping, XIE Huilin, WEN Lirong,
ZHAO Lihong, LIU Ailing, ZHOU Yang, SUN Wen, WEI Haiying, SHI Guihong (73
SHUI Qingxia). (Coach: YUANAN Ma).
Denmark: Dorthe LARSEN Nielsen, Lene TERP, Rikke BRINK Holm, Louise
HANSEN, Anne DOT EGGERS NIELSEN *(YC56)*, Katrine Søndergaard
PEDERSEN (43 Bettina ALLENTOFT), Birgit CHRISTENSEN, Gitte KROGH,
Lene MADSEN (79 Christina PETERSEN), Christina HANSEN, Helle JENSEN (26
Christina BONDE). (Coach: Keld GANTZHORN).
Goals: SHI Guihong (21), SUN Wen (76), WEI Haiying (90) / Christina BONDE (44)
Referee: Eduardo GAMBOA Martinez (Chile)   Attendance: 1,619

10.06.1995 Olympia, Helsingborg: United States – Australia 4-1 (0-0)
United States: Saskia Johanna WEBBER, Joy Lynn FAWCETT Biefeld, Carla
Werden OVERBECK, Thori Yvette STAPLES BRYAN, Linda HAMILTON,
Kristine Marie LILLY Heavey, Tisha Lea VENTURINI Hoch *(YC55)*, Holly Jean
MANTHEI (46 Carin Jennings GABARRA), Amanda Caryl CROMWELL (61 Julie
Maurine FOUDY), Tiffeny Carleen MILBRETT (78 Debbie KELLER), Mariel
Margaret (Mia) HAMM. (Coach: Tony DiCICCO).
Australia: Tracey WHEELER, Sarah COOPER, Anissa TANN DARBY, Jane
OAKLEY (75 Sacha WAINWRIGHT), Sonia GEGENHUBER, Lisa
CASAGRANDE (67 Lizzy CLAYDON), Angela IANNOTTA *(YC82)*, Alison
FORMAN *(YC42)*, Kim LEMBRYK (82 Kaylene JANSSEN), Julie MURRAY
(YC88), Sunni HUGHES. (Coach: Tom SERMANNI).
Goals: Julie Maurine FOUDY (69), Joy Lynn FAWCETT Biefeld (72), Carla Werden
OVERBECK (90+2 pen), Debbie KELLER (90+4) / Lisa CASAGRANDE (54)
Referee: Pirom UN PRASERT (Thailand)   Attendance: 1,105

Team	Pld	W	D	L	GF	GA	GD	Pts
United States	*3*	*2*	*1*	*0*	*9*	*4*	*+5*	*7*
China PR	*3*	*2*	*1*	*0*	*10*	*6*	*+4*	*7*
Denmark	*3*	*1*	*0*	*2*	*6*	*5*	*+1*	*3*
Australia	3	0	0	3	3	13	-10	0

QUARTER FINALS

13.06.1995 Strömvallen, Gävle: Japan – United States 0-4 (0-3)
Japan: Junko OZAWA, Yumi OBE, Rie YAMAKI *(YC72)*, Kae NISHINA, Yumi
TOMEI, Maki HANETA, Asako Takemoto TAKAKURA, Futaba KIOKA, Etsuko
HANDA (46 Nami OTAKE), Tamaki UCHIYAMA, Akemi NODA.
(Coach: Tamotsu SUZUKI).
United States: Briana Collette SCURRY, Joy Lynn FAWCETT Biefeld, Carla Werden
OVERBECK, Linda HAMILTON, Kristine Marie LILLY Heavey (68 Thori Yvette
STAPLES BRYAN), Tiffany Marie ROBERTS Sahaydak *(YC47)*, Julie Maurine
FOUDY, Tisha Lea VENTURINI Hoch (80 Amanda Caryl CROMWELL), Tiffeny
Carleen MILBRETT, Mariel Margaret (Mia) HAMM (61 Debbie KELLER), Carin
Jennings GABARRA. (Coach: Tony DiCICCO).
Goals: Kristine Marie LILLY Heavey (8, 42), Tiffeny Carleen MILBRETT (45),
Tisha Lea VENTURINI Hoch (80)
Referee: Eduardo GAMBOA Martinez (Chile) Attendance: 3,756

13.06.1995 Tingvalla IP, Karlstad: Norway – Denmark 3-1 (1-0)
Norway: Bente NORDBY, Linda MEDALEN *(YC23)*, Anne NYMARK
ANDERSEN, Tina SVENSSON, Gro ESPESETH, Merete MYKLEBUST, Hege
RIISE, Ann Kristin AARØNES (76 Agnete CARLSEN), Tone HAUGEN, Heidi
STØRE, Marianne PETTERSEN (84 Randi LEINAN).
(Coach: Even Jostein PELLERUD).
Denmark: Dorthe LARSEN Nielsen, Lene TERP, Rikke BRINK Holm *(YC90)*,
Kamma FLÆNG, Louise HANSEN (63 Anette LAURSEN), Anne DOT EGGERS
NIELSEN, Katrine Søndergaard PEDERSEN, Jeanne AXELSEN (46 Gitte KROGH),
Birgit CHRISTENSEN, Lene MADSEN (86 Christina BONDE), Helle JENSEN.
(Coach: Keld GANTZHORN).
Goals: Gro ESPESETH (21), Linda MEDALEN (64), Hege RIISE (85) / Gitte
KROGH (86)
Referee: Pirom UN PRASERT (Thailand) Attendance: 4,655

13.06.1995   Arosvallen, Västerås: Germany – England 3-0 (1-0)
Germany: Manuela GOLLER, Sandra MINNERT, Anouschka BERNHARD, Ursula
LOHN, Silva NEID, Maren MEINERT (85 Pia WUNDERLICH), Martina VOSS-
TECKLENBURG, Bettina WIEGMANN, Dagmar POHLMANN, Birgit PRINZ (67
Patricia BROCKER Grigoli), Heidi MOHR. (Coach: Gero BISANZ).
England: Pauline COPE Boanas, Tina Ann MAPES (79 Louise WALLER), Clare
Elizabeth TAYLOR (87 Samantha BRITTON), Brenda SEMPARE *(YC70)*, Karen
BURKE, Gillian COULTARD (46 Rebecca EASTON *(YC57)*), Marieanne SPACEY,
Deborah (Debbie) BAMPTON, Kerry DAVIS, Karen FARLEY, Karen WALKER.
(Coach: Ted COPELAND).
Goals: Martina VOSS-TECKLENBURG (41), Maren MEINERT (55), Heidi MOHR
(82)
Referee: Bente Ovedie SKOGVANG (Norway)   Attendance: 2,317

13.06.1995   Olympia, Helsingborg: Sweden – China PR 1-1 (0-1,1-1) (a.e.t.)
Sweden: Elisabeth LEIDINGE, Gärd Kristin BENGTSSON (65 Annika
NESSVOLD), Malin Elisabeth ANDERSSON, Anna POHJANEN, Lena
VIDEKULL, Susanne HEDBERG, Eva ZEIKFALVY (46 Åsa LÖNNQVIST), Pia
Mariane SUNDHAGE, Anneli ANDELÉN (71 Malin FLINK), Ulrika KALTE, Helen
NILSSON. (Coach: Bengt SIMONSSON).
China PR: GAO Hong, FAN Yunjie, WANG Liping (103 SHUI Qingxia), XIE Huilin
(YC22), WEN Lirong, ZHAO Lihong (119 CHEN Yufeng), LIU Ailing *(YC77)*,
ZHOU Yang, SUN Qingmei, SUN Wen, SHI Guihong (51 WEI Haiying).
(Coach: YUANAN Ma).
Goals: Ulrika KALTE (90+3) / SUN Qingmei (29)
Referee: Sonia DENONCOURT (Canada)   Attendance: 7,537

*Penalties: SUN Wen 0-1, Malin Elisabeth ANDERSSON missed, XIE Huilin 0-2,
Lena VIDEKULL 1-2, CHEN Yufeng 1-3, Anna POHJANEN 2-3, SHUI
Qingxia 2-4, Pia Mariane SUNDHAGE 3-4, LIU Ailing missed, Annika
NESSVOLD missed.*

China PR qualified after extra time on penalties (4:3).

SEMI-FINALS

15.06.1995   Arosvallen, Västerås: United States – Norway 0-1 (0-1)
United States: Briana Collette SCURRY, Joy Lynn FAWCETT Biefeld, Carla Werden
OVERBECK, Linda HAMILTON, Kristine Marie LILLY Heavey, Tiffany Marie
ROBERTS Sahaydak (53 Tiffeny Carleen MILBRETT), Julie Maurine FOUDY,
Michelle Anne AKERS, Tisha Lea VENTURINI Hoch, Mariel Margaret (Mia)
HAMM, Carin Jennings GABARRA. (Coach: Tony DiCICCO).
Norway: Bente NORDBY, Linda MEDALEN, Anne NYMARK ANDERSEN, Nina
NYMARK ANDERSEN Jakobsen, Tina SVENSSON *(YC6)*, Gro ESPESETH,
Merete MYKLEBUST, Hege RIISE, Ann Kristin AARØNES, Tone HAUGEN (69
Marianne PETTERSEN), Heidi STØRE. (Coach: Even Jostein PELLERUD).
Goal: Ann Kristin AARØNES (10)
Referee: Alain HAMER (Luxembourg)   Attendance: 2,893

Sent-off: 76' Heidi STØRE.

15.06.1995   Olympia, Helsingborg: Germany – China PR 1-0 (0-0)
Germany: Manuela GOLLER, Anouschka BERNHARD, Birgitt AUSTERMÜHL,
Ursula LOHN, Silva NEID, Maren MEINERT, Martina VOSS-TECKLENBURG,
Bettina WIEGMANN, Dagmar POHLMANN, Birgit PRINZ (83 Pia
WUNDERLICH), Heidi MOHR. (Coach: Gero BISANZ).
China PR: GAO Hong, FAN Yunjie (86 CHEN Yufeng), WANG Liping, XIE Huilin,
WEN Lirong *(YC52)*, ZHAO Lihong, LIU Ailing, ZHOU Yang, SUN Qingmei, SUN
Wen, SHI Guihong *(YC65)*. (Coach: YUANAN Ma).
Goal: Bettina WIEGMANN (88)
Referee: Petros MATHABELA (South Africa)   Attendance: 3,693

THIRD PLACE PLAY-OFF

17.06.1995   Strömvallen, Gävle: China PR – United States 0-2 (0-1)
China PR: GAO Hong, FAN Yunjie (72 CHEN Yufeng), WANG Liping, XIE Huilin
(YC45), WEN Lirong, NIU Lijie, ZHAO Lihong, LIU Ailing, SUN Qingmei, SUN
Wen (59 WEI Haiying), SHI Guihong. (Coach: YUANAN Ma).
United States: Briana Collette SCURRY, Joy Lynn FAWCETT Biefeld, Carla Werden
OVERBECK, Thori Yvette STAPLES BRYAN, Linda HAMILTON (54 Tiffeny
Marie ROBERTS Sahaydak), Kristine Marie LILLY Heavey, Julie Maurine FOUDY,
Tisha Lea VENTURINI Hoch, Tiffeny Carleen MILBRETT (68 Debbie KELLER),
Mariel Margaret (Mia) HAMM, Carin Jennings GABARRA (80 Sarah RAFANELLI).
(Coach: Tony DiCICCO).
Goals: Tisha Lea VENTURINI Hoch (24), Mariel Margaret (Mia) HAMM (55)
Referee: Sonia DENONCOURT (Canada)   Attendance: 4,335

FINAL

18.06.1995 Råsundastadion, Solna: Germany –Norway 0-2 (0-2)
Germany: Manuela GOLLER, Anouschka BERNHARD *(YC2)*, Birgitt
AUSTERMÜHL, Ursula LOHN, Silva NEID, Maren MEINERT (86 Sandra
SMISEK), Martina VOSS-TECKLENBURG, Bettina WIEGMANN, Dagmar
POHLMANN (75 Pia WUNDERLICH), Birgit PRINZ (83 Patricia BROCKER
Grigoli), Heidi MOHR. (Coach: Gero BISANZ).
Norway: Bente NORDBY, Linda MEDALEN *(YC58)*, Anne NYMARK ANDERSEN
(YC22), Nina NYMARK ANDERSEN Jakobsen, Tina SVENSSON, Gro ESPESETH,
Merete MYKLEBUST, Hege RIISE, Ann Kristin AARØNES *(YC70)*, Tone
HAUGEN, Marianne PETTERSEN. (Coach: Even Jostein PELLERUD).
Goals: Hege RIISE (37), Marianne PETTERSEN (40)
Referee: Ingrid JONSSON (Sweden) Attendance: 17,158

NORWAY BECAME WORLD CHAMPIONS

THIRD EDITION FIFA WOMEN'S WORLD CUP 1999

QUALIFYING TOURNAMENTS

CAF AFRICAN WOMEN'S CHAMPIONSHIP 1998

The tournament was held in Nigeria between 17 & 31 october 1998. The winner and runner-up will qualify for the FIFA Women's World Cup 1999.

QUALIFICATION

28.03.1998 Mozambique – Lesotho 3-0
29.03.1998 Johannesburg: South Africa – Swaziland 9-0
Goals: Khumalo, Thabethe (2x), Mtokwane, Phewa, Solomon (3x), ?? (og)
29.03.1998 Cairo: Egypt – Uganda 1-1
29.03.1998 Accra Sports Stadium, Accra: Ghana – Guinea 11-0 (7-0)
Goals: Gyamfuah (4, 22, 35, 90), Mensah (17, 24, 1H), Bayor (1H), Sackey (73, 80), Quartey (78)
10.04.1998 Nakivubo Stadium, Kampala: Uganda – Egypt 0-1
11.04.1998 Somhlolo: Swaziland – South Africa 0-6
Goals: Phewa (2x), Solomon (4x)
12.04.1998 Lesotho – Mozambique 2-4
12.04.1998 Conakry: Guinea – Ghana 0-8

Namibia withdrew, **DR Congo** qualified.
Sierra Leone withdrew, **Cameroon** qualified.
Kenya withdrew, **Morocco** qualified.

DR Congo, Egypt and Morocco made their first appearances in the tournament. Mozambique was also qualified, but failed to arrive for the tournament. Lesotho, which was drafted in as a late replacement, equally failed to show up.

FINAL TOURNAMENT
FIRST ROUND
GROUP A

17.10.1998 Ahmadu Bello Stadium, Kaduna: Nigeria – Morocco 8-0 (3-0)
Goals: Okosieme (17, 1H), Avre (30, 2H), Nwadike (2H, 2H), Omagbemi (2H), Akide (2H)
17.10.1998 Ahmadu Bello Stadium, Kaduna: DR Congo – Egypt 4-1
20.10.1998 Ahmadu Bello Stadium, Kaduna: Morocco – Egyp1 4-1
20.10.1998 Ahmadu Bello Stadium, Kaduna: Nigeria – DR Congo 6-0
23.10.1998 Ahmadu Bello Stadium, Kaduna: Morocco – DR Congo 0-0
23.10.1998 Ahmadu Bello Stadium, Kaduna: Nigeria – Egypt 6-0

Team	Pld	W	D	L	GF	GA	GD	Pts
Nigeria	*3*	*3*	*0*	*0*	*20*	*0*	*+20*	*9*
DR Congo	*3*	*1*	*1*	*1*	*4*	*7*	*-3*	*4*
Morocco	3	1	1	1	4	9	-5	4
Egypt	3	0	0	3	2	14	-12	0

GROUP B

18.10.1998 Gateway Stadium, Ijebu Ode: Ghana – South Africa 4-0
21.10.1998 Gateway Stadium, Ijebu Ode: Cameroon – South Africa 3-2
24.10.1998 Gateway Stadium, Ijebu Ode: Ghana – Cameroon 3-1

Team	Pld	W	D	L	GF	GA	GD	Pts
Ghana	*2*	*2*	*0*	*0*	*7*	*1*	*+6*	*6*
Cameroon	*2*	*1*	*0*	*1*	*4*	*5*	*-1*	*3*
South Africa	2	0	0	2	2	7	-5	0
Mozambique **withdrew**	0	0	0	0	0	0		0

KNOCKOUT STAGE
SEMI-FINALS

27.10.1998 Ahmadu Bello Stadium, Kaduna: Nigeria – Cameroon 6-0
27.10.1998 Ahmadu Bello Stadium, Kaduna: Ghana – DR Congo 4-1 (a.e.t.)

THIRD PLACE PLAY-OFF

30.10.1998 Gateway Stadium, Ijebu Ode: DR Congo – Cameroon 3-3 (a.e.t.)

DR Congo winner after extra time on penalties (3:1).

FINAL

31.10.1998 Gateway Stadium, Ijebu Ode: Nigeria – Ghana 2-0 (1-0)
Goals: Okosieme (43), Mbachu (64)

Nigeria and **Ghana** both qualified for the FIFA Women's World Cup 1999.

AFC ASIAN WOMEN'S CHAMPIONSHIP 1997

The tournament was held in Guangdong, China between 5 & 14 December 1997.
Three teams will qualify for the FIFA Women's World Cup 1999, the two finalists
and the winner of the third place play-off.

GROUP STAGE
GROUP A

05.12.1997 India – Hong Kong 3-0

05.12.1997 Japan – Guam 21-0
Goals: Gakei Nishina, Homare Sawa, Yuko Morimoto, Miyuki Yanagida, Mayumi
Daimatsu, Nami Otake, Tamaki Uchiyama
07.12.1997 Hong Kong – Guam 1-0
07.12.1997 Japan – India 1-0
Goal: Homare Sawa
09.12.1997 Japan – Hong Kong 9-0
Goals: Rie Yamaki, Yumi Toumei, Homare Sawa,Yuko Morimoto, Miyuki Yanagida,
Tomomi Mitsui, Tamaki Uchiyama
09.12.1998 India – Guam 10-0

Team	Pld	W	D	L	GF	GA	GD	Pts
Japan	*3*	*3*	*0*	*0*	*31*	*0*	*+31*	*9*
India	3	2	0	1	13	1	+12	6
Hong Kong	3	1	0	2	1	12	-11	3
Guam	3	0	0	3	0	32	-32	0

GROUP B

05.12.1997 China PR – North Korea 3-1 (2-0)
Goals: Liu Ailing (3, 88), Fan Yunjie (17) / Kim Kun-sil (83)
05.12.1997 Uzbekistan – Philippines 2-1
07.12.1997 China PR – Uzbekistan 8-0
Goals: Jin Yan (15, 46, 62, 74), ??
07.12.1997 North Korea – Philippines 14-1
09.12.1997 China PR – Philippines 16-0
09.12.1997 North Korea – Uzbekistan 8-0

Team	Pld	W	D	L	GF	GA	GD	Pts
China PR	*3*	*3*	*0*	*0*	*27*	*1*	*+26*	*9*
North Korea	*3*	*2*	*0*	*1*	*23*	*4*	*+19*	*6*
Uzbekistan	3	1	0	2	2	17	-15	3
Philippines	3	0	0	3	2	32	-30	0

GROUP C

05.12.1997 Chinese Taipei – South Korea 1-0
Goal: Hsu Ching-Hsin
07.12.1997 South Korea – Kazakhstan 11-0
09.12.1997 Chinese Taipei – Kazakhstan 6-0

Team	Pld	W	D	L	GF	GA	GD	Pts
Chinese Taipei	*2*	*2*	*0*	*0*	*7*	*0*	*+7*	*6*
South Korea	2	1	0	1	11	1	+10	3
Kazakhstan	2	0	0	2	0	17	-17	0

KNOCKOUT STAGE
SEMI-FINALS

12.12.1997   North Korea – Japan 1-0 (1-0)
Goal: Kim Kum-sil (3)
12.12.1997   China PR – Chinese Taipei 10-0
Goals: Sun Wen (2, 5), Liu Ailing (36, 43, 45, 85), Sun Qingmei (42, ??),
Shui Qingxia (46), Jin Yan.

THIRD PLACE PLAY-OFF

14.12.1997   Japan – Chinese Taipei 2-0 (2-0)
Goals: Homare Sawa (20, 39)

FINAL

14.12.1997   China PR – North Korea 2-0 (0-0)
Goals: Liu Ailing (49, 65)

China PR, North Korea and **Japan** qualified for the FIFA Women's World Cup
1999.

UEFA WOMEN'S WORLD CUP QUALIFICATION 1999

The tournament was held between 21 August 1997 and 11 October 1998. The 16
teams belonging to Class A of European women's football were drawn info four
groups. The four group winners qualify for the FIFA Women's World Cup 1999. The
four runners-up will drawn into two home-and-away knock-out matches. The winners
of those matches will also qualify.

GROUP STAGE
GROUP 1

30.08.1997   Iceland – Sweden 1-3
07.09.1997   Iceland – Ukraine 3-2
28.09.1997   Sweden – Ukraine 3-2
01.11.1997   Estadi La Bòbila, Gavà: Spain – Ukraine 1-2 (0-2)
Goals: Mateos (82) / Zinchenko (40, 45)
03.05.1998   Motril: Spain – Sweden 1-2
Goals: ?? / Ljungberg, Sandell
24.05.1998   Söderstadion, Stockholm: Sweden – Spain 3-1
Goals: Törnqvist, Sandell, ?? / ??
31.05.1998   Spain – Iceland 0-0
07.06.1998   Kiev: Ukraine – Spain 2-1
14.06.1998   Kópavogur: Iceland – Spain 1-1
08.08.1998   Ukraine – Sweden 0-5
26.08.1998   Sweden – Iceland 2-0
30.08.1998   Ukraine – Iceland 1-0

Team	Pld	W	D	L	GF	GA	GD	Pts
Sweden	*6*	*6*	*0*	*0*	*18*	*5*	*+13*	*18*
Ukraine	6	3	0	3	9	13	-4	9
Iceland	6	1	2	3	5	9	-4	5
Spain	6	0	2	4	5	10	-5	2

GROUP 2

06.09.1997 Finland – Switzerland 1-0
04.10.1997 Switzerland – France 1-2
18.10.1997 France – Finland 2-2
01.11.1997 Switzerland – Italy 1-3
22.11.1997 Italy – France 0-0
11.04.1998 France – Italy 2-3
02.05.1998 France – Switzerland 3-0
05.05.1998 Italy – Finland 1-0
16.05.1998 Italy – Switzerland 2-0
23.05.1998 Finland – France 1-0
06.06.1998 Switzerland – Finland 0-1
27.06.1998 Finland – Italy 1-2

Team	Pld	W	D	L	GF	GA	GD	Pts
Italy	*6*	*5*	*1*	*0*	*11*	*4*	*+7*	*16*
Finland	6	3	1	2	6	5	+1	10
France	6	2	2	2	9	7	+2	8
Switzerland	6	0	0	6	2	12	-10	0

GROUP 3

25.09.1997 Paul Greifzu Stadium, Dessau: Germany – England 3-0 (1-0)
Goals: Meyer (13), Smisek (68), Prinz (75)
01.10.1997 Bislett Stadion, Oslo: Norway – Netherlands 6-1 (3-0)
Goals: Pettersen (4, 9, 76), Riise (33), Medalen (79), Lehn (86) / Roos (60)
30.10.1997 Upton Park, London: England – Netherlands 1-0 (0-0)
Goal: Smith (60)
06.11.1997 Germany – Norway 1-0
13.11.1997 Polman Stadion, Almelo: Netherlands – Germany 1-0 (0-0)
Goals: Noom (64)
08.03.1998 The Den Stadium, Millwall: England – Germany 0-1 (0-1)
Goals: Smisek (33)
02.04.1998 Friedrich-Ludwig-Jahn-Stadion, Herford:
            Germany – Netherlands 2-1 (0-1)
Goals: Voss (80), Koning (82 og) / Migchelsen (45)
18.04.1998 De Baandert, Sittard: Netherlands – Norway 0-0
14.05.1998 Oldham Stadium, Oldham: England – Norway 1-2 (1-1)
Goals: White (45) / Knudsen (39), Haugenes (90)

47

23.05.1998   Sportpark Olympia, Waalwijk: Netherlands – England 2-1 (1-1)
Goals: Noom (1, 46) / Walker (19).
17.06.1998   Norway – Germany 3-2
15.08.1998   Åråsen Stadion, Lillestrøm: Norway – England 2-0 (0-0)
Goals: Pettersen (70), Sandaune (89)

Team	Pld	W	D	L	GF	GA	GD	Pts
Norway	6	4	1	1	13	5	+8	13
Germany	6	4	0	2	9	5	+4	12
Netherlands	6	2	1	3	5	10	-5	7
England	6	1	0	5	3	10	-7	3

GROUP 4

21.08.1997   Denmark – Russia 3-1
27.09.1997   Belgium – Denmark 1-2
11.10.1997   Belgium – Russia 3-4
29.10.1997   Hjørring Stadium, Hjørring: Denmark – Portugal 4-0 (1-0)
Goals: Krogh (28, 87), Flæng (48), Anne Nielsen (78)
08.11.1997   Complexo Desportivo Fernando Mamede, Beja:
              Portugal – Russia 0-2 (0-1)
Goals: Barbashina (12), Kamarova (90)
28.02.1998   Estádio Municipal de Cantanhede, Cantanhede:
              Portugal – Belgium 2-0 (1-0)
Goals: Carla Couto (8), Paula Reis (68)
04.04.1998   King Baudouin Stadium, Brussels: Belgium – Portugal 0-2 (0-1)
Goals: Ana Rita (7), Anabela (61)
25.04.1998   Arsenal Stadium, Tula: Russia – Portugal 2-0 (2-0)
Goals: Barbashina (10), Kamarova (24)
16.05.1998   Estádio-João-Paulo-II, Angra do Heroísmo (Azores):
              Portugal – Denmark 0-7 (0-4)
Goals: Christina B.Petersen (1), Merete Pedersen (4, 62), Monica (24 og),
Anne Nielsen (38), Krogh (69), Rasmussen (76)
23.05.1998   Russia – Belgium 5-1
22.08.1998   Russia – Denmark 1-2
29.08.1998   Denmark – Belgium 4-0

Team	Pld	W	D	L	GF	GA	GD	Pts
Denmark	6	6	0	0	22	3	+19	18
Russia	6	4	0	2	15	9	+6	12
Portugal	6	2	0	4	4	15	-11	6
Belgium	6	0	0	6	5	19	-14	0

PLAY-OFF A

12.09.1998   Russia – Finland 2-1
17.09.1998   Germany – Ukraine 5-0
11.10.1998   Finland – Russia 1-2
11.10.1998   Ukraine – Germany 1-1

48

The four group winners **Sweden**, **Italy**, **Norway**, **Denmark** and the two winners of the play-off matches **Russia** and **Germany** qualified for the FIFA Women's World Cup 1999.

CONCACAF WOMEN'S CHAMPIONSHIP 1998

United States was directly qualified for the FIFA Women's World Cup 1999 as hosts of the event. The winner of the tournament will qualify for the FIFA Women's World Cup 1999. The runner-up has to play two play-off matches against the second-placed team of CONMEBOL Sudamericano Femenino 1998. The winner of these play-off matches will also qualify for the FIFA Women's World Cup 1999.

QUALIFICATION

UNCAF QUALIFYING TOURNAMENT 1998

The UNCAF Qualifying Tournament 1998 (Central American Zone) was held in Guatemala City between 19 & 25 July 1998.

GROUP A

19.07.1998 Estadio Mateo Flores, Guatemala City: Costa Rica – Guatemala B 17-0
Goals: Mora (5x), Alemán (4x), Contreras (3x), Araya (2x), Carmona, Castro, Álvarez
21.07.1998 Estadio Mateo Flores, Guatemala City: Haiti – Costa Rica 2-1
23.07.1998 Estadio Mateo Flores, Guatemala City: Haiti – Guatemala B 7-1

Team	Pld	W	D	L	GF	GA	GD	Pts
Haiti	*2*	*2*	*0*	*0*	*9*	*2*	*+7*	*6*
Costa Rica	2	1	0	1	18	2	+16	3
Guatemala B	2	0	0	2	1	24	-23	0

GROUP B

19.07.1998 Estadio Mateo Flores, Guatemala City: Guatemala – Honduras 11-0
21.07.1998 Estadio Mateo Flores, Guatemala City: El Salvador – Honduras 1-1
23.07.1998 Estadio Mateo Flores, Guatemala City: Guatemala – El Salvador 4-1

Team	Pld	W	D	L	GF	GA	GD	Pts
Guatemala	*2*	*2*	*0*	*0*	*15*	*1*	*+14*	*6*
El Salvador	2	0	1	1	2	5	-3	1
Honduras	2	0	1	1	1	12	-11	1

THIRD PLACE PLAY-OFF

25.07.1998 Estadio Mateo Flores, Guatemala City: Costa Rica – El Salvador 5-1

FINAL

25.07.1998   Estadio Mateo Flores, Guatemala City: Guatemala – Haiti 1-0

Guatemala, Haiti and **Costa Rica** qualified for the CONCACAF Final Stage 1998.

CFU QUALIFYING ROUND

The CFU Qualifying Round (Caribbean Zone) consisted of home-and-away ties.

07.08.1998   Central of Excellence Ground, Macoya:
             Trinidad and Tobago – Guyana 9-0
09.08.1998   Central of Excellence Ground, Macoya:
             Trinidad and Tobago – Guyana 7-1

Bahamas withdrew, **Haiti** qualified.
It is not clear whether Martinique and Puerto Rico received a bye to the finals, or whether their unknown opponents withdrew.

Martinique, Puerto Rico and **Trinidad and Tobago** qualified for the CONCACAF Final Stage 1998.

CONCACAF FINAL STAGE 1998

The final stage of the tournament was held at Etobicoke and Scarborough in Toronto, Canada.

GROUP A

28.08.1998   Canada – Puerto Rico 21-0
28.08.1998   Guatemala – Martinique 2-0
30.08.1998   Puerto Rico – Guatemala 0-8
30.08.1998   Canada – Martinique 14-0
01.09.1998   Puerto Rico – Martinique 0-9
01.09.1998   Canada – Guatemala 4-0

Team	Pld	W	D	L	GF	GA	GD	Pts
Canada	*3*	*3*	*0*	*0*	*39*	*0*	*+39*	*9*
Guatemala	*3*	*2*	*0*	*1*	*10*	*4*	*+6*	*6*
Martinique	3	1	0	2	9	16	-7	3
Puerto Rico	3	0	0	3	0	38	-38	0

GROUP B

29.08.1998   Trinidad and Tobago – Haiti 2-1
29.08.1998   Mexico – Costa Rica 3-2
31.08.1998   Haiti – Mexico 1-7
31.08.1998   Costa Rica – Trinidad and Tobago 3-1

50

02.09.1998   Costa Rica – Haiti 2-1
02.09.1998   Trinidad and Togago – Mexico 2-2

Team	Pld	W	D	L	GF	GA	GD	Pts
Mexico	*3*	*2*	*1*	*0*	*12*	*5*	*+7*	*7*
Costa Rica	*3*	*2*	*0*	*1*	*7*	*5*	*+2*	*6*
Trinidad and Tobago	3	1	1	1	5	6	-1	4
Haiti	3	0	0	3	3	11	-8	0

KNOCKOUT STAGE
SEMI-FINALS

04.09.1998   Guatemala – Mexico 0-8
04.09.1998   Canada – Costa Rica 2-0

THIRD PLACE PLAY-OFF

06.09.1998   Costa Rica – Guatemala 4-0

FINAL

06.09.1998   Canada – Mexico 1-0

Canada qualified for the FIFA Women's World Cup 1999. Runner-up Mexico had to play a two-leg play-off against Argentina in December 1998 in the CONMEBOL/CONCACAF Intercontinental play-off.

OFC WOMEN'S CHAMPIONSHIP 1998

The OFC Women's Championship 1998, also known as the VI Ladies Oceania Nations Cup was held in Auckland, New Zealand between 9 & 17 October 1998. Only the winner will qualify for the FIFA Women's World Cup 1999.

FIRST ROUND
GROUP A

09.10.1998   Mt Smart Stadium, Auckland: New Zeland – Samoa 21-0
Goals: Andersen (9, 11, 18, 38, 45, ??), Henderson (16, 75, 78, 86), Haskell (12, 28, 40, 67), ?? (22 og), Cox (52, 83), Smith (62, 66), Crawford (64), Jackman (82)
11.10.1998   Mt Smart Stadium, Auckland: New Zeland – Fiji 14-0
Goals: Andersen (6, 9, ??, 45+, 47, 77, ??), Haskell (17, 29, 32), Ruscoe (31), Cox (45+), Crawford (65), Smith (??)
13.10.1998   Mt Smart Stadium, Auckland: Fiji – Samoa 5-0
Goals: Kubulala, ??

51

Team	Pld	W	D	L	GF	GA	GD	Pts
New Zealand	*2*	*2*	*0*	*0*	*35*	*0*	*+35*	*6*
Fiji	*2*	*1*	*0*	*1*	*5*	*14*	*-9*	*3*
Samoa	2	0	0	2	0	26	-26	0

GROUP B

09.10.1998   Mt Smart Stadium, Auckland: Australia – American Samoa 21-0 (7-0)
Goals: Thomas (4, 35, 55), Casagrande (19, 59), Tann-Darby (28), Salisbury (29, 58, 72, 81, 90+3), Black (37, 68, 88, 90+5), Ferguson (44, 79), Taylor (50), Forman (66), Peters (78), Boyd (90+6)
11.10.1998   Mt Smart Stadium, Auckland: Australia – Papua New Guinea 8-0 (4-0)
Goals: Black (3, 18, 22), Casagrande (28), Salisbury (66, 67, 86), Boyd (90+2)
13.10.1998   Mt Smart Stadium, Auckland:
            Papua New Guinea – American Samoa 9-0
Goals: Taman, ??

Team	Pld	W	D	L	GF	GA	GD	Pts
Australia	*2*	*2*	*0*	*0*	*29*	*0*	*+29*	*6*
Papua New Guinea	*2*	*1*	*0*	*1*	*9*	*8*	*+1*	*3*
American Samoa	2	0	0	2	0	30	-30	0

KNOCKOUT STAGE
SEMI-FINALS

15.10.1998   Mt Smart Stadium, Auckland:
            New Zealand – Papua New Guinea 5-0 (4-0)
Goals: Andersen (6, 55 (p)), Henderson (38), Carlisle (??), Cox (40)
15.10.1998   Mt Smart Stadium, Auckland: Australia – Fiji 17-0 (8-0)
Goals: Murray (3, 23, 47), Iannotta (7, 43), Boyd (23, 39), Black (33, 40, 55), Peters (49, 53, 58, 81), Ferguson (69, 72), Salisbury (83)

THIRD PLACE PLAY-OFF

17.10.1998   Mt Smart Stadium, Auckland: Papua New Guinea – Fiji 7-1

FINAL

17.10.1998   Mt Smart Stadium, Auckland: New Zealand – Australia 1-3 (0-2)
Goals: Smith (77) / Murray (2), Starr (13), Casagrande (66)

Australia qualified for FIFA Women's World Cup 1999.

CONMEBOL SUDAMERICANO FEMENINO 1998

The South America (CONMEBOL) Sudamericano Femenino 1998 tournament was held in Mar del Plata, Argentina between 1 & 15 March 1998. The winner will qualify for the FIFA Women's World Cup 1999. The runner-up has to play two play-off matches against the second-placed team of CONCACAF Women's Championship 1998.

GROUP STAGE
GROUP A

02.03.1998   Estadio José María Minella, Mar del Plata: Colombia – Venezuela 4-1
02.03.1998   Estadio José María Minella, Mar del Plata: Brazil – Peru 15-0
04.03.1998   Estadio José María Minella, Mar del Plata: Chile – Venezuela 5-0 (1-0)
Goals: Lazo (6, 63), González (60, 74, 76)
05.03.1998   Estadio José María Minella, Mar del Plata: Brazil – Colombia 12-1
06.03.1998   Estadio José María Minella, Mar del Plata: Chile – Peru 0-1
Goal: Quintana.
06.03.1998   Estadio José María Minella, Mar del Plata: Brazil – Venezuela 14-0
Goals: Kátia (4x), Roseli (3x), Suzana (2x), Nenê, Pretinha, Elsi, Elane, Maycon
08.03.1998   Estadio José María Minella, Mar del Plata: Venezuela – Peru 1-2
Goals: Infante / Arce, Hoyle
08.03.1998   Estadio José María Minella, Mar del Plata: Chile – Colombia 1-5
Goals: Alburquerque (pen) / Valencia (3x), Grisales, Chala
10.03.1998   Estadio José María Minella, Mar del Plata: Colombia – Peru 1-2 (1-0)
Goals: Valencia (39) / Salinas (80), Quintana (83)
10.03.1998   Estadio José María Minella, Mar del Plata: Brazil – Chile 7-0

Team	Pld	W	D	L	GF	GA	GD	Pts
Brazil	*4*	*4*	*0*	*0*	*48*	*1*	*+47*	*12*
Peru	*4*	*3*	*0*	*1*	*5*	*17*	*-12*	*9*
Colombia	4	2	0	2	11	16	-5	6
Chile	4	1	0	3	6	13	-7	3
Venezuela	4	0	0	4	2	25	-23	0

GROUP B

01.03.1998   Estadio José María Minella, Mar del Plata: Paraguay – Uruguay 3-2
Goals: Giménez, Cuevas (2x) / Arrúa, Soria
01.03.1998   Estadio José María Minella, Mar del Plata: Argentina – Bolivia 9-0 (3-0)
Goals: Achával (37), Villanueva (38), Morales (45, 71), Gaitán (52, 68), Trujillo (57), Núñez (76), Ochotorena (79)
03.03.1998   Estadio José María Minella, Mar del Plata: Uruguay – Ecuador 2-2
03.03.1998   Estadio José María Minella, Mar del Plata: Argentina – Paraguay 3-0
Goals: Villanueva, Baca, Núñez
05.03.1998   Estadio José María Minella, Mar del Plata: Argentina – Uruguay 2-1
05.03.1998   Estadio José María Minella, Mar del Plata: Ecuador – Bolivia 5-2
07.03.1998   Estadio José María Minella, Mar del Plata: Ecuador – Paraguay 3-0

53

07.03.1998   Estadio José María Minella, Mar del Plata: Uruguay – Bolivia 1-1
09.03.1998   Estadio José María Minella, Mar del Plata: Bolivia – Paraguay 2-3
Goals: ?? / Cuevas (2x), ??
09.03.1998   Estadio José María Minella, Mar del Plata: Argentina – Ecuador 2-0
Goals: Morales, Baca

Team	Pld	W	D	L	GF	GA	GD	Pts
Argentina	*4*	*4*	*0*	*0*	*16*	*1*	*+15*	*12*
Ecuador	*4*	*2*	*1*	*1*	*10*	*6*	*+4*	*7*
Paraguay	4	2	0	2	6	10	-4	6
Uruguay	4	0	2	2	6	8	-2	2
Bolivia	4	0	1	3	5	18	-13	1

KNOCKOUT STAGE

SEMI-FINALS

13.03.1998   Estadio José María Minella, Mar del Plata: Brazil – Ecuador 11-1
13.03.1998   Estadio José María Minella, Mar del Plata:
             Argentina – Peru 1-1 (1-0,1-1) (a.e.t.)
Goals: Villanueva (1H) / Salinas (2H)

Argentina won after extra time on penalties (4:3).

THIRD PLACE PLAY-OFF

15.03.1998   Estadio José María Minella, Mar del Plata: Peru – Ecuador 3-3 (a.e.t.)

Peru won after extra time on penalties (5:4).

FINAL

15.03.1998   Estadio José María Minella, Mar del Plata: Brazil – Argentina 7-1 (3-0)
Goals: Roseli (10, 21 pen, 59), Formiga (18 pen), Pretinha (54), Cidinha (65),
Sissi (76) / Gerez (58)

Brazil qualified for the FIFA Women's World Cup 1999. Runner-up Argentina will
play in the CONMEBOL/CONCACAF Intercontinental play-off.

CONMEBOL/CONCACAF INTERCONTINENTAL PLAY-OFF

14.12.1998   Toluca: Mexico – Argentina 3-1
19.12.1998   Buenos Aires: Argentina – Mexico 2-3

Mexico qualified for the FIFA Women's World Cup 1999.

FIFA WOMEN'S WORLD CUP FINAL TOURNAMENT IN USA 1999

GROUP STAGE
GROUP A

19.06.1999 Giants Stadium, East Rutherford: United States – Denmark 3-0 (1-0)
United States: Briana Collette SCURRY, Kathryn Michele MARKGRAF Sobrero,
Joy Lynn FAWCETT Biefeld, Carla Werden OVERBECK, Kristine Marie LILLY
Heavey, Brandi Denise CHASTAIN, Julie Maurine FOUDY, Michelle Anne AKERS,
Tiffeny Carleen MILBRETT (82 Shannon Ann MACMILLAN), Mariel Margaret
(Mia) HAMM, Cynthia Marie (Cindy) PARLOW Cone. (Coach: Tony DiCICCO).
Denmark: Dorthe LARSEN Nielsen, Karina CHRISTENSEN, Lene TERP, Katrine
Søndergaard PEDERSEN, Jeanne AXELSEN, Janne RASMUSSEN (YC11),
Christina PETERSEN (83 Lise SØNDERGAARD), Lene REVSBECK JENSEN (78
Louise HANSEN), Merete PEDERSEN, Gitte KROGH, Mikka HANSEN (63 Janni
LUND JOHANSEN). (Coach: Jørgen HVIDEMOSE).
Goals: Mariel Margaret (Mia) HAMM (17), Julie Maurine FOUDY (73),
Kristine Marie LILLY Heavey (89)
Referee: Sonia DENONCOURT (Canada) Attendance: 78,972

21.06.1999 Rose Bowl, Pasadena: North Korea – Nigeria 1-2 (0-0)
North Korea: KYE Yong-Sun, YUN In-Sil, KIM Sun-Hui (61 JO Jong-Ran), KIM
Hye-Ran, RI Ae-Gyong, RI Hyang-Ok (YC1), SOL Yong-Suk (55 RI Kyong-Ae),
KIM Kum-Sil (29 PAK Jong-Ae), RI Kum-Suk (YC5), JIN Pyol-Hui (YC88), JO
Song-Ok. (Coach: TONG Chan).
Nigeria: Ann CHIEJINE, Yinka KUDAISI (86 Adanna NWANERI (YC88)), Florence
Kikelomo AJAYI, Florence OMAGBEMI, Eberechi OPARA (YC81), Prisca
EMEAFU, Nkiru OKOSIEME, Patience AVRE, Ifeanyi CHIEJINE (70 Nkechi
EGBE), Mercy AKIDE (YC90+3), Rita NWADIKE. (Coach: Mabo ISMAILA).
Goals: JO Song-Ok (74) / Mercy AKIDE (50), Rita NWADIKE (79)
Referee: Katriina ELOVIRTA (Finland) Attendance: 17,100

25.06.1999 Providence Park, Portland: North Korea – Denmark 3-1 (2-0)
North Korea: KYE Yong-Sun, YUN In-Sil, KIM Sun-Hui (YC34) (46 KIM Hye-Ran),
RI Ae-Gyong, RI Hyang-Ok, SOL Yong-Suk, KIM Kum-Sil, PAK Jong-Ae
(YC49,RC86), RI Kum-Suk (YC81), JIN Pyol-Hui, JO Song-Ok (YC83).
(Coach: TONG Chan).
Denmark: Dorthe LARSEN Nielsen, Marlene KRISTENSEN (9 Hanne SAND
CHRISTENSEN), Lene TERP (YC36), Louise HANSEN, Katrine Søndergaard
PEDERSEN, Jeanne AXELSEN, Janne RASMUSSEN, Christina PETERSEN, Lene
REVSBECK JENSEN (46 Janni LUND JOHANSEN), Merete PEDERSEN (63
Mikka HANSEN), Gitte KROGH. (Coach: Jørgen HVIDEMOSE).
Goals: JIN Pyol-Hui (15), JO Song-Ok (39), KIM Kum-Sil (73) /
Janni LUND JOHANSEN (74)
Referee: Martha TORO (Colombia) Attendance: 20,129

Sent-off: 86' PAK Jong-Ae.

25.06.1999 Soldier Field, Chicago: United States – Nigeria 7-1 (6-1)
United States: Briana Collette SCURRY, Kathryn Michele MARKGRAF Sobrero
(46' Sara Eve WHALEN Hess), Joy Lynn FAWCETT Biefeld, Carla Werden
OVERBECK, Kristine Marie LILLY Heavey, Brandi Denise CHASTAIN, Julie
Maurine FOUDY, Michelle Anne AKERS (46 Lorraine Ming (Lorrie) FAIR), Tiffeny
Carleen MILBRETT, Mariel Margaret (Mia) HAMM (57 Shannon Ann
MACMILLAN), Cynthia Marie (Cindy) PARLOW Cone. (Coach: Tony DiCICCO).
Nigeria: Ann CHIEJINE, Yinka KUDAISI, Florence Kikelomo AJAYI *(YC45)*,
Florence OMAGBEMI, Eberechi OPARA, Prisca EMEAFU (84 Gloria USIETA),
Nkiru OKOSIEME, Patience AVRE *(YC30)* (53 Stella MBACHU), Ifeanyi
CHIEJINE (43 Nkechi EGBE), Mercy AKIDE, Rita NWADIKE.
(Coach: Mabo ISMAILA).
Goals: Ifeanyi CHIEJINE (2 og), Mariel Margaret (Mia) HAMM (20), Tiffeny
Carleen MILBRETT (23, 83), Kristine Marie LILLY Heavey (32), Michelle Anne
AKERS (39), Cynthia Marie (Cindy) PARLOW Cone (42) / Nkiru OKOSIEME (3)
Referee: Nicole PETIGNAT (Switzerland) Attendance: 65,080

27.06.1999 FedEx Field, Landover: Nigeria – Denmark 2-0 (1-0)
Nigeria: Ann CHIEJINE, Yinka KUDAISI, Florence OMAGBEMI, Eberechi
OPARA, Prisca EMEAFU *(YC90+1)*, Nkiru OKOSIEME, Patience AVRE, Ifeanyi
CHIEJINE (81 Adanna NWANERI), Mercy AKIDE, Nkechi EGBE (54 Stella
MBACHU *(YC88)*), Rita NWADIKE. (Coach: Mabo ISMAILA).
Denmark: Dorthe LARSEN Nielsen, Lene TERP, Katrine Søndergaard PEDERSEN,
Jeanne AXELSEN, Janne RASMUSSEN, Christina PETERSEN, Janni LUND
JOHANSEN, Hanne SAND CHRISTENSEN, Mikka HANSEN (58 Merete
PEDERSEN), Hanne NØRREGAARD (32 Lene REVSBECK JENSEN), Gitte
KROGH *(YC50)* (66 Louise HANSEN). (Coach: Jørgen HVIDEMOSE).
Goals: Mercy AKIDE (25), Nkiru OKOSIEME (81)
Referee: MARIA Edilene SIQUEIRA (Brazil) Attendance: 22,109

28.06.1999 Foxboro Stadium, Fosborough: United States – North Korea 3-0 (0-0)
United States: Briana Collette SCURRY, Joy Lynn FAWCETT Biefeld, Carla Werden
OVERBECK, Sara Eve WHALEN Hess, Kristine Marie LILLY Heavey, Brandi
Denise CHASTAIN, Tiffany Marie ROBERTS Sahaydak (73 Christie PEARCE),
Tisha Lea VENTURINI Hoch, Shannon Ann MACMILLAN, Mariel Margaret (Mia)
HAMM (46 Tiffeny Carleen MILBRETT), Cynthia Marie (Cindy) PARLOW Cone
(46 Julie Maurine FOUDY). (Coach: Tony DiCICCO).
North Korea: KYE Yong-Sun, YUN In-Sil, KIM Sun-Hui, KIM Sun-Hye *(YC8)*, KIM
Hye-Ran, RI Ae-Gyong (71 YANG Kyong-Hui), RI Hyang-Ok, SOL Yong-Suk, KIM
Kum-Sil *(YC74)*, JIN Pyol-Hui (61 JO Jong-Ran), JO Song-Ok *(YC24)*.
(Coach: TONG Chan).
Goals: Shannon Ann MACMILLAN (56), Tisha Lea VENTURINI Hoch (68, 76)
Referee: Katriina ELOVIRTA (Finland) Attendance: 50,484

Team	Pld	W	D	L	GF	GA	GD	Pts
United States	*3*	*3*	*0*	*0*	*13*	*1*	*+12*	*9*
Nigeria	*3*	*2*	*0*	*1*	*5*	*8*	*-3*	*6*
North Korea	3	1	0	2	4	6	-2	3
Denmark	3	0	0	3	1	8	-7	0

GROUP B

19.06.1999   Giants Stadium, East Rutherford: Brazil – Mexico 7-1 (5-1)
Brazil: Marlisa Wahlbrink "MARAVILHA", Alissandra Cavalcante "NENÊ", ELANE
dos Santos Rego, SUZANA Ferreira da Silva, Rosilane Camargo Mota "FANTA" (82
JULIANA Ribeiro Cabral), MARISA Pires Nogueira, Sisleide do Amor Lima
"SISSI", Maria Dias Aparecida de Souza "CIDINHA" (46 ANDRÉIA dos Santos),
RAQUEL de Souza Noronha, Delma Gonçalves "PRETINHA", KÁTIA Cilene
Teixeira da Silva (72 Miraildes Maciel Mota "FORMIGA").
(Coach: WILSON DE OLIVEIRA Riça).
Mexico: Linnea Andrea QUIÑONES Sandland, Susana MORA Chávez, Martha
Ofelia MOORE Camacho (73 Patricia PÉREZ Peña), Regina Marie OCEGUERA
Schmul, Fátima LEYVA Morán (46 Laurie Anne HILL Rozenel), Andrea
RODEBAUGH Huitrón, María del Carmen Denise IRETA Gonzalez *(YC4)*, Maribel
Guadalupe DOMÍNGUEZ Castelán *(YC74)*, Lisa Anne NÁÑEZ Stromberg *(YC53)*,
Mónica Marie GERARDO Moran (78 Iris Adriana MORA Vallejo *(YC81)*), Mónica
Christine GONZÁLEZ Canales. (Coach: Leonardo CUÉLLAR Rivera).
Goals: Delma Gonçalves "PRETINHA" (3, 12, 90+1), Sisleide do Amor Lima
"SISSI" (29, 42, 50), KÁTIA Cilene Teixeira da Silva (35 pen) / Maribel Guadalupe
DOMÍNGUEZ Castelán (10)
Referee: Nicole PETIGNAT (Switzerland)   Attendance: 78,972

20.06.1999   Rose Bowl, Pasadena: Germany – Italy 1-1 (0-1)
Germany: Silke ROTTENBERG, Kerstin STEGEMANN, Doris FITSCHEN, Ariane
HINGST, Stephanie JONES, Pia WUNDERLICH, Maren MEINERT (82 Monika
MEYER), Bettina WIEGMANN, Birgit PRINZ, Inka GRINGS, Sandra SMISEK (86
Renate LINGOR). (Coach: Tina THEUNE).
Italy: Giorgia BRENZAN, Roberta STEFANELLI, Daniela TAVALAZZI, Luisa
MARCHIO, Anna DUO, Adele FROLLANI (71 Paola ZANNI), Manuela TESSE (68
Damiana DE IANA), Federica D'ASTOLFO *(YC32)*, Antonella CARTA, Patrizia
PANICO, Rita GUARINO (89 Silvia FIORINI). (Coach: Carlo FACCHIN).
Goals: Bettina WIEGMANN (61 pen) / Patrizia PANICO (36)
Referee: Bola ABIDOYE (Nigeria)   Attendance: 17,100

24.06.1999 Soldier Field, Chicago: Brazil – Italy 2-0 (1-0)
Brazil: Marlisa Wahlbrink "MARAVILHA", TÂNIA Maria Pereira Ribeiro *(YC74)*,
Alissandra Cavalcante "NENÊ" *(YC84)* (89 JULIANA Ribeiro Cabral), ELANE dos
Santos Rego, SUZANA Ferreira da Silva *(YC35)*, MARISA Pires Nogueira, Sisleide
do Amor Lima "SISSI", Maria Dias Aparecida de Souza "CIDINHA", RAQUEL de
Souza Noronha (46 Miraildes Maciel Mota "FORMIGA"), Delma Gonçalves
"PRETINHA", KÁTIA Cilene Teixeira da Silva (75 ANDRÉIA dos Santos).
(Coach: WILSON DE OLIVEIRA Riça).
Italy: Giorgia BRENZAN, Roberta STEFANELLI, Daniela TAVALAZZI, Luisa
MARCHIO, Anna DUO *(YC13)*, Adele FROLLANI (55 Damiana DE IANA),
Manuela TESSE, Federica D'ASTOLFO *(YC21)*, Antonella CARTA (58 Silvia
FIORINI), Patrizia PANICO, Rita GUARINO *(YC71)* (74 Silvia TAGLIACARNE).
(Coach: Carlo FACCHIN).
Goals: Sisleide do Amor Lima "SISSI" (3, 63)
Referee: Gitte NIELSEN (Denmark) Attendance: 65,080

25.06.1999 Providence Park, Portland: Germany – Mexico 6-0 2-0)
Germany: Silke ROTTENBERG, Sandra MINNERT, Doris FITSCHEN, Ariane
HINGST, Stephanie JONES, Pia WUNDERLICH, Maren MEINERT *(YC21)* (64
Renate LINGOR), Bettina WIEGMANN (69 Melanie HOFFMANN), Birgit PRINZ
(75 Claudia MÜLLER), Inka GRINGS, Sandra SMISEK. (Coach: Tina THEUNE).
Mexico: Linnea Andrea QUIÑONES Sandland, Susana MORA Chávez, Regina Marie
OCEGUERA Schmul, Fátima LEYVA Morán, Mónica VERGARA Rubio (62
Mónica Marie GERARDO Moran), Patricia PÉREZ Peña, Andrea RODEBAUGH
Huitrón (57 Mónica Christine GONZÁLEZ Canales), Laurie Anne HILL Rozenel,
María del Carmen Denise IRETA Gonzalez, Maribel Guadalupe DOMÍNGUEZ
Castelán, Lisa Anne NÁÑEZ Stromberg. (Coach: Leonardo CUÉLLAR Rivera).
Goals: Inka GRINGS (10, 57, 90+2), Sandra SMISEK (45+1), Ariane HINGST (49),
Renate LINGOR (89)
Referee: IM Eun-Ju (South Korea) Attendance: 20,129

27.06.1999 FedEx Field, Landover: Germany – Brazil 3-3 (1-2)
Germany: Silke ROTTENBERG, Sandra MINNERT *(YC68)*, Doris FITSCHEN,
Ariane HINGST, Stephanie JONES, Pia WUNDERLICH (46 Tina WUNDERLICH
(YC85)), Maren MEINERT, Martina VOSS-TECKLENBURG (29 Sandra SMISEK),
Bettina WIEGMANN, Birgit PRINZ, Inka GRINGS (89 Monika MEYER).
(Coach: Tina THEUNE).
Brazil: Marlisa Wahlbrink "MARAVILHA", TÂNIA Maria Pereira Ribeiro,
Alissandra Cavalcante "NENÊ", ELANE dos Santos Rego, SUZANA Ferreira da
Silva (65 ANDRÉIA dos Santos), MARISA Pires Nogueira (33 Rosilane Camargo
Mota "FANTA"), Sisleide do Amor Lima "SISSI", Maria Dias Aparecida de Souza
"CIDINHA", RAQUEL de Souza Noronha (60 Miraildes Maciel Mota "FORMIGA"
(YC79)), Delma Gonçalves "PRETINHA", KÁTIA Cilene Teixeira da Silva.
(Coach: WILSON DE OLIVEIRA Riça).
Goals: Birgit PRINZ (8), Bettina WIEGMANN (46 pen), Stephanie JONES (58) /
KÁTIA Cilene Teixeira da Silva (15), Sisleide do Amor Lima "SISSI" (20),
ANDRÉIA dos Santos (90+4)
Referee: IM Eun-Ju (South Korea) Attendance: 22,109

27.06.1999   Foxboro Stadium, Foxborough: Mexico – Italy 0-2 (0-1)
Mexico: Linnea Andrea QUIÑONES Sandland, Susana MORA Chávez, Martha
Ofelia MOORE Camacho (42 Mónica Christine GONZÁLEZ Canales), Regina Marie
OCEGUERA Schmul, Fátima LEYVA Morán (66 María del Carmen Denise IRETA
Gonzalez), Mónica VERGARA Rubio (55 Laurie Anne HILL Rozenel), Patricia
PÉREZ Peña, Andrea RODEBAUGH Huitrón *(YC74)*, Maribel Guadalupe
DOMÍNGUEZ Castelán, Lisa Anne NÁÑEZ Stromberg, Mónica Marie GERARDO
Moran. (Coach: Leonardo CUÉLLAR Rivera).
Italy: Giorgia BRENZAN, Daniela TAVALAZZI, Paola ZANNI, Luisa MARCHIO,
Anna DUO (46 Roberta STEFANELLI), Adele FROLLANI, Alessandra PALLOTTI,
Tatiana ZORRI, Damiana DE IANA, Patrizia PANICO, Rita GUARINO (46 Silvia
TAGLIACARNE). (Coach: Carlo FACCHIN).
Goals: Patrizia PANICO (37), Paola ZANNI (51)
Referee: Bola ABIDOYE (Nigeria)   Attendance: 50,484

Team	Pld	W	D	L	GF	GA	GD	Pts
Brazil	*3*	*2*	*1*	*0*	*12*	*4*	*+8*	*7*
Germany	*3*	*1*	*2*	*1*	*10*	*4*	*+6*	*5*
Italy	3	1	1	1	3	3	0	4
Mexico	3	0	0	3	1	15	-14	0

GROUP C

20.06.1999   Spartan Stadium, San Jose: Japan – Canada 1-1 (0-1)
Japan: Nozomi YAMAGO, Hiromi ISOZAKI, Kae NISHINA, Yumi TOMEI, Ayumi
HARA, Tomomi MIYAMOTO, Tomoe KATO, Homare SAWA, Tamaki
UCHIYAMA, Nami OTAKE, Mito ISAKA (52 Yayoi KOBAYASHI).
(Coach: Satoshi MIYAUCHI).
Canada: Nicole (Nicci) WRIGHT, Sharolta Louisa NONEN, Isabelle MORNEAU,
Charmaine HOOPER *(YC5)*, Janine HELLAND Wood, Amy Heather WALSH, Tanya
FRANCK, Geraldine DONNELLY, Silvana BURTINI (55 Andrea NEIL), Shannon
ROSENOW, Isabelle HARVEY. (Coach: Neil TURNBULL).
Goals: Nami OTAKE (64) / Silvana BURTINI (32)
Referee: MARIA Edilene SIQUEIRA (Brazil)   Attendance: 23,298

20.06.1999 Foxboro Stadium, Foxborough: Norway – Russia 2-1 (1-0)
Norway: Bente NORDBY, Brit SANDAUNE, Gøril KRINGEN, Linda MEDALEN,
Anne NYMARK ANDERSEN, Unni LEHN (61 Tone Gunn FRUSTØL), Hege
RIISE, Monica KNUDSEN (86 Anita RAPP), Silje JØRGENSEN, Ragnhild Øren
GULBRANDSEN (74 Dagny MELLGREN), Marianne PETTERSEN.
(Coach: Per-Mathias HØGMO).
Russia: Svetlana PETKO, Marina BURAKOVA, Natalia FILIPPOVA, Tatiana
CHEVERDA, Natalia BARBASHINA, Natalia KARASEVA, Tatiana EGOROVA,
Alexandra SVETLITSKAYA (84 Elena FOMINA), Olga KARASSEVA (46 Galina
KOMAROVA), Irina GRIGORIEVA, Olga LETYUSHOVA (73 Larissa SAVINA).
(Coach: Yuri BYSTRITSKIY).
Goals: Brit SANDAUNE (28), Marianne PETTERSEN (68) /
Galina KOMAROVA (78)
Referee: ZUO Xiudi (China PR) Attendance: 14,873

24.06.1999 FedEx Field, Landover: Norway – Canada 7-1 (2-1)
Norway: Bente NORDBY, Brit SANDAUNE, Gøril KRINGEN (YC45+1), Linda
MEDALEN, Anne NYMARK ANDERSEN (46 Tone Gunn FRUSTØL), Unni LEHN
(70 Solveig GULBRANDSEN), Hege RIISE, Monica KNUDSEN (62 Linda
ØRMEN), Silje JØRGENSEN, Ann Kristin AARØNES, Marianne PETTERSEN.
(Coach: Per-Mathias HØGMO).
Canada: Nicole (Nicci) WRIGHT, Sharolta Louisa NONEN, Isabelle MORNEAU,
Charmaine HOOPER (YC5), Janine HELLAND Wood, Amy Heather WALSH, Tanya
FRANCK, Geraldine DONNELLY, Jeanette HAAS (16 Andrea NEIL), Shannon
ROSENOW (70 Mary Beth BOWIE), Isabelle HARVEY.
(Coach: Neil TURNBULL).
Goals: Ann Kristin AARØNES (8, 36), Unni LEHN (49), Hege RIISE (54), Linda
MEDALEN (68), Marianne PETTERSEN (76), Ragnhild Øren GULBRANDSEN
(87) / Charmaine HOOPER (31)
Referee: Tammy Nicole OGSTON (Australia) Attendance: 16,448

24.06.1999 Providence Park, Portland: Japan – Russia 0-5 (0-1)
Japan: Nozomi YAMAGO, Hiromi ISOZAKI, Kae NISHINA, Yumi TOMEI, Ayumi
HARA, Tomomi MIYAMOTO, Tomoe KATO (69 Rie YAMAKI), Homare SAWA
(YC72), Tamaki UCHIYAMA, Nami OTAKE (57 Miyuki YANAGITA), Mito
ISAKA (64 Yayoi KOBAYASHI). (Coach: Satoshi MIYAUCHI).
Russia: Svetlana PETKO, Marina BURAKOVA, Natalia FILIPPOVA, Tatiana
CHEVERDA, Natalia KARASEVA, Galina KOMAROVA, Tatiana EGOROVA (79
Elena FOMINA), Alexandra SVETLITSKAYA (46 Olga KARASSEVA), Irina
GRIGORIEVA, Olga LETYUSHOVA, Larissa SAVINA (72 Natalia
BARBASHINA). (Coach: Yuri BYSTRITSKIY).
Goals: Larissa SAVINA (29), Olga LETYUSHOVA (52, 90), Natalia KARASEVA
(58), Natalia BARBASHINA (80)
Referee: Sandra HUNT (United States) Attendance: 17,668

60

26.06.1999 Giants Stadium, East Rutherford: Canada – Russia 1-4 (0-0)
Canada: Nicole (Nicci) WRIGHT, Sharolta Louisa NONEN, Isabelle MORNEAU,
Charmaine HOOPER, Janine HELLAND Wood, Amy Heather WALSH, Tanya
FRANCK *(YC32)*, Geraldine DONNELLY, Mary Beth BOWIE (55 Silvana
BURTINI), Shannon ROSENOW (80 Sarah MAGLIO), Isabelle HARVEY *(YC49)*.
(Coach: Neil TURNBULL).
Russia: Svetlana PETKO, Marina BURAKOVA, Natalia FILIPPOVA, Tatiana
CHEVERDA (72 Yulia YUSHEKIVITCH), Natalia BARBASHINA (56 Larissa
SAVINA), Natalia KARASEVA *(YC77)*, Galina KOMAROVA, Tatiana EGOROVA
(61 Elena FOMINA), Olga KARASSEVA, Irina GRIGORIEVA, Olga
LETYUSHOVA. (Coach: Yuri BYSTRITSKIY).
Goals: Charmaine HOOPER (76) / Irina GRIGORIEVA (54), Elena FOMINA (66,
86), Olga KARASSEVA (90+1)
Referee: ZUO Xiudi (China PR) Attendance: 29,401

27.06.1999 Soldier Field, Chicago: Norway – Japan 4-0 (3-0)
Norway: Bente NORDBY, Brit SANDAUNE, Anne TØNNESSEN *(YC83)*, Linda
MEDALEN (11 Gøril KRINGEN, 57 Henriette VIKER), Unni LEHN, Hege RIISE,
Monica KNUDSEN, Silje JØRGENSEN *(YC73)*, Tone Gunn FRUSTØL, Ann Kristin
AARØNES (38 Solveig GULBRANDSEN), Dagny MELLGREN.
(Coach: Per-Mathias HØGMO).
Japan: Nozomi YAMAGO, Hiromi ISOZAKI, Rie YAMAKI, Kae NISHINA, Yumi
TOMEI, Ayumi HARA (86 Kozue ANDO), Tomomi MIYAMOTO, Homare SAWA
(YC65), Tamaki UCHIYAMA (78 Miyuki YANAGITA), Nami OTAKE, Mito
ISAKA (60 Yayoi KOBAYASHI). (Coach: Satoshi MIYAUCHI).
Goals: Hege RIISE (8 pen), Hiromi ISO (26 og), Ann Kristin AARØNES (36), Dagny
MELLGREN (61)
Referee: Marisela CONTRERAS (Venezuela) Attendance: 34,256

Team	Pld	W	D	L	GF	GA	GD	Pts
Norway	*3*	*3*	*0*	*0*	*13*	*2*	*+11*	*9*
Russia	*3*	*2*	*0*	*1*	*10*	*3*	*+7*	*6*
Canada	3	0	1	2	3	12	-9	1
Japan	3	0	1	2	1	19	-9	1

61

GROUP D

19.06.1999   Spartan Stadium, San Jose: China PR – Sweden 2-1 (1-1)
China PR: GAO Hong, FAN Yunjie, WANG Liping, XIE Huilin (59 ZHANG Ouying), WEN Lirong, ZHAO Lihong, LIU Ying, LIU Ailing, BAI Jie, SUN Wen (74 PU Wei), JIN Yan. (Coach: YUANAN Ma).
Sweden: Ulrika KARLSSON, Karolina WESTBERG, Jane TÖRNQVIST, Gärd Kristin BENGTSSON (88 Tina NORDLUND), Åsa LÖNNQVIST, Cecilia SANDELL, Malin Sofi MOSTRÖM (77 Linda FAGERSTRÖM), Malin Elisabeth ANDERSSON, Hanna Carolina LJUNGBERG, Victoria Margareta Sandell SVENSSON, Therese LUNDIN (46 Malin GUSTAFSSON).
(Coach: Marika Susan DOMANSKI LYFORS).
Goals: JIN Yan (17), LIU Ailing (69) / Gärd Kristin BENGTSSON (2)
Referee: Virginia TOVAR Dias (Mexico)   Attendance: 23,298

20.06.1999   Foxboro Stadium, Foxborough: Australia – Ghana 1-1 (0-0)
Australia: Tracey WHEELER, Dianne ALAGICH, Cheryl SALISBURY, Bridgette STARR, Sarah COOPER, Traci BARTLETT *(YC89)*, Joanne PETERS (89 Kelly GOLEBIOWSKI), Sharon BLACK, Angela IANNOTTA (59 Lisa CASAGRANDE *(YC65)*), Alison FORMAN, Julie MURRAY. (Coach: Greg BROWN).
Ghana: Memunatu SULEMANA, Patience SACKEY, Elizabeth BAIDU, Rita YEBOAH *(YC11)*, Regina ANSAH *(YC4)*, Adjoa BAYOR (79 Lydia ANKRAH), Genevive CLOTTEY *(YC80)*, Barikisu TETTEY QUAO *(RC26)*, Alberta SACKEY *(YC15)*, Mavis DGAJMAH (32 Sheila OKAI, 65 Nana GYAMFUAH), Vivian MENSAH. (Coach: Emmanuel AFRANI).
Goals: Julie MURRAY (74) / Nana GYAMFUAH (76)
Referee: Kari SEITZ (United States)   Attendance: 14,873

Sent-off: 26' Barikisu TETTEY QUAO.

24.06.1999   FedEx Field, Landover: Australia – Sweden 1-3 (1-2)
Australia: Bellinda KITCHING, Dianne ALAGICH, Cheryl SALISBURY, Bridgette STARR (87 Anissa TANN DARBY), Sarah COOPER (76 Angela IANNOTTA), Traci BARTLETT, Joanne PETERS, Sharon BLACK (58 Kelly GOLEBIOWSKI *(YC79)*), Lisa CASAGRANDE, Alison FORMAN *(YC85)*, Julie MURRAY.
(Coach: Greg BROWN).
Sweden: Ulrika KARLSSON, Karolina WESTBERG, Jane TÖRNQVIST (75 Jessika SUNDH), Gärd Kristin BENGTSSON *(YC53)* (57 Therese LUNDIN), Åsa LÖNNQVIST, Cecilia SANDELL, Malin Sofi MOSTRÖM, Malin Elisabeth ANDERSSON, Linda GREN (46 Malin GUSTAFSSON), Hanna Carolina LJUNGBERG, Victoria Margareta Sandell SVENSSON.
(Coach: Marika Susan DOMANSKI LYFORS).
Goals: Julie MURRAY (32) / Jane TÖRNQVIST (8), Hanna Carolina LJUNGBERG (21, 69)
Referee: Fatou GAYE (Senegal)   Attendance: 16,448

24.06.1999   Providence Park, Portland: China PR – Ghana 7-0 (3-0)
China PR: GAO Hong, PU Wei (73 XIE Huilin), FAN Yunjie, WANG Liping, WEN
Lirong, ZHAO Lihong, LIU Ying, LIU Ailing (58 QIU Haiyan), BAI Jie, SUN Wen,
JIN Yan (51 ZHANG Ouying). (Coach: YUANAN Ma).
Ghana: Memunatu SULEMANA, Patience SACKEY *(YC28)*, Elizabeth BAIDU, Rita
YEBOAH *(YC16)*, Regina ANSAH, Adjoa BAYOR (56 Lydia ANKRAH), Genevive
CLOTTEY, Stella QUARTEY, Alberta SACKEY, Nana GYAMFUAH (74 Mavis
DGAJMAH), Vivian MENSAH. (Coach: Emmanuel AFRANI).
Goals: SUN Wen (9, 21, 54), JIN Yan (16), ZHANG Ouying (82, 90+1), ZHAO
Lihong (90+2)
Referee: Elke GÜNTHER (Germany)   Attendance: 17,668

26.06.1999   Giants Stadium, East Rutherford: China PR – Australia 3-1 (1-0)
China PR: GAO Hong, PU Wei, FAN Yunjie *(YC4)*, WANG Liping, WEN Lirong
(YC70), ZHAO Lihong (75 XIE Huilin), LIU Ying, LIU Ailing, BAI Jie, SUN Wen
(63 QIU Haiyan), JIN Yan (46 ZHANG Ouying). (Coach: YUANAN Ma).
Australia: Bellinda KITCHING, Dianne ALAGICH, Cheryl SALISBURY (86 Peita-
Claire HEPPERLIN), Bridgette STARR, Traci BARTLETT, Anissa TANN DARBY,
Alicia FERGUSON, Kelly GOLEBIOWSKI, Lisa CASAGRANDE (72 Angela
IANNOTTA), Alison FORMAN, Julie MURRAY. (Coach: Greg BROWN).
Goals: SUN Wen (39, 51), LIU Ying (73) / Cheryl SALISBURY (66)
Referee: Sandra HUNT (United States)   Attendance: 29,401

Sent-off: 2' Alicia FERGUSON.

26.06.1999   Soldier Field, Chicago: Ghana – Sweden 0-2 (0-0)
Ghana: Memunatu SULEMANA, Lydia ANKRAH (65 Sheila OKAI *(YC81)*),
Patience SACKEY, Elizabeth BAIDU, Adjoa BAYOR, Genevive CLOTTEY,
Barikisu TETTEY QUAO, Stella QUARTEY, Alberta SACKEY, Vivian MENSAH,
Nana GYAMFUAH *(YC10)* (84 Mercy TAGOE). (Coach: Emmanuel AFRANI).
Sweden: Ulrika KARLSSON, Karolina WESTBERG, Jane TÖRNQVIST, Gärd
Kristin BENGTSSON (60 Tina NORDLUND), Åsa LÖNNQVIST, Cecilia
SANDELL, Malin Sofi MOSTRÖM, Malin Elisabeth ANDERSSON, Hanna Carolina
LJUNGBERG (6 Therese LUNDIN), Victoria Margareta Sandell SVENSSON, Malin
GUSTAFSSON (87 Linda FAGERSTRÖM).
(Coach: Marika Susan DOMANSKI LYFORS).
Goals: Victoria Margareta Sandell SVENSSON (58, 86)
Referee: Sonia DENONCOURT (Canada)   Attendance: 34,256

Team	Pld	W	D	L	GF	GA	GD	Pts
China PR	*3*	*3*	*0*	*0*	*12*	*2*	*+10*	*9*
Sweden	*3*	*2*	*0*	*1*	*6*	*3*	*+3*	*6*
Australia	3	0	1	2	3	7	-4	1
Ghana	3	0	1	2	1	10	-9	1

63

QUARTER-FINALS

30.06.1999 Spartan Stadium, San Jose: China PR – Russia 2-0 (1-0)
China PR: GAO Hong, PU Wei (80 QIU Haiyan *(YC90+2)*), FAN Yunjie, WANG
Liping, WEN Lirong, ZHAO Lihong, LIU Ying, LIU Ailing, BAI Jie, SUN Wen, JIN
Yan (89 ZHANG Ouying). (Coach: YUANAN Ma).
Russia: Svetlana PETKO, Marina BURAKOVA, Natalia FILIPPOVA, Tatiana
CHEVERDA *(YC35)*, Natalia BARBASHINA (68 Larissa SAVINA), Natalia
KARASEVA, Galina KOMAROVA (88 Alexandra SVETLITSKAYA), Tatiana
EGOROVA (46 Elena FOMINA), Olga KARASSEVA, Irina GRIGORIEVA, Olga
LETYUSHOVA. (Coach: Yuri BYSTRITSKIY).
Goals: PU Wei (37), JIN Yan (56)
Referee: Nicole PETIGNAT (Switzerland)   Attendance: 21,411

30.06.1999 Spartan Stadium, San Jose: Norway – Sweden 3-1 (0-0)
Norway: Bente NORDBY, Brit SANDAUNE, Gøril KRINGEN, Linda MEDALEN,
Unni LEHN (77 Dagny MELLGREN), Hege RIISE, Monica KNUDSEN, Silje
JØRGENSEN, Tone Gunn FRUSTØL (46 Solveig GULBRANDSEN *(YC55)*), Ann
Kristin AARØNES (81 Anita RAPP), Marianne PETTERSEN.
(Coach: Per-Mathias HØGMO).
Sweden: Ulrika KARLSSON, Karolina WESTBERG, Jane TÖRNQVIST, Gärd
Kristin BENGTSSON (46 Therese LUNDIN), Åsa LÖNNQVIST, Cecilia
SANDELL, Malin Sofi MOSTRÖM, Malin Elisabeth ANDERSSON, Tina
NORDLUND (81 Minna HEPONIEMI), Victoria Margareta Sandell SVENSSON,
Malin GUSTAFSSON (72 Jessika SUNDH).
(Coach: Marika Susan DOMANSKI LYFORS).
Goals: Ann Kristin AARØNES (51), Marianne PETTERSEN (58), Hege RIISE
(72 pen), / Malin Sofi MOSTRÖM (90+1)
Referee: IM Eun-Ju (South Korea)   Attendance: 21,411

01.07.1999 FedEx Field, Landover: United States – Germany 3-2 (1-2)
United States: Briana Collette SCURRY, Kathryn Michele MARKGRAF Sobrero,
Joy Lynn FAWCETT Biefeld, Carla Werden OVERBECK, Kristine Marie LILLY
Heavey, Brandi Denise CHASTAIN (73 Lorraine Ming (Lorrie) FAIR), Julie Maurine
FOUDY (65 Shannon Ann MACMILLAN), Michelle Anne AKERS, Tiffeny Carleen
MILBRETT, Mariel Margaret (Mia) HAMM, Cynthia Marie (Cindy) PARLOW Cone
(85 Tiffany Marie ROBERTS Sahaydak). (Coach: Tony DiCICCO).
Germany: Silke ROTTENBERG, Sandra MINNERT, Doris FITSCHEN *(YC53)*,
Ariane HINGST, Stephanie JONES, Pia WUNDERLICH (53 Monika MEYER),
Maren MEINERT, Bettina WIEGMANN, Birgit PRINZ, Inka GRINGS (90+2
Melanie HOFFMANN), Sandra SMISEK (84 Renate LINGOR).
(Coach: Tina THEUNE).
Goals: Tiffeny Carleen MILBRETT (16), Brandi Denise CHASTAIN (49), Joy Lynn
FAWCETT Biefeld (66) / Brandi Denise CHASTAIN (5 og), Bettina WIEGMANN
(45+1)
Referee: Martha TORO (Colombia)   Attendance: 54,642

01.07.1999   FedEx Field, Landover: Brazil – Nigeria 4-3 (3-0,3-3) (a.e.t.)
Brazil: Marlisa Wahlbrink "MARAVILHA", TÂNIA Maria Pereira Ribeiro,
Alissandra Cavalcante "NENÊ", ELANE dos Santos Rego, SUZANA Ferreira da
Silva *(YC81)*, Miraildes Maciel Mota "FORMIGA", Sisleide do Amor Lima "SISSI",
Maria Dias Aparecida de Souza "CIDINHA", RAQUEL de Souza Noronha (66
ANDRÉIA dos Santos), Delma Gonçalves "PRETINHA", KÁTIA Cilene Teixeira da
Silva. (Coach: WILSON DE OLIVEIRA Riça).
Nigeria: Ann CHIEJINE (40 Judith CHIME), Yinka KUDAISI (77 Adanna
NWANERI *(YC102)*), Florence OMAGBEMI *(YC28)*, Eberechi OPARA, Prisca
EMEAFU, Nkiru OKOSIEME, Patience AVRE *(RC87)*, Ifeanyi CHIEJINE (26
Florence Kikelomo AJAYI), Mercy AKIDE, Nkechi EGBE, Rita NWADIKE *(YC12)*.
(Coach: Mabo ISMAILA).
Goals: Maria Dias Aparecida de Souza "CIDINHA" (4, 22), Alissandra Cavalcante
"NENÊ" (35), Sisleide do Amor Lima "SISSI" (104) / Prisca EMEAFU (63), Nkiru
OKOSIEME (72), Nkechi EGBE (85)
Referee: Virginia TOVAR Dias (Mexico)   Attendance: 54,642

Sent-off: 87' Patience AVRE.

Brazil won after extra time.

SEMI-FINALS

04.07.1999   Stanford Stadium, Stanford: United States – Brazil 2-0 (1-0)
United States: Briana Collette SCURRY, Kathryn Michele MARKGRAF Sobrero,
Joy Lynn FAWCETT Biefeld, Carla Werden OVERBECK, Kristine Marie LILLY
Heavey, Brandi Denise CHASTAIN, Julie Maurine FOUDY, Michelle Anne AKERS
(YC90), Tiffeny Carleen MILBRETT (88 Danielle Ruth Garrett FOTOPOULOS),
Mariel Margaret (Mia) HAMM (85 Lorraine Ming (Lorrie) FAIR), Cynthia Marie
(Cindy) PARLOW Cone (62 Shannon Ann MACMILLAN).
(Coach: Tony DiCICCO).
Brazil: Marlisa Wahlbrink "MARAVILHA", TÂNIA Maria Pereira Ribeiro *(YC13)*,
JULIANA Ribeiro Cabral, Alissandra Cavalcante "NENÊ", ELANE dos Santos Rego,
SUZANA Ferreira da Silva (70 ANDRÉIA dos Santos), Miraildes Maciel Mota
"FORMIGA", Sisleide do Amor Lima "SISSI" *(YC41)*, Maria Dias Aparecida de
Souza "CIDINHA", Delma Gonçalves "PRETINHA", KÁTIA Cilene Teixeira da
Silva *(YC90+2)*. (Coach: WILSON DE OLIVEIRA Riça).
Goals: Cynthia Marie (Cindy) PARLOW Cone (5), Michelle Anne AKERS (80 pen).
Referee: Katriina ELOVIRTA (Finland)   Attendance: 73,123

65

05.07.1999 Foxboro Stadium, Foxborough: Norway – China PR 0-5 (0-2)
Norway: Bente NORDBY, Brit SANDAUNE, Gøril KRINGEN, Linda MEDALEN,
Solveig GULBRANDSEN, Unni LEHN (46 Dagny MELLGREN), Hege RIISE,
Monica KNUDSEN (76 Tone Gunn FRUSTØL), Silje JØRGENSEN, Ann Kristin
AARØNES (46 Ragnhild Øren GULBRANDSEN), Marianne PETTERSEN.
(Coach: Per-Mathias HØGMO).
China PR: GAO Hong, PU Wei (76 ZHANG Ouying), FAN Yunjie, WANG Liping,
WEN Lirong, ZHAO Lihong (78 QIU Haiyan), LIU Ying, LIU Ailing, BAI Jie, SUN
Wen, JIN Yan. (Coach: YUANAN Ma).
Goals: SUN Wen (3, 72 pen), LIU Ailing (14, 51), FAN Yunjie (65)
Referee: Sonia DENONCOURT (Canada) Attendance: 8,986

THIRD PLACE PLAY-OFF

10.07.1999 Rose Bowl, Pasadena: Brazil – Norway 0-0 (a.e.t.)
Brazil: Marlisa Wahlbrink "MARAVILHA", TÂNIA Maria Pereira Ribeiro *(YC55)*,
JULIANA Ribeiro Cabral, Alissandra Cavalcante "NENÊ", ELANE dos Santos Rego,
SUZANA Ferreira da Silva (72 ANDRÉIA dos Santos), Miraildes Maciel Mota
"FORMIGA", Sisleide do Amor Lima "SISSI", Maria Dias Aparecida de Souza
"CIDINHA", Delma Gonçalves "PRETINHA", KÁTIA Cilene Teixeira da Silva.
(Coach: WILSON DE OLIVEIRA Riça).
Norway: Bente NORDBY, Brit SANDAUNE, Gøril KRINGEN, Henriette VIKER,
Linda MEDALEN, Solveig GULBRANDSEN, Hege RIISE, Monica KNUDSEN,
Silje JØRGENSEN, Ragnhild Øren GULBRANDSEN (62 Ann Kristin AARØNES),
Marianne PETTERSEN (58 Dagny MELLGREN). (Coach: Per-Mathias HØGMO).
Referee: IM Eun-Ju (South Korea) Attendance: 90,185

Penalties: Hege RIISE 0-1, Delma Gonçalves "PRETINHA" missed, Marianne
PETTERSEN 0-2, Maria Dias Aparecida de Souza "CIDINHA" 1-2, Silje
JØRGENSEN missed, KÁTIA Cilene Teixeira da Silva 2-2, Brit
SANDAUNE 2-3, ANDRÉIA dos Santos 3-3, Solveig GULBRANDSEN 3-4,
Alissandra Cavalcante "NENÊ" 4-4, Ann Kristin AARØNES missed,
Miraildes Maciel Mota "FORMIGA" 5-4.

Brazil won after extra time on penalties (5:4).

FINAL

10.07.1999   Rose Bowl, Pasadena: United States – China PR 0-0 (a.e.t.)
United States: Briana Collette SCURRY, Kathryn Michele MARKGRAF Sobrero,
Joy Lynn FAWCETT Biefeld, Carla Werden OVERBECK, Kristine Marie LILLY
Heavey, Brandi Denise CHASTAIN, Julie Maurine FOUDY, Michelle Anne AKERS
(YC74) (91 Sara Eve WHALEN Hess), Tiffeny Carleen MILBRETT (115 Tisha Lea
VENTURINI Hoch), Mariel Margaret (Mia) HAMM, Cynthia Marie (Cindy)
PARLOW Cone (57 Shannon Ann MACMILLAN). (Coach: Tony DiCICCO).
China PR: GAO Hong, PU Wei (59 ZHANG Ouying *(YC70)*), FAN Yunjie, WANG
Liping, WEN Lirong, ZHAO Lihong (114 QIU Haiyan), LIU Ying, LIU Ailing
(YC80), BAI Jie, SUN Wen, JIN Yan (119 XIE Huilin). (Coach: YUANAN Ma).
Referee: Nicole PETIGNAT (Switzerland)   Attendance: 90.185

Penalties: XIE Huilin 0-1, Carla Werden OVERBECK 1-1, QIU Haiyan 1-2, Cynthia
Marie (Cindy) PARLOW Cone 2-2, LIU Ying missed, Kristine Marie LILLY
Heavey 3-2, ZHANG Ouying 3-3, Mariel Margaret (Mia) HAMM 4-3, SUN
Wen 4-4, Brandi Denise CHASTAIN 5-4.

United States won after extra time on penalties (5:4).

UNITED STATES BECAME WORLD CHAMPIONS

FOURTH EDITION FIFA WOMEN'S WORLD CUP 2003

QUALIFYING TOURNAMENTS

CAF AFRICAN WOMEN'S CHAMPIONSHIP 2002

The winner and the runner-up of CAF African Women's Championship 2002 will qualify for the FIFA Women's World Cup 2003.

QUALIFICATION

FIRST ROUND

10/11.08.2002   Zambia – Botswana **Cancelled**
10/11.08.2002   Ethiopia – Swaziland **Cancelled**
10/11.08.2002   Senegal – Guinea-Bissau **Cancelled**
10.08.2002   Asmara: Eritrea – Tanzania 2-3 (1-3)
Goals: Mebrahtu (3), Debessay (47) / Kavena (20), Paul (31), Chambruma (45)
10.08.2002   São Tomé: São Tomé and Príncipe – Gabon 0-2 (0-1)
Goals: Okawe (36 pen), Etoua (48)
10.08.2002   Abidjan: Ivory Coast – Mali 3-3 (1-2)
Goals: Bancouly (27, 71), Koudougnon (48) / Konate (7, 45), N'Diaye (74)
11.08.2002   Luanda: Angola – Equatorial Guinea 3-0 (1-0)
Goals: Ramos (3, 78), Mvunbio (83)
24.08.2002   Dar es Salaam: Tanzania – Eritrea 2-2 (0-2)
Goals: Mosi (54), Chambruma (89) / Tekeste (7), Bereket-ab (17)
24.08.2002   Malabo: Equatorial Guinea – Angola 1-3 (1-2)
Goals: Añonma (10) / Mvunbio (20), Ramos (39), de Souza (86)
24.08.2002   Libreville: Gabon – São Tomé and Príncipe 6-0 (3-0)
Goals: Okawe (24, 71, 81), Etoua (25), Nisame (45), Mapangou (85)
24.08.2002   Bamako: Mali – Ivory Coast 1-1 (0-1)
Goals: N'Diaye (59) / Bancouly (35)
Mali won on away goals.

Botswana, Guinea-Bissau and Swaziland withdrew; **Zambia**, *Ethiopia and* **Senegal** *advanced to the Second Round.*

SECOND ROUND

21.09.2002   Lusaka: Zambia – South Africa 1-4 (0-2)
Goals: Muchindu (64) / Solomon (19, 40, 62), Phewa (80)
21.09.2002   Dar es Salaam: Tanzania – Zimbabwe 0-5 (0-4)
Goals: Mpala (10), Moyo (11, 40, 48), Zulu (43)
21.09.2002   Libreville: Gabon – Camroon 0-0
22.09.2002   Addis Ababa: Ethiopia – Uganda 2-0
Goals: Adois (13), Endegene-Leme

22.09.2002   Lubango: Angola – DR Congo 1-0 (1-0)
Goal: Ramos (38)
22.09.2002   Stade Iba Mar Diop, Dakar: Senegal – Ghana 0-3 (0-2)
Goals: Amoah-Tetteh (24, 56), Darku (29)
22.09.2002   Bamako: Mali – Morocco 0-0
11.10.2002   Kinshasa: DR Congo – Angola 1-0 (1-0,1-0) (a.e.t.)
Angola won after extra time on penalties (4:5)
11.10.2002   Rabat: Morocco – Mali 0-0 (a.e.t.)
Mali won after extra time on penalties (4:5)
12.10.2002   Seisa Ramabodu Stadium, Bloemfontein:
          South Africa – Zambia 4-0 (3-0)
Goals: Solomon (13), Nteso (17), Mlomo (36), Phewa (47)
12.10.2002   Stade de la Réunification, Douala: Cameroon – Gabon 4-0 (1-0)
Goals: Belemgoto (20 pen), Mekongo (72 pen), Anounga (90+1),
Mvie Manga (90+4)
12.10.2002   Kumasi: Ghana – Senegal 3-1 (1-0)
Goals: Okah (30), Ohenewaa (51, 67) / Gueye (81)
13.10.2002   Kampala: Uganda – Ethiopia 2-2 (1-0)
Goals: Nakimbugwe (20), Mbekeka (51) / Endegene-Leme (54), Teramah (72)
13.10.2002   Harare: Zimbabwe – Tanzania 5-0 (3-0)
Goals: Zulu (2, 76), Moyo (9), Mpala (34), Phiri (62)

FINAL TOURNAMENT

The Final Tournament was held in Nigeria between 7 & 20 December 2002. Nigeria
was qualified automatically as both hosts and defending champion.

GROUP STAGE
GROUP A

07.12.2002   Warri Township Stadium, Warri: Nigeria – Ethiopia 3-0 (1-0)
Goals: Mbachu (15), Akide (63, 66)
07.12.2002   Warri Township Stadium, Warri: Mali – Ghana 0-2 (0-0)
Goals: Sackey (55), Dgajmah (78)
10.12.2002   Warri Township Stadium, Warri: Ethiopia – Mali 2-2 (0-2)
Goals: Endegene-Leme (61, 70) / Konate (20), Samake (44)
10.12.2002   Warri Township Stadium, Warri: Nigeria – Ghana 0-1 (0-1)
Goal: Sackey (33)
13.12.2002   Warri Township Stadium, Warri: Nigeria – Mali 5-1 (2-0)
Goals: Akide (38), Nkwocha (40, 70), Iweta (49), Chiejine (82) / Samake (60)
13.12.2002   Oghara Township Stadium, Oghara: Ghana – Ethiopia 3-0 (1-0)
Goals: Sackey (30, 60), Gyamfuah (75)

Team	Pld	W	D	L	GF	GA	GD	Pts
Ghana	*3*	*3*	*0*	*0*	*6*	*0*	*+6*	*9*
Nigeria	*3*	*2*	*0*	*1*	*8*	*2*	*+6*	*6*
Mali	3	0	1	2	3	9	-6	1
Ethiopia	3	0	1	2	2	8	-6	1

GROUP B

08.12.2002   Oghara Township Stadium, Oghara: South Africa – Cameroon 2-1 (0-0)
Goals: Phewa (70), Carelse (71) / Anounga (72)
08.12.2002   Oghara Township Stadium, Oghara: Angola – Zimbabwe 1-1 (1-0)
Goals: Gonçalves (16) / Talent (48)
11.12.2002   Oghara Township Stadium, Oghara: Cameroon – Zimbabwe 0-0
11.12.2002   Oghara Township Stadium, Oghara: South Africa – Angola 1-1 (1-0)
Goals: Monyepao (9) / Ramos (75)
14.12.2002   Oghara Township Stadium, Oghara: Cameroon – Angola 1-0 (0-0)
Goal: Ngono Mani (89)
14.12.2002   Warri Township Stadium, Warri: South Africa – Zimbabwe 3-1 (2-0)
Goals: Phewa (27, 33, 61) / Talent (50)

Team	Pld	W	D	L	GF	GA	GD	Pts
South Africa	3	2	1	0	6	3	+3	7
Cameroon	3	1	1	1	2	2	0	4
Angola	3	0	2	1	2	3	-1	2
Zimbabwe	3	0	2	1	2	4	-2	2

KNOCKOUT STAGE

SEMI-FINALS

17.12.2002   Warri Township Stadium, Warri:
          Ghana – Cameroon 3-2 (1-0,2-2) (a.e.t.)
Goals: Dgajmah (2), Gyamfuah (75), Bayor (120) / Pokam (83), Belemgoto (90 pen)
Ghana won after extra time
18.12.2002   Warri Township Stadium, Warri: South Africa – Nigeria 0-5 (0-1)
Goals: Yusuf (31), Chiejine (47), Mbachu (56, 81), Nkwocha (69)

THIRD PLACE PLAY-OFF

20.12.2002   Warri Township Stadium, Warri: Cameroon – South Africa 3-0

FINAL

20.12.2002   Warri Township Stadium, Warri: Ghana – Nigeria 0-2 (0-2)
Goals: Nkwocha (25), Effionwan (25)

The match was held up for about 5 minutes after fans pelted a linesman with sachets of water after Alberta Sackey had not given offside (but missed the chance anayway).

Nigeria and runner-up **Ghana** qualified for the FIFA Women's World Cup 2003.

AFC ASIAN WOMEN'S CHAMPIONSHIP 2003

The tournament was held in Thailand between 8 & 21 June 2003. Four teams will qualify for the FIFA Women's World Cup 2003.

GROUP STAGE

GROUP A

08.06.2003 Rajamangala Stadium, Bangkok: Singapore – Thailand 0-3
08.06.2003 Rajamangala Stadium, Bangkok: South Korea – Hong Kong 8-0
10.06.2003 Rajamangala Stadium, Bangkok: South Korea – Thailand 6-0
10.06.2003 Rajamangala Stadium, Bangkok: North Korea – Hong Kong 13-0
12.06.2003 Rajamangala Stadium, Bangkok: South Korea – Singapore 4-0
12.06.2003 Rajamangala Stadium, Bangkok: North Korea – Thailand 14-0
14.06.2003 Rajamangala Stadium, Bangkok: Hong Kong – Thailand 1-3
14.06.2003 Rajamangala Stadium, Bangkok: North Korea – Singapore 16-0
16.06.2003 Rajamangala Stadium, Bangkok: North Korea – South Korea 2-2
16.06.2003 Rajamangala Stadium, Bangkok: Hong Kong – Singapore 1-0

Team	Pld	W	D	L	GF	GA	GD	Pts
North Korea	4	3	1	0	45	2	+43	10
South Korea	4	3	1	0	20	2	+18	10
Thailand	4	2	0	2	6	21	-15	6
Hong Kong	4	1	0	3	2	24	-22	3
Singapore	4	0	0	4	0	24	-24	0

GROUP B

09.06.2003 Rajamangala Stadium, Bangkok: Japan – Philippines 15-0
09.06.2003 Rajamangala Stadium, Bangkok: Guam – Chinese Taipei 1-2
11.06.2003 Rajamangala Stadium, Bangkok: Philippines – Myanmar 0-6
11.06.2003 Rajamangala Stadium, Bangkok: Japan – Guam 7-0
13.06.2003 Rajamangala Stadium, Bangkok: Philippines – Chinese Taipei 0-4
13.06.2003 Rajamangala Stadium, Bangkok: Japan – Myanmar 7-0
15.06.2003 Rajamangala Stadium, Bangkok: Guam – Myanmar 0-4
15.06.2003 Rajamangala Stadium, Bangkok: Japan – Chinese Taipei 5-0
17.06.2003 Rajamangala Stadium, Bangkok: Chinese Taipei – Myanmar 1-1
17.06.2003 Rajamangala Stadium, Bangkok: Philippines – Guam 2-1

Team	Pld	W	D	L	GF	GA	GD	Pts
Japan	4	4	0	0	34	0	+34	12
Myanmar	4	2	1	1	11	8	+3	7
Chinese Taipei	4	2	1	1	7	7	0	7
Philippines	4	1	0	3	2	26	-24	3
Guam	4	0	0	4	2	15	-13	0

71

GROUP C

09.06.2003 Nakhon Sawan Province Stadium, Bangkok: China PR – Vietman 6-0
09.06.2003 Nakhon Sawan Province Stadium, Bangkok: India – Uzbekistan 6-0
11.06.2003 Nakhon Sawan Province Stadium, Bangkok: Vietnam – Uzbekistan 4-2
11.06.2003 Nakhon Sawan Province Stadium, Bangkok: China PR – India 12-0
13.06.2003 Nakhon Sawan Province Stadium, Bangkok: Vietnam – India 2-1
13.06.2003 Nakhon Sawan Province Stadium, Bangkok:
China PR – Uzbekistan 11-0

Team	Pld	W	D	L	GF	GA	GD	Pts
China PR	3	3	0	0	29	0	+29	9
Vietnam	3	2	0	1	6	9	-3	6
India	3	1	0	2	7	14	-7	3
Uzbekistan	3	0	0	3	2	21	-19	0

KNOCKOUT STAGE
SEMI-FINALS

19.06.2003 Rajamangala Stadium, Bangkok: North Korea – Japan 3-0
19.06.2003 Rajamangala Stadium, Bangkok: China PR – South Korea 3-1

THIRD PLACE PLAY-OFF

21.06.2003 Rajamangala Stadium, Bangkok: Japan – South Korea 0-1 (0-1)
Goal: Hwang In-sun (18)

FINAL

21.06.2003 Rajamangala Stadium, Bangkok:
North Korea – China PR 2-1 (1-0,1-1) (a.e.t.)
Goals: Ri Kum-suk (41, 112 pen) / Gao Hongxia (61)

North Korea won after extra time

North Korea, China PR (as original host nation automatically qualified) and **South Korea** qualified for the FIFA Women's World Cup 2003. Japan had to play two play-off matches against the runner-up of the CONCACAF Women's Gold Cup 2002.

UEFA WOMEN'S WORLD CUP QUALIFICATION 2003

The tournament was held between 18 August 2001 and 16 November 2002. The 16 teams belonging to Class A of European women's football were drawn info four groups. The four group winners will qualify for the FIFA Women's World Cup 2003. The four runners-up will play in play-off matches for the 5th berth.

GROUP STAGE
GROUP 1

25.08.2001 Kolos, Boryspíl: Ukraine – Czech Republic 4-1 (2-0)
Goals: Verezoubova (10), Pekur (31), Ivanova (51), Zinchenko (77) / Urbancová (83)
08.09.2001 Åråsen, Lilleström: Norway – Ukraine 4-0 (2-0)
Goals: Ørmen (23, 90), Gulbrandsen (27), Mellgren (47)
11.09.2001 Gjemselund, Kongsvinger: Norway – Czech Republic 5-0 (3-0)
Goals: Mellgren (26), Ørmen (38), Gulbrandsen (41), Risse (62), Bugge-Paulsen (90)
13.10.2001 Pierre de Coubertin, Cannes-la-Bocca: France – Norway 0-3 (0-2)
Goals: Lehn (2, 29), Mellgren (55)
28.10.2001 Kolos, Boryspíl: Ukraine – France 0-2 (0-2)
Goals: Pichon (3, 7)
17.11.2001 FK Drnovice, Drnovice: Czech Republic – France 1-2 (0-2)
Goals: Chlumecká (59) / Pichon (7, 28)
24.03.2002 TJ Slany, Slany: Czech Republic – Norway 1-5 (1-3)
Goals: Dudová (18) / Papp (19), Gulbrandsen (23), Lehn (32), Sæthre (60),
Ørmen (64)
20.04.2002 La Meinau, Strasbourg: France – Czech Republic 4-1 (3-0)
Goals: Soubeyrand (5), Pichon (30), Mugneret-Béghé (39), Blouin (48) /
Scasná (90 pen)
09.05.2002 Halden Stadion, Halden: Norway – France 3-1 (2-1)
Goals: Mellgren (3, 25, 55) / Pichon (10)
12.05.2002 Kolos, Boryspíl: Ukraine- Norway 1-1 (0-0)
Goals: Mykhailenko (60) / Gulbrandsen (53)
26.05.2002 FK Chmel, Bisany: Czech Republic – Ukraine 2-3 (1-1)
Goals: Chlumecká (12), Penicková (86) / Mykhailenko (32), Zinchenko (46),
Frishko (76)
01.06.2002 Gaston Petit, Châteauroux: France – Ukraine 2-1 (0-0)
Goals: Pichon (60), Soubeyrand (73) / Verezoubova (51)

Team	Pld	W	D	L	GF	GA	GD	Pts
Norway	*6*	*5*	*1*	*0*	*21*	*3*	*+18*	*16*
France	6	4	0	2	11	9	+2	12
Ukraine	6	2	1	3	9	12	-3	7
Czech Republic	6	0	0	6	6	23	-17	0

GROUP 2

04.09.2001 Lättich, Baar: Switzerland – Finland 1-0 (1-0)
Goal: Di Fonzo (24)
08.09.2001 Odense Stadion, Odense: Denmark – Switzerland 4-0 (2-0)
Goals: Bonde (5 pen), Kjældgaard (20, 47), Madsen (90+3)
09.09.2001 Gammliavallen, Umeå: Sweden – Finland 8-1 (5-1)
Goals: Svensson (10, 45), Mostström (22), Andersson (25 pen), Ljungberg (43),
Bengtsson (72, 89), Sjöström (80) / Uusi-Luomalahti (19 pen)
30.09.2001 Idrottsplats, Malmö: Sweden – Denmark 4-1 (1-1)
Goals: Bengtsson (5), Ljungberg (68), Andersson (71), Björn (75) / Pedersen (43)

13.10.2001   Pohjola, Vantaa: Finland – Denmark 0-6 (0-4)
Goals: Rydahl (7), Hansen (8), Pedersen (43, 89), Andersson (39), Bonde (85 pen)
03.11.2001   Au-Stadion, Brugg: Switzerland – Sweden 0-5 (0-1)
Goals: Ljungberg (28), Björn (60, Larsson (68, 90+2), Sjöström (79)
20.04.2002   Gemeinde Sportplatz, Gossau: Switzerland – Denmark 1-4 (1-2)
Goals: Di Fonzo (43) / Andersen (12), Bonde (42, 79), Pedersen (56)
05.05.2002   Pohjola, Vantaa: Finland – Switzerland 1-0 (0-0)
Goal: Mustonen (65)
08.05.2002   Råsunda, Solna: Sweden – Switzerland 4-0 (2-0)
Goals: Svensson (2, 54), Ljungberg (42, 88)
26.05.2002   Odense Stadion, Odense: Denmark – Finland 4-2 (1-1)
Goals: Jensen (22, 61), Jokmusen (82, 90) / Heikari (16), Kalmari (84)
09.06.2002   Ballerup Idrætspark, Copenhagen: Denmark – Sweden 2-1 (0-0)
Goals: Terp (75), Sørensen (88) / Andersson (60 pen)
26.06.2002   Centralplan, Jakobstad: Finland – Sweden 0-5 (0-2)
Goals: Eriksson (20, 43), Ljungberg (46), Svensson (48, 78)

Team	Pld	W	D	L	GF	GA	GD	Pts
Sweden	*6*	*5*	*0*	*1*	*27*	*4*	*+23*	*15*
Denmark	6	5	0	1	21	8	+13	15
Switzerland	6	1	0	5	2	18	-16	3
Finland	6	1	0	5	4	24	-20	3

GROUP 3

18.08.2001   KR-Völlur, Reykjavik: Iceland – Russia 1-1 (0-1)
Goals: Færseth (49) / Barbachina (8)
08.09.2001   Laugardalsvöllur, Reykjavik: Iceland – Italy 2-1 (1-0)
Goals: Færseth (40, 52) / Helgadóttir (80 og)
30.09.2001   Pinilla, Teruel: Spain – Iceland 6-1 (3-0)
Goals: Del Rio (4, 30), Jiménez (43, 59), Gimbert (86 pen), Ferreira (87) /
Ólafsdóttir (63)
10.10.2001   Stadio Artemio Franchi, Siena: Italy – Russia 1-3 (0-1)
Goals: Guarino (58) / Bosikova (31), Fomina (60), Barbachina (84)
28.10.2001   Stroitel, Selyatino: Russia – Spain 2-0
Goals: Svetliskaia (11), Bosikova
28.11.2001   Città di Castello: Italy – Spain 3-0 (1-0)
Goals: Camporese (7), Pasqui (65), Zorri (78)
24.03.2002   Pozoblanco: Spain – Italy 0-1 (0-0)
Goal: Guarino (77)
29.04.2002   Spain – Russia 2-1 (2-0)
Goals: Jiménez (10), Del Rio (33) / Saenko (62)
18.05.2002   Russia – Iceland 1-1
22.05.2002   Moscow: Russia – Italy 2-1 (1-0)
Goals: Zorri (9), Barbachina (65 pen) / Saenko (73 pen)
30.05.2002   Iceland – Spain 3-0
08.06.2002   Italy – Iceland 0-0

Team	Pld	W	D	L	GF	GA	GD	Pts
Russia	*6*	*3*	*2*	*1*	*10*	*6*	*+4*	*11*
Iceland	6	2	3	1	8	9	-1	9
Italy	6	2	1	3	7	7	0	7
Spain	6	2	0	4	8	11	-3	6

GROUP 4

27.09.2001 Auestadion, Kassel: Germany – England 3-1 (3-0)
Goals: M.Müller (3), Smisek (7, 11) / Yankey (49)
25.10.2001 VfL-Stadion, Wolfsburg: Germany – Portugal 9-0 (5-0)
Goals: Pohlers (2, 25, 57, 63, 84), Künzer (6), M.Müller (12, 26, 90)
04.11.2001 Blundell Park, Cleethorpes: England – Netherlands 0-0
17.11.2001 De Grolsch Veste, Enschede: Netherlands – Germany 0-3 (0-1)
Goals: Wunderlich (9), Prinz (53), Mensink (62 og)
24.11.2001 Complexo Desportivo, Gafanha da Nazaré: Portugal – England 1-1 (1-1)
Goals: Anabela (5) / Walker (38)
08.12.2001 Estádio Municipal de Tábua, Tábua: Portugal – Netherlands 2-1 (0-1)
Goals: Sónia (80, 90) / Muller (14)
24.02.2002 Fratton Park, Portsmouth: England – Portugal 3-0 (1-0)
Goals: Williams (29), Smith (58, 60)
23.03.2002 Zuiderpark Stadion, The Hague: Netherlands – England 1-4 (0-2)
Goals: Kiesel-Griffioen (55) / Chapman (16), Burke (24), Smith (73), Walker (89)
18.04.2002 Stadion am Schönbusch, Aschaffenburg:
Germany – Netherlands 6-0 (3-0)
Goals: Wiegmann (4 pen, 32, 90), Prinz (41, 49, 84)
04.05.2002 Estádio Adelino Ribeiro Novo, Barcelos: Portugal – Germany 0-8 (0-3)
Goals: Wunderlich (6, 59), Lingor (12, 56), Stegemann (40), Mónica (50 og),
Grings (62), Prinz (85)
19.05.2002 Sportpark Molenbroek, Gemert: Netherlands – Portugal 4-1 (1-0)
Goals: Smith (24), Ran (58), Noom (72), Burger (76) / Bé (51)
19.05.2002 Selhurst Park, London: England – Germany 0-1 (0-1)
Goal: Gottschlich (41)

Team	Pld	W	D	L	GF	GA	GD	Pts
Germany	*6*	*6*	*0*	*0*	*30*	*1*	*+29*	*18*
England	6	2	2	2	9	6	+3	8
Netherlands	6	1	1	4	6	16	-10	4
Portugal	6	1	1	4	4	26	-22	4

PLAY-OFF A
SEMI-FINALS

23.08.2002 Stade Félix-Bollaert, Lens: France – Denmark 2-0 (2-0)
Goals: Pichon (32), Bompastor (36)
15.09.2002 Odense Stadion, Odense: Denmark – France 1-1 (1-0)
Goals: Hansen (9) / Lecouflé (89)

16.09.2002   Laugardalsvöllur, Reykjavik: Iceland – Engeland 2-2 (1-1)
Goals: Færseth (42), Hendriksdóttir (56) / Walker (44,88)
22.09.2002   St. Andrews, Birmingham: England – Iceland 1-0 (0-0)
Goal: Barr (87)

FINALS

17.10.2002   Selhurst Park, London: England – France 0-1 (0-0)
Goal: Pichon (75)
16.11.2002   Stade Geoffroy Guichard, Saint-Étienne: France – England 1-0 (0-0)
Goal: Diacre (54)

Group winners **Norway, Sweden, Russia** and **Germany** qualified. **France** qualified as the winner of the final of the runners-up play-off matches.

CONCACAF WOMEN'S GOLD CUP 2002

United States was directly qualified for the FIFA Women's World Cup 2003 as hosts of the event.

QUALIFICATION

UNCAF QUALIFYING TOURNAMENT 2002

The UNCAF Qualifying Tournament 2002 was held in El Salvador between 29 July and 6 August 2002.

29.07.2002   Panama – Guatemata 2-1
29.07.2002   Costa Rica – Honduras 5-2
01.08.2002   Panama – El Salvador 3-1
01.08.2002   Guatemala – Honduras 2-1
03.08.2002   Costa Rica – Guatemala 4-0
03.08.2002   El Salvador – Honduras 1-0
04.08.2002   Costa Rica – Panama 4-1
04.08.2002   Guatemala – El Salvador 5-1
06.08.2002   Costa Rica – El Salvador 3-0
06.08.2002   Panama – Honduras 2-6

Team	Pld	W	D	L	GF	GA	GD	Pts
Costa Rica	*4*	*4*	*0*	*0*	*16*	*3*	*+13*	*12*
Panama	*4*	*2*	*0*	*2*	*8*	*12*	*-4*	*6*
Guatemala	4	2	0	2	8	8	0	6
El Salvador	4	1	0	3	3	11	-8	3
Honduras	4	1	0	3	9	10	-1	3
Nigaragua	0	0	0	0	0	0		0
Belize	0	0	0	0	0	0		0

Nigaragua and Belize withdrew.

Costa Rica and **Panama** qualified for the CONCACAF Women's Gold Cup 2002.

CFU QUALIFYING TOURNAMENT 2002

FIRST ROUND

GROUP 1

05.07.2002   Trinidad and Tobago: Dominica – Trinidad and Tobago 0-13
06.07.2002   Trinidad and Tobago: Trinidad and Tobago – Dominica 9-0
13.07.2002   Jamaica: Jamaica – Puerto Rico 8-0
21.07.2002   Puerto Rico: Puerto Rico – Jamaica 0-3

Trinidad and Tobago and **Jamaica** qualified for Final Round.

GROUP 2

All matches in this group were played in Haiti.

10.07.2002   Bahamas – Haiti 0-9
10.07.2002   Dominican Republic – Saint Lucia 2-2
12.07.2002   Saint Lucia – Haiti 0-2
12.07.2002   Dominican Republic – Bahamas 3-0
14.07.2002   Saint Lucia – Bahamas 7-1
14.07.2002   Haiti – Dominican Republic 2-0

Team	Pld	W	D	L	GF	GA	GD	Pts
Haiti	*3*	*3*	*0*	*0*	*13*	*0*	*+13*	*9*
Saint Lucia	3	1	1	1	9	5	+4	4
Dominican Republic	3	1	1	1	5	4	+1	4
Bahamas	3	0	0	3	1	19	-18	0

Haiti qualified for the Final Round.

GROUP 3

Guyana and Montserrat withdrew, causing **Suriname** and **U.S. Virgin Islands** to win by walkover.

08.08.2002   Suriname: Suriname – U.S. Virgin Islands 6-1
10.08.2002   Suriname: U.S. Virgin Islands – Suriname 0-2

Suriname qualified for Final Round.

FINAL ROUND

SEMI-FINALS

04.08.2002 Jamaica: Jamaica – Haiti 2-0
13.08.2002 Suriname: Suriname – Trinidad and Tobago 1-3
15.08.2002 Suriname: Trinidad and Tobago – Suriname 2-1
18.08.2002 Haiti: Haiti – Jamaica 0-0

THIRD PLACE PLAY-OFF

08.09.2002 Haiti: Haiti – Suriname 3-0 (2-0)
Goals: Bien-Aime (28), Nord (42), J.Pierre (80)
10.09.2002 Haiti: Suriname – Haiti 1-2 (1-1)
Goals: Vliet (4) / Hilaire (45), Teleus (48)

Trinidad and Tobago and **Jamaica** qualified for the CONCACAF Women's Gold Cup 2002.

CONCACAF WOMEN'S GOLD CUP 2002

The tournament was held in Seattle, Washington, United States and Vancouver, British Columbia, Canada.

FINAL TOURNAMENT

FIRST ROUND
GROUP A

27.10.2002 Pasadena, United States: Trinidad and Tobago – Panama 2-4 (1-2)
Goals: Attin-Johnson (42), St. Louis (66) / Bedoya (42), de Mera (35, 61, 64)
27.10.2002 Pasadena, United States: United States – Trinidad and Tobago 3-0 (1-0)
Goals: Parlow (19), Chastain (54), Milbrett (63)
29.10.2002 Fullerton, United States: Mexico – Panama 5-1 (3-1)
Goals: Gómez (4, 22 pen), Sandoval (37), Leyva (65), Dominguez (78) / Valderrama (26)
02.11.2002 Seattle, United States: Mexico – Trinidad and Tobago 2-0 (1-0)
Goals: Gerardo (3, 60)
02.11.2002 Seattle, United States: United States – Panama 9-0 (8-0)
Goals: Milbrett (3, 5, 9, 23, 34), MacMillan (11, 14), Roberts (40), Wambach (86)

Team	Pld	W	D	L	GF	GA	GD	Pts
United States	*3*	*3*	*0*	*0*	*15*	*0*	*+15*	*9*
Mexico	*3*	*2*	*0*	*1*	*7*	*4*	*+3*	*6*
Panama	3	1	0	2	5	16	-11	3
Trinidad and Tobago	3	0	0	3	2	9	-7	0

78

GROUP B

30.10.2002   Victoria, Canada: Jamaica – Costa Rica 0-2 (0-1)
Goals: Chavez (43, 69)
30.10.2002   Victoria, Canada: Canada – Haiti 11-1 (7-1)
Goals: Hooper (6, 26, 32), Burtini (11, 84), Sinclair (16, 43, 71, 86), Chapman (30),
Fenelon (79 og) / Marseille (14)
01.11.2002   Victoria, Canada: Haiti – Costa Rica 0-5 (0-0)
Goals: Cruz (53, 68), Chavez (62, 87), Briceño (90)
01.11.2002   Victoria, Canada: Canada – Jaimaica 9-0 (4-0)
Goals: Sinclair (13, 78), Hooper (20), Walsh (42), Lang (45, 63, 84, 90), Hermus (55)
03.11.2002   Victoria, Canada: Jamaica – Haiti 1-2 (0-1)
Goals: Sinclair (59) / Gilles (13, 56)
03.11.2002   Victoria, Canada: Canada – Costa Rica 3-0 (2-0)
Goals: Hooper (28, 42), Sinclair (47)

Team	Pld	W	D	L	GF	GA	GD	Pts
Canada	3	3	0	0	23	1	+22	9
Costa Rica	3	2	0	1	7	3	+4	6
Haiti	3	1	0	2	3	17	-14	3
Jamaica	3	0	0	3	1	13	-12	0

KNOCKOUT STAGE
SEMI-FINALS

06.11.2002   Seattle, United States: Canada – Mexico 2-0
06.11.2002   Seattle, United States: United States – Costa Rica 7-0

THIRD PLACE PLAY-OFF

09.11.2002   Pasadena, United States: Mexico – Costa Rica 4-1

FINAL

09.11.2002   Rose Bowl, Pasadena, United States: United States – Canada 2-1

Second-place team **Canada** qualified for the FIFI Women's World Cup 2003. The
winner **United States** qualified as hosts. The third-placed Mexico had to play against
Japan two play-off matches for qualification.

OFC WOMEN'S CHAMPIONSHIP 2003

The OFC Women's Championship 2003 was held in Canberra, Australia between 5 &
13 April 2003. Originally the tournament was scheduled for 19-29 November 2002,
but was postponed after withdrawal by American Samoa, Tahiti and Tonga. A
rescheduled tournament with seven teams in two groups was arranged, however Fiji
and Vanuatu withdrew, resulting in a five nation championship of one group. Only the
winner of the tournament will qualify for the FIFA Women's World Cup 2003.

05.04.2003   Belconnen Soccer Centre, Canberra:
            Cook Islands – Papua New Guinea 1-5 (1-4)
Goals: Rakei (29) / Matthies (21), Konalalai (23), Limbai (40, 87), Banabas (42)
05.04.2003   Belconnen Soccer Centre, Canberra: Australia – Samoa 19-0 (6-0)
Goals: Peters (5, 35, 50, 79), Goleboiwski (16, 42, 46, 61), Davies (18), Small (41,
78), Mann (53, 58, 85, 87), Wainwright (55), Slatyer (56, 57), Garriock (72)
07.04.2003   Belconnen Soccer Centre, Canberra: Australia – Cook Islands 11-0 (5-0)
Goals: Crawford (8, 17), Davies (11), Alagich (34, 62 pen), Karp (37, 81), Hohnke
(59), Small (65), Wilson (71, 82)
07.04.2003   Belconnen Soccer Centre, Canberra: Samoa – New Zealand 0-15 (0-10)
Goals: Jackman (5, 9, 24, 50), Ferrara (7, 10, 32), Smith (11, 12, 42, 65, 87),
Moorwood (41), Michele (80, 82)
09.04.2003   Belconnen Soccer Centre, Canberra:
            Cook Islands – New Zealand 0-9 (0-5)
Goals: Ferrara (4, 22), Jackman (13, 33, 49), Smith (30), Henderson (53), Simpson
(59), McCahill (88)
09.04.2003   Belconnen Soccer Centre, Canberra:
            Australia – Papua New Guinea 13-0 (4-0)
Goals: Mann (5, 41, 49, 55), Peters (17), Salisbury (29, 81 pen), Alagich (46),
Golebiowski (59, 71), Garriock (60, 78, 89)
11.04.2003   Belconnen Soccer Centre, Canberra: Papua New Guinea – New Zealand
0-5 (0-2)
Goals: Smith (7), Jackman (12, 47, 59), Duncan (68)
11.04.2003   Belconnen Soccer Centre, Canberra: Cook Islands – Samoa 0-1 (0-0)
Goal: Laumea (77)
13.04.2003   Belconnen Soccer Centre, Canberra:
            Papua New Guinea – Samoa 5-2 (2-0)
Goals: Banabas (27, 80), Matthies (30), Nombe (51), Lanta (71) / Talai (74),
Peresia (87)
13.04.2003   Belconnen Soccer Centre, Canberra: Australia – New Zealand 2-0 (1-0)
Goals: Peters (24), Small (49)

Team	Pld	W	D	L	GF	GA	GD	Pts
Australia	*4*	*4*	*0*	*0*	*45*	*0*	*+45*	*12*
New Zealand	4	3	0	1	29	2	+27	9
Papua New Guinea	4	2	0	2	10	21	-11	6
Samoa	4	1	0	3	3	39	-36	3
Cook Islands	4	0	0	4	1	26	-25	0

Australia qualified for the FIFA Women's World Cup 2003.

CONMEBOL SUDAMERICANO FEMENINO 2003

The South America (CONMEBOL) Sudamericano Femenino 2003 tournament was
held between 9 & 27 April 2003. Three venues, located in three different countries,
were used to the tournament, Salta in Argentina, Loja in Ecuador and Lima in Peru.

Originally the tournament was scheduled to take place between 5 & 16 April 2002 in Córdoba, Argentina. Later, it was moved to Peru, to be played in January and February 2003, with Lima and Chincha as venues.

The winner and the runner-up will qualify for the FIFA Women's World Cup 2003.

FIRST ROUND

GROUP A

09.04.2003 Estadio Monumental "U", Lima: Peru – Bolivia 3-1 (1-1)
Goals: Salinas (18, 70 pen), Mori (55) / Zamorano (34)
11.04.2003 Estadio Monumental "U", Lima: Bolivia – Chile 7-1 (3-0)
Goals: Zamorano (13, 20, 43), Moreno (54), E.Pérez (56), S.Pérez (62), Urgel (77) / Galvez (90 pen)
13.04.2003 Estadio Monumental "U", Lima: Peru – Chile 2-1 (0-1)
Goals: Bosmans (51), Veruzhka (80) / Castro (44)

Team	Pld	W	D	L	GF	GA	GD	Pts
Peru	*2*	*2*	*0*	*0*	*5*	*2*	*+3*	*6*
Bolivia	2	1	0	1	8	4	+4	3
Chile	2	0	0	2	2	9	-7	0

GROUP B

09.04.2003 Estadio Federativo Reina del Cisne, Loja: Ecuador – Venezuela 2-0 (0-0)
Goals: Villón (71, 90)
11.04.2003 Estadio Federativo Reina del Cisne, Loja:
Colombia – Venezuela 8-0 (2-0)
Goals: Valencia (10, 86), Imbachi (33), Miranda (49), Garzón (58, 59), Gutiérrez (80), Munera (90)
13.04.2003 Estadio Federativo Reina del Cisne, Loja: Ecuador – Colombia 1-1 (1-0)
Goals: Campi (45) / Valencia (46)

Team	Pld	W	D	L	GF	GA	GD	Pts
Colombia	*2*	*1*	*1*	*0*	*9*	*1*	*+8*	*4*
Ecuador	2	1	1	0	3	1	+2	4
Venezuela	2	0	0	2	0	10	-10	0

GROUP C

09.04.2003 Estadio Padre Ernesto Martearena, Salta: Argentina – Paraguay 3-0 (1-0)
Goals: Jiménez (41), Medina (65, 72)
11.04.2003 Estadio Padre Ernesto Martearena, Salta: Uruguay – Paraguay 1-3 (1-1)
Goals: Lemos (27) / Agüero (11), Rodas (56), Román (72)
13.04.2003 Estadio Padre Ernesto Martearena, Salta: Argentina – Uruguay 8-0 (3-0)
Goals: Jiménez (5), Gatti (32), Alvariza (35 pen, 79), Medina (46, 49, 51, 81)

Team	Pld	W	D	L	GF	GA	GD	Pts
Argentina	*2*	*2*	*0*	*0*	*11*	*0*	*+11*	*6*
Paraguay	2	1	0	1	3	4	-1	3
Uruguay	2	0	0	2	1	11	-10	0

FINAL ROUND

All matches were played in Lima, Peru.
Brazil got a bye to the Final Round after winning the previous edition.

23.04.2003   Estadio Monumental "U", Lima: Brazil – Argentina 3-2 (2-0)
Goals: Kátia (1), Pretinha (7), Rosana (54) / Gatti (49), Almeida (71)
23.04.2003   Estadio Monumental "U", Lima: Peru – Colombia 0-1 (0-1)
Goal: Valencia (18)
25.04.2003   Estadio Monumental "U", Lima: Colombia – Argentina 2-3 (2-2)
Goals: Ordónez (5), Valencia (33) / Gómez (25), Alvariza (43), Gerez (71)
25.04.2003   Estadio Monumental "U", Lima: Brazil – Peru 3-0 (2-0)
Goals: Formiga (26), Pretinha (30), Marta (53)
27.04.2003   Estadio Monumental "U", Lima: Brazil – Colombia 12-0 (6-0)
Goals: Pretinha (7, 15), Formiga (22), Marta (34, 50, 70 pen), Kátia (42, 44, 74, 82, 89), Cristiane (80)
27.04.2003   Estadio Monumental "U", Lima: Peru – Argentina 1-1 (1-0)
Goals: Dávila (7) / Medina (88)

Team	Pld	W	D	L	GF	GA	GD	Pts
Brazil	*3*	*3*	*0*	*0*	*18*	*2*	*+16*	*9*
Argentina	*3*	*1*	*1*	*1*	*6*	*6*	*0*	*4*
Colombia	3	1	0	2	3	15	-12	3
Peru	3	0	1	2	1	5	-4	1

Winner **Brazil** and runner-up **Argentina** qualified for the FIFA Women's World Cup 2003.

AFC/CONCACAF PLAY-OFF

05.07.2003   Estadio Azteca, Mexico City: Mexico – Japan 2-2 (0-0)
Goals: Mora (60, Sandoval (76) /Kobayashi (51), Miyamoto (74)
12.07.2003   National Stadium, Tokyo: Japan – Mexico 2-0 (0-0)
Goals: Sawa (56), Maruyama (83)

Japan qualified for the FIFA Women's World Cup 2003.

FIFA WOMEN'S WORLD CUP FINAL TOURNAMENT IN USA 2003

The tournament was originally scheduled for China from 23 September to 11 October 2003. On 3 May 2003, FIFA announced that they would move the tournament to an alternate host country because of the 2003 SARS outbreak in China. At the same time the FIFA announced that the FIFA Women's World Cup 2007 would be awarded to China in its place. On 26 ay 2003, FIFA announced the United States would host the tournament. Because the United States had hosted the FIFA Women's World Cup 1999, it was thought the United States could best organize the tournament in the little time remaining before October 2003 scheduled start. In compensation for losing the tournament, China retained its automatic qualification as host and was named as host for the 2007 event.

GROUP STAGE

GROUP A

20.09.2003   Lincoln Financial Field, Philadelphia: Nigeria – North Korea 0-3 (0-1)
Nigeria: Predious Uzoaru DEDE, Bunmi KAYODE, Florence Kikelomo AJAYI
(YC28), Florence IWETA, Florence OMAGBEMI (44 Maureen MMADU),
Efioanwan EKPO, Perpetua Ijeoma NKWOCHA, Stella MBACHU, Ifeanyi
CHIEJINE (85 Onome EBI), Mercy AKIDE *(YC22)*, Nkechi EGBE (46 Patience
AVRE). (Coach: Samuel OKPODU).
North Korea: RI Jong-Hui, YUN In-Sil, RA Mi-Ae, JANG Ok-Gyong, JON Hye-
Yong *(YC71)*, RI Un-Gyong, YUN Yong-Hui (57 PAK Kyong-Sun), O Kum-Ran, RI
Hyang-Ok *(YC25)*, RI Kum-Suk (81 HO Sun-Hui), JIN Pyol-Hui.
(Coach: RI Song-Gun).
Goals: JIN Pyol-Hui (13, 88), RI Un-Gyong (73)
Referee: Nicole PETIGNAT (Switzerland)   Attendance: 24,346

21.09.2003   Robert F. Kennedy Memorial Stadium, Washington:
            United States – Sweden 3-1 (2-0)
United States: Briana Collette SCURRY *(YC13)*, Christie PEARCE, Kathryn Michele
MARKGRAF Sobrero, Joy Lynn FAWCETT Biefeld, Shannon BOXX, Kristine
Marie LILLY Heavey, Brandi Denise CHASTAIN (46 Catherine WHITEHILL), Julie
Maurine FOUDY, Abby WAMBACH (56 Tiffeny Carleen MILBRETT), Mariel
Margaret (Mia) HAMM, Cynthia Marie (Cindy) PARLOW Cone (70 Alyson Kay
(Aly) WAGNER *(YC72)*). (Coach: April HEINRICHS).
Sweden: Caroline JÖNSSON, Karolina WESTBERG, Jane TÖRNQVIST, Sara
LARSSON, Hanna Gunilla MARKLUND, Kerstin Ingrid Therese SJÖGRAN (46
Frida Christina ÖSTBERG), Linda FAGERSTRÖM, Malin Sofi MOSTRÖM, Malin
Elisabeth ANDERSSON (77 Anna SJÖSTRÖM *(YC90+3)*), Hanna Carolina
LJUNGBERG (83 Josefine ÖQVIST), Victoria Margareta Sandell SVENSSON.
(Coach: Marika Susan DOMANSKI LYFORS).
Goals: Kristine Marie LILLY Heavey (27), Cynthia Marie (Cindy) PARLOW Cone
(36), Shannon BOXX (78) / Victoria Margareta Sandell SVENSSON (58)
Referee: ZHANG Dongqing (China PR)   Attendance: 34,144

83

25.09.2003   Lincoln Financial Field, Philadelphia: Sweden – North Korea 1-0 (1-0)
Sweden: Caroline JÖNSSON, Karolina WESTBERG *(YC52)*, Jane TÖRNQVIST,
Sara LARSSON, Hanna Gunilla MARKLUND, Frida Christina ÖSTBERG, Linda
FAGERSTRÖM (56 Anna SJÖSTRÖM), Malin Sofi MOSTRÖM, Malin Elisabeth
ANDERSSON (65 Gärd Kristin BENGTSSON), Hanna Carolina LJUNGBERG (86
Josefine ÖQVIST), Victoria Margareta Sandell SVENSSON.
(Coach: Marika Susan DOMANSKI LYFORS).
North Korea: RI Jong-Hui, SIN Kum-Ok (55 YUN In-Sil), RA Mi-Ae (62 SONG
Jong-Sun), JANG Ok-Gyong *(YC56)*, JON Hye-Yong, RI Un-Gyong, YUN Yong-Hui
(36 HO Sun-Hui), O Kum-Ran, RI Hyang-Ok, RI Kum-Suk, JIN Pyol-Hui.
(Coach: RI Song-Gun).
Goal: Victoria Margareta Sandell SVENSSON (7)
Referee: Tammy Nicole OGSTON (Australia)   Attendance: 31,553

25.09.2003   Lincoln Financial Field, Philadelphia: United States – Nigeria 5-0 (2-0)
United States: Briana Collette SCURRY, Catherine WHITEHILL, Kathryn Michele
MARKGRAF Sobrero, Kylie Elizabeth BIVENS, Joy Lynn FAWCETT Biefeld,
Shannon BOXX (71 Tiffany Marie ROBERTS Sahaydak), Alyson Kay (Aly)
WAGNER (46 Abby WAMBACH), Kristine Marie LILLY Heavey, Julie Maurine
FOUDY, Mariel Margaret (Mia) HAMM, Cynthia Marie (Cindy) PARLOW Cone (57
Tiffeny Carleen MILBRETT). (Coach: April HEINRICHS).
Nigeria: Predious Uzoaru DEDE, Bunmi KAYODE, Florence Kikelomo AJAYI,
Florence OMAGBEMI *(YC76)*, Maureen MMADU, Nkiru OKOSIEME, Patience
AVRE, Perpetua Ijeoma NKWOCHA, Stella MBACHU, Ifeanyi CHIEJINE, Mercy
AKIDE. (Coach: Samuel OKPODU).
Goals: Mariel Margaret (Mia) HAMM (6 pen, 12), Cynthia Marie (Cindy) PARLOW
Cone (47), Abby WAMBACH (65), Julie Maurine FOUDY (89 pen)
Referee: Florencia ROMANO (Argentina)   Attendance: 31,553

28.09.2003   MAPFRE Stadium, Columbus: Sweden – Nigeria 3-0 (0-0)
Sweden: Caroline JÖNSSON, Karolina WESTBERG, Gärd Kristin BENGTSSON (46
Anna SJÖSTRÖM), Sara LARSSON, Hanna Gunilla MARKLUND, Sara CALL,
Frida Christina ÖSTBERG, Malin Sofi MOSTRÖM, Malin Elisabeth ANDERSSON
(66 Kerstin Ingrid Therese SJÖGRAN), Hanna Carolina LJUNGBERG, Victoria
Margareta Sandell SVENSSON (85 Josefine ÖQVIST).
(Coach: Marika Susan DOMANSKI LYFORS).
Nigeria: Predious Uzoaru DEDE, Florence Kikelomo AJAYI, Florence IWETA (83
Onome EBI), Florence OMAGBEMI, Maureen MMADU, Nkiru OKOSIEME (65
Efioanwan EKPO), Patience AVRE (89 Olaitan YUSUF), Perpetua Ijeoma
NKWOCHA, Stella MBACHU, Ifeanyi CHIEJINE, Mercy AKIDE.
(Coach: Samuel OKPODU).
Goals: Hanna Carolina LJUNGBERG (56, 79), Malin Sofi MOSTRÖM (81)
Referee: Sonia DENONCOURT (Canada)   Attendance: 22,828

28.09.2003   MAPFRE Stadium, Columbus: North Korea – United States 0-3 (0-1)
North Korea: RI Jong-Hui, YUN In-Sil, SIN Kum-Ok (26 JON Hye-Yong), RA Mi-Ae, JANG Ok-Gyong, RI Un-Gyong, YUN Yong-Hui (74 PAK Kyong-Sun *(YC90+1)*), O Kum-Ran *(YC16)* (53 SONG Jong-Sun), RI Hyang-Ok, RI Kum-Suk, JIN Pyol-Hui. (Coach: RI Song-Gun).
United States: Briana Collette SCURRY, Christie PEARCE, Catherine WHITEHILL, Kathryn Michele MARKGRAF Sobrero (73 Danielle SLATON), Kylie Elizabeth BIVENS, Joy Lynn FAWCETT Biefeld, Alyson Kay (Aly) WAGNER, Kristine Marie LILLY Heavey (46 Julie Maurine FOUDY), Tiffany Marie ROBERTS Sahaydak, Tiffeny Carleen MILBRETT *(YC40)*, Abby WAMBACH *(YC22)* (56 Shannon Ann MACMILLAN). (Coach: April HEINRICHS).
Goals: Abby WAMBACH (17 pen), Catherine WHITEHILL (48, 66)
Referee: SUELI Terezinha TORTURA (Brazil)   Attendance: 22,828

Team	Pld	W	D	L	GF	GA	GD	Pts
United States	*3*	*3*	*0*	*0*	*11*	*1*	*+10*	*9*
Sweden	*3*	*2*	*0*	*1*	*5*	*3*	*+2*	*6*
North Korea	3	1	0	2	3	4	-1	3
Nigeria	*3*	*0*	*0*	*3*	*0*	*11*	*-11*	*0*

GROUP B

20.09.2003   Lincoln Financial Field, Philidelphia: Norway – France 2-0 (0-0)
Norway: Bente NORDBY, Ane STANGELAND Horpestad, Gunhild Bentzen FØLSTAD, Brit SANDAUNE, Solveig GULBRANDSEN (80 Trine RØNNING), Unni LEHN (89 Hege RIISE), Monica KNUDSEN, Lise KLAVENESS *(YC90+1)*, Marianne PETTERSEN (90+1 Linda ØRMEN), Anita RAPP *(YC86)*, Dagny MELLGREN. (Coach: Åge STEEN).
France: Corinne DIACRE, Celine MARTY, Laura GEORGES, Sonia BOMPASTOR, Sabrina Marie-Christine VIGUIER, Peggy PROVOST, Sandrine SOUBEYRAND, Élodie WOOCK, Stéphanie MUGNERET-BÉGHÉ (82 Marie-Ange KRAMO), Hoda LATTAF (72 Laëtitia Françoise Andree (Toto) TONAZZI), Marinette PICHON. (Coaches: Corinne DIACRE & Élisabeth LOISEL).
Goals: Anita RAPP (47), Dagny MELLGREN (66)
Referee: Kari SEITZ (United States)   Attendance: 24,346

21.09.2003   Robert F. Kennedy Memorial Stadium, Washington:
Brazil – South Korea 3-0 (1-0)
Brazil: ANDRÉIA Suntaque, TÂNIA Maria Pereira Ribeiro, Renata Aparecida da
Costa "KÓKI", JULIANA Ribeiro Cabral, ROSANA dos Santos Augusto, Miraildes
Maciel Mota "FORMIGA" *(YC2)* (89 PRISCILA Faria de Oliveira), SIMONE Gomes
Jatobá, DANIELA Alves Lima, ANDRÉIA dos Santos (78 CRISTIANE Rozeira de
Souza Silva), MARTA Vieira da Silva, KÁTIA Cilene Teixeira da Silva.
(Coach: PAULO GONÇALVES).
South Korea: KIM Jung-Mi, KIM Yu-Mi *(YC22)* (46 JIN Suk-Hee *(YC71)*), SONG
Ju-Hee, SHIN Sun-Nam, KIM Yu-Jin, YOO Young-Sil, KIM Kyul-Sil (65 HWANG
Insun), KIM Jin-Hee (49 SUNG Hyun-Ah), HAN Jin-Sook, PARK Eun-Sun, LEE Ji-
Eun. (Coach: AN Jong-Goan).
Goals: MARTA Vieira da Silva (14 pen), KÁTIA Cilene Teixeira da Silva (55, 62)
Referee: Tammy Nicole OGSTON (Australia)   Attendance: 34,144

24.09.2003   Robert F. Kennedy Memorial Stadium, Washington:
Norway – Brazil 1-4 (1-2)
Norway: Bente NORDBY, Ane STANGELAND Horpestad, Trine RØNNING
(YC77), Gunhild Bentzen FØLSTAD, Brit SANDAUNE, Solveig GULBRANDSEN
(74 Lise KLAVENESS), Unni LEHN (74 Hege RIISE), Monica KNUDSEN,
Marianne PETTERSEN, Anita RAPP (46 Linda ØRMEN), Dagny MELLGREN.
(Coach: Åge STEEN).
Brazil: ANDRÉIA Suntaque, TÂNIA Maria Pereira Ribeiro, Renata Aparecida da
Costa "KÓKI" *(YC51)*, JULIANA Ribeiro Cabral, ROSANA dos Santos Augusto,
Miraildes Maciel Mota "FORMIGA" (88 RAFAELA Andrade de Moraes), SIMONE
Gomes Jatobá, DANIELA Alves Lima (90 PRISCILA Faria de Oliveira), ANDRÉIA
dos Santos (80 CRISTIANE Rozeira de Souza Silva), MARTA Vieira da Silva,
KÁTIA Cilene Teixeira da Silva. (Coach: PAULO GONÇALVES).
Goals: Marianne PETTERSEN (45) / DANIELA Alves Lima (26), ROSANA dos
Santos Augusto (37), MARTA Vieira da Silva (59),
KÁTIA Cilene Teixeira da Silva (68)
Referee: Xonam AGBOYI (Togo)   Attendance: 16,316

24.09.2003   Robert F. Kennedy Memorial Stadium, Washington:
France – South Korea 1-0 (0-0)
France: Corinne DIACRE *(YC65)*, Celine MARTY, Laura GEORGES, Sonia
BOMPASTOR, Anne-Laure CASSELEUX (81 Emmanuelle SYKORA), Peggy
PROVOST, Sandrine SOUBEYRAND, Marie-Ange KRAMO, Élodie WOOCK
(YC37) (89 Virginie DESSALLE), Stéphanie MUGNERET-BÉGHÉ (68 Laëtitia
Françoise Andree (Toto) TONAZZI), Marinette PICHON.
(Coaches: Corinne DIACRE & Élisabeth LOISEL).
South Korea: KIM Jung-Mi, KIM Yu-Mi, SONG Ju-Hee, SHIN Sun-Nam (85 KIM
Ju-Hee), KIM Yu-Jin, YOO Young-Sil *(YC45)* (83 JIN Suk-Hee), KIM Kyul-Sil (75
LEE Myung-Hwa *(YC83)*), KIM Jin-Hee, HAN Jin-Sook, PARK Eun-Sun, LEE Ji-
Eun. (Coach: AN Jong-Goan).
Goal: Marinette PICHON (84)
Referee: ZHANG Dongqing (China PR)   Attendance: 16,316

27.09.2003 Gilette Stadium, Foxborough: South Korea – Norway 1-7 (0-4)
South Korea: KIM Jung-Mi, KIM Yu-Mi, SONG Ju-Hee, KIM Yu-Jin (55 JIN Suk-Hee), YOO Young-Sil, KIM Ju-Hee, KIM Kyul-Sil, KIM Jin-Hee, HAN Jin-Sook (30 KIM Yoo-Jin), PARK Eun-Sun (59 HONG Kyung-Suk), LEE Ji-Eun.
(Coach: AN Jong-Goan).
Norway: Bente NORDBY, Marit Helene Fiane GRØDUM CHRISTENSEN, Ane STANGELAND Horpestad, Trine RØNNING (69 Linda ØRMEN), Brit SANDAUNE, Solveig GULBRANDSEN (73 Ingrid Camilla Fosse SÆTHRE), Unni LEHN, Monica KNUDSEN, Lise KLAVENESS (81 Hege RIISE), Marianne PETTERSEN, Dagny MELLGREN. (Coach: Åge STEEN).
Goals: KIM Jin-Hee (75) / Solveig GULBRANDSEN (5), Dagny MELLGREN (24, 31), Marianne PETTERSEN (40), Brit SANDAUNE (52), Linda ØRMEN (80, 90)
Referee: Tammy Nicole OGSTON (Australia)   Attendance: 14,356

27.09.2003 Robert F. Kennedy Memorial Stadium, Washington:
France – Brazil 1-1 (0-0)
France: Corinne DIACRE, Celine MARTY, Laura GEORGES, Sonia BOMPASTOR, Sabrina Marie-Christine VIGUIER (85 Hoda LATTAF), Peggy PROVOST *(YC72)*, Sandrine SOUBEYRAND, Marie-Ange KRAMO, Élodie WOOCK (73 Amelie COQUET), Stéphanie MUGNERET-BÉGHÉ (46 Laëtitia Françoise Andree (Toto) TONAZZI), Marinette PICHON. (Coaches: Corinne DIACRE & Élisabeth LOISEL).
Brazil: ANDRÉIA Suntaque, TÂNIA Maria Pereira Ribeiro (88 MÔNICA Angélica de Paula), JULIANA Ribeiro Cabral, ROSANA dos Santos Augusto, SIMONE Gomes Jatobá, DANIELA Alves Lima *(YC51)*, ANDRÉIA dos Santos, RAFAELA Andrade de Moraes, PRISCILA Faria de Oliveira (46 CRISTIANE Rozeira de Souza Silva), MARTA Vieira da Silva, KÁTIA Cilene Teixeira da Silva.
(Coach: PAULO GONÇALVES).
Goals: Marinette PICHON (90+2) / KÁTIA Cilene Teixeira da Silva (58)
Referee: Floarea Cristina Ionescu BABADAC (Romania)   Attendance: 17,618

Team	Pld	W	D	L	GF	GA	GD	Pts
Brazil	*3*	*2*	*1*	*0*	*8*	*2*	*+6*	*7*
Norway	*3*	*2*	*0*	*1*	*10*	*5*	*+5*	*6*
France	3	1	1	1	2	3	-1	4
South Korea	3	0	0	3	1	11	-10	0

GROUP C

20.09.2003 MAPFRE Stadium, Columbus: Germany – Canada 4-1 (1-1)
Germany: Silke ROTTENBERG, Kerstin STEGEMANN, Sandra MINNERT,
Stefanie GOTTSCHLICH, Ariane HINGST (65 Nia Tsholofelo KÜNZER), Renate
LINGOR (73 Kerstin GAREFREKES), Linda BRESONIK *(YC45+1)*, Stephanie
JONES, Maren MEINERT *(YC78)*, Bettina WIEGMANN, Birgit PRINZ.
(Coach: Tina THEUNE).
Canada: Karina LEBLANC *(YC21)*, Kristina KISS, Tanya DENNIS, Sharolta Louisa
NONEN, Charmaine HOOPER *(YC38)*, Andrea NEIL, Diana MATHESON, Brittany
TIMKO, Christine SINCLAIR, Kara Elise LANG (46 Rhian WILKINSON), Cristine
LATHAM. (Coach: Even Jostein PELLERUD).
Goals: Bettina WIEGMANN (39 pen), Stefanie GOTTSCHLICH (47), Birgit PRINZ
(75), Kerstin GAREFREKES (90+2) / Christine SINCLAIR (4)
Referee: IM Eun-Ju (South Korea) Attendance: 16,409

20.09.2003 MAPFRE Stadium, Columbus: Japan – Argentina 6-0 (2-0)
Japan: Nozomi YAMAGO, Kyoko YANO, Yumi OBE, Yasuyo YAMAGISHI (73
Hiromi ISOZAKI), Tomomi MIYAMOTO, Tomoe KATO Sakai, Homare SAWA (80
Karina MARUYAMA), Emi YAMAMOTO, Yayoi KOBAYASHI (57 Eriko
ARAKAWA), Naoko KAWAKAMI, Mio OTANI. (Coach: Eiji UEDA).
Argentina: Romina FERRO, Sabrina BARBITTA *(YC59)*, Clarisa HUBER, Marisa
GEREZ, Mariela RICOTTI (76 Noelia LOPEZ), Andrea GONSEBATE, Rosana
GÓMEZ *(YC18)* (46 Valeria COTELO), Fabiana VALLEJOS, Mariela CORONEL,
Natalia GATTI (RC39), Maria VILLANUEVA *(YC16)* (46 Karina ALVARIZA).
(Coach: José Carlos BORRELLO).
Goals: Homare SAWA (13, 38), Emi YAMAMOTO (64), Mio OTANI (72, 75, 80)
Referee: Katriina ELOVIRTA (Finland) Attendance: 16,409

Sent-off: 39' Natalia GATTI.

24.09.2003 MAPFRE Stadium, Columbus: Germany – Japan 3-0 (2-0)
Germany: Silke ROTTENBERG, Kerstin STEGEMANN, Sandra MINNERT,
Stefanie GOTTSCHLICH (64 Sandra SMISEK), Ariane HINGST (72 Linda
BRESONIK), Renate LINGOR, Kerstin GAREFREKES, Stephanie JONES, Maren
MEINERT, Bettina WIEGMANN (78 Nia Tsholofelo KÜNZER *(YC80)*), Birgit
PRINZ. (Coach: Tina THEUNE).
Japan: Nozomi YAMAGO, Kyoko YANO (60 Hiromi ISOZAKI), Yumi OBE,
Yasuyo YAMAGISHI, Tomomi MIYAMOTO, Tomoe KATO Sakai (56 Miyuki
YANAGITA), Homare SAWA, Emi YAMAMOTO, Yayoi KOBAYASHI (56 Eriko
ARAKAWA), Naoko KAWAKAMI, Mio OTANI. (Coach: Eiji UEDA).
Goals: Sandra MINNERT (23), Birgit PRINZ (36, 66)
Referee: SUELI Terezinha TORTURA (Brazil) Attendance: 15,529

24.09.2003 MAPFRE Stadium, Columbus: Canada – Argentina 3-0 (1-0)
Canada: Taryn SWIATEK, Kristina KISS, Tanya DENNIS, Rhian WILKINSON
(YC62) (75 Silvana BURTINI), Sharolta Louisa NONEN, Charmaine HOOPER,
Diana MATHESON *(YC41)*, Brittany TIMKO, Christine SINCLAIR, Kara Elise
LANG, Cristine LATHAM (83 Sasha Ajua ANDREWS *(YC86)*).
(Coach: Even Jostein PELLERUD).
Argentina: Romina FERRO, Sabrina BARBITTA, Clarisa HUBER, Marisa GEREZ,
Mariela RICOTTI *(YC29)* (78 Noelia LOPEZ), Andrea GONSEBATE, Rosana
GÓMEZ, Fabiana VALLEJOS, Mariela CORONEL (84 Yanina GAITAN), Marisol
MEDINA, Maria VILLANUEVA (75 Karina ALVARIZA).
(Coach: José Carlos BORRELLO).
Goals: Charmaine HOOPER (19 pen), Cristine LATHAM (79, 82)
Referee: Nicole PETIGNAT (Switzerland) Attendance: 15,529

27.09.2003 Robert F. Kennedy Memorial Stadium, Washington:
            Argentina – Germany 1-6 (0-4)
Argentina: Romina FERRO, Sabrina BARBITTA, Clarisa HUBER, Marisa GEREZ,
Andrea GONSEBATE, Noelia LOPEZ, Rosana GÓMEZ (56 Yanina GAITAN),
Fabiana VALLEJOS, Mariela CORONEL, Marisol MEDINA, Maria VILLANUEVA
(85 Karina ALVARIZA). (Coach: José Carlos BORRELLO).
Germany: Silke ROTTENBERG, Kerstin STEGEMANN, Sandra MINNERT,
Stefanie GOTTSCHLICH (46 Conny POHLERS), Ariane HINGST, Renate LINGOR,
Kerstin GAREFREKES (46 Martina MÜLLER), Stephanie JONES (62 Sonja Beate
FUSS), Maren MEINERT, Bettina WIEGMANN, Birgit PRINZ.
(Coach: Tina THEUNE).
Goals: Yanina GAITAN (71) / Maren MEINERT (3, 43), Bettina WIEGMANN (24
pen), Birgit PRINZ (32), Conny POHLERS (89), Martina MÜLLER (90+2)
Referee: Bola ABIDOYE (Nigeria) Attendance: 17,618

27.09.2003 Gillette Stadium, Foxborough: Canada – Japan 3-1 (1-1)
Canada: Taryn SWIATEK, Tanya DENNIS, Sharolta Louisa NONEN, Isabelle
MORNEAU *(YC45+1)*, Charmaine HOOPER, Andrea NEIL (77 Kristina KISS),
Diana MATHESON, Brittany TIMKO, Christine SINCLAIR, Kara Elise LANG (85
Rhian WILKINSON), Cristine LATHAM (60 Silvana BURTINI).
(Coach: Even Jostein PELLERUD).
Japan: Nozomi YAMAGO, Hiromi ISOZAKI, Yumi OBE, Yasuyo YAMAGISHI,
Tomomi MIYAMOTO, Tomoe KATO Sakai (62 Miyuki YANAGITA), Homare
SAWA, Emi YAMAMOTO (89 Aya MIYAMA), Yayoi KOBAYASHI (54 Eriko
ARAKAWA), Naoko KAWAKAMI, Mio OTANI. (Coach: Eiji UEDA).
Goals: Christine SINCLAIR (36, 49), Kara Elise LANG (72) / Homare SAWA (20)
Referee: IM Eun-Ju (South Korea) Attendance: 14,356

Team	Pld	W	D	L	GF	GA	GD	Pts
Germany	*3*	*3*	*0*	*0*	*13*	*2*	*+11*	*9*
Canada	*3*	*2*	*0*	*1*	*7*	*5*	*+2*	*6*
Japan	3	1	0	2	7	6	+1	3
Argentina	3	0	0	3	1	15	-14	0

89

GROUP D

20.09.2003 Stubhub Center, Carson: China PR – Ghana 1-0 (1-0)
China PR: ZHAO Yan, LI Jie, PU Wei, FAN Yunjie, WANG Liping, PAN Lina (36 QU Feifei), ZHAO Lihong (88 REN Liping), LIU Ying, HAN Duan (59 LIU Yali), BAI Jie, SUN Wen. (Coach: MA Liangxing).
Ghana: Memunatu SULEMANA, Mavis DANSO, Yaa AVOE (58 Belinda KANDA), Lydia ANKRAH, Patience SACKEY, Elizabeth BAIDU, Florence OKOE, Adjoa BAYOR, Genevive CLOTTEY, Alberta SACKEY (83 Myralyn OSEI AGYEMANG), Mavis DGAJMAH *(YC90)* (90+2 Akua ANOKYEWAA).
(Coach: Oko ARYEE).
Goal: SUN Wen (29)
Referee: Sonia DENONCOURT (Canada)   Attendance: 15,239

21.09.2003 Stubhub Center, Carson: Australia – Russia 1-2 (1-1)
Australia: Cassandra KELL, Dianne ALAGICH, Cheryl SALISBURY, Rhian DAVIES, Sacha WAINWRIGHT (46 Bryony DUUS), Heather GARRIOCK, Joanne PETERS, Danielle SMALL, Tal KARP (90+1 April MANN), Gillian FORSTER, Kelly GOLEBIOWSKI. (Coach: Adrian SANTRAC).
Russia: Alla VOLKOVA, Oksana SHMACHKOVA, Marina SAENKO, Tatiana ZAYTSEVA, Marina BURAKOVA, Anastasia PUSTOVOITOVA (67 Vera STROUKOVA), Natalia BARBASHINA, Elena FOMINA *(YC83)*, Galina KOMAROVA, Tatiana EGOROVA (68 Tatiana SKOTNIKOVA), Olga LETYUSHOVA *(YC87)*. (Coach: Yuri BYSTRITSKIY).
Goals: Kelly GOLEBIOWSKI (38) / Dianne ALAGICH (39 og), Elena FOMINA (89)
Referee: Bola ABIDOYE (Nigeria)   Attendance: 15.239

25.09.2003 Stubhub Center, Carson: Ghana – Russia 0-3 (0-1)
Ghana: Memunatu SULEMANA, Mavis DANSO, Yaa AVOE (58 Alberta SACKEY), Lydia ANKRAH, Patience SACKEY (78 Belinda KANDA), Elizabeth BAIDU, Florence OKOE, Adjoa BAYOR, Genevive CLOTTEY, Myralyn OSEI AGYEMANG (52 Akua ANOKYEWAA), Mavis DGAJMAH.
(Coach: Oko ARYEE).
Russia: Alla VOLKOVA, Marina SAENKO (74 Anastasia PUSTOVOITOVA), Elena DENCHTCHIK (46 Alexandra SVETLITSKAYA), Tatiana ZAYTSEVA, Marina BURAKOVA, Vera STROUKOVA, Natalia BARBASHINA, Elena FOMINA, Galina KOMAROVA, Tatiana EGOROVA (59 Tatiana SKOTNIKOVA), Olga LETYUSHOVA. (Coach: Yuri BYSTRITSKIY).
Goals: Marina SAENKO (36), Natalia BARBASHINA (54), Olga LETYUSHOVA (80)
Referee: Kari SEITZ (United States)   Attendance: 13,929

25.09.2003   Stubhub Center, Carson: China PR – Australia 1-1 (0-1)
China PR: ZHAO Yan, LI Jie, PU Wei, LIU Yali, FAN Yunjie, WANG Liping,
ZHAO Lihong (85 QU Feifei), LIU Ying *(YC55)*, ZHANG Ouying (74 REN Liping),
BAI Jie (90 TENG Wei), SUN Wen. (Coach: MA Liangxing).
Australia: Cassandra KELL, Dianne ALAGICH *(YC89)*, Cheryl SALISBURY, Rhian
DAVIES, Karla REUTER, Heather GARRIOCK, Joanne PETERS, Danielle SMALL
(76 Bryony DUUS), Tal KARP, Gillian FORSTER, Kelly GOLEBIOWSKI
(YC90+1). (Coach: Adrian SANTRAC).
Goals: BAI Jie (46) / Heather GARRIOCK (28)
Referee: Katriina ELOVIRTA (Finland)   Attendance: 13,929

28.09.2003   Providence Park, Portland: Ghana – Australia 2-1 (2-0)
Ghana: Memunatu SULEMANA, Mavis DANSO (75 Yaa AVOE), Lydia ANKRAH
(YC59), Patience SACKEY, Elizabeth BAIDU, Florence OKOE, Adjoa BAYOR,
Genevive CLOTTEY, Gloria FORIWA (67 Myralyn OSEI AGYEMANG, 90+1 Akua
ANOKYEWAA), Alberta SACKEY, Mavis DGAJMAH. (Coach: Oko ARYEE).
Australia: Melissa BARBIERI HUDSON, Dianne ALAGICH, Cheryl SALISBURY,
Rhian DAVIES, Karla REUTER (90 Pamela GRANT), Heather GARRIOCK *(YC52)*,
Joanne PETERS, Danielle SMALL, Tal KARP (33 Bryony DUUS), Gillian
FORSTER (43 April MANN), Kelly GOLEBIOWSKI. (Coach: Adrian SANTRAC).
Goals: Alberta SACKEY (34, 39) / Heather GARRIOCK (61)
Referee: Xonam AGBOYI (Togo)   Attendance: 19,132

28.09.2003   Providence Park, Portland: China PR – Russia 1-0 (1-0)
China PR: HAN Wenxia, LI Jie, PU Wei, LIU Yali, FAN Yunjie, WANG Liping, BI
Yan (55 QU Feifei), ZHAO Lihong (62 REN Liping), LIU Ying, BAI Jie, SUN Wen.
(Coach: MA Liangxing).
Russia: Alla VOLKOVA, Marina SAENKO, Tatiana ZAYTSEVA, Marina
BURAKOVA, Vera STROUKOVA, Natalia BARBASHINA, Elena FOMINA
(YC90), Galina KOMAROVA, Tatiana EGOROVA, Alexandra SVETLITSKAYA,
Olga LETYUSHOVA (66 Tatiana SKOTNIKOVA). (Coach: Yuri BYSTRITSKIY).
Goal: BAI Jie (16)
Referee: Florencia ROMANO (Argentina)   Attendance: 19,132

Team	Pld	W	D	L	GF	GA	GD	Pts
China PR	3	2	1	0	3	1	+2	7
Russia	3	2	0	1	5	2	+3	6
Ghana	3	1	0	2	2	5	-3	3
Australia	3	0	1	2	3	5	-2	1

QUARTER FINALS

01.10.2003 Gillette Stadium, Foxborough: Brazil – Sweden 1-2 (1-1)
Brazil: ANDRÉIA Suntaque, TÂNIA Maria Pereira Ribeiro, Renata Aparecida da
Costa "KÓKI", JULIANA Ribeiro Cabral *(YC52)*, ROSANA dos Santos Augusto,
Miraildes Maciel Mota "FORMIGA" (81 KELLY Christina Pereira da Silva),
SIMONE Gomes Jatobá (58 CRISTIANE Rozeira de Souza Silva), DANIELA Alves
Lima *(YC37)*, ANDRÉIA dos Santos, MARTA Vieira da Silva, KÁTIA Cilene
Teixeira da Silva. (Coach: PAULO GONÇALVES).
Sweden: Sofia LUNDGREN *(YC43)*, Karolina WESTBERG, Jane TÖRNQVIST,
Sara LARSSON (90 Sara CALL), Hanna Gunilla MARKLUND, Frida Christina
ÖSTBERG, Malin Sofi MOSTRÖM, Malin Elisabeth ANDERSSON (72 Kerstin
Ingrid Therese SJÖGRAN), Hanna Carolina LJUNGBERG, Victoria Margareta
Sandell SVENSSON, Anna SJÖSTRÖM *(YC15)*.
(Coach: Marika Susan DOMANSKI LYFORS).
Goals: MARTA Vieira da Silva (44) / Victoria Margareta Sandell SVENSSON (23),
Malin Elisabeth ANDERSSON (53)
Referee: ZHANG Dongqing (China PR) Attendance: 25,103

01.10.2003 Gillette Stadium, Foxborough: United States – Norway 1-0 (1-0)
United States: Briana Collette SCURRY, Christie PEARCE, Catherine WHITEHILL,
Kathryn Michele MARKGRAF Sobrero, Joy Lynn FAWCETT Biefeld, Shannon
BOXX, Kristine Marie LILLY Heavey, Julie Maurine FOUDY (81 Kylie Elizabeth
BIVENS), Abby WAMBACH, Mariel Margaret (Mia) HAMM, Cynthia Marie
(Cindy) PARLOW Cone (72 Tiffeny Carleen MILBRETT).
(Coach: April HEINRICHS).
Norway: Bente NORDBY *(YC66)*, Marit Helene Fiane GRØDUM CHRISTENSEN
(77 Linda ØRMEN), Ane STANGELAND Horpestad, Trine RØNNING (24 Anita
RAPP), Brit SANDAUNE, Solveig GULBRANDSEN, Unni LEHN *(YC80)* (84 Hege
RIISE *(YC86)*), Monica KNUDSEN, Lise KLAVENESS *(YC75)*, Marianne
PETTERSEN, Dagny MELLGREN. (Coach: Åge STEEN).
Goal: Abby WAMBACH (24)
Referee: Nicole PETIGNAT (Switzerland) Attendance: 25,103

02.10.2003 Providence Park, Portland: Germany – Russia 7-1 (1-0)
Germany: Silke ROTTENBERG, Kerstin STEGEMANN, Sandra MINNERT,
Stefanie GOTTSCHLICH, Ariane HINGST, Renate LINGOR (82 Viola
ODEBRECHT), Kerstin GAREFREKES, Maren MEINERT, Bettina WIEGMANN
(66 Nia Tsholofelo KÜNZER), Birgit PRINZ, Martina MÜLLER (57 Pia
WUNDERLICH *(YC66)*). (Coach: Tina THEUNE).
Russia: Alla VOLKOVA, Marina SAENKO, Tatiana ZAYTSEVA, Marina
BURAKOVA, Vera STROUKOVA, Natalia BARBASHINA, Tatiana
SKOTNIKOVA, Galina KOMAROVA, Tatiana EGOROVA (75 Marina
KOLOMIETS), Alexandra SVETLITSKAYA (34 Elena DENCHTCHIK), Olga
LETYUSHOVA (46 Elena DANILOVA). (Coach: Yuri BYSTRITSKIY).
Goals: Martina MÜLLER (25), Sandra MINNERT (57), Pia WUNDERLICH (60),
Kerstin GAREFREKES (62, 85), Birgit PRINZ (80, 89) / Elena DANILOVA (70)
Referee: IM Eun-Ju (South Korea) Attendance: 20,012

92

02.10.2003 Providence Park, Portland: China PR – Canada 0-1 (0-1)
China PR: HAN Wenxia, LI Jie, PU Wei, LIU Yali (82 TENG Wei *(YC90+2)*), FAN
Yunjie, WANG Liping, BI Yan, ZHAO Lihong (58 REN Liping), LIU Ying (65
ZHANG Ouying), BAI Jie, SUN Wen. (Coach: MA Liangxing).
Canada: Taryn SWIATEK, Tanya DENNIS, Sharolta Louisa NONEN, Isabelle
MORNEAU (12 Silvana BURTINI), Charmaine HOOPER *(YC76)*, Andrea NEIL
(YC53), Diana MATHESON, Brittany TIMKO, Christine SINCLAIR, Kara Elise
LANG *(YC42)* (90 Kristina KISS), Cristine LATHAM (73 Rhian WILKINSON).
(Coach: Even Jostein PELLERUD).
Goal: Charmaine HOOPER (7)
Referee: Kari SEITZ (United States) Attendance: 20,012

SEMI-FINALS

04.10.2003 Providence Park, Portland: Sweden – Canada 2-1 (0-0)
Sweden: Caroline JÖNSSON, Karolina WESTBERG, Jane TÖRNQVIST *(YC64)*,
Gärd Kristin BENGTSSON (75 Sara JOHANSSON), Hanna Gunilla MARKLUND,
Frida Christina ÖSTBERG, Malin Sofi MOSTRÖM, Malin Elisabeth ANDERSSON
(70 Kerstin Ingrid Therese SJÖGRAN), Hanna Carolina LJUNGBERG, Victoria
Margareta Sandell SVENSSON, Anna SJÖSTRÖM (70 Josefine ÖQVIST).
(Coach: Marika Susan DOMANSKI LYFORS).
Canada: Taryn SWIATEK, Tanya DENNIS, Sharolta Louisa NONEN, Charmaine
HOOPER, Andrea NEIL, Diana MATHESON, Brittany TIMKO, Christine
SINCLAIR, Kara Elise LANG, Cristine LATHAM (74 Rhian WILKINSON), Silvana
BURTINI (55 Kristina KISS). (Coach: Even Jostein PELLERUD).
Goals: Anna SJÖSTRÖM (79), Josefine ÖQVIST (86) / Kara Elise LANG (64)
Referee: Katriina ELOVIRTA (Finland) Attendance: 27,623

05.10.2003 Providence Park, Portland: United States – Germany 0-3 (0-1)
United States: Briana Collette SCURRY, Catherine WHITEHILL, Kathryn Michele
MARKGRAF Sobrero, Kylie Elizabeth BIVENS (70 Tiffeny Carleen MILBRETT),
Joy Lynn FAWCETT Biefeld, Shannon BOXX, Kristine Marie LILLY Heavey, Julie
Maurine FOUDY, Abby WAMBACH, Mariel Margaret (Mia) HAMM, Cynthia
Marie (Cindy) PARLOW Cone (52 Alyson Kay (Aly) WAGNER).
(Coach: April HEINRICHS).
Germany: Silke ROTTENBERG, Kerstin STEGEMANN, Sandra MINNERT,
Stefanie GOTTSCHLICH, Ariane HINGST, Renate LINGOR, Kerstin
GAREFREKES, Pia WUNDERLICH, Maren MEINERT, Bettina WIEGMANN,
Birgit PRINZ. (Coach: Tina THEUNE).
Goals: Kerstin GAREFREKES (15), Maren MEINERT (90+1), Birgit PRINZ (90+3)
Referee: Sonia DENONCOURT (Canada) Attendance: 27,623

THIRD PLACE FINAL

11.10.2003   Stubhub Center, Carson: United States – Canada 3-1 (1-1)
United States: Briana Collette SCURRY, Christie PEARCE, Catherine WHITEHILL, Kathryn Michele MARKGRAF Sobrero (84 Shannon Ann MACMILLAN), Joy Lynn FAWCETT Biefeld, Shannon BOXX, Kristine Marie LILLY Heavey, Julie Maurine FOUDY (78 Kylie Elizabeth BIVENS), Abby WAMBACH, Mariel Margaret (Mia) HAMM, Cynthia Marie (Cindy) PARLOW Cone (43 Tiffeny Carleen MILBRETT). (Coach: April HEINRICHS).
Canada: Taryn SWIATEK, Kristina KISS, Sharolta Louisa NONEN, Sasha Ajua ANDREWS (84 Isabelle MORNEAU), Charmaine HOOPER *(YC76)*, Andrea NEIL (90 Carmelina MOSCATO), Diana MATHESON, Brittany TIMKO, Christine SINCLAIR, Kara Elise LANG *(YC65)* (89 Rhian WILKINSON), Cristine LATHAM. (Coach: Even Jostein PELLERUD).
Goals: Kristine Marie LILLY Heavey (22), Shannon BOXX (51), Tiffeny Carleen MILBRETT 80) / Christine SINCLAIR (38)
Referee: Tammy Nicole OGSTON (Australia)   Attendance: 25,253

FINAL

12.10.2003   Stubhub Center, Carson: Germany – Sweden 2-1 (0-1,1-1) (a.e.t.)
Germany: Silke ROTTENBERG, Kerstin STEGEMANN, Sandra MINNERT, Stefanie GOTTSCHLICH, Ariane HINGST, Renate LINGOR, Kerstin GAREFREKES (76 Martina MÜLLER), Pia WUNDERLICH (88 Nia Tsholofelo KÜNZER), Maren MEINERT, Bettina WIEGMANN, Birgit PRINZ. (Coach: Tina THEUNE).
Sweden: Caroline JÖNSSON, Karolina WESTBERG, Jane TÖRNQVIST, Sara LARSSON (76 Gärd Kristin BENGTSSON), Hanna Gunilla MARKLUND, Frida Christina ÖSTBERG, Malin Sofi MOSTRÖM, Malin Elisabeth ANDERSSON (53 Kerstin Ingrid Therese SJÖGRAN), Hanna Carolina LJUNGBERG, Victoria Margareta Sandell SVENSSON, Anna SJÖSTRÖM (53 Linda FAGERSTRÖM). (Coach: Marika Susan DOMANSKI LYFORS).
Goals: Maren MEINERT (46), Nia Tsholofelo KÜNZER (98) / Hanna Carolina LJUNGBERG (41)
Referee: Floarea Cristina Ionescu BABADAC (Romania)   Attendance: 26,137

Germany won after extra time.

GERMANY BECAME WORLD CHAMPIONS

FIFTH EDITION FIFA WOMEN'S WORLD CUP 2007

QUALIFYING TOURNAMENTS

CAF AFRICAN WOMEN'S CHAMPIONSHIP 2006

The African Women's Championship was held in Nigeria between 28 October and 11 November 2006.

Originally this tournament was scheduled to be held in Gabon, but due to organizational reasons Gabon withdrew from hosting the competition. The CAF awarded the hosting of the competition to Nigeria in May 2006. Initially the tournament was scheduled for September 2006, but is was moved to October due to weather considerations.

The winner and the runner-up of CAF African Women's Championship 2006 will qualify for the FIFA Women's World Cup 2007.

PRELIMINARY ROUND

xx.02.2006 Libya – Swaziland **Cancelled**
xx.02.2006 Djibouti – Lesotho **Cancelled**
xx.02.2006 Zambia – Botswana **Cancelled**
19.02.2006 Benin – Malawi 1-0
19.02.2006 Mozambique – Namibia 9-0
19.02.2006 São Tomé and Príncipe – Togo 0-3
19.02.2006 Senegal – Central African Republic 4-0
26.02.2006 Malawi – Benin 0-0
xx.02.2006 Namibia – Mozambique **Cancelled**
26.02.2006 Togo – São Tomé and Príncipe 6-0
xx.02.2006 Central African Republic – Senegal **Cancelled**

Swaziland withdrew, Libya advanced.
Lesotho withdrew, Djibouti advanced.
Botswana withdrew, Zambia advanced.
Namibia withdrew, Mozambique advanced.
Central African Republic withdrew, Senegal advanced.

FIRST ROUND

xx.03.2006 Algeria – Libya **Cancelled**
xx.03.2006 Eritrea – Egypt **Cancelled**
xx.03.2006 Uganda – Tanzania **Cancelled**
11.03.2006 Stade de FUS, Rabat: Morocco – Mali 0-2 (0-0)
Goals: N'Diaye (60), Samake (75)
11.03.2006 South Africa – Mozambique 6-2

11.03.2006 Lubumbashi: DR Congo – Zambia 3-0 (1-0)
Goals: Bosangi (23), Zuma (80), Panda (80)
12.03.2006 Benin – Ivory Coast 1-1
12.03.2006 Angola – Equatorial Guinea 3-2
12.03.2006 Congo – Togo 9-0
12.03.2006 Senegal – Guinea 7-0
25.03.2006 Stade de Modibo Kéïta, Bamako: Mali – Morocco 4-1 (2-0)
Goals: N'Diaye (2), Coulibaly (4, 67), Diarra (47) / Sanae (52)
25.03.2006 Ivory Coast – Benin 1-1 (a.e.t.)
Benin won on penalties (3:4)
25.03.2006 Nyayo National Stadium, Nairobi: Kenya – Djibouti 7-0
Goals: Mureu (7), Adhiambo (1H, 52, 84), Wanjala (36), Nabwire (44, 2H)
Only one leg was played, Kenya advanced
25.03.2006 Chingola: Zambia – DR Congo 2-3 (2-3)
Goals: Lisaka (23, 43) / Balembo (6), Masevo (11), Mukanu (15)
26.03.2006 Equatorial Guinea – Angola 3-1
26.03.2006 Mozambique – South Africa 1-6
26.03.2006 Togo – Congo 1-3
26.03.2006 Guinea – Senegal 1-5

Libya withdrew, Algeria advanced.
Eritrea withdrew, Egypt advanced.
Uganda withdrew, Tanzania advanced.
Ethiopia and Zimbabwe also withdrew, both had originally received byes.

Bye: South Africa.

SECOND ROUND

xx.07.2006 Nigeria – Equatorial Guinea **Called Off**
Match was called off after Nigeria were awarded the hosting of the final tournament.
Equatorial Guinea qualified by default for the final tournament.
xx.07.2006 Obuasi: Ghana – Congo **Cancelled**
22.07.2006 Stade Modibo Kéïta, Bamako: Mali – Benin 3-1 (1-0)
Goals: Doumbia (45), Diarra (51), N'Diaye (65) / Bathily (90)
22.07.2006 Ahmadou Ahidjo Stadium, Yaoundé: Cameroon – Kenya 4-0 (2-0)
Goals: Ngono Mani (5, 30), Mbida (71), Ndoumbouk (89)
23.07.2006 Annaba: Algeria – Egypt 1-0 (0-0)
Goal: Zerrouki (55)
23.07.2006 Johannesburg: South Africa – Tanzania 3-0 (2-0)
Goals: Phewa (10), Mosebo (17), Makanye (90)
23.07.2006 Kinshasa: DR Congo – Senegal 3-0 (3-0)
Goals: Vavadio (12), Malembo (22), Diasilwa (45)
04.08.2006 Dar es Salaam: Tanzania – South Africa 0-4 (0-2)
Goals: Makanye (24), Mametja (31), Nyandeni (51), Phewa (85)
05.08.2006 Alexandria: Egypt – Algeria 0-3 (0-1)
Goals: Bouhenni (44), Imloul (54), Laïfa (88)
05.08.2006 Moi International Sports Centre, Kasarani: Kenya – Cameroon 0-5
05.08.2006 Dakar: Senegal – DR Congo 2-0

96

06.08.2006   Cotonou: Benin – Mali 0-1 (0-0)
Goal: N'Diaye (48)

Congo withdrew, Ghana advanced.

FINAL TOURNAMENT
FIRST ROUND
GROUP A

Equatorial Guinea arrived at Murtala Mohammed Airport in a private chartered plane, which did not have clearance to land. The players were not allowed to disembark for three hours and despite organising officials trying to remedy the situation, the Equatorial Guinea players apparently left for home, unhappy with the treatment they received by airport officials. However, their first match went ahead on time.

28.10.2006   Warri Township Stadium, Warri: South Africa – Algeria 4-0 (3-0)
Goals: Phewa (1, 35), Monpumelolo (38), Solomon (90)
28.10.2006   Oleh, Delta: Nigeria – Equatorial Guinea 4-2 (3-2)
Goals: Uwak (4, 9), Nkwocha (34), Ajayi (89) / Chinasa Okoro (16), Essiane (22)
31.10.2006   Warri Township Stadium, Warri: Algeria – Nigeria 0-6 (0-3)
Goals: Ajayi (8), Nkwocha (20, 90+), Madu (35), Ekpo (56), Uwak (89)
31.10.2006   Oleh, Delta: Equatorial Guinea – South Africa 0-2 (0-0)
Goals: Nkosi (63), Solomon (75)
03.11.2006   Oghara Township Stadium, Oghara:
              Equatorial Guinea – Algeria 3-3 (1-1)
Goals: Añonma (2), Essiane (72, 78) / Boumrar (35), Bouhani (56, 76)
03.11.2006   Oleh, Delta: Nigeria – South Africa 2-0 (2-0)
Goals: Uwak (4, 43)

Team	Pld	W	D	L	GF	GA	GD	Pts
Nigeria	*3*	*3*	*0*	*0*	*12*	*2*	*+10*	*9*
South Africa	*3*	*2*	*0*	*1*	*6*	*2*	*+4*	*6*
Equatorial Guinea	3	0	1	2	5	9	-4	1
Algeria	3	0	1	2	3	13	-10	1

GROUP B

29.10.2006   Oghara: Mali – Ghana 0-1 (0-0)
Goal: Rumanatu (56)
29.10.2006   Ughelli: Cameroon – DR Congo 1-1 (1-0)
Goals: Ngono (1) / Milandu (57)
01.11.2006   Ughelli: Ghana – Cameroon 2-1 (1-0)
Goals: Aminkwa (28, 90+) / Francoise (53)
01.11.2006   Oghara: Mali – DR Congo 3-2 (1-1)
Goals: Doumbia (36), Diarra (69, 90) / Zuma (28), Mafuta (85)
04.11.2006   Ughelli: DR Congo – Ghana 1-3 (0-2)
Goals: Vumongo (51) / Amankwa (22, 32), Okoe (84)

04.11.2006 <u>Warri Township Stadium, Warri</u>: Cameroon – Mali 2-0 (1-0)
Goals: Bekombo (42), Ngo (74)

Team	Pld	W	D	L	GF	GA	GD	Pts
Ghana	*3*	*3*	*0*	*0*	*6*	*2*	*+4*	*9*
Cameroon	*3*	*1*	*1*	*1*	*4*	*3*	*+1*	*4*
Mali	3	1	0	2	3	5	-2	3
DR Congo	3	0	1	2	4	7	-3	1

SEMI-FINALS

07.11.2006 <u>Warri Township Stadium, Warri</u>: Nigeria – Cameroon 5-0 (2-0)
Goals: Uwak (33), Nkwocha (45, 46, 54), Ekpo (61)
07.11.2006 <u>Oghara</u>: Ghana – South Africa 1-0 (0-0)
Goal: Okoe (88 pen)

THIRD PLACE PLAY-OFF

10.11.2006 <u>Oleh, Delta</u>: Cameroon – South Africa 2-2 (0-1)
Goals: Bella (48 pen), Ngono (81) / Modise (4), Makhanya (61)
South Africa won on penalties (4:5)

FINAL

11.11.2006 <u>Warri Township Stadium, Warri</u>: Nigeria – Ghana 1-0 (1-0)

Nigeria and **Ghana** both qualified for the FIFA Women's World Cup 2007.

AFC ASIAN WOMEN'S CHAMPIONSHIP 2006

The tournament was originally scheduled to be held in Japan, but after the Football
Federation Australia moved from the Oceania Football Confederation (OFC) to the
Asian Football Confederation (AFC), the Australian team entered the qualifying
series. They were awarded hosting rights in February 2006. The Championship (Main
Tournament) took place between 16 & 30 July 2006.

QUALIFICATION
GROUP A

12.06.2005 <u>My Dinh Stadium, Hanoi</u>: Vietnam – Philippines 6-1
14.06.2005 <u>My Dinh Stadium, Hanoi</u>: Myanmar – Philippines 4-1
16.06.2005 <u>My Dinh Stadium, Hanoi</u>: Vietnam – Myanmar 1-0

Team	Pld	W	D	L	GF	GA	GD	Pts
Vietnam	*2*	*2*	*0*	*0*	*7*	*1*	*+6*	*6*
Myanmar	*2*	*1*	*0*	*1*	*4*	*2*	*+2*	*3*
Philippines	2	0	0	2	2	10	-8	0

GROUP B

12.06.2005   My Dinh Stadium, Hanoi: India – Guam 10-0
14.06.2005   My Dinh Stadium, Hanoi: Chinese Taipei – India 2-1
16.06.2005   My Dinh Stadium, Hanoi: Chinese Taipei – Guam 11-0

Team	Pld	W	D	L	GF	GA	GD	Pts
Chinese Taipei	2	2	0	0	13	1	+12	6
India	2	1	0	1	11	2	+9	3
Guam	2	0	0	2	0	21	-21	0

GROUP C

13.06.2005   My Dinh Stadium, Hanoi: Uzbekistan – Maldives 6-0
15.06.2005   My Dinh Stadium, Hanoi: Uzbekistan – Hong Kong 3-0
17.06.2005   My Dinh Stadium, Hanoi: Hong Kong – Maldives 4-0

Team	Pld	W	D	L	GF	GA	GD	Pts
Uzbekistan	2	2	0	0	9	0	+9	6
Hong Kong	2	1	0	1	4	3	+1	3
Maldives	2	0	0	2	0	10	-10	0

GROUP D

13.06.2005   My Dinh Stadium, Hanoi: Indonesia – Singapore 0-0
15.06.2005   My Dinh Stadium, Hanoi: Thailand – Singapore 5-1
17.06.2005   My Dinh Stadium, Hanoi: Thailand – Indonesia 4-0

Team	Pld	W	D	L	GF	GA	GD	Pts
Thailand	2	2	0	0	8	0	+8	6
Singapore	2	0	1	1	1	5	-4	1
Indonesia	2	0	1	1	0	4	-4	1

Singapore advanced on a coin toss

SECOND ROUND

19.06.2005   My Dinh Stadium, Hanoi: Vietnam – Hong Kong 4-1
19.06.2005   My Dinh Stadium, Hanoi: Chinese Taipei – Singapore 3-0
20.06.2005   My Dinh Stadium, Hanoi: Uzbekistan – Myanmar 1-2
20.06.2005   My Dinh Stadium, Hanoi: Thailand – India 3-2

The winners of each match qualified for the main tournament.

MAIN TOURNAMENT
GROUP STAGE
GROUP A

19.07.2006   Hindmarsch Stadium, Adelaide: China PR – Chinese Taipei 2-0 (1-0)
Goals: Han Duan (11), Pu Wei (64)
19.07.2006   Hindmarsch Stadium, Adelaide: Japan – Vietnam 5-0 (1-0)
Goals: Homare Sawa (39, 52), Mizuho Sakaguchi (65, 78), Yuki Nagasato (81)
21.07.2006   Hindmarsch Stadium, Adelaide: Japan – Chinese Taipei 11-1 (4-1)
Goals: Shinobu Ohno (9), Yuki Nagasato (29, 33, 46, 71, 90+2), Homare Sawa (38,
80), Mizuho Sakaguchi (48, 89), Miyuki Yanagita (68) / Hsieh I-ling (35)
21.07.2006   Hindmarsch Stadium, Adelaide: Vietnam – China PR 0-2 (0-1)
Goals: Ma Xiaoxu (20, 58)
23.07.2006   Hindmarsch Stadium, Adelaide: China PR – Japan 0-1 (0-1)
Goal: Aya Miyama (18)
23.07.2006   Marden Stadium, Adelaide: Chinese Taipei – Vietnam 0-1 (0-0)
Goal: Vu Thi Huyen Linh (70)

Team	Pld	W	D	L	GF	GA	GD	Pts
Japan	*3*	*3*	*0*	*0*	*17*	*1*	*+16*	*9*
China PR	*3*	*2*	*0*	*1*	*4*	*1*	*+3*	*6*
Vietnam	3	1	0	2	1	7	-6	3
Chinese Taipei	3	0	0	3	1	14	-13	0

GROUP B

16.07.2006   Hindmarsch Stadium, Adelaide: Myanmar – Thailand 1-2 (0-1)
Goals: Daw My Nilar Htwe (60) / Pitsamai Sornsai (34, 55)
16.07.2006   Hindmarsch Stadium, Adelaide: Australia – South Korea 4-0 (1-0)
Goals: Shin Sun-nam (30 og), Sarah Walsh (66), Caitlin Munoz (75),
Lisa De Vanna (87)
18.07.2006   Hindmarsch Stadium, Adelaide: Thailand – North Korea 0-9 (0-5)
Goals: Ri Kum-suk (8, 34), Ri Un-suk (31), Kim Tan-sil (36, 73), Ho Sun-hui (43),
Jo Yun-mi (59), Kim Yong-ae (67, 87)
18.07.2006   Hindmarsch Stadium, Adelaide: Myanmar – Australia 0-2 (0-1)
Goals: Sally Shipard (31), Lisa De Vanna (77)
20.07.2006   Hindmarsch Stadium, Adelaide: North Korea – Myanmar 3-0 (2-0)
Goals: Ri Un-suk (23, 37), Ri Un-gyong (85)
20.07.2006   Hindmarsch Stadium, Adelaide: South Korea – Thailand 11-0 (4-0)
Goals: Cha Yun-hee (30, 44), Jung Jung-suk (39, 50, 71, 80, 83, 86),
Kim Joo-hee (42), Kim Jin-hee (69), Jung Sey-hwa (87)
22.07.2006   Hindmarsch Stadium, Adelaide: South Korea – Myanmar 3-1 (2-0)
Goals: Kim Joo-hee (7), Jun Suk-hee (35), Jung Jung-suk (64) / Hlaing (90)
22.07.2006   Hindmarsch Stadium, Adelaide: Australia – North Korea 0-0
24.07.2006   Marden Stadium, Adelaide: Thailand – Australia 0-5 (0-2)
Goals: Alicia Ferguson (3), Joanne Burgess (27), Sarah Walsh (53), Kathryn Gill (62),
Lisa De Vanna (81)

24.07.2006   Hindmarsch Stadium, Adelaide: North Korea – South Korea 1-0 (0-0)
Goal: Kim Yong-ae (76)

Team	Pld	W	D	L	GF	GA	GD	Pts
North Korea	*4*	*3*	*1*	*0*	*13*	*0*	*+13*	*10*
Australia	*4*	*3*	*1*	*9*	*11*	*0*	*+11*	*10*
South Korea	4	2	0	2	14	6	+8	6
Thailand	4	1	0	3	2	26	-24	3
Myanmar	4	0	0	4	2	10	-8	0

KNOCKOUT STAGES
SEMI-FINALS

27.07.2006   Hindmarsch Stadium, Adelaide: Australia – Japan 2-0 (2-0)
Goals: Caitlin Munoz (10), Joanne Peters (45)
27.07.2006   Hindmarsch Stadium, Adelaide: China PR – North Korea 1-0 (0-0)
Goal: Ma Xiaoxu (58)

THIRD PLACE PLAY-OFF

30.07.2006   Hindmarsch Stadium, Adelaide: Japan – North Korea 2-3 (1-3)
Goals: Kozue Ando (43), Yuki Nagasato (89) / Ri Un-suk (23), Ri Un-gyong (33, 39)

FINAL

30.07.2006   Hindmarsch Stadium, Adelaide: Australia – China PR 2-2 (2-0) (a.e.t.)
Goals: Caitlin Munoz (29), Joanne Peters (33) / Han Duan (68), Ma Xiaoxu (73)

China PR won after extra time on penalties (2:4).

Since **China PR**, the host nation of the FIFA Women's World Cup 2007, proceeded
to the final, another finalist, **Australia** and third-placed **North Korea**, were qualified
for the FIFA Women's World Cup final tournament 2007. Fourth-placed Japan will
play an AFC-CONCACAF PLAY-OFF against the third-placed team from the
CONCACAF Women's Gold Cup 2006.

UEFA WOMEN'S WORLD CUP QUALIFICATION 2007

The 25 teams belonging to the First Category of European women's football were
drawn into five groups, from which the group winners will qualify for the FIFA
Women's World Cup 2007. The qualifiers begun on 9 July 2005 and concluded on 30
September 2006.

GROUP STAGE
GROUP 1

27.08.2005   Åråsen, Lilleström: Norway – Ukraine 4-1 (1-1)
Goals: Mellgren (28, 54 pen), Christensen (47), Klaveness (58) / Verezoubova (45)

24.09.2005   Kolubara, Lazarevac: Serbia and Montenegro – Norway 0-4 (0-1)
Goals: S.Gulbrandsen (31, 86), Rønning (55, 63)
24.09.2005   Brianteo, Monza: Italy – Ukraine 3-1 (1-1)
Goals: Zorri (20), Panico (47), Marsico (78) / Zinchenko (8)
29.10.2005   Brann, Bergen: Norway – Italy 1-0 (0-0)
Goals: Klaveness (60)
29.10.2005   Doxa Dramas: Greece – Serbia and Montenegro 0-2 (0-0)
Goals: Podovac (85, 90+1)
02.11.2005   Sesto al Reghena: Italy – Serbia and Montenegro 6-0 (3-0)
Goals: Boni (21, 29), Panico (41, 85), Marsico (75), Zorri (83)
05.11.2005   Zeleznicar, Lajkovac: Serbia and Montenegro – Ukraine 0-4 (0-1)
Goals: Zinchenko (34, 84), Apanashenko (47), Frisco (73)
09.11.2005   Kavala Stadium, Kavala: Greece – Ukraine 1-3 (0-2)
Goals: Papadopoulou (64) / Korniyevets (13, 37), Frisco (83)
25.03.2006   Georgios Kamaras, Athens: Greece – Norway 0-3 (0-1)
Goals: R.Gulbrandsen (2, 90+2), Lehn (81)
29.03.2006   Comunale Rinascita, Aversa: Italy – Greece 2-0 (1-0)
Goals: Zorri (38), Greco (69)
15.04.2006   Zeleznicar, Lajkovac: Serbia and Montenegro – Greece 3-1 (1-1)
Goals: Jovanovic (13), Stojanovic (68, 79) / Arvanitaki (26)
22.04.2006   Kesariani, Athens: Greece – Italy 0-5 (0-2)
Goals: Panico (15 pen, 83, 86, 89), Di Filippo (37)
06.05.2006   Ukrajina, Lviv: Ukraine – Serbia and Montenegro 2-1 (1-1)
Goals: Frisco (35), Pekur (81) / Stojanovic (15)
10.05.2006   Storstadion, Sandefjord: Norway – Serbia and Montenegro 3-0 (3-0)
Goals: Lehn (11), Stangeland (16), Følstad (21)
17.06.2006   Illychivets, Mariupol: Ukraine – Italy 2-1 (0-0)
Goals: Hodyreva (47), Frisco (57) / Marsico (75)
20.06.2006   Halden Stadion, Halden: Norway – Greece 4-0 (2-0)
Goals: R.Gulbrandsen (14, 45), Knutsen (59), Giske (85)
21.06.2006   Stadium Vozdovac: Serbia and Montenegro – Italy 0-7 (0-3)
Goals: Zorri (4, 15), Di Filippo (26), Marsico (56, 63, 68), Pini (73)
23.06.2006   Illychivets, Mariupol: Ukraine – Greece 6-0 (2-0)
Goals: Frisco (17, 42 pen), Verezoubova (49, 58), Soukhoroukova (51), Pekur (86)
27.08.2006   Ukrajina, Lviv: Ukraine – Norway 1-1 (1-1)
Goals: Verezoubova (28) / Lehn (45)
23.09.2006   Romeo Neri, Rimini: Italy – Norway 1-2 (0-0)
Goals: Panico (83) / R.Gulbrandsen (60), Knutsen (63)

Team	Pld	W	D	L	GF	GA	GD	Pts
Norway	8	7	1	0	22	3	+19	22
Ukraine	8	5	1	2	20	11	+9	16
Italy	8	5	0	3	25	6	+19	15
Serbia and Montenegro	8	2	0	6	6	27	-21	6
Greece	8	0	0	8	2	28	-26	0

GROUP 2

21.08.2005   Laugardalsvöllur, Reykjavik: Iceland – Belarus 3-0 (1-0)
Goals: Lárusdóttir (31, 58), M.L.Vidarsdóttir (56)
27.08.2005   Darida Stadium, Minsk: Belarus – Czech Republic 1-1 (0-0)
Goals: Tatarynova (73) / Hejlova (76)
28.08.2005   Nobelstadion, Karlskoga: Sweden – Iceland 2-2 (1-0)
Goals: Ljungberg (34), Schelin (73) / A.Helgadóttir (49), M.L.Vidarsdóttir (75)
24.09.2005   Stadion SK Kravere: Czech Republic – Iceland 1-0 (1-0)
Goal: Penicková (8)
24.09.2005   Norrvalla, Skellefteå: Sweden – Belarus 6-0 (3-0)
Goals: Ljungberg (14, 24, 90, 90+1), Schelin (20), Lundin (83)
01.11.2005   Alcochelense, Setúbal: Portugal – Sweden 1-4 (0-1)
Goals: Fernandes (71) / Ljungberg (9, 53), Sjöström (49), Moström (90+2)
05.11.2005   Primero de Maio, Lisbon: Portugal – Czech Republic 0-3 (0-2)
Goals: Martinkova (15), Chlumecka (38), Penicková (87)
22.04.2006   Frantiska Kloze, Kladno: Czech Republic – Sweden 2-3 (1-1)
Goals: Scasná (4), Mouchová (67) / Larsson (23), Schelin (62, 69)
06.05.2006   Darida Stadium, Minsk: Belarus – Iceland 1-2 (0-1)
Goals: Aniskoutsava (54) / K.Jónsdóttir (27), A.Helgadóttir (51)
07.05.2006   Vångavallen, Trelleborg: Sweden – Portugal 5-1 (2-1)
Goals: Lundin (10, 64, 79), Schelin (30), Sjögran (72) / Fernandes (17)
11.05.2006   Estadio Municipal, Beja: Portugal – Belarus 0-1 (0-1)
Goal: Ryzhevich (11)
04.06.2006   Roudnice nad Labem: Czech Republic – Portugal 6-0 (5-0)
Goals: Knavova (9), Scasná (16, 24), Martinková (29), Chlumecká (35),
Penicková (46)
18.06.2006   Darida Stadium, Minsk: Belarus – Sweden 0-6 (0-1)
Goals: Schelin (45), Svensson (48, 82, 86), Seger (52), Öqvist (75)
18.06.2006   Laugardalsvöllur, Reykjavik: Iceland – Portugal 3-0 (1-0)
Goals: M.L.Vidarsdóttir (40, 90), Samúelsdóttir (85)
19.08.2006   Laugardalsvöllur, Reykjavik: Iceland – Czech Republic 2-4 (2-2)
Goals: Á.Helgadóttir (6), M.L.Vidarsdóttir (35) / Martinková (2), Scasná (37),
Mouchová (57), J.Jónsdóttir (72 og)
26.08.2006   Laugardalsvöllur, Reykjavik: Iceland – Sweden 0-4
Goals: Moström (13 pen), Thunebro, Svensson (80), Ljungberg
27.08.2006   Mestsky stadion, Celákovice: Czech Republic – Belarus 3-0 (1-0)
Goals: Scasná (5), Chlumecká (48), Kladrubská (79)
23.09.2006   Darida Stadium, Minsk: Belarus – Portugal 3-2 (3-1)
Goals: Aniskoutsava (17, 20 pen), Tatarynova (34) / Martins (5), Azavedo (46)
24.09.2006   Värendsvallen, Växjö: Sweden – Czech Republic 2-0 (2-0)
Goals: Ljungberg (5, 30)
28.09.2006   Primero de Maio, Lisbon: Portugal – Iceland 0-6 (0-2)
Goals: J.Jónsdóttir (9, 55), M.L.Vidarsdóttir (21, 67, 79, 86)

Team	Pld	W	D	L	GF	GA	GD	Pts
Sweden	*8*	*7*	*1*	*0*	*32*	*6*	*+26*	*22*
Czech Republic	8	5	1	2	20	8	+12	16
Iceland	8	4	1	3	18	12	+6	13
Belasrus	8	2	1	5	6	23	-17	7
Portugal	8	0	0	8	4	31	-27	0

GROUP 3

27.08.2005   Stadion Miejski, Slupsk: Poland – Denmark 1-5 (0-4)
Goals: Gawronska (74) / M.Pedersen (8, 10, 39, 67), Sørensen (13)
31.08.2005   Sportcomplex de Singel, Strombeek: Belgium – Finland 0-3 (0-2)
Goals: Kackur (3), Kalmari (45), Mustonen (64)
24.09.2005   Hietalahti, Vaasa: Finland – Poland 3-1 (1-0)
Goals: Salmén (45), Kalmari (69), Talonen (84) / Gawronska (68)
25.09.2005   Farum Park: Denmark – Belgium 3-0 (3-0)
Goals: M.Pedersen (13, 24), Eggers Nielsen (34)
29.09.2005   City Stadium, Kutno: Poland – Spain 3-2 (0-2)
Goals: Rytwinska (49), Gurrutxaga (53 og), Pozerska (61) / del Rio (6, 40)
30.10.2005   Olympiastadion, Helsinki: Finland – Spain 0-1 (0-1)
Goal: Cabezón (34)
30.11.2005   Oud-Heverlee, Leuven: Belgium – Poland 2-3 (1-2)
Goals: Van Humbeeck (43), Zeler (68) / Gawronska (13), Nazarczyk (31),
Otrebska (60)
05.11.2005   Pabellón, Madrid: Spain – Belgium 3-2 (1-0)
Goals: Cabezón (2), De Cock (90+1), Gimbert (90+2) / Maes (67), Verelst (81)
10.11.2005   Pabellón, Madrid: Spain – Denmark 2-2 (2-1)
Goals: Vilanova (13), Martín (31) / Sørensen (18), Rasmussen (52)
26.03.2006   Des Géants, Ath: Belgium – Denmark 0-2 (0-0)
Goals: M.Pedersen (63, 72)
30.03.2006   El Montecillo, Aranda: Spain – Poland 7-0 (3-0)
Goals: Martín (9, 28, 52, 63, 85), Cabezón (32), Azagra (54)
22.04.2006   Miejski, Jaworzno: Poland – Finland 1-5 (0-3)
Goals: Zelazko (55) / Kalmari (23, 49, 74), Talonen (27, 36)
22.04.2006   Joseph Marien, Brussels: Belgium – Spain 2-4 (0-4)
Goals: Maes (64), Callebaut (75) / Martín (5, 40), Gurrutxaga (16), del Rio (29)
27.04.2006   Viborg Stadion, Viborg: Denmark – Spain 5-0 (0-0)
Goals: M.Pedersen (50), Pape (62 pen, 88), Sørensen (68), Rasmussen (75)
06.05.2006   Ratina, Tampere: Finland – Belgium 3-0 (2-0)
Goals: Kalmari (8, 18), Sjölund (82)
07.05.2006   Brøndby Stadium, Brøndby: Denmark – Poland 3-1 (1-0)
Goals: M.Pedersen (40), Pape (47), Madsen (71) / Zelazko (66)
11.05.2006   Estadio Municipal Pozoblanco, Pozoblanco: Spain – Finland 0-0
26.08.2006   Ratina, Tampere: Finland – Denmark 2-1 (1-1)
Goals: Österberg Kalmari (26), Mustonen (78) / Sørensen (38)
23.09.2006   City Stadium, Kutno: Poland – Belgium 4-2 (1-1)
Goals: Zelazko (35, 67), Rytwinsko (46), Makowska (87 pen) / Heiremans (26, 72)

104

27.09.2006 Viborg Stadion, Viborg: Denmark – Finland 1-0 (0-0)
Goal: Pape (56)

Team	Pld	W	D	L	GF	GA	GD	Pts
Denmark	*8*	*6*	*1*	*1*	*22*	*6*	*+16*	*19*
Finland	8	5	1	2	16	5	+11	16
Spain	8	4	2	2	19	14	+5	14
Poland	8	3	0	5	14	29	-15	9
Belgium	8	0	0	8	8	25	-17	0

GROUP 4

09.07.2005 Moskvich, Moscow: Russia – Republic of Ireland 5-1 (4-0)
Goals: Kurochkina (2), Zaitseva (33), Boyle (35 og), Mokshanova (42),
Barbashina (48) / O'Brien (70)
28.08.2005 Moskvich, Moscow: Russia – Scotland 6-0 (3-0)
Goals: Morozova (13), Barbashina (24), Skotnikova (25), Danilova (52),
Letyushova (82), Savchenkova (84)
01.09.2005 Herti-Allmend, Zug: Switzerland – Russia 0-2 (0-1)
Goals: Morozova (3), Kurochkina (54)
25.09.2005 Leimbach, Siegen: Germany – Russia 5-1 (3-0)
Goals: Lingo (6 pen), Grings (8), Minnert (43), Prinz (87), Smisek (90) /
Komarova (60)
25.09.2005 McDiarmid Park, Perth: Scotland – Republic of Ireland 0-0
20.10.2005 Hans-Waller Wild Stadion, Bayreuth: Germany – Scotland 4-0 (1-0)
Goals: Grings (24), Stegemann (57), Prinz (61, 78)
12.11.2005 Donaustadion, Ulm: Germany – Switzerland 4-0 (3-0)
Goals: Jones (10), Carlson (20, 62), Wimbersky (36)
25.03.2006 Gurzelen, Biel: Switzerland – Republic of Ireland 2-0 (2-0)
Goals: Dickenmann (23, 44)
22.04.2006 Richmond Park, Dublin: Republic of Ireland – Switzerland 2-0 (1-0)
Goals: Grant (23), O'Toole (90)
26.04.2006 McDiarmid Park, Perth: Scotland – Switzerland 1-0 (0-0)
Goal: Grant (61)
06.05.2006 Richmond Park, Dublin: Republic of Ireland – Scotland 0-2 (0-0)
Goals: Love (47), Fleeting (81)
10.05.2006 Stadion der Freundschaft, Cottbus:
Germany – Republic of Ireland 1-0 (1-0)
Goal: Wimbersky (3)
24.05.2006 McDiarmid Park, Perth: Scotland – Russia 0-4
Goals: Morozova, Kurochkina (2x), Savchenkova.
17.06.2006 Richmond Park, Dublin: Republic of Ireland – Russia 0-2 (0-1)
Goals: Kurochkina (17), Barbashina (81)
26.08.2006 Scholssfeld, Willisau: Switzerland – Scotland 1-1 (1-0)
Goals: Gailard (17 pen) / Fleeting (71)
26-08-2006 Richmond Park, Dublin: Republic of Ireland – Germany 0-3 (0-3)
Goals: Wimbersky (2), Prinz (16), Garefrekes (45)

30.08.2006   Breite Stadion, Schaffhausen: Switzerland – Germany 0-6 (0-1)
Goals: Pohlers (1), Prinz (57), Wimbersky (73), Lingor (78), M.Müller (89),
Garefrekes (90+2)
23.09.2006   McDiarmid Park, Perth: Scotland – Germany 0-5 (0-3)
Goals: Prinz (26, 53), Lingor (36), Garefrekes (44), Smisek (67)
23.09.2006   Moskvich, Moscow: Russia – Switzerland 2-0 (1-0)
Goals: Kremleva (27 pen), Morozova (68)
27.09.2006   Eduard Streltsov Stadium, Moscow: Russia – Germany 2-3 (0-3)
Goals: Barbashina (83), Kremleva (90) / Smisek (32), Garefrekes (36), Prinz (45)

Team	Pld	W	D	L	GF	GA	GD	Pts
Germany	*8*	*8*	*0*	*0*	*31*	*3*	*+28*	*24*
Russia	8	6	0	2	24	9	+15	18
Scotland	8	2	2	4	4	20	-16	8
Republic of Ireland	8	1	1	6	3	15	-12	4
Switzerland	8	1	1	6	3	18	-15	4

GROUP 5

01.09.2005   Ertl Glas, Amstetten: Austria – England 1-4 (1-2)
Goals: Celouch (21) / Williams (23 pen), K.Smith (35, 90+2), Barr (56)
24.09.2005   Jean-Bouin Stadium, Angers: France – Netherlands 0-1 (0-0)
Goal: de Boer (65)
24.09.2005   Bük Stadium, Bük: Hungary – Austria 0-3 (0-2)
Goals: Burger (10, 79), Aigner (32)
27.10.2005   Tapolca Stadium, Tapolca: Hungary – England 0-13 (0-7)
Goals: K.Smith (3, 43, 80), Yankey (5), Aluko (12, 50), Scott (15, 38), Chapman (30),
Williams (61, 88 pen), Potter (75), Handley (79)
29.10.2005   Franz Fekete Stadium, Kapfenberg: Austria – Netherlands 0-1 (0-1)
Goal: Louwaars (32)
05.11.2005   Neue Sportanlage Langenrohr, Langenrohr: Austria – France 1-3 (1-2)
Goals: Aigner (7 pen) / Pichon (24), Soubeyrand (42, 56)
09.11.2005   Les Allées, Blois: France – Hungary 2-0 (0-0)
Goals: Soubeyrand (67), Tonazzi (81)
17.11.2005   Oosterenkstadion, Zwolle: Netherlands – England 0-1 (0-0)
Goal: Williams (55 pen)
25.03.2006   Municipal, Andrashida: Hungary – Netherlands 0-5 (0-3)
Goals: Louwaars (21, 61), Smith (33), Delies (41), Hoogendijk (55)
26.03.2006   Ewood Park, Blackburn: England – France 0-0
20.04.2006   Priestfield, Gillingham: England – Austria 4-0 (1-0)
Goals: Carney (36), Williams (85), K.Smith (87), Handley (90+2)
22.04.2006   Ezsperantó Út, Dunaujvaros: Hungary – France 0-5 (0-4)
Goals: Pichon (17, 27), Bompastor (19), Soubeyrand (36), Lattaf (66)
11.05.2006   St Mary's, Southampton: England – Hungary 2-0 (1-0)
Goals: Exley (40), Scott (90+1)
13.05.2006   Oosterenkstadion, Zwolle: Netherlands – France 0-2 (0-1)
Goals: Soubeyrand (7, 63)

26.08.2006   Parkstadion, Bruckneudorf: Austria – Hungary 1-1 (0-0)
Goals: Burger (85) / Nagy (55)
31.08.2006   The Valley, Chariton, London: England – Netherlands 4-0 (2-0)
Goals: K.Smith (9, 24 pen, 65), Yankey (67)
20.09.2006   Oosterenkstadion, Zwolle: Netherlands – Austria 4-0 (0-0)
Goals: Demarteau (58), Delies (88), Smit (90+1, 90+4)
23.09.2006   l'Aube, Troyes: France – Austria 2-1 (2-1)
Goals: Bussaglia (31, 38) / Burger (35)
24.09.2006   Oosterenkstadion, Zwolle: Netherlands – Hungary 4-0 (2-0)
Goals: Stevens (26, 36, 89), Smit (90)
30.09.2006   Route de Lorient, Rennes: France – England 1-1 (0-0)
Goals: Diguelman (88) / Lattaf (63 og)

Team	Pld	W	D	L	GF	GA	GD	Pts
England	*8*	*6*	*2*	*0*	*29*	*2*	*+27*	*20*
France	8	5	2	1	15	4	+11	17
Netherlands	8	5	0	3	15	7	+8	15
Austria	8	1	1	6	7	19	-12	4
Hungary	8	0	1	7	1	35	-34	1

The five group winners **Norway, Sweden, Denmark, Germany** and **England** qualified for the FIFA Women's World Cup 2007.

CONCACAF WOMEN'S GOLD CUP 2006

The CONCACAF Women's Gold Cup 2006 finals took place between 19 & 26 November 2006.

QUALIFICATION
UNCAF/NAFU QUALIFYING
GROUP A

10.05.2006   Mexico: Mexico – Nicaragua 9-0
12.05.2006   Mexico: Nicaragua – El Salvador 2-1
14.05.2006   Mexico: Mexico – El Salvador 8-0

Team	Pld	W	D	L	GF	GA	GD	Pts
Mexico	*2*	*2*	*0*	*0*	*17*	*0*	*+17*	*6*
Nicaragua	2	1	0	1	2	10	-8	3
El Salvador	2	0	0	2	1	10	-9	0
Belize	0	0	0	0	0	0		0

Belize withdrew

GROUP B

24.05.2006   Panama: Guatemala – Costa Rica 2-1
26.05.2006   Panama: Panama – Costa Rica 2-0
28.05.2006   Panama: Panama – Guatemala 3-0

Team	Pld	W	D	L	GF	GA	GD	Pts
Panama	*2*	*2*	*0*	*0*	*5*	*0*	*+5*	*6*
Guatemala	2	1	0	1	2	4	-2	3
Costa Rica	2	0	0	2	1	4	-3	0
Honduras	0	0	0	0	0	0		0

Honduras withdrew

CFU QUALIFYING
PRELIMINARY ROUND

Bahamas, Guyana and Montserrat withdrew.

12.03.2006 Barbados: Barbados – Antigua and Barbuda 0-1
18.03.2006 Antigua and Barbuda: Antigua and Barbuda – Barbados 0-0
18.03.2006 Cayman Islands: Cayman Islands – Netherlands Antilles 1-2
25.03.2006 Netherlands Antilles: Netherlands Antilles – Cayman Islands 1-0
01.04.2006 British Virgin Islands: British Virgin Islands – U.S. Virgin Islands 1-3
09.04.2006 U.S. Virgin Islands: U.S. Virgin Islands – British Virgin Islands 5-0

FIRST ROUND
GROUP A

04.05.2006 Dominican Republic: Dominian Republic – U.S. Virgin Islands 3-1
04.05.2006 Dominican Republic: Bermuda – Turks and Caicos Islands 4-0
06.05.2006 Dominican Republic: Bermuda – U.S. Virgin Islands 4-1
06.05.2006 Dominican Republic:
            Dominican Republic – Turks and Caicos Islands 5-0
08.05.2006 Dominican Republic: U.S. Virgin Islands – Turks and Caicos Islands 2-0
08.05.2006 Dominican Republic: Dominican Republic – Bermuda 3-1

Team	Pld	W	D	L	GF	GA	GD	Pts
Dominican Republic	*3*	*3*	*0*	*0*	*11*	*2*	*+9*	*9*
Bermuda	3	2	0	1	9	4	+5	6
U.S. Virgin Islands	3	1	0	2	4	7	-3	3
Turks and Caicos Islands	3	0	0	0	0	11	-11	0

GROUP B

03.05.2006 Aruba: Suriname – Netherlands Antilles 7-1
05.05.2006 Aruba: Aruba – Netherlands Antilles 1-2
07.05.2006 Aruba: Aruba – Suriname 0-3

Haiti were denied entry, but were allowed play-off with group winners Suriname.

108

Team	Pld	W	D	L	GF	GA	GD	Pts
Suriname	*2*	*2*	*0*	*0*	*10*	*1*	*+9*	*6*
Netherlands Antilles	2	1	0	1	3	8	-5	3
Aruba	2	0	0	2	1	5	-4	0

PLAY-OFF

29.05.2006   Suriname: Suriname – Haiti 0-3

Haiti also qualified for the Final Round.

GROUP C

08.05.2006   Jamaica: Saint Kitts and Nevis – Antigua and Barbuda 3-2
08.05.2006   Jamaica: Jamaica – Saint Lucia 5-0
10.05.2006   Jamaica: Saint Lucia – Saint Kitts and Nevis 3-2
10.05.2006   Jamaica: Jamaica – Antigua and Barbuda 10-0
12.05.2006   Jamaica: Antigua and Barbuda – Saint Lucia 1-2
12.05.2006   Jamaica: Jamaica – Saint Kitts and Nevis 11-0

Team	Pld	W	D	L	GF	GA	GD	Pts
Jamaica	*3*	*3*	*0*	*0*	*27*	*0*	*+27*	*9*
Saint Lucia	3	2	0	1	5	8	-3	6
Saint Kitts and Nevis	3	1	0	2	5	16	-11	3
Antigua and Barbuda	3	0	0	3	3	16	-13	0

GROUP D

19.05.2006   Trinidad and Tobago: Saint Vincent and the Grenadines – Dominica 2-0
19.05.2006   Trinidad and Tobago: Trinidad and Tobago – Grenada 10-0
21.05.2006   Trinidad and Tobago: Dominica – Grenada 2-2
21.05.2006   Trinidad and Tobago:
                 Trinidad and Tobago – Saint Vincent and the Grenadines 4-1
23.05.2006   Trinidad and Tobago: Grenada – Saint Vincent and the Grenadines 0-5
23.05.2006   Trinidad and Tobago: Trinidad and Tobago – Dominica 6-0

Team	Pld	W	D	L	GF	GA	GD	Pts
Trinidad and Tobago	*3*	*3*	*0*	*0*	*20*	*1*	*+19*	*9*
Saint Vincent and the Grenadines	3	2	0	1	8	4	+4	6
Dominica	3	0	1	2	2	10	-8	1
Grenada	3	0	1	2	2	17	-15	1

FINAL ROUND

Trinidad and Tobago hosted the Final Round, which was played between 6 & 10 September 2006. The winner of each group will qualify for the CONCACAF Women's Gold Cup final tournament

GROUP A

06.09.2006   Larry Gomes Stadium, Arima:
             Trinidad and Tobago – Suriname 5-1 (2-1)
Goals: James (13), Russell (36), St.Louis (62, 77), Douglas (66) / Rigters (7)
08.09.2006   Hasely Crawford Stadium, Port of Spain:
             Suriname – Dominican Republic 0-2 (0-0)
Goals: Jiménez (76), Valerio (90)
10.09.2006   Larry Gomes Stadium, Arimam:
             Dominican Republic – Trinidad and Tobago 0-7 (0-3)
Goals: St.Louis (10, 53 pen, 57 pen), James (13), Mascall (45), Russell (68)

Team	Pld	W	D	L	GF	GA	GD	Pts
Trinidad and Tobago	*2*	*2*	*0*	*0*	*12*	*1*	*+11*	*6*
Dominican Republic	2	1	0	1	2	7	-5	3
Suriname	2	0	0	2	1	7	-6	0

GROUP B

06.09.2006   Larry Gomes Stadium, Arimam: Jamaica – Bermuda 7-0 (2-0)
Goals: Davis (19, 76), Reid (33, 61, 83, 88), Duncan (89)
08.09.2006   Hasely Crawford Stadium, Port of Spain: Bermuda – Haiti 0-5 (0-2)
Goals: Joseph (16, 74), Libertin (42, 65), dolce (76)
10.09.2006   Larry Gomes Stadium, Arimam: Haiti – Jamaica 0-3 (0-1)
Goals: Mitchel (38), Reid (48), Duncan (89)

Team	Pld	W	D	L	GF	GA	GD	Pts
Jamaica	*2*	*2*	*0*	*0*	*10*	*0*	*+10*	*6*
Haiti	2	1	0	1	5	3	+2	3
Bermuda	2	0	0	2	0	12	-12	0

CONCACAF WOMEN'S GOLD CUP FINAL TOURNAMENT
FIRST ROUND

19.11.2006   Tropical Park Stadium, Miami, Florida: Jamaica – Panama 2-0 (1-0)
Goals: Sullivan (4), Reid (59)
19.11.2006   Tropical Park Stadium, Miami, Florida:
             Mexico – Trinidad and Tobago 3-0 (2-0)
Goals: P.Pérez (20), González (45), Domínguez (67)

Byes: United States and Canada.

SEMI-FINALS

22.11.2006   The HomeDepot Center, Carson, California: Canada – Jamaica 4-0 (1-0)
Goals: Sinclair (40, 71), Wilkinson (51), Booth (88)
22.11.2006   The HomeDepot Center, Carson, California:
United States – Mexico 2-0 (1-0)
Goals: Wambach (10, 64)

THIRD PLACE PLAY-OFF

26.11.2006   The HomeDepot Center, Carson, California: Jamaica – Mexico 0-3 (0-3)
Goals: Ocampo (19 pen, 37), Domínguez (22)

FINAL

26.11.2006   The HomeDepot Center, Carson, California:
Canada – United States 1-2 (1-1,1-1) (a.e.t.)
Goals: Hermuss (44) / Osobrne (6), Lilly (120 pen)

Winner **United States** and runner-up **Canada** both qualified for the FIFA Women's
World Cup 2007. Third place winner Mexico will play an AFC-CONCACAF PLAY-
OFF against the fourth-place team of the AFC Asian Women's Championship.

OFC WOMEN'S CHAMPIONSHIP 2007

The OFC Women's Championship 2007 was held in Papua New Guinea between 9 &
13 April 2007. Only the winner will qualify for the FIFA Women's World Cup 2007.

The Cook Islands, Fiji, New Caledonia, Samoa, Tahiti and Vanuatu would take part,
but withdrew before the tournament was organised.

09.04.2007   Sir Ignatius Kilage Stadium, Lae: New Zealand – Tonga 6-1 (3-0)
Goals: Yallop (8, 73), Henderson (13, 53), Erceg (17), Thompson (81) / Feke (85)
09.04.2007   Sir Ignatius Kilage Stadium, Lae:
Papua New Guinea – Solomon Islands 6-1 (3-1)
Goals: Chalau (8, 48), Siniu (40, 50, 66), Galo (45 og) / Fula (44)
11.04.2007   Sir Ignatius Kilage Stadium, Lae:
New Zealand – Solomon Islands 8-0 (5-0)
Goals: Ferrara (4, 22), N.Smith (32, 45+2, 62), Percival (38), R.Smith (52),
Kete (90+1)
11.04.2007   Sir Ignatius Kilage Stadium, Lae: Papua New Guinea – Tonga 1-0 (0-0)
Goal: Niukapu (63 og)
13.04.2007   Sir Ignatius Kilage Stadium, Lae:
Papua New Guinea – New Zealand 0-7 (0-4)
Goals N.Smith (20), Thompson (23), Percival (26), Yallop (30, 65), Green (63),
Moorwood (85)
13.04.2007   Sir Ignatius Kilage Stadium, Lae: Tonga – Solomon Islands 0-0

Team	Pld	W	D	L	GF	GA	GD	Pts
New Zealand	*3*	*3*	*0*	*0*	*21*	*1*	*+20*	*9*
Papua New Guinea	3	2	0	1	7	8	-1	6
Tonga	3	0	1	2	1	7	-6	1
Solomon Islands	3	0	1	2	1	14	-13	1

The winner **New Zealand** qualified for the FIFA Women's World Cup 2007

CONMEBOL SUDAMERICANO FEMENINO 2006

Originally, a women's football tournament at the 2006 South American Games in Buenos Aires would serve as qualifier tournament, but the South American Games committee scrapped football from the games, forcing the Argentine Football Association to organize a tournament on short notice. The tournament was held between 10 & 26 November 2006 in Argentina.

FIRST ROUND

GROUP A

10.11.2006   Estadio José María Minella, Mar del Plata: Chile – Ecuadar 1-2 (1-1)
Goals: Reyes (34) / Velarde (39, 50)
10.11.2006   Estadio José María Minella, Mar del Plata:
Argentina – Uruguay 2-1 (1-1)
Goals: Almeida (4), Potassa (63) / Souza (11)
12.11.2006   Estadio José María Minella, Mar del Plata:
Colombia – Uruguay 1-0 (1-0)
Goal: Moscoso (17)
12.11.2006   Estadio José María Minella, Mar del Plata: Chile – Argentina 0-8 (0-5)
Goals: Potassa (4, 22), Coronel (8), Almeida (27), Ojeda (30), Gómez (70),
Huber (79), Hirmbruchner (86)
14.11.2006   Estadio José María Minella, Mar del Plata:
Ecuador – Argentina 0-1 (0-0)
Goal: Gómez (54)
14.11.2006   Estadio José María Minella, Mar del Plata: Colombia – Chile 1-3 (0-1)
Goals: Gaete (71 og) / Arias (8), Quezada (81, 87)
16.11.2006   Estadio José María Minella, Mar del Plata: Uruguay – Chile 2-1 (1-1)
Goals: Quinteros (43), Barrera (76 og) / Quezada (4)
16.11.2006   Estadio José María Minella, Mar del Plata:
Ecuador – Colombia 2-2 (1-0)
Goals: Velarde (28), Vivas (47) / Saavedra (62), Molina (69)
18.11.2006   Estadio José María Minella, Mar del Plata:
Argentina – Colombia 6-0 (3-0)
Goals: Gómez (3), Vallejos (21, 52), Quiñones (27), Huber (46), Ojeda (57)
18.11.2006   Estadio José María Minella, Mar del Plata: Uruguay – Ecuador 1-0 (0-0)
Goal: Laborda (67)

Team	Pld	W	D	L	GF	GA	GD	Pts
Argentina	4	4	0	0	17	1	+16	12
Uruguay	4	2	0	2	4	4	0	6
Ecuador	4	1	1	2	4	5	-1	4
Colombia	4	1	1	2	4	11	-7	4
Chile	4	1	0	3	5	13	-8	3

GROUP B

11.11.2006   Estadio José María Minella, Mar del Plata: Bolivia – Venezuela 1-1 (0-0)
Goals: Rios (52) / Espinosa (53)
11.11.2006   Estadio José María Minella, Mar del Plata: Paraguay – Brazil 1-4 (0-1)
Goals: Alarcón (69) / Cristiane (19, 53), Daniela Alves (46), Aline (59)
13.11.2006   Estadio José María Minella, Mar del Plata: Peru – Brazil 0-2 (0-1)
Goals: Cristiane (6), Elaine (80)
13.11.2006   Estadio José María Minella, Mar del Plata: Bolivia – Paraguay 1-5 (1-3)
Goals: Morón (40) / Ortiz (1), Quintana (8, 43), Alarcón (56 pen), Martínez (83)
15.11.2006   Estadio José María Minella, Mar del Plata:
             Venezuela – Paraguay 1-3 (1-0)
Goals: Lovera (20) / Cuevas (63, 81), Vega (66)
15.11.2006   Estadio José María Minella, Mar del Plata: Peru – Bolivia 2-1 (0-1)
Goals: Chinchilla (61 og), Dorador (63) / Zamorano (8)
17.11.2006   Estadio José María Minella, Mar del Plata: Brazil – Bolivia 6-1 (5-1)
Goals: Daniela Alves (7), Cristiane (8, 22, 60), Mônica (13), Elaine (44) /
Morón (43 pen)
17.11.2006   Estadio José María Minella, Mar del Plata: Venezuela – Peru 2-0 (1-0)
Goals: Ferrer (29, 73)
19.11.2006   Estadio José María Minella, Mar del Plata: Paraguay – Peru 2-1 (0-0)
Goals: Vega (67, 81 pen) / Veruzhka (87 pen)
19.11.2006   Estadio José María Minella, Mar del Plata: Brazil – Venezuela 6-0 (4-0)
Goals: Daniela Alves (1), Renata Costa (12), Michele (27, 45), Cristiane (56),
Daniele (81)

Team	Pld	W	D	L	GF	GA	GD	Pts
Brazil	4	4	0	0	18	2	+16	12
Paraguay	4	3	0	1	11	7	+4	9
Venezuela	4	1	1	2	4	10	-6	4
Peru	4	1	0	3	3	7	-4	3
Bolivia	4	0	1	3	4	14	-10	1

FINAL ROUND

22.11.2006   Estadio José María Minella, Mar del Plata: Argentina – Paraguay 0-0
22.11.2006   Estadio José María Minella, Mar del Plata: Brazil – Uruguay 6-0 (2-0)
Goals: Daniela Alves (11, 23 pen), Grazielle (47, 86), Elaine (64), Cristiane (72 pen)

24.11.2006   Estadio José María Minella, Mar del Plata:
             Argentina – Uruguay 2-0 (0-0)
Goals: Gerez (71), Manicier (76)
24.11.2006   Estadio José María Minella, Mar del Plata: Brazil – Paraguay 6-0 (3-0)
Goals: Cristiane (6, 27 pen, 62, 64), Daniela Alves (36), Renata Costa (68)
26.11.2006   Estadio José María Minella, Mar del Plata:
             Uruguay – Paraguay 3-2 (1-2)
Goals: Souza (27, 62, 67) / Cuevas (17, 44)
26.11.2006   Estadio José María Minella, Mar del Plata: Argentina – Brazil 2-0 (0-0)
Goals: González (66), Potassa (68)

Team	Pld	W	D	L	GF	GA	GD	Pts
Argentina	*3*	*2*	*1*	*0*	*4*	*0*	*+4*	*7*
Brazil	*3*	*2*	*0*	*1*	*12*	*2*	*+10*	*6*
Uruguay	3	1	0	2	3	10	-7	3
Paraguay	3	0	1	2	2	9	-7	1
Bolivia	4	0	1	3	4	14	-10	1

The winner **Argentina** and the runner-up **Brazil** both qualified for the FIFA Women's
World Cup 2007.

AFC-CONCACAF PLAY-OFF

10.03.2007   National Stadium, Tokyo: Japan – Mexico 2-0 (1-0)
Goals: Sawa (37), Miyama (69)
17.03.2007   Estadio Nemesio Díez, Toluca: Mexico – Japan 2-1 (2-1)
Goals: Leyva (18 pen), Domínguez (29) / Arakawa (12)

Japan qualified for the FIFA Women's World Cup 2007.

FIFA WOMEN'S WORLD CUP FINAL TOURNAMENT IN CHINA PR 2007

GROUP STAGE
GROUP A

10.09.2007 Hongkou Stadium, Shanghai: Germany – Argentina 11-0 (5-0)
Germany: Nadine ANGERER, Kerstin STEGEMANN, Sandra MINNERT, Ariane
HINGST, Renate LINGOR, Kerstin GAREFREKES (84 Anja MITTAG), Melanie
BEHRINGER (68 Petra WIMBERSKY), Linda BRESONIK, Simone LAUDEHR (74
Saskia BARTUSIAK *(YC86)*), Birgit PRINZ, Sandra SMISEK.
(Coach: Silva NEID).
Argentina: Vanina CORREA, Eva Nadia GONZÁLEZ *(YC56)*, Valeria COTELO,
Gabriela CHAVEZ *(YC20)*, Sabrina BARBITTA, Clarisa HUBER (74 Florencia
MANDRILE), Rosana GÓMEZ *(YC16)* (66 Mercedes PEREYRA), María Florencia
QUIÑONES *(YC90+2)*, Fabiana VALLEJOS, Analia ALMEYDA (53 Ludmila
MANICLER), Belén POTASSA. (Coach: José Carlos BORRELLO).
Goals: Vanina CORREA (12 og), Kerstin GAREFREKES (17), Melanie
BEHRINGER (24), Birgit PRINZ (29, 45+1, 59), Renate LINGOR (51, 90+1), Sandra
SMISEK (57, 70, 79)
Referee: Tammy Nicole OGSTON (Australia)   Attendance: 28,098

11.09.2007 Hongkou Stadium, Shanghai: Japan – England 2-2 (0-0)
Japan: Miho FUKUMOTO, Hiromi ISOZAKI (86 Yuki NAGASATO), Yukari
KINGA (46 Kozue ANDO), Azusa IWASHIMIZU, Tomomi MIYAMOTO (71
Ayumi HARA), Tomoe KATO Sakai, Homare SAWA, Aya MIYAMA, Rumi
UTSUGI, Eriko ARAKAWA, Shinobu OHNO. (Coach: Hiroshi OHASHI).
England: Rachel Laura BROWN, Alexandra SCOTT (89 Lindsay JOHNSON), Casey
STONEY, Faye Deborah WHITE, Mary Rose PHILLIP, Katie CHAPMAN *(YC23)*,
Fara WILLIAMS, Karen CARNEY, Eniola ALUKO (74 Jill SCOTT), Kelly SMITH
(YC90+4), Rachel YANKEY. (Coach: Hope Patricia POWELL).
Goals: Aya MIYAMA (55, 90+5) / Kelly SMITH (81, 83)
Referee: Kari SEITZ (United States)   Attendance: 27,146

14.09.2007 Hongkou Stadium, Shanghai: Argentina – Japan 0-1 (0-0)
Argentina: Romina FERRO, Eva Nadia GONZÁLEZ, Gabriela CHAVEZ, Clarisa
HUBER (53 Andrea Susana OJEDA), Catalina PÉREZ, María Florencia QUIÑONES
(61 Emilia MENDIETA), Florencia MANDRILE, Fabiana VALLEJOS, Analia
ALMEYDA, Mercedes PEREYRA, Belén POTASSA (77 Ludmila MANICLER).
(Coach: José Carlos BORRELLO).
Japan: Miho FUKUMOTO, Hiromi ISOZAKI *(YC57)*, Kyoko YANO (50 Rumi
UTSUGI), Azusa IWASHIMIZU, Tomomi MIYAMOTO, Tomoe KATO Sakai,
Homare SAWA, Aya MIYAMA, Kozue ANDO (79 Yukari KINGA), Yuki
NAGASATO, Shinobu OHNO (57 Eriko ARAKAWA). (Coach: Hiroshi OHASHI).
Goal: Yuki NAGASATO (90+1)
Referee: Dagmar DAMKOVA (Czech Republic)   Attendance: 27,730

14.09.2007 Hongkou Stadium, Shanghai: England – Germany 0-0
England: Rachel Laura BROWN, Alexandra SCOTT, Casey STONEY, Faye Deborah
WHITE, Mary Rose PHILLIP, Anita Amma Ankyewah ASANTE, Katie CHAPMAN
(YC16), Fara WILLIAMS (YC55), Jill SCOTT, Karen CARNEY (57 Rachel
YANKEY), Kelly SMITH. (Coach: Hope Patricia POWELL).
Germany: Nadine ANGERER, Kerstin STEGEMANN, Annike KRAHN (YC36),
Ariane HINGST, Renate LINGOR, Kerstin GAREFREKES, Melanie BEHRINGER
(63 Fatmire ALUSHI (YC85)), Linda BRESONIK, Simone LAUDEHR (YC84),
Birgit PRINZ, Sandra SMISEK. (Coach: Silva NEID).
Referee: Jenny PALMQVIST (Sweden) Attendance: 27,730

17.09.2007 Chengdu Sports Center, Chengdu: England – Argentina 6-1 (2-0)
England: Rachel Laura BROWN, Alexandra SCOTT (YC4) (68 Sue SMITH), Casey
STONEY, Faye Deborah WHITE, Mary Rose PHILLIP, Anita Amma Ankyewah
ASANTE, Fara WILLIAMS (YC61), Jill SCOTT, Eniola ALUKO (80 Jodie
HANDLEY), Kelly SMITH (80 Vicky EXLEY), Rachel YANKEY.
(Coach: Hope Patricia POWELL).
Argentina: Romina FERRO, Eva Nadia GONZÁLEZ (YC42), Gabriela CHAVEZ,
Clarisa HUBER (52 Valeria COTELO), Catalina PÉREZ (YC41,YC49), María
Florencia QUIÑONES (76 Emilia MENDIETA), Florencia MANDRILE, Fabiana
VALLEJOS, Analia ALMEYDA (62 Natalia GATTI), Mercedes PEREYRA, Belén
POTASSA. (Coach: José Carlos BORRELLO).
Goals: Eva Nadia GONZÁLEZ (9 og), Jill SCOTT (10), Fara WILLIAMS (50 pen),
Kelly SMITH (64, 77), Vicky EXLEY (90 pen) / Eva Nadia GONZÁLEZ (60)
Referee: Dianne FERREIRA-JAMES (Guyana) Attendance: 30,730

Sent-off: 49' Catalina PÉREZ.

17.09.2007 Yellow Dragon Sports Center, Hangzhou: Germany – Japan 2-0 (1-0)
Germany: Nadine ANGERER, Kerstin STEGEMANN, Annike KRAHN, Ariane
HINGST, Renate LINGOR, Kerstin GAREFREKES (YC82), Melanie BEHRINGER
(57 Fatmire ALUSHI), Linda BRESONIK, Petra WIMBERSKY, Birgit PRINZ,
Sandra SMISEK (78 Martina MÜLLER (YC88)). (Coach: Silva NEID).
Japan: Miho FUKUMOTO, Hiromi ISOZAKI, Yukari KINGA, Azusa
IWASHIMIZU, Miyuki YANAGITA, Ayumi HARA, Tomoe KATO Sakai (YC16),
Homare SAWA, Aya MIYAMA (46 Eriko ARAKAWA, 63 Shinobu OHNO), Rumi
UTSUGI, Yuki NAGASATO (76 Tomomi MIYAMOTO).
(Coach: Hiroshi OHASHI).
Goals: Birgit PRINZ (21), Renate LINGOR (87 pen)
Referee: Adriana CORREA (Colombia) Attendance: 39,817

Team	Pld	W	D	L	GF	GA	GD	Pts
Germany	*3*	*2*	*1*	*0*	*13*	*0*	*+13*	*7*
England	*3*	*1*	*2*	*0*	*8*	*3*	*+5*	*5*
Japan	3	1	1	1	3	4	-1	4
Argentina	3	0	0	3	1	18	-17	0

GROUP B

11.09.2007   Chengdu Sports Center, Chengdu: United States – North Korea 2-2 (0-0)
United States: Hope Amelia SOLO, Christie PEARCE *(YC45)*, Catherine
WHITEHILL, Stephanie COX, Kathryn Michele MARKGRAF Sobrero, Shannon
BOXX, Kristine Marie LILLY Heavey, Lori CHALUPNY, Heather O'REILLY
(90+2 Natasha KAI), Carli LLOYD, Abby WAMBACH. (Coach: Greg RYAN).
North Korea: JON Myong-Hui, OM Jong-Ran, SONG Jong-Sun, SONU Kyong-Sun,
KONG Hye-Ok, KIM Kyong-Hwa, HO Sun-Hui (22 KIM Yong-Ae, 90 JONG Pok-
Sim *(YC90+1)*), RI Un-Suk, RI Un-Gyong, KIL Son-Hui, RI Kum-Suk.
(Coach: KIM Kwang-Min).
Goals: Abby WAMBACH (50), Heather O'REILLY (69) / KIL Son-Hui (58),
KIM Yong-Ae (62)
Referee: Nicole PETIGNAT (Switzerland)   Attendance: 35,100

11.09.2007   Chengdu Sports Center, Chengdu: Nigeria – Sweden 1-1 (0-0)
Nigeria: Predious Uzoaru DEDE, Faith IKIDI, Onome EBI, Ulunma JEROME, Rita
CHIKWELU, Maureen MMADU (59 Efioanwan EKPO), Christie GEORGE,
Perpetua Ijeoma NKWOCHA, Ifeanyi CHIEJINE, Chi-Chi IGBO (35 Stella
MBACHU), Cynthia UWAK. (Coach: Ntiero EFFIOM).
Sweden: Rut Hedvig LINDAHL, Anna PAULSON, Sara Kristina THUNEBRO, Stina
SEGERSTRÖM, Hanna Gunilla MARKLUND, Frida Christina ÖSTBERG, Sara
Caroline SEGER, Kerstin Ingrid Therese SJÖGRAN *(YC12)*, Hanna Carolina
LJUNGBERG (69 Sara JOHANSSON), Victoria Margareta Sandell SVENSSON,
Lotta Eva SCHELIN (83 Linda FORSBERG). (Coach: Thomas DENNERBY).
Goals: Cynthia UWAK (82) / Victoria Margareta Sandell SVENSSON (50)
Referee: NIU Huijun (China PR)   Attendance: 35,600

14.09.2007   Chengdu Sports Center, Chengdu: Sweden- United States 0-2 (0-1)
Sweden: Rut Hedvig LINDAHL, Anna PAULSON, Stina SEGERSTRÖM *(YC34)* (81
Therese LUNDIN), Hanna Gunilla MARKLUND, Frida Christina ÖSTBERG, Sara
Caroline SEGER *(YC90+3)*, Kerstin Ingrid Therese SJÖGRAN (65 Nilla FISCHER),
Hanna Carolina LJUNGBERG, Linda FORSBERG, Victoria Margareta Sandell
SVENSSON, Lotta Eva SCHELIN. (Coach: Thomas DENNERBY).
United States: Hope Amelia SOLO, Christie PEARCE, Catherine WHITEHILL,
Stephanie COX, Kathryn Michele MARKGRAF Sobrero, Leslie OSBORNE, Kristine
Marie LILLY Heavey, Lori CHALUPNY, Lindsay TARPLEY (67 Heather
O'REILLY), Carli LLOYD (46 Shannon BOXX), Abby WAMBACH.
(Coach: Greg RYAN).
Goals: Abby WAMBACH (34 pen, 58)
Referee: Gyöngyi Krisztina GAÁL (Hungary)   Attendance: 35,600

14.09.2007   Chengdu Sports Center, Chengdu: North Korea – Nigeria 2-0 (2-0)
North Korea: JON Myong-Hui, OM Jong-Ran, SONG Jong-Sun, SONU Kyong-Sun,
KONG Hye-Ok, KIM Kyong-Hwa (77 JONG Pok-Sim), RI Un-Suk, RI Un-Gyong,
KIL Son-Hui, RI Kum-Suk *(YC77)*, KIM Yong-Ae. (Coach: KIM Kwang-Min).
Nigeria: Predious Uzoaru DEDE, Faith IKIDI, Onome EBI (30 Lilian COLE),
Ulunma JEROME *(YC52)*, Rita CHIKWELU (61 Maureen MMADU), Efioanwan
EKPO, Christie GEORGE, Perpetua Ijeoma NKWOCHA, Stella MBACHU, Ifeanyi
CHIEJINE *(YC35)* (80 Chi-Chi IGBO), Cynthia UWAK. (Coach: Ntiero EFFIOM).
Goals: KIM Kyong-Hwa (17), RI Kum-Suk (21)
Referee: Tammy Nicole OGSTON (Australia)   Attendance: 35,600

18.09.2007   Tianjin Olympic Center Stadium, Tianjin:
            North Korea – Sweden 1-2 (1-1)
North Korea: JON Myong-Hui *(YC88)*, OM Jong-Ran, SONG Jong-Sun, SONU
Kyong-Sun, KONG Hye-Ok, KIM Kyong-Hwa (56 HONG Myong-Gum), RI Un-
Suk, RI Un-Gyong, KIL Son-Hui (85 KIM Ok-Sim), RI Kum-Suk, KIM Yong-Ae
(YC32) (60 JONG Pok-Sim). (Coach: KIM Kwang-Min).
Sweden: Rut Hedvig LINDAHL, Anna PAULSON (69 Sara JOHANSSON), Karolina
WESTBERG, Nilla FISCHER, Hanna Gunilla MARKLUND, Frida Christina
ÖSTBERG *(YC31)*, Sara Caroline SEGER, Kerstin Ingrid Therese SJÖGRAN, Hanna
Carolina LJUNGBERG (40 Sara Kristina THUNEBRO, 89 Therese LUNDIN),
Victoria Margareta Sandell SVENSSON, Lotta Eva SCHELIN *(YC82)*.
(Coach: Thomas DENNERBY).
Goals: RI Un-Suk (22) / Lotta Eva SCHELIN (4, 54)
Referee: Christine BECK (Germany)   Attendance: 33,196

18.09.2007   Hongkou Stadium, Shanghai: Nigeria – United States 0-1 (0-1)
Nigeria: Predious Uzoaru DEDE, Faith IKIDI, Ulunma JEROME, Rita CHIKWELU,
Lilian COLE *(YC14)*, Efioanwan EKPO, Christie GEORGE, Perpetua Ijeoma
NKWOCHA, Stella MBACHU, Chi-Chi IGBO (22 Ifeanyi CHIEJINE), Cynthia
UWAK (83 Ogonna CHUKWUDI). (Coach: Ntiero EFFIOM).
United States: Hope Amelia SOLO, Christie PEARCE (77 Tina ELLERTSON),
Catherine WHITEHILL, Stephanie COX, Kathryn Michele MARKGRAF Sobrero,
Shannon BOXX, Kristine Marie LILLY Heavey (84 Lindsay TARPLEY), Lori
CHALUPNY, Heather O'REILLY, Carli LLOYD (64 Leslie OSBORNE), Abby
WAMBACH. (Coach: Greg RYAN).
Goal: Lori CHALUPNY (1)
Referee: Mayumi OIWA (Japan)   Attendance: 6,100

Team	Pld	W	D	L	GF	GA	GD	Pts
United States	*3*	*2*	*1*	*0*	*5*	*2*	*+3*	*7*
North Korea	*3*	*1*	*1*	*1*	*5*	*4*	*+1*	*4*
Sweden	3	1	1	1	3	4	-1	4
Nigeria	3	0	1	2	1	4	-3	1

GROUP C

12.09.2007   Yellow Dragon Sports Center, Hangzhou: Ghana – Australia 1-4 (0-1)
Ghana: Memunatu SULEMANA, Aminatu IBRAHIM, Mavis DANSO, Olivia
AMOAKO, Yaa AVOE (67 Belinda KANDA), Lydia ANKRAH, Florence OKOE,
Adjoa BAYOR, Memuna DARKU, Anita AMENUKU (67 Hamdya ABASS), Anita
AMANKWA. (Coach: Isaac PAHA).
Australia: Melissa BARBIERI HUDSON, Kate McSHEA *(YC87)*, Dianne
ALAGICH, Cheryl SALISBURY *(YC90)*, Clare POLKINGHORNE (83 Thea
SLATYER), Heather GARRIOCK, Joanne PETERS (62 Alicia FERGUSON), Sally
SHIPARD, Caitlin MUNOZ (46 Lisa DE VANNA), Collette McCALLUM, Sarah
WALSH *(YC53)*. (Coach: Tom SERMANNI).
Goals: Anita AMANKWA (70) / Sarah WALSH (15), Lisa DE VANNA (57, 81),
Heather GARRIOCK (69)
Referee: Adriana CORREA (Colombia)   Attendance: 30,752

12.09.2007   Yellow Dragon Sports Center, Hangzhou: Norway – Canada 2-1 (0-1)
Norway: Bente NORDBY, Siri Kristine NORDBY (46 Camilla HUSE), Ane
STANGELAND Horpestad, Trine RØNNING, Gunhild Bentzen FØLSTAD, Ingvild
STENSLAND, Leni LARSEN KAURIN, Solveig GULBRANDSEN, Lene Glesåsen
STORLØKKEN (76 Marie KNUTSEN), Ragnhild Øren GULBRANDSEN, Lindy
Melissa Wiik LØVBRÆK (66 Lene MYKJÅLAND). (Coach: Bjarne BERNTSEN).
Canada: Erin McLEOD, Kristina KISS, Tanya DENNIS, Candace Marie CHAPMAN
(73 Amy Heather WALSH), Martina FRANKO, Randee HERMAS, Diana
MATHESON, Sophie SCHMIDT, Christine SINCLAIR, Melissa TANCREDI (46
Rhian WILKINSON), Kara Elise LANG (83 Jodi-Ann ROBINSON).
(Coach: Even Jostein PELLERUD).
Goals: Ragnhild Øren GULBRANDSEN (52), Ane STANGELAND Horpestad (81) /
Candace Marie CHAPMAN (33)
Referee: Christine BECK (Germany)   Attendance: 30,752

15.09.2007   Yellow Dragon Sports Center, Hangzhou: Canada – Ghana 4-0 (1-0)
Canada: Erin McLEOD, Kristina KISS, Tanya DENNIS *(YC8)*, Candace Marie
CHAPMAN, Martina FRANKO, Randee HERMAS, Diana MATHESON (84 Andrea
NEIL), Katie THORLAKSON (45 Jodi-Ann ROBINSON), Sophie SCHMIDT,
Christine SINCLAIR, Kara Elise LANG (63 Rhian WILKINSON).
(Coach: Even Jostein PELLERUD).
Ghana: Memunatu SULEMANA, Aminatu IBRAHIM, Mavis DANSO, Olivia
AMOAKO *(YC78)*, Yaa AVOE (35 Hamdya ABASS), Florence OKOE, Adjoa
BAYOR (71 Safia ABDULRAHMAN), Memuna DARKU (77 Lydia ANKRAH),
Gloria FORIWA *(YC39)*, Rumanatu TAHIRU, Anita AMANKWA *(YC21)*.
(Coach: Isaac PAHA).
Goals: Christine SINCLAIR (16, 62), Sophie SCHMIDT (55), Martina FRANKO (77)
Referee: Nicole PETIGNAT (Switzerland)   Attendance: 33,835

119

15.09.2007   Yellow Dragon Sports Center, Hangzhou: Australia – Norway 1-1 (0-1)
Australia: Melissa BARBIERI HUDSON, Dianne ALAGICH, Cheryl SALISBURY,
Thea SLATYER, Alicia FERGUSON, Heather GARRIOCK, Lauren Elizabeth
COLTHORPE (76 Caitlin MUNOZ), Danielle SMALL (46 Lisa DE VANNA),
Joanne BURGESS, Collette McCALLUM, Kathryn GILL (61 Sarah WALSH).
(Coach: Tom SERMANNI).
Norway: Bente NORDBY, Ane STANGELAND Horpestad, Trine RØNNING,
Camilla HUSE, Gunhild Bentzen FØLSTAD, Ingvild STENSLAND, Leni LARSEN
KAURIN (74 Guro KNUTSEN Mienna), Marie KNUTSEN, Solveig
GULBRANDSEN (86 Lene Glesåsen STORLØKKEN), Ragnhild Øren
GULBRANDSEN, Lindy Melissa Wiik LØVBRÆK (46 Lene MYKJÅLAND).
(Coach: Bjarne BERNTSEN).
Goals: Lisa DE VANNA (83) / Solveig GULBRANDSEN (5)
Referee: NIU Huijun (China PR)   Attendance: 33,835

20.09.2007   Yellow Dragon Sports Center, Hangzhou: Norway – Ghana 7-2 (3-0)
Norway: Bente NORDBY, Marit Helene Fiane GRØDUM CHRISTENSEN, Siri
Kristine NORDBY, Ane STANGELAND Horpestad, Camilla HUSE, Ingvild
STENSLAND, Leni LARSEN KAURIN (61 Lise KLAVENESS), Lene
MYKJÅLAND (46 Isabell HERLOVSEN), Solveig GULBRANDSEN (46 Madeleine
GISKE), Lene Glesåsen STORLØKKEN, Ragnhild Øren GULBRANDSEN.
(Coach: Bjarne BERNTSEN).
Ghana: Gladys ENTI (64 Memunatu SULEMANA), Aminatu IBRAHIM (YC15),
Mavis DANSO, Olivia AMOAKO, Yaa AVOE, Doreen AWUAH (58 Memuna
DARKU), Florence OKOE, Adjoa BAYOR, Anita AMENUKU (46 Sheila OKAI
(YC80)), Rumanatu TAHIRU, Anita AMANKWA. (Coach: Isaac PAHA).
Goals: Lene Glesåsen STORLØKKEN (4), Ragnhild Øren GULBRANDSEN (39, 59,
62), Ane STANGELAND Horpestad (45 pen), Isabell HERLOVSEN (56), Lise
KLAVENESS (69) / Adjoa BAYOR (73), Florence OKOE (80 pen)
Referee: Jennifer BENNETT (United States)   Attendance: 43,817

20.09.2007   Chengdu Sports Center, Chengdu: Australia – Canada 2-2 (0-1)
Australia: Melissa BARBIERI HUDSON, Kate McSHEA, Dianne ALAGICH, Cheryl
SALISBURY, Heather GARRIOCK, Joanne PETERS (76 Alicia FERGUSON), Sally
SHIPARD, Lauren Elizabeth COLTHORPE (46 Lisa DE VANNA), Caitlin MUNOZ
(62 Joanne BURGESS), Collette McCALLUM (YC90), Sarah WALSH.
(Coach: Tom SERMANNI).
Canada: Erin McLEOD (79 Taryn SWIATEK), Tanya DENNIS, Rhian
WILKINSON, Candace Marie CHAPMAN, Martina FRANKO, Randee HERMAS
(YC89), Diana MATHESON, Sophie SCHMIDT, Christine SINCLAIR, Melissa
TANCREDI (68 Jodi-Ann ROBINSON), Kara Elise LANG (90+2 Brittany TIMKO).
(Coach: Even Jostein PELLERUD).
Goals: Collette McCALLUM (53), Cheryl SALISBURY (90+2) /
Melissa TANCREDI (1), Christine SINCLAIR (85)
Referee: Gyöngyi Krisztina GAÁL (Hungary)   Attendance: 29,300

Team	Pld	W	D	L	GF	GA	GD	Pts
Norway	*3*	*2*	*1*	*0*	*10*	*4*	*+6*	*7*
Australia	*3*	*1*	*2*	*0*	*7*	*4*	*+3*	*5*
Canada	3	1	1	1	7	4	+3	4
Ghana	3	0	0	3	3	15	-12	0

GROUP D

12.09.2007   Wuhan Sports Center Stadium, Wuhan: New Zealand – Brazil 0-5 (0-1)
New Zealand: Jenny Lynn BINDON, Rebecca Katie SMITH, Ria PERCIVAL
(YC25), Abby ERCEG, Alexandra RILEY, Maia Giselle JACKMAN, Katie
DUNCAN (66 Priscilla DUNCAN), Hayley Rose MOORWOOD, Emma
HUMPHRIES (72 Zoe Victoria THOMPSON), Emily McCOLL, Wendi Judith
HENDERSON (46 Rebecca TEGG). (Coach: John HERDMAN).
Brazil: ANDRÉIA Suntaque, ALINE Pellegrino, TÂNIA Maria Pereira Ribeiro,
Renata Aparecida da Costa "KÓKI", Miraildes Maciel Mota "FORMIGA", ESTER
Aparecida dos Santos, SIMONE Gomes Jatobá, DANIELA Alves Lima, ANDRÉIA
dos Santos (78 ROSANA dos Santos Augusto), MARTA Vieira da Silva,
CRISTIANE Rozeira de Souza Silva (84 Delma Gonçalves "PRETINHA").
(Coach: JORGE BARCELLOS).
Goals: DANIELA Alves Lima (10), CRISTIANE Rozeira de Souza Silva (54),
MARTA Vieira da Silva (74, 90+3), Renata Aparecida da Costa "KÓKI" (86)
Referee: Pannipar KAMNUENG (Thailand)   Attendance: 50,800

12.09.2007   Wuhan Sports Center Stadium, Wuhan: China PR – Denmark 3-2 (1-0)
China PR: HAN Wenxia, LI Jie (90+3 LIU Yali), WANG Kun, PU Wei, ZHOU
Gaoping (68 ZHANG Ying), XIE Caixia *(YC89)*, BI Yan, PAN Lina, QU Feifei (58
SONG Xiaoli), HAN Duan, MA Xiaoxu.
(Coach: Marika Susan DOMANSKI LYFORS).
Denmark: Heidi ELGAARD-JOHANSEN, Gitte ANDERSEN, Bettina FALK
HANSEN, Mia Birkehøj BROGAARD Olsen, Julie RYDAHL BUKH, Catherine
PAASKE SØRENSEN *(YC80)*, Mariann GAJHEDE Knudsen (75 Stine KJÆR
DIMUN), Johanna Maria Baltensberger RASMUSSEN (75 Merete PEDERSEN),
Anne DOT EGGERS NIELSEN, Katrine Søndergaard PEDERSEN, Maiken With
PAPE *(YC86)*. (Coach: Kenneth HEINER-MØLLER).
Goals: LI Jie (30), BI Yan (50), SONG Xiaoli (88) / Anne DOT EGGERS NIELSEN
(51), Catherine PAASKE SØRENSEN (87)
Referee: Dianne FERREIRA-JAMES (Guyana)   Attendance: 50,800

15.09.2007   Wuhan Sports Center Stadium, Wuhan:
Denmark – New Zealand 2-0 (0-0)
Denmark: Heidi ELGAARD-JOHANSEN, Gitte ANDERSEN, Bettina FALK
HANSEN, Mia Birkehøj BROGAARD Olsen, Julie RYDAHL BUKH, Catherine
PAASKE SØRENSEN (86 Janne MADSEN), Mariann GAJHEDE Knudsen (46
Maiken With PAPE), Johanna Maria Baltensberger RASMUSSEN (72 Camilla
SAND ANDERSEN), Anne DOT EGGERS NIELSEN, Katrine Søndergaard
PEDERSEN, Merete PEDERSEN. (Coach: Kenneth HEINER-MØLLER).
New Zealand: Jenny Lynn BINDON *(YC90+2)*, Rebecca Katie SMITH, Ria
PERCIVAL (70 Emma HUMPHRIES), Abby ERCEG *(YC88)*, Marlies OOSTDAM,
Alexandra RILEY, Maia Giselle JACKMAN *(YC60)*, Hayley Rose MOORWOOD
(87 Annalie LONGO), Priscilla DUNCAN, Emily McCOLL, Wendi Judith
HENDERSON (64 Rebecca TEGG). (Coach: John HERDMAN).
Goals: Katrine Søndergaard PEDERSEN (61), Catherine PAASKE SØRENSEN (66)
Referee: Mayumi OIWA (Japan)   Attendance: 54,000

15.09.2007   Wuhan Sports Center Stadium, Wuhan: Brazil – China PR 4-0 (1-0)
Brazil: ANDRÉIA Suntaque, ELAINE Estrela Moura, ALINE Pellegrino *(YC41)*,
TÂNIA Maria Pereira Ribeiro, Renata Aparecida da Costa "KÓKI" *(YC61)*, Miraildes
Maciel Mota "FORMIGA" (89 SIMONE Gomes Jatobá), ESTER Aparecida dos
Santos, DANIELA Alves Lima *(YC10)* (79 ROSANA dos Santos Augusto),
ANDRÉIA dos Santos, MARTA Vieira da Silva, CRISTIANE Rozeira de Souza Silva
(85 KÁTIA Cilene Teixeira da Silva). (Coach: JORGE BARCELLOS).
China PR: HAN Wenxia, LI Jie, WANG Kun, PU Wei *(YC27)*, LIU Yali (57 ZHOU
Gaoping), SONG Xiaoli, XIE Caixia (67 LIU Sa), BI Yan, PAN Lina (52 ZHANG
Tong *(YC53)*), HAN Duan, MA Xiaoxu.
(Coach: Marika Susan DOMANSKI LYFORS).
Goals: MARTA Vieira da Silva (42, 70), CRISTIANE Rozeira de Souza Silva (47,
48)
Referee: Jennifer BENNETT (United States)   Attendance: 54,000

20.09.2007   Yellow Dragon sports Center, Hangzhou: Brazil – Denmark 1-0 (0-0)
Brazil: ANDRÉIA Suntaque, ELAINE Estrela Moura, TÂNIA Maria Pereira Ribeiro,
MÔNICA Angélica de Paula *(YC76)*, Miraildes Maciel Mota "FORMIGA", ESTER
Aparecida dos Santos, SIMONE Gomes Jatobá, DANIELA Alves Lima (88 ROSANA
dos Santos Augusto), ANDRÉIA dos Santos, MARTA Vieira da Silva, CRISTIANE
Rozeira de Souza Silva (61 Delma Gonçalves "PRETINHA").
(Coach: JORGE BARCELLOS).
Denmark: Heidi ELGAARD-JOHANSEN, Gitte ANDERSEN, Christina Øyangen
ØRNTOFT, Mia Birkehøj BROGAARD Olsen, Julie RYDAHL BUKH (65 Johanna
Maria Baltensberger RASMUSSEN), Catherine PAASKE SØRENSEN, Mariann
GAJHEDE Knudsen (79 Merete PEDERSEN), Camilla SAND ANDERSEN (65
Stine KJÆR DIMUN), Anne DOT EGGERS NIELSEN, Katrine Søndergaard
PEDERSEN *(YC42)*, Maiken With PAPE. (Coach: Kenneth HEINER-MØLLER).
Goal: Delma Gonçalves "PRETINHA" (90+1)
Referee: Kari SEITZ (United States)   Attendance: 43,817

20.09.2007   Tianjin Olympic Center Stadium, Tianjin:
China PR – New Zealand 2-0 (0-0)
China PR: ZHANG Yanru, LI Jie, WANG Kun, PU Wei, ZHOU Gaoping (65 LIU Yali *(YC72)*), XIE Caixia, BI Yan, PAN Lina (60 ZHANG Tong), HAN Duan, ZHANG Ouying (88 LIU Sa), MA Xiaoxu.
(Coach: Marika Susan DOMANSKI LYFORS).
New Zealand: Jenny Lynn BINDON, Rebecca Katie SMITH, Ria PERCIVAL (73 Merissa Louise SMITH), Abby ERCEG, Marlies OOSTDAM, Alexandra RILEY, Maia Giselle JACKMAN, Hayley Rose MOORWOOD *(YC25)*, Priscilla DUNCAN *(YC56)*, Emily McCOLL (82 Simone CARMICHAEL Ferrara), Wendi Judith HENDERSON (62 Zoe Victoria THOMPSON). (Coach: John HERDMAN).
Goals: LI Jie (57), XIE Caixia (79)
Referee: Dagmar DAMKOVA (Czech Republic)   Attendance: 55,832

Team	Pld	W	D	L	GF	GA	GD	Pts
Brazil	*3*	*3*	*0*	*0*	*10*	*0*	*+10*	*9*
China PR	*3*	*2*	*0*	*1*	*5*	*6*	*-1*	*6*
Denmark	3	1	0	2	4	4	0	3
New Zealand	3	0	0	3	0	9	-9	0

QUARTER FINALS

22.09.2007   Wuhan Sports Center Stadium, Wuhan:
Germany – North Korea 3-0 (1-0)
Germany: Nadine ANGERER, Kerstin STEGEMANN, Annike KRAHN, Ariane HINGST, Renate LINGOR, Kerstin GAREFREKES, Melanie BEHRINGER, Linda BRESONIK (77 Sandra MINNERT), Simone LAUDEHR, Birgit PRINZ, Sandra SMISEK (74 Martina MÜLLER). (Coach: Silva NEID).
North Korea: JON Myong-Hui, OM Jong-Ran, SONG Jong-Sun *(YC51)*, SONU Kyong-Sun, KONG Hye-Ok, HONG Myong-Gum (74 JONG Pok-Sim), RI Un-Suk, RI Un-Gyong, KIL Son-Hui, RI Kum-Suk, KIM Yong-Ae (50 KIM Kyong-Hwa). (Coach: KIM Kwang-Min).
Goals: Kerstin GAREFREKES (44), Renate LINGOR (67), Annike KRAHN (72)
Referee: Tammy Nicole OGSTON (Australia)   Attendance: 37,200

22.09.2007   Tianjin Olympic Center Stadium, Tianjin:
United States – England 3-0 (0-0)
United States: Hope Amelia SOLO, Christie PEARCE, Catherine WHITEHILL, Stephanie COX, Kathryn Michele MARKGRAF Sobrero, Shannon BOXX (82 Carli LLOYD), Leslie OSBORNE, Kristine Marie LILLY Heavey, Lori CHALUPNY, Heather O'REILLY, Abby WAMBACH (86 Natasha KAI). (Coach: Greg RYAN).
England: Rachel Laura BROWN, Alexandra SCOTT, Casey STONEY, Faye Deborah WHITE, Mary Rose PHILLIP (80 Lianne SANDERSON), Anita Amma Ankyewah ASANTE, Katie CHAPMAN, Jill SCOTT, Karen CARNEY, Eniola ALUKO (46 Rachel YANKEY), Kelly SMITH. (Coach: Hope Patricia POWELL).
Goals: Abby WAMBACH (48), Shannon BOXX (57), Kristine Marie LILLY Heavey (60)
Referee: Jenny PALMQVIST (Sweden)   Attendance: 29,586

23.09.2007   Wuhan Sports Center Stadium, Wuhan: Norway – China PR 1-0 (1-0)
Norway: Bente NORDBY, Ane STANGELAND Horpestad, Trine RØNNING (YC85), Camilla HUSE, Gunhild Bentzen FØLSTAD (YC59), Ingvild STENSLAND, Leni LARSEN KAURIN (64 Lise KLAVENESS), Marie KNUTSEN, Solveig GULBRANDSEN (75 Lene Glesåsen STORLØKKEN), Ragnhild Øren GULBRANDSEN (YC83), Isabell HERLOVSEN (90+3 Marit Helene Fiane GRØDUM CHRISTENSEN). (Coach: Bjarne BERNTSEN).
China PR: ZHANG Yanru, LI Jie, WANG Kun (YC69), PU Wei, LIU Yali, XIE Caixia (71 ZHANG Ouying), BI Yan, PAN Lina, ZHANG Tong (75 LIU Sa), HAN Duan, MA Xiaoxu. (Coach: Marika Susan DOMANSKI LYFORS).
Goal: Isabell HERLOVSEN (32)
Referee: Gyöngyi Krisztina GAÁL (Hungary)   Attendance: 52,000

23.09.2007   Tianjin Olympic Center Stadium, Tianjin: Brazil – Australia 3-2 (2-1)
Brazil: ANDRÉIA Suntaque, ELAINE Estrela Moura, ALINE Pellegrino, TÂNIA Maria Pereira Ribeiro, Renata Aparecida da Costa "KÓKI", Miraildes Maciel Mota "FORMIGA" (90+2 SIMONE Gomes Jatobá), ESTER Aparecida dos Santos, DANIELA Alves Lima, ANDRÉIA dos Santos, MARTA Vieira da Silva, CRISTIANE Rozeira de Souza Silva. (Coach: JORGE BARCELLOS).
Australia: Melissa BARBIERI HUDSON, Dianne ALAGICH, Cheryl SALISBURY (20 Kate McSHEA), Thea SLATYER, Heather GARRIOCK, Joanne PETERS (YC63) (81 Joanne BURGESS), Sally SHIPARD (78 Caitlin MUNOZ (YC85)), Lauren Elizabeth COLTHORPE, Collette McCALLUM, Sarah WALSH, Lisa DE VANNA. (Coach: Tom SERMANNI).
Goals: Miraildes Maciel Mota "FORMIGA" (4), MARTA Vieira da Silva (23 pen), CRISTIANE Rozeira de Souza Silva (75) / Lisa DE VANNA (36), Lauren Elizabeth COLTHORPE (68)
Referee: Christine BECK (Germany)   Attendance: 35,061

SEMI-FINALS

26.09.2007   Tianjin Olympic Center Stadium, Tianjin: Germany – Norway 3-0 (1-0)
Germany: Nadine ANGERER, Kerstin STEGEMANN, Annike KRAHN, Ariane
HINGST, Renate LINGOR, Kerstin GAREFREKES, Melanie BEHRINGER (40
Fatmire ALUSHI), Linda BRESONIK (81 Sandra MINNERT), Simone LAUDEHR,
Birgit PRINZ, Sandra SMISEK (65 Martina MÜLLER). (Coach: Silva NEID).
Norway: Bente NORDBY, Ane STANGELAND Horpestad, Trine RØNNING,
Camilla HUSE, Gunhild Bentzen FØLSTAD (48 Siri Kristine NORDBY), Ingvild
STENSLAND, Leni LARSEN KAURIN (YC14), Marie KNUTSEN, Solveig
GULBRANDSEN (56 Lene Glesåsen STORLØKKEN), Ragnhild Øren
GULBRANDSEN, Isabell HERLOVSEN (46 Lise KLAVENESS).
(Coach: Bjarne BERNTSEN).
Goals: Trine RØNNING (42 og), Kerstin STEGEMANN (72), Martina MÜLLER
(75)
Referee: Dagmar DAMKOVA (Czech Republic)   Attendance: 53,819

27.09.2007   Yellow Dragon Sports Center, Hangzhou:
       United States – Brazil 0-4 (0-2)
United States: Briana Collette SCURRY, Christie PEARCE, Catherine WHITEHILL,
Stephanie COX (46 Carli LLOYD), Kathryn Michele MARKGRAF Sobrero (74
Marian DOUGHERTY), Shannon BOXX (YC14,YC45+1), Leslie OSBORNE,
Kristine Marie LILLY Heavey, Lori CHALUPNY (YC26), Heather O'REILLY (60
Tina ELLERTSON), Abby WAMBACH (YC49). (Coach: Greg RYAN).
Brazil: ANDRÉIA Suntaque, ELAINE Estrela Moura, ALINE Pellegrino (YC28),
TÂNIA Maria Pereira Ribeiro, Renata Aparecida da Costa "KÓKI" (YC45), Miraildes
Maciel Mota "FORMIGA", ESTER Aparecida dos Santos, DANIELA Alves Lima,
ANDRÉIA dos Santos, MARTA Vieira da Silva, CRISTIANE Rozeira de Souza
Silva. (Coach: JORGE BARCELLOS).
Goals: Leslie OSBORNE (20 og), MARTA Vieira da Silva (27, 79), CRISTIANE
Rozeira de Souza Silva (56)
Referee: Nicole PETIGNAT (Switzerland)   Attendance: 47,818

Sent-off: 45+1' Shannon BOXX.

THIRD PLACE FINAL

30.09.2007 Hongkou Stadium, Shanghai: Norway – United States 1-4 (0-1)
Norway: Bente NORDBY, Marit Helene Fiane GRØDUM CHRISTENSEN, Ane
STANGELAND Horpestad, Camilla HUSE, Gunhild Bentzen FØLSTAD (57
Madeleine GISKE), Ingvild STENSLAND, Marie KNUTSEN, Solveig
GULBRANDSEN, Lene Glesåsen STORLØKKEN (61 Guro KNUTSEN Mienna),
Ragnhild Øren GULBRANDSEN, Lindy Melissa Wiik LØVBRÆK (78 Isabell
HERLOVSEN). (Coach: Bjarne BERNTSEN).
United States: Briana Collette SCURRY, Marian DOUGHERTY, Christie PEARCE
(46 Tina ELLERTSON), Catherine WHITEHILL, Stephanie COX, Alyson Kay (Aly)
WAGNER (59 Lindsay TARPLEY), Leslie OSBORNE, Kristine Marie LILLY
Heavey (89 Natasha KAI), Lori CHALUPNY *(YC28)*, Heather O'REILLY, Abby
WAMBACH. (Coach: Greg RYAN).
Goals: Ragnhild Øren GULBRANDSEN (63) / Abby WAMBACH (30, 46), Lori
CHALUPNY (58), Heather O'REILLY (59)
Referee: Gyöngyi Krisztina GAÁL (Hungary) Attendance: 31,000

FINAL

30.09.2007 Hongkou Stadium, Shanghai: Germany – Brazil 2-0 (0-0)
Germany: Nadine ANGERER, Kerstin STEGEMANN, Annike KRAHN, Ariane
HINGST, Renate LINGOR, Kerstin GAREFREKES *(YC7)*, Melanie BEHRINGER
(74 Martina MÜLLER), Linda BRESONIK *(YC63)*, Simone LAUDEHR, Birgit
PRINZ, Sandra SMISEK (80 Fatmire ALUSHI). (Coach: Silva NEID).
Brazil: ANDRÉIA Suntaque, ELAINE Estrela Moura, ALINE Pellegrino (88 KÁTIA
Cilene Teixeira da Silva), TÂNIA Maria Pereira Ribeiro (81 Delma Gonçalves
"PRETINHA"), Renata Aparecida da Costa "KÓKI", Miraildes Maciel Mota
"FORMIGA", ESTER Aparecida dos Santos (63 ROSANA dos Santos Augusto),
DANIELA Alves Lima *(YC59)*, ANDRÉIA dos Santos, MARTA Vieira da Silva,
CRISTIANE Rozeira de Souza Silva. (Coach: JORGE BARCELLOS).
Goals: Birgit PRINZ (52), Simone LAUDEHR (86)
Referee: Tammy Nicole OGSTON (Australia) Attendance: 31,000

GERMANY BECAME WORLD CHAMPIONS

SIXTH EDITION FIFA WOMEN'S WORLD CUP 2011

QUALIFYING TOURNAMENTS

CAF AFRICAN WOMEN'S CHAMPIONSHIP 2010

The African Women's Championship final tournament was held in South Africa between 31 October and 14 November 2010. The two finalists will qualify for the FIFA Women's World Cup 2011.

PRELIMINARY ROUND

Egypt withdrew, Algeria advanced.
Togo withdrew, Mali advanced.
Kenya withdrew, Eritrea advanced.

06.03.2010   Stade Alassane Djigo, Pikine: Senegal – Morocco 0-0
06.03.2010   Addis Ababa Stadium, Addis Ababa: Ethiopia – Tanzania 1-3 (0-1)
Goals: Yassin (67 pen) / Chabruma (23), Omar (53), Rashid (88)
07.03.2010   Sam Nujoma Stadium, Windhoek: Namibia – Angola 2-1 (0-1)
Goals: Adams (73), Fredericks (85) / Goncalves (37)
07.03.2010   University of Botswana Stadium, Gaborone:
            Botswana – DR Congo 0-2 (0-2)
Goals: Malembo (11), Diantseo (17)
07.03.2010   Stade Augustin Monédan de Sibang, Libreville:
            Gabon – Ivory Coast 1-2 (1-1)
Goals: Glwadis (27) / Bankouly (7), Diakité (90+1)
07.03.2010   Stade du 28 Septembre, Conakry: Guinea – Sierra Leone 3-2 (2-0)
Goals: ?? (1H), ?? (1H), ?? (2H) / Moriba (2H), ?? (2H)
19.03.2010   Stade des Martyrs, Kinshasa: DR Congo – Botswana 5-2 (4-1)
Goals: Malembo (20, 27), Nzuzi (24, 28), Mafutu (88) / Ramasi (21, 55)
19.03.2010   Stade Robert Champroux, Abidjan: Ivory Coast – Gabon 3-1 (2-1)
Goals: Rachelle (3, 31, 46) / Mapangou (8)
20.03.2010   Stade Abou Bakr Ammar, Salé: Morocco – Senegal 0-1 (0-1)
Goal: Ndiaye (10)
20.03.2010   National Stadium, Freetown: Sierra Leone – Guinea 1-1
20.03.2010   Uhuru Stadium, Dar es Salaam: Tanzania – Ethiopia 1-1 (0-0)
Goals: Rashid (77) / Ware (73)
21.03.2010   Ombaka National Stadium, Benguela: Angola – Namibia 1-1 (0-0)
Goals: Goncalves (51) / Kleihtjia (87)

FIRST ROUND

21.05.2010   Stade des Martyrs, Kinshasa: DR Congo – Cameroon 0-2 (0-2)
Goals: Mani (4), Mbella (35)

22.05.2010   Stade de Koléa, Koléa: Algeria – Tunesia 1-1 (0-0)
Goals: Laouadi (90+4) / Chebbi (73 pen)
22.05.2010   Stade Demba Diop, Dakar: Senegal – Ghana 0-1 (0-1)
Goal: Ankomah (43)
23.05.2010   Sam Nujoma Stadium, Windhoek:
             Namibia – Equatorial Guinea 1-5 (1-5)
Goals: Skrywer (3) / Carol (19, 36), Añonma (25), Simporé (42), Chinasa (45+1)
*The return match was called of due to inability of the Namibian side to obtain
transport to Equatorial Guinea after their initial flight was cancelled. Equatorial
Guinea advanced*
23.05.2010   Stade Robert Champroux, Abidjan: Ivory Coast – Nigeria 1-2 (0-2)
Goals: N'Guessan (78) / Nkwocha (21), Ohadugha (45+1)
23.05.2010   Stade du 28 Septembre, Conakry: Guinea – Mali 0-2 (0-1)
Goals: Sako (43 og), Touré (90)
23.05.2010   Uhuru Stadium, Dar es Salaam: Tanzania – Eritrea 8-1 (5-0)
Goals: Omary (6, 27, 64, 80), Mwasikili (19), Rashidi (21, 60, 74) / Ghebresa (90)
05.06.2010   Stade El Menzah, Tunis: Tunesia – Algeria 0-1 (0-0)
Goal: Wadah (65)
05.06.2010   Stade Ahmadou Ahidjo, Yaoundé: Cameroon – DR Congo 3-0 (2-0)
Goals: Mani (23), Enganamouit (45), Onguene (86)
05.06.2010   Abuja National Stadium, Abuja: Nigeria – Ivory Coast 3-1 (1-0)
Goals: Chikwelu (13), Nkwocha (72, 89) / Diakité (50)
05.06.2010   Bamako: Mali – Guinea 1-2
05.06.2010   Cicero Stadium, Asmara: Eritrea – Tanzania 3-3 (1-0)
Goals: Mehari (1), Zerihani (48, 52) / Rashidi (76, 78, 88)
06.06.2010   Ohene Djan Stadium, Accra: Ghana – Senegal 3-0 (2-0)
Goals: Boakye (23), Ankomah (34), Okoe (65)

FINAL TOURNAMENT

The Final Tournament was held in Gauteng, South Africa between 31 October and 14
November 2010.

GROUP A

31.10.2010   Sinaba Stadium, Daveyton: South Africa – Tanzania 2-1 (1-1)
Goals: Popela (35), Mamello (87 pen) / Chabruma (43)
01.11.2010   Sinaba Stadium, Daveyton: Nigeria – Mali 5-0 (3-0)
Goals: Nkwocha (15, 16, 42), Mbachu (70), Ordega (84)
04.11.2010   Sinaba Stadium, Daveyton: South Africa – Nigeria 1-2 (1-2)
Goals: van Wyk (44) / Nkwocha (33, 39)
04.11.2010   Sinaba Stadium, Daveyton: Mali – Tanzania 3-2 (2-2)
Goals: Konate (25), Diarra (31), N'Diaye (67) / Mwasikili (30), Swalehe (32)
07.11.2010   Sinaba Stadium, Daveyton: Mali – South Africa 0-4 (0-1)
Goals: Amanda (32, 76, 90), Jermaine (84)
07.11.2010   Makhulong Stadium, Tembesa: Tanzania – Nigeria 0-3 (0-2)
Goals: Nkwocha (12, 32), Oparanozie (82)

Team	Pld	W	D	L	GF	GA	GD	Pts
Nigeria	*3*	*3*	*0*	*0*	*10*	*1*	*+9*	*9*
South Africa	*3*	*2*	*0*	*1*	*7*	*3*	*+4*	*6*
Mali	3	1	0	2	3	11	-8	3
Tanzania	3	0	0	3	3	8	-5	0

GROUP B

02.11.2010 Sinaba Stadium, Daveyton: Equatorial Guinea – Cameroon 2-2 (2-1)
Goals: Jade (2), Jumária (30) / Patience (45+1), Michele (57)
02.11.2010 Sinaba Stadium, Daveyton: Algeria – Ghana 1-2 (1-0)
Goals: Ouadah (4) / Agnes (62, 73)
05.11.2010 Sinaba Stadium, Daveyton: Equatorial Guinea – Algeria 1-0 (1-0)
Goal: Chinasa (31)
05.11.2010 Sinaba Stadium, Daveyton: Ghana – Cameroon 1-2 (1-2)
Goals: Agnes (31) / Manie (24), Ngo-Ndoumbouk (37)
08.11.2010 Sinaba Stadium, Daveyton: Ghana – Equatorial Guinea 1-3 (1-1)
Goals: Agnes (40 pen) / Añonma (12 pen), S.Simporé (58), Chinasa (68)
08.11.2010 Makhulong Stadium, Tembisa: Cameroon – Algeria 2-1 (0-0)
Goals: Onguene (50), Ejangue (65) / Bouhenni (55)

Team	Pld	W	D	L	GF	GA	GD	Pts
Equatorial Guinea	*3*	*2*	*1*	*0*	*6*	*3*	*+3*	*7*
Cameroon	*3*	*2*	*1*	*0*	*6*	*4*	*+2*	*7*
Ghana	3	1	0	2	4	6	-2	3
Algeria	3	0	0	3	2	5	-3	0

KNOCKOUT STAGES
SEMI-FINALS

11.11.2010 Sinaba Stadium, Daveyton: Nigeria – Cameroon 5-1 (2-0)
Goals: Helen Ukaonu (33), Oparanozie (45+1), Nkwocha (58, 74, 81 pen) /
Ngock (47)
11.11.2010 Sinaba Stadium, Daveyton:
          Equatorial Guinea – South Africa 3-1 (0-0,0-0) (a.e.t.)
Goals: S.Simporé (103, 120+5), Jade (109) / Dlamini (120+8)

THIRD PLACE PLAY-OFF

14.11.2010 Sinaba Stadium, Daveyton: Cameroon – South Africa 0-2 (0-2)
Goals: Skiti (8), Dlamini (38)

FINAL

14.11.2010 Sinaba Stadium, Daveyton: Nigeria – Equatorial Guinea 4-2 (1-0)
Goals: Nkwocha (8), Oparanozie (76), Nke (77 og), Carol (84 og) / Carol 62,
Jade (81)

129

The winner **Nigeria** and the runner-up **Equatorial Guinea** qualified for the FIFA Women's World Cup 2011.

AFC WOMEN'S ASIAN CUP 2010

North Korea, China PR, Australia, Japan and South Korea were automatic qualified for the Final Tournament which was held in Chengdu, China PR between 19 & 30 May 2010. The winner, runner-up and the third-place team will qualify for the FIFA Women's World Cup 2011.

QUALIFICATION
FIRST ROUND

Myanmar, Chinese Taipei, Thailand, Iran, Vietnam and Hong Kong had a bye to the Second Round. Bangladesh withdrew before the start of qualification. The First Round was held in Kuala Lumpur, Malaysia and was played between 25 April and 3 May 2009.

25.04.2009   KLFA Stadium, Kuala Lumpur: Kyrgyzstan – Jordan 1-7 (0-6)
Goals: Pokachalova (75) / Al-Azab (1), Al-Naber (11, 38), Taalaibek (14 og), Jbarah (18, 36), Jebreen (90+2)
25.04.2009   KLFA Stadium, Kuala Lumpur: Palestine – Maldives 4-0 (2-0)
Goals: Sohgian (40), Hussein (45, 53), Jorban (60)
27.04.2009   KLFA Stadium, Kuala Lumpur: Maldives – Uzbekistan 0-5 (0-4)
Goals: Sarikova (7), Usmanova (14), Abdurasulova (28 pen, 31, 75)
27.04.2009   KLFA Stadium, Kuala Lumpur: Palestine – Kyrgyzstan 1-4 (0-1)
Goals: Shaheen (90) / Litvinenko (7, 53, 81), Pokachalova (55)
29.04.2009   KLFA Stadium, Kuala Lumpur: Uzbekistan – Palestine 5-0 (3-0)
Goals: Abdurasulova (10, 14, 85), Sarikova (42), Senina (74)
29.04.2009   KLFA Stadium, Kuala Lumpur: Jordan – Maldives 9-0 (4-0)
Goals: Al-Nahar (9, 26, 67), Jbarah (15, 27), Al-Naber (52, 50, 71 pen, 90+2)
01.05.2009   KLFA Stadium, Kuala Lumpur: Jordan – Palestine 5-0 (4-0)
Goals:Al-Naber (24, 50), Jbarah (35, 42), Al-Âzb (44)
01.05.2009   KLFA Stadium, Kuala Lumpur: Kyrgyzstan – Uzbekistan 0-2 (0-0)
Goals: Umanova (75), Abdurasulova (90+2)
03.05.2009   KLFA Stadium, Kuala Lumpur: Maldives – Kyrgyzstan 0-2 (0-1)
Goals: Pokachalova (8, 90+1)
03.05.2009   KLFA Stadium, Kuala Lumpur: Uzbekistan – Jordan 2-2 (1-1)
Goals: Turapova (24), Sarikova (56) / Al-Naber (31 pen), Jbarah (74)

Team	Pld	W	D	L	GF	GA	GD	Pts
Jordan	*4*	*3*	*1*	*0*	*23*	*3*	*+20*	*10*
Uzbekistan	*4*	*3*	*1*	*0*	*14*	*2*	*+12*	*10*
Kyrgyzstan	*4*	*2*	*0*	*2*	*7*	*10*	*-3*	*6*
Palestine	4	1	0	3	5	14	-9	3
Maldives	4	0	0	4	0	20	-20	0

SECOND ROUND
GROUP A

All matches in Group A were played in Hsinying City, Chinese Taipei.

10.07.2009   Tainan County Stadium, Hsinying City:
             Jordan – Chinese Taipei 1-0 (0-0)
Goal: Jebreen (74)
12.07.2009   Tainan County Stadium, Hsinying City: Myanmar – Jordan 3-0 (2-0)
Goals: Khin Mariar Tun (18), Than Than Htwe (33), Myint Myint Aye (57)
14.07.2009   Tainan County Stadium, Hsinying City:
             Chinese Taipei – Myanmar 2-5 (1-2)
Goals: Tsai Hsin-Yun (21), Lin Man-Ting (68) / Aye Nandar Hlaing (10), My Nilar
Htwe (34, 50, 76), Khin Marlar Tun (48)

Team	Pld	W	D	L	GF	GA	GD	Pts
Myanmar	*2*	*2*	*0*	*0*	*8*	*2*	*+6*	*6*
Jordan	2	1	0	1	1	3	-2	3
Chinese Taipei	2	0	0	2	2	6	-4	0

GROUP B

All matches were played in Bangkok, Thailand.

04.07.2009   Rajamangala Stadium, Bangkok: Uzbekistan – Thailand 1-6 (1-1)
Goals: Abdurasulova (15) / Maijarern (9, 77), Romyen (57, 64), Seesraum (89, 90+1)
06.07.2009   Rajamangala Stadium, Bangkok: Iran – Uzbekistan 1-4 (0-1)
Goals: Karimi (51) / Abdurasulova (8), Juraeva (70), Usmanova (76, 78)
08.07.2009   Rajamangala Stadium, Bangkok: Thailand – Iran 8-1 (4-1)
Goals: Chawong (14), Romyen (21, 49, 63), Maijarem (37, 42), Seesraum (70),
Peangthem (90+2) / Karimi (45+1)

Team	Pld	W	D	L	GF	GA	GD	Pts
Thailand	*2*	*2*	*0*	*0*	*14*	*2*	*+12*	*6*
Uzbekistan	2	1	0	1	5	7	-2	3
Iran	2	0	0	2	2	12	-10	0

GROUP C

All matches were played in Ho Chi Minh City, Vietnam.

04.07.2009   Thánh Long Sports Centre, Ho Chi Minh City:
             Kyrgyzstan – Vietnam 1-10 (0-4)
Goals: Pokachalova (78 pen) / Kim Chi (10), Ngoc Châm (21, 24, 57, 62, 72, 87),
Nguyen Thi Nga (28), Minh Nguyêt (59), Lê Thi Oanh (83)
06.07.2009   Thánh Long Sports Centre, Ho Chi Minh City:
             Hong Kong – Kyrgyzstan 2-0 (0-0)
Goals: Fung Kam Mui (48), Ng Wing Kum (50)

131

08.07.2009   Thánh Long Sports Centre, Ho Chi Minh City:
Vietnam – Hong Kong 7-0 (4-0)
Goals: Van Thi Thanh (9, 23), Do Thi Ngoc Châm (11, 39, 70), Doàn Thi Kim Chi
(56), Nguyen Thi Muôn (80)

Team	Pld	W	D	L	GF	GA	GD	Pts
Vietnam	*2*	*2*	*0*	*0*	*17*	*1*	*+16*	*6*
Hong Kong	2	1	0	1	2	7	-5	3
Kyrgyzstan	2	0	0	2	1	12	-11	0

The three group winners Myanmar, Thailand and Vietnam qualified for the Final
tournament.

FINAL TOURNAMENT
GROUP STAGES

The Final Tournament was held in Chengdu, China PR between 19 & 30 May 2010.

GROUP A

20.05.2010   Chengdu Sports Center, Chengdu: North Korea – Thailand 3-0 (2-0)
Goals: Jon Myong-hwa (1), Kim Yong-ae (2), Jo Yun-mi (73)
20.05.2010   Chengdu Sports Center, Chengdu: Japan – Myanmar 8-0 (3-0)
Goals: Azusa Iwashimizu (4), Homare Sawa (10, 71), Mami Yamaguchi (28 pen, 60),
Aya Sameshima (50), Aya Miyama (54), Megumi Kamionobe (85)
22.05.2010   Chengdu Sports Center, Chengdu: Thailand – Japan 0-4 (0-3)
Goals: Megumi Takase (28), Manami Nakano (42), Rumi Utsugi (45+3),
Kozue Ando (55)
22.05.2010   Chengdu Sports Center, Chengdu: Myanmar – North Korea 0-2 (0-1)
Goals: Yun Song-mi (17), Jo Yun-mi (84)
24.05.2010   Chengdu Sports Center, Chengdu: North Korea – Japan 1-2 (0-2)
Goals: Ra Un-sim (70) / Kozue Ando (4 pen), Yuki Nagasato (14)
24.05.2010   Shuangliu Sports Centre Stadium, Chengdu: Myanmar – Thailand 0-2
(0-1)
Goals: Junpen Seesraum (15), Waranya Chaikantree (89)

Team	Pld	W	D	L	GF	GA	GD	Pts
Japan	*3*	*3*	*0*	*0*	*14*	*1*	*+13*	*9*
North Korea	*3*	*2*	*0*	*1*	*6*	*2*	*+4*	*6*
Thailand	3	1	0	2	2	7	-5	3
Myanmar	3	0	0	3	0	12	-12	0

GROUP B

19.05.2010   Chengdu Sports Center, Chengdu: Australia – Vietnam 2-0 (1-0)
Goals: Leena Khamis (29), Kylie Ledbrook (51 pen)
19.05.2010   Chengdu Sports Center, Chengdu: China PR – South Korea 0-0
21.05.2010   Chengdu Sports Center, Chengdu: South Korea – Australia 1-3 (0-0)

Goals: Kang Sun-mi (71) / Kim Carroll (52), Lisa De Vanna (59), Samantha Kerr (66)
21.05.2010   Shuangliu Sports Centre Stadium, Chengdu:
            Vietnam – China PR 0-5 (0-4)
Goals: Li Danyang (8), Yuan Fan (12), Zhang Rui (37), Bi Yan (45+1 pen),
Han Duan (51)
23.05.2010   Chengdu Sports Center, Chengdu: China PR – Australia 1-0 (1-0)
Goal: Zhang Rui (9)
23.05.2010   Shuangliu Sports Centre Stadium, Chengdu:
            Vietnam – South Korea 0-5 (0-4)
Goals: Yoo Young-a (20, 21, 66), Cha Yun-hee (28), Jung Hye-in (36)

Team	Pld	W	D	L	GF	GA	GD	Pts
China PR	3	2	1	0	6	0	+6	7
Australia	3	2	0	1	5	2	+3	6
South Korea	3	1	1	1	6	3	+3	4
Vietnam	3	0	0	3	0	12	-12	0

KNOCKOUT STAGES
SEMI-FINALS

27.05.2010   Chengdu Sports Center, Chengdu: Japan – Australia 0-1 (0-1)
Goal: Kate Gill (45+1)
27.05.2010   Chengdu Sports Center, Chengdu:
            China PR – North Korea 0-1 (0-0,0-0) (a.e.t.)
Goal: Kim Kyong-hwa (109)

THIRD PLACE PLAY-OFF

30.05.2010   Chengdu Sports Center, Chengdu: Japan – China PR 2-0 (1-0)
Goals: Kozue Ando (18), Homare Sawa (62)

FINAL

30.05.2010   Chengdu Sports Center, Chengdu:
            Australia – North Korea 1-1 (1-0,1-1) (a.e.t.)
Goals: Samantha Kerr (19) / Jo Yun-mi (73)

Australia won after extra time on penalties (5:4).

The winner **Australia**, the runner-up **North Korea** and the third-place team **Japan**
qualified for the FIFA Women's World Cup 2011.

UEFA WOMEN'S WORLD CUP QUALIFICATION 2011

Forty-one teams from Europe were drawn into eight groups. These groups were
played between August 2009 and August 2010. The group winners advanced to four
home-and-away play-offs, which were palyed in September 2010, with the winners
advancing to the World Cup finals. The four losing teams competed in repechage

133

play-offs the following month to determine a team to play against the third-place CONCACAF team for the 16th place in the finals.

QUALIFYING ROUND
GROUP 1

15.08.2009   Laugardalsvöllur, Reykjavik: Iceland – Serbia 5-0 (1-0)
Goals: M.Vidarsdóttir (32, 49, 72, 84), K.Jónsdóttir (80)
17.09.2009   Laugardalsvöllur, Reykjavik: Iceland – Estonia 12-0 (7-0)
Goals: M.Vídarsdóttir (4, 9 pen, 38), Lárusdóttir (7), K.Jónsdóttir (16, 18), Gardarsdóttir (33), Magnúsdóttir (49, 64, 74), S.Gunnarsdóttir (54), Hönnudóttir (76)
23.09.2009   Stadion NK Inter Zapresic, Zapresic: Croatia – France 0-7 (0-3)
Goals: Soubeyrand (25), Franco (38, 55), Delie (45+2), Le Sommer (65), Abily (73), Thomis (90+3)
26.09.2009   Masinac Stadium, Nis: Serbia – Croatia 1-1 (0-1)
Goals: Pesic (54) / Joscak (22)
24.10.2009   Stadion NK Inter Zapresic, Zapresic:
             Croatia – Northern Ireland 0-1 (0-1)
Goal: Furness (26)
24.10.2009   Stade de Gerland, Lyon: France – Iceland 2-0 (1-0)
Goals: Thiney (23), Thomis (79)
28.10.2009   Stade Jules Deschaseaux, Le Havre: France – Estonia 12-0 (6-0)
Goals: Herbert (27, 57), Necib (31), Abily (36), Thiney (37, 41, 47), Franco (40), Thomis (79), Delie (80, 90+1), Prants (90+4 og)
28.10.2009   The Oval, Belfast: Northern Ireland – Iceland 0-1 (0-0)
Goal: Ómarsdóttir (79)
21.11.2009   Stadion FK Indjija, Indjija: Serbia – France 0-2 (0-2)
Goals: Thiney (27), Abily (45+3)
27.03.2010   Mirko Vucurevic Stadium, Banatski Dvor: Serbia – Iceland 0-2 (0-0)
Goals: Magnúsdóttir (52, 81)
27.03.2010   Gradski Stadion kraj Sajmista, Vrbovec: Coratia – Estonia 0-3 (0-2)
Goals: Aarna (10, 84), Morkovkina (33)
27.03.2010   Stade de la Libération, Boulogne-sur-Mer:
             France – Northern Ireland 6-0 (2-0)
Goals: Franco (31), Bompastor (34), Le Sommer (47), Delie (50), Necib (54), Hutton (71 og)
31.03.2010   Mirko Vucurevic Stadium, Banatski Dvor: Serbia – Estonia 4-0 (1-0)
Goals: Damnjanovic (14), Sretenovic (54), Stojkanovic (73), Podovac (89)
31.03.2010   Gradski Stadion kraj Sajmista, Vrbovec: Croatia – Iceland 0-3 (0-2)
Goals: K.Jónsdóttir (3), M.Vidarsdóttir (37), Logadóttir (84)
31.03.2010   Windsor Park, Belfast: Northern Ireland – France 0-4 (0-2)
Goals: Bompastor (17), Abily (19), Le Sommer (52), Delie (90)
09.05.2010   Gradski Stadion kraj Sajmista, Vrbovec: Croatia – Serbia 1-2 (1-1)
Goals: Bokanovic (39) / Damnjanovic (13), Krstic (54)
05.06.2010   Kadrioru Stadium, Tallinn: Estonia – Northern Ireland 2-1 (2-0)
Goals: Morkovkina (15), Palmaru (30) / Hurst (59)
19.06.2010   Rakvere Linnastaadion, Rakvere: Estonia – Serbia 1-0 (0-0)
Goal: Paulus (61)

134

19.06.2010   Laugardalsvöllur, Reykjavik: Iceland – Northern Ireland 2-0 (1-0)
Goals: S.Gunnarsdóttir (15), K.Jónsdóttir (59)
20.06.2010   Stade Léo Lagrange, Besançon: France – Croatia 3-0 (1-0)
Goals: Thiney (22), Le Sommer (57), Delie (62)
22.06.2010   Laugardalsvöllur, Reykjavik: Iceland – Croatia 3-0 (2-0)
Goals: Magnúsdóttir (20, 42), K.Jónsdóttir (75)
23.06.2010   Kadrioru Stadium, Tallinn: Estonia – France 0-6 (0-1)
Goals: Thiney (21), Thomis (53), Bussaglia (54), Le Sommer (60), Delie (61, 90)
23.06.2010   The Showgrounds, Coleraine: Northern Ireland – Serbia 0-0
24.07.2010   The Showgrounds, Coleraine: Northern Ireland – Estonia 3-0 (0-0)
Goals: McKenna (53, 62), Nelson (69)
21.08.2010   Vasariste, Pozarevac: Serbia – Northern Ireland 0-0
21.08.2010   Laugardalsvöllur, Reykjavik: Iceland – France 0-1 (0-0)
Goal: Thiney (60)
22.08.2010   A. Le Coq Arena, Tallinn: Estonia – Croatia 1-1 (1-0)
Goals: Palmaru (16) / Lojna (81)
25.08.2010   Rakvere Linnastaadion, Rakvere: Estonia – Iceland 0-5 (0-2)
Goals: M.Vidarsdóttir (9, 17), S.Gunnarsdóttir (56, 86), Morkovkina (58 og)
25.08.2010   Stade de l'Aube, Troyes: France – Serbia 7-0 (3-0)
Goals: Thomis (5), Thiney (32, 63, 87), Bussaglia (45), Delie (60), Abily (79)
25.08.2010   The Oval, Belfast: Northern Ireland – Croatia 3-1 (1-0)
Goals: Furness (1, 51, 59) / Landeka (50)

Team	Pld	W	D	L	GF	GA	GD	Pts
France	*10*	*10*	*0*	*0*	*50*	*0*	*+50*	*30*
Iceland	10	8	0	2	33	3	+30	24
Northern Ireland	10	3	2	5	8	16	-8	11
Estonia	10	3	1	6	7	44	-37	10
Serbia	10	2	3	5	7	19	-12	9
Croatia	10	0	2	8	4	27	-23	2

GROUP 2

19-09-2009   NTC Stadion, Senec: Slovakia – Macedonia 9-0 (5-0)
Goals: Budosová (9), Fecková (31, 42, 65, 70, 73), Klechová (36, 39 pen),
Ondrusová (55)
24.10.2009   Nadderud stadion, Bærum: Norway – Netherlands 3-0 (2-0)
Goals: Rønning (44 pen), Gulbrandsen (45+1), Herlovsen (87)
25.10.2009   Gradski Stadion, Kumanovo: Macedonia – Belarus 1-6 (0-3)
Goals: Spirovska (51) / Lis (3), Aukhimovich (5, 65), Vasilyeva (12), Krylowa (90+1
pen), Pilipenka (90+3)
28.10.2009   Skagerak Arena, Skien: Norway – Slovakia 1-0 (0-0)
Goal: Bíróová (51 og)
29.10.2009   Oosterenkstadion, Zwolle: Netherlands – Macedonia 13-1 (6-0)
Goals: Kiesel-Griffioen (9, 36, 67, 78), Smit (11, 38, 41, 83, 87, 90+2), Melis (30),
Koster (53), Spitse (62) / Salihi (74)
21.11.2009   Den Haag Stadion, The Hague: Netherlands – Belarus 1-1 (1-0)
Goals: Slegers (22) / Aukhimovich (63)

27.03.2010   AKA Arena, Hønefoss: Norway – Macedonia 14-0 (8-0)
Goals: Herlovsen (1, 16, 17, 41, 74, 81), Rønning (13), Stensland (21), Mykjåland (25, 90+1), Klaveness (26), Pedersen (71), Woods (80, 90+3)
27.03.2010   Polman Stadion, Almelo: Netherlands – Slovakia 2-0 (1-0)
Goals: Smit (16 pen), Koster (78)
30.03.2010   Neman Stadium, Grodno: Belarus – Norway 0-5 (0-2)
Goals: Giske (24), Klaveness (33), Herlovsen (57), Mykjåland (64), Gulbrandsen (74)
01.04.2010   NTC Stadion, Senec: Slovakia – Netherlands 0-1 (0-0)
Goal: Kiesel-Griffioen (90+2)
22.04.2010   Gradski Stadion, Kumanovo: Macedonia – Netherlands 0-7 (0-6)
Goals: Hoogendijk (2), Pieëte (4), Smit (7), Meulen (21), Melis (23), de Ridder (44), Slegers (84)
28.04.2010   City Stadium, Molodechno: Belarus – Macedonia 6-0 (2-0)
Goals: Lis (18, 20, 66), Shramok (53), Nikolaeva (77), Buzinova (81)
19.06.2010   Stadión FC ViOn, Zlaté Moravce: Slovakia – Belarus 0-2 (0-2)
Goals: Aukhimovich (22), Krylova (40)
19.06.2010   Oosternenstadion, Zwolle: Netherlands – Norway 2-2 (1-1)
Goals: Melis (2), Dekker (80) / Herlovsen (5), Vikestad (48)
23.06.2010   Goce Delcev Stadium, Prilep: Macedonia – Slovakia 1-6 (0-2)
Goals: Andonova (90) / Klechová (11), Fecková (45+2), Budosová (57), Harsányová (61, 70), Kolenová (63)
23.06.2010   Skagerak Arena, Skien: Norway – Belarus 3-0 (1-0)
Goals: Klaveness (11), Woods (64), Haavi (88)
21.08.2010   NTC Stadion, Senec: Slovakia – Norway 0-4 (0-3)
Goals: Rønning (22 pen), Gulbrandsen (28), Woods (34), Korenciová (78 og)
21.08.2010   City Stadium, Molodechno: Belarus – Netherlands 0-4 (0-1)
Goals: van de Ven (21), Melis (55, 60), de Ridder (70)
25.08.2010   City Stadium, Molodechno: Belarus – Slovakia 2-0 (0-0)
Goals: Urazaeva (66), Lis (79)
25.08.2010   Goce Delcev Stadium, Prilep: Macedonia – Norway 0-7 (0-4)
Goals: Haavi (25, 68), Woods (28), Stensland (36), Thorsnes (43), Gulbrandsen (73), Rønning (78)

Team	Pld	W	D	L	GF	GA	GD	Pts
Norway	*8*	*7*	*1*	*0*	*39*	*2*	*+37*	*22*
Netherlands	8	5	2	1	30	7	+23	17
Belarus	8	4	1	3	17	14	+3	13
Slovakia	8	2	0	6	15	13	+2	6
Macedonia	8	0	0	8	3	68	-65	0

GROUP 3

23.09.2009   Yiannis Pathiakakis Stadium, Ano Liossia: Greece – Denmark 0-6 (0-4)
Goals: Paaske-Sørensen (12, 71), Veje (17), Pape (23), Sand Andersen (25), Rydahl Bukh (59)
21.10.2009   Gradski Lovech Stadium, Lovech: Bulgaria – Greece 0-1 (0-0)
Goal: Panteleiadou (53)

24.10.2009   Vejle Stadion, Vejle: Denmark – Georgia 15-0 (7-0)
Goals: Sand Andersen (13, 56), J.Rasmussen (17, 52), Harder (21, 44, 74), Munk (28, 32, 48), Veje (38), Brogaard (53, 81 pen), Troelsgaard Nielsen (84, 90+2)
24.10.2009   Yiannis Pathiakakis Stadium, Ano Liossia: Greece – Scotland 0-1 (0-0)
Goal: Beattie (53)
28.10.2009   Gradski Lovech Stadium, Lovech: Bulgaria – Denmark 0-0
29.10.2009   Tynecastle Stadium, Edinburgh: Scotland – Georgia 3-1 (0-0)
Goals: Grant (50, 80), Little (51) / Pogosian (59)
21.11.2009   Gradski Lovech Stadium, Lovech: Bulgaria – Georgia 5-0 (2-0)
Goals: Nadirashvili (28 og), Pasikashvili (31 og), Kostova (51), Boyanova (65), Gospodinova (90+1)
26.11.2009   Michalis Kritikopoulos Stadium, Athens: Greece – Georgia 5-0 (2-0)
Goals: Katsaiti (31 pen), Kontomichi (42, 67, 70), Papadopoulou (53)
27.03.2010   Mikheil Meskhi Stadium, Tbilisi: Georgia – Scotland 1-3 (1-1)
Goals: Chichinadze (21) / Beattie (45+4), Corsie (52), Ross (82)
27.03.2010   Vejle Stadion, Vejle: Denmark – Bulgaria 9-0 (5-0)
Goals: J.Rasmussen (6, 21), K.Søndergaard Pedersen (10), Munk (37), Troelsgaard Nielsen (45), Paaske-Sørensen (53 pen, 78), J.Jensen (55), Pedersen (90)
01.04.2010   Mikheil Meskhi Stadium, Tbilisi: Georgia – Denmark 0-7 (0-4)
Goals: J.Rasmussen (11, 33, 39, 52), Paaske-Sørensen (31, 87), Røddik Hansen (90 pen)
01.04.2010   Falkirk Stadium, Falkirk: Scotland – Bulgaria 8-1 (2-1)
Goals: Little (39, 87), Hamill (40), Fleeting (53, 58, 64, 90), Grant (60) / Liliane Kostova (21)
15.04.2010   Mikheil Meskhi Stadium, Tbilisi: Georgia – Greece 0-3 (0-2)
Goals: Gkatzogianni (23), Chalkiadaki (28), Sidira (60)
19.06.2010   Vejle Stadion, Vejle: Denmark – Greece 7-0 (2-0)
Goals: Røddik Hansen (7), J.Rasmussen (45+1, 80), Pape (49 pen), Kakambouki (50 og), Paaske-Sørensen (77), Gajhede (79)
19.06.2010   Georgi Asparuhov Stadium, Sofia: Bulgaria – Scotland 0-5 (0-2)
Goals: Beattie (17), Fleeting (35), Little (62 pen), Corsie (66), Hamill (90+2)
24.06.2010   Rugby Park, Kilmarnock: Scotland – Denmark 0-1 (0-1)
Goal: Røddik Hansen (22)
21.08.2010   Mikheil Meskhi Stadium, Tbilisi: Georgia – Bulgaria 1-1 (1-0)
Goals: Matveeva (24) / Koshuleva (50)
21.08.2010   Strathclyde Homes Stadium, Dumbarton: Scotland – Greece 4-1 (2-1)
Goals: Beattie (22), Fleeting (24), Corsie (81), Grant (83) / Sidira (6 pen)
25.08.2010   Municipal Stadium Arta, Arta: Greece – Bulgaria 1-2 (1-0)
Goals: Kakambouki (5) / Radoyska (69), Kostova (80 pen)
25.08.2010   Vejle Stadion, Vejle: Denmark – Scotland 0-0

Team	Pld	W	D	L	GF	GA	GD	Pts
Denmark	*8*	*6*	*2*	*0*	*45*	*0*	*+45*	*20*
Scotland	8	6	1	1	24	5	+19	19
Greece	8	3	0	5	11	20	-9	9
Bulgaria	8	2	2	4	9	25	-16	8
Georgia	8	0	1	7	3	42	-39	1

GROUP 4

19.09.2009   Stadion im. Ojca Wladyslawa Augustynka, Nowy Sacz:
Poland – Ukraine 4-1 (3-0)
Goals: Winczo (7, 30, 55), Lesnik (38) / Pekur (83)
19.09.2009   Asim Ferhatovic Hase Stadium, Sarajevo:
Bosnia and Herzegovina – Hungary 0-2 (0-0)
Goals: Padár (77), Krenács (84)
23.09.2009   Stadionul Buftea, Buftea: Romania – Bornia and Herzegovina 4-0 (3-0)
Goals: Pavel (37 pen), Dusa (42, 45), Spânu (65)
24.09.2009   Stadion Városi, Sopron: Hungary – Poland 4-2 (1-1)
Goals: Méry (34), Tóth (67), Padár (87), Vagó (90+2 pen) / Zyla (25), Pozerska (52)
24.10.2009   Stadion Dyskobolii, Grodzisk Wielkopolski: Poland – Romania 2-0 (1-0)
Goals: Winczo (19), Zelazko (71)
25.10.2009   Stadion Yuri Gagarin, Chernihiv:
Ukraine – Bosnia and Herzegovina 7-0 (6-0)
Goals: Pekur (9, 43), Apanaschenko (13, 42), Dyatel (36), Khodyreva (41),
Chorna (48)
28.10.2009   Stadion Városi, Sopron: Hungary – Romania 1-1 (0-0)
Goals: Méry (82) / Dusa (68)
29.10.2009   Asim Ferhatovic Hase Stadium, Sarajevo:
Bosnia and Herzegovina – Poland 0-4 (0-1)
Goals: Stobba (24), Zyla (47), Tarczynska (55), Pozerska (70)
14.11.2009   Stadion Városi, Sopron: Hungary – Ukraine 1-1 (1-0)
Goals: Jakabfi (16) / Chorna (63)
27.03.2010   Asim Ferhatovic Hase Stadium, Sarajevo:
Bosnia and Herzegovina – Romania 0-5 (0-1)
Goals: Vatafu (25), Dusa (50), Rus (65), Laiu (66), Sarghe (77)
31.03.2010   Stadionul Mogosoaia, Mogosoaia: Romania – Poland 1-4 (1-2)
Goals: Laiu (39) / Winczo (13, 63, 82), Tarczynska (29)
31.03.2010   Stadion Városi, Sopron: Hungary – Bosnia and Herzegovina 2-0 (2-0)
Goals: Vágó (9), Pádár (37)
20.05.2010   Stadion Yuri Gagarin, Chernihiv: Ukraine – Hunagry 4-2 (2-1)
Goals: Apanaschenko (6, 36), Khodyreva (81), Boychenko (85) / Jakabfi (38, 71)
19.06.2010   Asim Ferhatovic Hase Stadium, Sarajevo:
Bosnia and Herzegovina – Ukraine 0-5 (0-2)
Goals: Apanaschenko (11, 57), Dyatel (23), Boychenko (73, 77)
19.06.2010   Arena Kielc, Kielce: Poland – Hungary 0-0
23.06.2010   Stadionul Mogosoaia, Mogosoaia: Romania – Ukraine 0-0
24.06.2010   OSiR-u, Racibórz: Poland – Bosnia and Herzegovina 1-0 (0-0)
Goal: Pozerska (74)
21.08.2010   Stadion Yuri Gagarin, Chernihiv: Ukraine – Romania 3-1 (1-0)
Goals: Apanaschenko (24, 66), Boychenko (49) / Dusa (56)
25.08.2010   Stadionul Mogosoaia, Mogosoaia: Romania – Hunagry 2-3 (1-2)
Goals: Spanu (38), Olar (48) / Jakabfi (15, 34, 90+1 pen)
25.08.2010   Stadion Yuri Gagarin, Chernihiv: Ukraine – Poland 3-1 (0-1)
Goals: Boychenko (61), Apanaschenko (67, 72) / Tarczynska (18)

138

Team	Pld	W	D	L	GF	GA	GD	Pts
Ukraine	*8*	*5*	*2*	*1*	*24*	*9*	*+15*	*17*
Poland	8	5	1	2	18	9	+9	16
Hungary	8	4	3	1	15	10	+5	15
Romania	8	2	2	4	14	13	+1	8
Bosnia and Herzegovina	8	0	0	8	0	30	-30	0

GROUP 5

19.09.2009   Centenary Stadium, Ta'Qali: Malta – Spain 0-13 (0-8)
Goals: Meseguer (6), Martín (11, 19, 30, 51), Bermúdez (26, 36, 38), Romero (31, 68, 90+3), Boquete (53, 75)
24.10.2009   Estadio Nuevo Arcángel, Córdoba: Spain – Austria 2-0 (2-0)
Goals: Bermúdez (20), Martín (32)
25.10.2009   Bloomfield Road, Blackpool: England – Malta 8-0 (4-0)
Goals: White (8), F.Williams (21, 39, 66), Clarke (37, 76), Westwood (78), Unitt (87)
29.10.2009   Ertl Glas Stadion, Amstetten: Austria – Spain 0-1 (0-0)
Goal: Martín (49)
18.11.2009   Centenary Stadium, Ta'Qali: Malta – Austria 0-2 (0-1)
Goals: Aigner (11, 48)
21.11.2009   Manisa 19 Mayis Stadium, Manisa: Turkey – Spain 0-5 (0-0)
Goals: Martín (47, 50 pen, 53), Bermúdez (78), Boquete (82)
26.11.2009   Buca Arena, Izmir: Turkey – England 0-3 (0-0)
Goals: A.Scott (77), Sanderson (81), Unitt (85)
25.03.2010   Loftus Road, London: England – Austria 3-0 (1-0)
Goals: Sanderson (16), Aluko (67), White (90)
27.03.2010   Centenary Stadium, Ta'Qali: Malta – Turkey 0-2 (0-1)
Goals: Uraz (22, 57)
01.04.2010   The New Den, London: England – Spain 1-0 (1-0)
Goal: Chapman (30)
07.04.2010   Estadio Pedro Escartín, Guadalajara: Spain – Turkey 5-1 (4-0)
Goals: Bermúdez (29), Martín (31, 70), Torrejón (36), Olabarrieta (40) / Elgalp (55)
11.04.2010   Hüseyin Avni Aker Stadium, Trabzon: Turkey – Malta 5-1 (4-0)
Goals: Yag (7, 41), Uraz (39, 61), Defterli (45+2) / Pace (49)
20.05.2010   Centenary Stadium, Ta'Qali: Malta – England 0-6 (0-3)
Goals: White (7), K.Smith (15), F.Williams (29, 82), Clarke (56), White (67)
09.06.2010   Donaustadion, Ottensheim: Austria – Malta 6-0 (2-0)
Goals: Makas (3, 53, 68), Gröbner (10, 90+1), Hanschitz (59)
19.06.2010   Estadio El Montecillo, Aranda de Duero: Spain – England 2-2 (1-0)
Goals: Martín (16), Bermúdez (67) / Unitt (78), F.White (88)
23.06.2010   Anger Stadium, Anger: Austria – Turkey 4-0 (3-0)
Goals: Burger (8), Makas (10), Feiersinger (45), Gröbner (49)
24.06.2010   Estadio La Albuera, Segovia: Spain – Malta 9-0 (1-0)
Goals: Martín (17, 47, 61, 72), Ibarra (49, 80), Casado (77), Pace (86 og), Boquete (90)

139

20.07.2010   Bescot Stadium, Walsall: England – Turkey 3-0 (1-0)
Goals: Yankey (23), E.White (62), Clarke (78)
21.08.2010   Sepp-Doll-Stadion, Krems an der Donau: Austria – England 0-4 (0-3)
Goals: K.Smith (7, 30), A.Scott (40), F.White (80)
25.08.2010   Samsun 19 Mayis Stadium, Samsun: Turkey – Austria 2-2 (1-0)
Goals: Defterli (22), Yag (51 pen) / Burger (66), Makas (82)

Team	Pld	W	D	L	GF	GA	GD	Pts
England	*8*	*7*	*1*	*0*	*30*	*2*	*+28*	*22*
Spain	8	6	1	1	37	4	+33	19
Austria	8	3	1	4	14	12	+2	10
Turkey	8	2	1	5	10	23	-13	7
Malta	8	0	0	8	1	51	-50	0

GROUP 6

19.09.2009   Stadion Niedermatten, Wohlen:
Switzerland – Republic of Ireland 2-0 (0-0)
Goals: Moser (56), Dickenmann (64 pen)
23.09.2009   Esp Stadiu, Fislisbach: Switzerland – Russia 1-2 (0-2)
Goals: Meyer (87) / Skotnikova (8), Danilova (16)
24.09.2009   Turners Cross, Cork: Republic of Ireland – Kazakhstan 2-1 (1-0)
Goals: O'Sullivan (43), Roche (87) / Krassyukova (64)
24.10.2009   Ness Ziona Stadium, Ness Ziona: Israel – Kazakhstan 1-0 (1-0)
Goal: Erez (42)
25.10.2009   Krasnoarmeysk Stadium, Krasnoarmeysk:
Russia – Republic of Ireland 3-0 (1-0)
Goals: Morozova (12), Savchenkova (52), Petrova (90+1)
28.10.2009   Ness Ziona Stadium, Ness Ziona: Israel – Switzerland 1-2 (0-0)
Goals: Abbé (76 og) / Maendly (55), Abbé (90+1)
29.10.2009   Zhetysu Stadium, Taldykorgan:
Kazakhstan – Republic of Ireland 1-2 (1-0)
Goals: Yalova (6) / Roche (64), Tracy (70)
17.11.2009   Ramat Gan Stadium, Ramat Gan: Israel – Russia 1-6 (0-2)
Goals: Cohen (47) / Poryadina (10), Fomina (29, 89), Savchenkova (62), Kurochkina (81), Kozhnikova (85)
21.03.2010   Ness Ziona Stadium, Ness Ziona: Israel – Republic of Ireland 0-3 (0-1)
Goals: O'Sullivan (32, 52), O'Brien (81)
27.03.2010   Stadion Niedermatten, Wohlen: Switzerland – Israel 6-0 (2-0)
Goals: Abbé (8, 64), Barqui (14 og), Stein (68), Dickenmann (71), Crnogorcevic (90+3)
28.03.2010   Zhetysu Stadium, Taldykorgan: Kazakhstan – Russia 0-6 (0-2)
Goals: Kurochkina (42, 56 pen, 71 pen, 89), Savchenkova (44), Terekhova (52)
31.03.2010   Richmond Park, Dublin: Republic of Ireland – Switzerland 1-2 (0-1)
Goals: Grant (57) / Maendly (21), Beney (54)
19.06.2010   Astana Arena, Astana: Kazakhstan – Israel 0-1 (0-0)
Goal: Sofer (71)

140

19.06.2010   Krasnoarmeysk Stadium, Krasnoarmeysk:
Russia – Switzerland 0-3 (0-1)
Goals: Kuster (18), Bachmann (77, 78)
23.06.2010   Shakhtyor Stadium, Karagandy: Kazakhstan – Switzerland 2-4 (2-2)
Goals: Yalova (16, 44) / Bachmann (15), Dickenmann (43, 56), Meyer (57)
24.06.2010   Krasnoarmeysk Stadium, Krasnoarmeysk: Russia – Israel 4-0 (3-0)
Goals: Kurochkina (5 pen), Skotnikova (24), Kozhnikova (31), Sochneva (80)
21.08.2010   Ferrycarrig Park, Wexford: Republic of Ireland – Russia 1-1 (0-0)
Goals: Grant (59 pen) / Kozhnikova (64)
21.08.2010   Stade Universitaire Saint-Léonard, Fribourg:
Switzerland – Kazakhstan 8-0 (5-0)
Goals: Crnogorcevic (4, 27, 44, 57, 77), Zumbühl (7), Moser (11, 56)
25.08.2010   Krasnoarmeysk Stadium, Krasnoarmeysk: Russia – Kazakhstan 8-0 (2-0)
Goals: Skotnikova (2), Sochneva (34, 88), Danilova (50, 55, 62, 72),
Semenchenko (64)
25.08.2010   Carlisle Grounds, Bray: Republic of Ireland – Israel 3-0 (0-0)
Goals: O'Sullivan (59, 64, 80)

Team	Pld	W	D	L	GF	GA	GD	Pts
Switzerland	*8*	*7*	*0*	*1*	*28*	*6*	*+22*	*21*
Russia	8	6	1	1	30	6	+24	19
Republic of Ireland	8	4	1	3	12	10	+2	13
Israel	8	2	0	6	4	24	-20	6
Kazakhstan	8	0	0	8	4	32	-28	0

GROUP 7

19.09.2009   Hrazdan Stadium, Yerevan: Armenia – Finland 0-4 (0-2)
Goals: Talonen (1, 40), Saari (78), Malaska (88)
19.09.2009   Sports Park, Domzale: Slovenia – Italy 0-8 (0-6)
Goals: conti (3, 13, 41), Gabbaidini (14, 29), Carissimi (40), Fuselli (81),
Panico (90+3)
23.09.2009   Stadio Centro d'Italy, Rieti: Italy – Portugal 2-0 (1-0)
Goals: Panico (45, 65)
24.10.2009   Hanrapetakan Stadium, Yerevan: Armenia – Italy 0-8 (0-4)
Goals: Tona (12), Conti (25, 83 pen), Gama (29, 68), Fuselli (55), Schiavi (70),
Panico (90+2)
24.10.2009   Stadion Matije Gbuca, Krsko: Slovenia – Finland 0-3 (0-0)
Goals: Österberg Kalmari (61), Salmén (67), Sjölund (68)
28.10.2009   Hanrapetakan Stadium, Yerevan: Armenia – Slovenia 1-5 (0-2)
Goals: Mangasaryan (74 pen) / Milenkovic (25), Tibaut (41), Zver (54, 75),
Vrabel (63)
28.10.2009   Estádio João Cardoso, Tondela: Portugal – Finland 0-1 (0-0)
Goal: Saari (49)
21.11.2009   Finnair Stadium, Helsinki: Finland – Armenia 7-0 (5-0)
Goals: Österberg Kalmari (2, 34, 77), Sjölund (19, 38, 83), Rantanen (45+1)
21.11.2009   Stadion Sportni Park, Nova Gorica: Slovenia – Portugal 0-4 (0-0)
Goals: Ana Borges (50), Carla Couto (68), Sónia Matias (76), Edite Fernandes (77)

25.11.2009   Stadio Comunale di Francavilla, Francavilla al Mare: Italy – Armenia 7-0 (2-0)
Goals: Tona (1), Conti (40), Gabbiadini (50, 80), Panico (52, 90+4), Camporese (77 pen)
27.03.2010   Ob Jezeru, Velenje: Slovenia – Armenia 1-0 (0-0)
Goal: Milenkovic (56)
27.03.2010   Complexo Desportivo da Tocha, Tocha: Portugal – Italy 1-3 (1-2)
Goals: Ana Borges (41) / Tona (24), Panico (43), Camporese (70)
31.03.2010   Stadio Cino e Lillo Del duca, Ascoli Piceno: Italy – Finland 1-1 (1-1)
Goals: Gabbiadini (18) / Tiilikainen (4)
31.03.2010   Complexo Desportivo da Tocha, Tocha: Portugal – Armenia 7-0 (5-0)
Goals: Edite Fernandes (22, 49, 86), Silvia Rebelo (27), Cláudia Neto (33), Sofia Vieira (40 pen), Carole Costa (44)
19.06.2010   ISS Stadion, Vantaa: Finland – Portugal 4-1 (2-1)
Goals: Österberg Kalmari (28, 44 pen, 58), Sällström (70) / Edite Fernandes (22)
19.06.2010   Stadio Sandro Pertini, Montereale Valcellina: Italy – Slovenia 6-0 (3-0)
Goals: Gabbiadini (2), Domenichetti (29), Camporese (37 pen), Golob (69 og), Conti (73), Panico (78)
23.06.2010   ISS Stadion, Vantaa: Finland – Italy 1-3 (0-1)
Goals: Sällström (49) / Conti (5), Gabbiadini (66), Parisi (70 pen)
23.06.2010   Municipal Stadium, Cartaxo: Portugal – Slovenia 1-0 (0-0)
Goal: Inês Borges (46)
25.08.2010   Mika Stadium, Yerevan: Armenia – Portugal 0-3 (0-1)
Goals: Dolores Silva (31, 64), Carole Costa (55)
25.08.2010   Wiklöf Holding Arena, Mariehamn: Finland – Slovenia 4-1 (1-1)
Goals: Sällström (16, 70, 89), Sjölund (79 pen) / Zver (27)

Team	Pld	W	D	L	GF	GA	GD	Pts
Italy	*8*	*7*	*1*	*0*	*38*	*3*	*+35*	*22*
Finland	8	6	1	1	25	6	+19	19
Portugal	8	4	0	4	17	10	+7	12
Slovenia	8	2	0	6	7	27	-20	6
Armenia	8	0	0	8	1	42	-41	0

GROUP 8

20.09.2009   Bridge Meadow Stadium, Haverfordwest: Wales – Belgium 0-1 (0-0)
Goal: Verelst (90+4)
23.09.2009   Gamla Ullevi, Gothenburg: Sweden – Belgium 2-1 (1-0)
Goals: Asllani (30), Landström (66) / Maes (68)
23.09.2009   Stebonheath Park, Llanelli: Wales – Czech Republic 2-0 (1-0)
Goals: Fishlock (16), Plewa (84)
24.10.2009   Ismet Qaibov Stadium, Baku: Azerbaijan – Sweden 0-3 (0-1)
Goals: Seger (38, 80), Landström (59)
25.10.2009   Dolícek Stadion, Prague: Czech Republic – Wales 2-1 (2-1)
Goals: Pincová (8, 22) / Fishlock (17)
28.10.2009   Ismet Qaibov Stadium, Baku: Azerbaijan – Wales 2-1 (2-1)
Goals: Atayeva (33), Kaziyeva (43) / Lander (29)

28.10.2009 Den Dreef, Heverlee: Belgium – Sweden 1-4 (0-1)
Goals: Maes (71) / Seger (23, 65), Landström (67), Lindén (86)
22.11.2009 Ismet Qaibov Stadium, Baku: Azerbaijan – Belgium 0-0
26.11.2009 Mestský sportovní areál, Písek: Czech Republic – Belgium 1-2 (0-2)
Goals: Pivonková (69) / Verelst (24), Maes (27)
27.03.2010 Tofik Bakhramov Stadium, Baku:
            Azerbaijan – Czech Republic 0-5 (0-3)
Goals: Nepokojova (11), Divisová (21), Heroldová (43), Mocová (53), Kruzová (87)
28.03.2010 Edmond Machtens Stadium, Brussels: Belgium – Wales 2-3 (0-2)
Goals: Philtjens (64), Zeler (72) / Dykes (19), Daley (42 pen), Jones (90+1)
31.03.2010 The Airfield, Broughton: Wales – Sweden 0-4 (0-0)
Goals: Fischer (69), Liljegård (78), Paulson (85), Landström (90)
01.04.2010 Edmond Machtens Stadium, Brussels:
            Belgium – Czech Republic 0-3 (0-2)
Goals: Divisová (29, 44, 49)
19.06.2010 Stade Leburton, Tubize: Belgium – Azerbaijan 11-0 (8-0)
Goals: De Cock (3, 11, 40, 42), Philtjens (10, 26), Heiremans (18, 54), Onzia (35, 90+1), Puttemans (89)
19.06.2010 Gamla Ullevi, Gothenburg: Sweden – Czech Republic 0-0
23.06.2010 Gamla Ullevi, Gothenburg: Sweden – Azerbaijan 17-0 (7-0)
Goals: Mirzaguliyeva (19 og), Forsberg (25, 31), Sjögran (33, 60), Seger (41, 45+1), Liljegård (44, 49, 62), Landström (52, 66), Asllani (55), Asadova (63 og), Lindén (72, 78), Paulson (72)
21.08.2010 Dolíček Stadion, Prague: Czech Republic – Sweden 0-1 (0-1)
Goal: Seger (26)
21.08.2010 Latham Park, Newtown: Wales – Azerbaijan 15-0 (7-0)
Goals: Lander (3, 7, 21, 36, 38, 72), Harries (13, 56, 66), Dutton (19), Fishlock (59), Ingle (65), Green (81, 83), Manley (90+2)
25.08.2010 Stadion Na Chvalech, Prague: Czech Republic – Azerbaijan 8-0 (5-0)
Goals: Divisová (6, 43), Mocová (7), Pivonková (14, 57), Martínková (17, 61), Dosková (54)
25.08.2010 Värendsvallen, Växjö: Sweden – Wales 5-1 (2-0)
Goals: Schelin (12, 60), Öqvist (45, 55, 71) / Harries (81)

Team	Pld	W	D	L	GF	GA	GD	Pts
Sweden	*8*	*7*	*1*	*0*	*36*	*3*	*+33*	*22*
Czech Republic	8	4	1	3	19	6	+13	13
Belgium	8	3	1	4	18	13	+5	10
Wales	8	3	0	5	23	16	+7	9
Azerbaijan	8	1	1	6	2	60	-58	4

PLAY-OFF STAGES

11.09.2010 Stade Léo Lagrange, Besançon: France – Italy 0-0
11.09.2010 Stadion Yuri Gagarin, Chernihiv: Ukraine – Norway 0-1 (0-1)
Goal: Mjelde (32)
11.09.2010 Gamla Ullevi, Gothenburg: Sweden – Denmark 2-1 (1-0)
Goals: Forsberg (12), Schelin (61) / Paaske-Sørensen (64)

12.09.2010   Greenhous Meadow, Shrewsbury: England – Switzerland 2-0 (2-0)
Goals: Williams (44), K.Smith (45+2)
15.09.2010   Stadio Pietro Barbetti, Gubbio: Italy – France 2-3 (1-0)
Goals: Panico (34), Domenichetti (90+3) / Bussaglia (54), Thiney (58),
Bompastor (90+2)
15.09.2010   Nadderud stadion, Bærum: Norway – Ukraine 2-0 (1-0)
Goals: Pedersen (6), Gulbrandsen (86)
16.09.2010   Stadion Niedermatten, Wohlen: Switzerland – England 2-3 (1-2)
Goals: Bachmann (41), Zumbühl (65) / K.Smith (32), Eniola Aluko (34),
Williams (50 pen)
16.09.2010   Vejle Stadion, Vejle: Denmark – Sweden 2-2 (2-0) (a.e.t.)
Goals: J.Rasmussen (41), Paaske-Sørensen (43) / Rohlin (73, 94)
Sweden qualified after extra time

France, **England**, **Norway** and **Sweden** qualified for the FIFA Women's World Cup
2011.

REPECHAGE QUALIFICATION
REPECHAGE I

02.10.2010   Stadion Yuri Gagarin, Chernihiv: Ukraine – Italy 0-3 (0-0)
Goals: Conti (60), Panico (81), Pini (89)
03.10.2010   Vejle Stadion, Vejle: Denmark – Switzerland 1-3 (0-1)
Goals: Harder (87) / Crnogorcevic (18), Zumbühl (50, Abbé (83 pen)
06.10.2010   Stadio Domenico Francioni, Latina: Italy – Ukraine 0-0
07.10.2010   Stadion Brügglifeld, Aarau: Switzerland – Denmark 0-0

REPECHAGE II

23.10.2010   Stadio Omobono Tenni, Treviso: Italy – Switzerland 1-0 (0-0)
Goal: Tuttuno (86)
27.10.2010   Stadion Brügglifeld, Aarau: Switzerland – Italy 2-4 (0-0)
Goals: Maendly (56, 79) / Panico (52), Camporese (61 pen, 63), Tona (89)

Italy advance to the UEFA-CONCACAF Play-off 2010.

CONCACAF WOMEN'S GOLD CUP 2010

QUALIFYING CENTRAL AMERICA

TRIANGULAR A

All matches played in Antigua Guatemala, Guatemala.

20.04.2010   Estadio Pensativo, Antigua Guatemala: El Salvador – Belize 9-0 (4-0)
Goals: Merino (9), Campos (15, 29), Landaverde (17, 68), Ramos (69, 86, 87, 90)
22.04.2010   Estadio Pensativo, Antigua Guatemala:
              Guatemala – El Salvador 2-1 (1-1)
Goals: Ramos (12), Cayetano (55) / Landaverde (35)

24.04.2010   Estadio Pensativo, Antigua Guatemala: Guatemala – Belize 5-1 (1-0)
Goals: Tobar (45), Ramos (48), Cayetano (61, 72), Lohaiza (70) / Hernandez (55)

Team	Pld	W	D	L	GF	GA	GD	Pts
Guatemala	*2*	*2*	*0*	*0*	*7*	*2*	*+5*	*6*
El Salvador	2	1	0	1	10	2	+8	3
Belize	2	0	0	2	1	14	-13	0

TRIANGULAR B

All matches played in Managua, Nicaragua.

26.04.2010   Estadio Nacional de la UNAN-Managua, Managua:
               Nicaragua – Honduras 2-1 (1-1)
Goals: Lovo (31), Acevedo (86) / Turcios (9)
28.04.2010   Estadio Nacional de la UNAN-Managua, Managua:
               Honduras – Costa Rica 0-2 (0-1)
Goals: C.Venegas (39), F.Sanchez (81)
30.04.2010   Estadio Nacional de la UNAN-Managua, Managua:
               Nicaragua – Costa Rica 0-2 (0-2)
Goals: Cedeño (24), C.Venegas (37)

Team	Pld	W	D	L	GF	GA	GD	Pts
Costa Rica	*2*	*2*	*0*	*0*	*4*	*0*	*+4*	*6*
Nicaragua	2	1	0	1	2	3	-1	3
Honduras	2	0	0	2	1	4	-3	0

QUALIFYING CARIBBEAN

FIRST ROUND

Cuba and Trinidad and Tobago received byes to the Second Round.
The winner of each group advanced to the Second Round, along with the best of the five runners-up.

GROUP A

All matches played in Georgetown, Guyana.

03.03.2010   Georgetown Cricket Club Ground, Georgetown:
               Suriname – Saint Vincent and the Grenadines 1-0 (0-0)
Goal: Smit (65 pen)
05.03.2010   Georgetown Cricket Club Ground, Georgetown:
               Guyana – Suriname 2-0 (1-0)
Goals: B.Persaud (19), Heydorn (47)
07.03.2010   Georgetown Cricket Club Ground, Georgetown:
               Guyana – Saint Vincent and the Grenadines 1-0 (0-0)
Goal: Heydorn (60)

Team	Pld	W	D	L	GF	GA	GD	Pts
Guyana	*2*	*2*	*0*	*0*	*3*	*0*	*+3*	*6*
Suriname	2	1	0	1	1	2	-1	3
Saint Vincent and the Grenadines	2	0	0	2	0	2	-2	0

GROUP B

All matches played in Bayamón, Puerto Rico.

17.03.2010   Juan Ramón Loubriel Stadium, Bayamón:
           Saint Kitts and Nevis – Dominica 2-0 (0-0)
Goals: Arthurton (84), Powell (89)
19.03.2010   Juan Ramón Loubriel Stadium, Bayamón:
           Puerto Rico – Saint Kitts and Nevis 7-0 (5-0)
Goals: Tirelli (5), Negron (6, 53, 84), Rodriguez (25), Reyes (31), Hernández (44)
21.03.2010   Juan Ramón Loubriel Stadium, Bayamón:
           Puerto Rico – Dominica 6-0 (1-0)
Goals: Cardona (31, 83), Hernández (62), Tousett (67, 89), Felix (70)

Team	Pld	W	D	L	GF	GA	GD	Pts
Puerto Rico	*2*	*2*	*0*	*0*	*13*	*0*	*+13*	*6*
Saint Kitts and Nevis	2	1	0	1	2	7	-5	3
Dominica	2	0	0	2	0	8	-8	0

GROUP C

All matches played in St.John's, Antigua and Barbuda.

10.03.2010   Antigua Recreation Ground, St.John's:
           Antigua and Barbuda – Saint Lucia 1-2 (1-2)
Goals: London (2) / Marquis (40), Jean (44)
12.03.2010   Antigua Recreation Ground, St.John's:
           U.S. Virgin Islands – Saint Lucia 0-7 (0-3)
Goals: Alphonse (8), Jean (27, 33, 60), Frederick (47, 61), Celestin (85)
14.03.2010   Antigua Recreation Ground, St.John's:
           Antigua and Barbuda – U.S. Virgin Islands 3-1 (0-0)
Goals: Lewis (52), Simon (58), H.Thomas (90) / Taylor (90)

Team	Pld	W	D	L	GF	GA	GD	Pts
Saint Lucia	*2*	*2*	*0*	*0*	*9*	*1*	*+8*	*6*
Antigua and Barbuda	2	1	0	1	4	3	+1	3
U.S. Virgin Islands	2	0	0	2	1	10	-9	0

GROUP D

All matches played in Santo Domingo, Dominican Republic.

26.03.2010   Estadio Panamericano San Cristóbal, Santo Domingo:
Dominican Republic – Turks and Caicos Islands 3-1 (1-1)
Goals: Mateo (29, 55), Quiterio (75) / Barnett (1)
28.03.2010   Estadio Panamericano San Cristóbal, Santo Domingo:
Turks and Caicos Islands – Haiti 0-5 (0-3)
Goals: Dolce (2), Saintilmond (25), Batard (45), Hilaire (71, 78)
30.03.2010   Estadio Panamericano San Cristóbal, Santo Domingo:
Dominican Republic – Haiti 1-2 (1-1)
Goals: Díaz (42 pen) / Saintilmond (28), Dolce (84)

Team	Pld	W	D	L	GF	GA	GD	Pts
Haiti	*2*	*2*	*0*	*0*	*7*	*1*	*+6*	*6*
Dominican Republic	2	1	0	1	4	3	+1	3
Turks and Caicos Islands	2	0	0	2	1	8	-7	0

GROUP E

All matches played in Bridgetown, Barbados.

28.03.2010   Barbados National Stadium, Bridgetown: Barbados – Anguilla 3-0 (1-0)
Goals: Hackette (17, 60, 83)
30.03.2010   Barbados National Stadium, Bridgetown: Anguilla – Grenada 2-0 (2-0)
Goals: Anderson (9), C.Richardson (12)
01.04.2010   Barbados National Stadium, Bridgetown: Barbados – Grenada 4-0 (1-0)
Goals: Brathwaite (9), Hackette (46, 87 pen), Thompson (83)

Team	Pld	W	D	L	GF	GA	GD	Pts
Barbados	*2*	*2*	*0*	*0*	*7*	*0*	*+7*	*6*
Anguilla	2	1	0	1	2	3	-1	3
Grenada	2	0	0	2	0	6	-6	0

Ranking of group runners-up

Top team advanced to the Second Round.

Gp	Team	Pld	W	D	L	GF	GA	GD	Pts
C	*Antigua and Barbuda*	*2*	*1*	*0*	*1*	*4*	*3*	*+1*	*3*
D	Dominican Republic	2	1	0	1	4	3	+1	3
E	Anguilla	2	1	0	1	2	3	-1	3
A	Suriname	2	1	0	1	1	2	-1	3
B	Saint Kitts and Nevis	2	1	0	1	2	7	-5	3

147

Antigua and Barbuda and the Dominican Republic finished equal as best runners-up.
Antigua and Barbuda won the draw taken to break the tie.

SECOND ROUND

The winner of each group afvanced to the CONCACAF Women's World Cup
Qualifying final tournament in late 2010. The runners-up advanced to the Carribean
play-off.

GROUP F

All matches played in Macoya, Trinidad and Tobago.

10.05.2010   Marvin Lee Stadium, Macoya: Guyana – Barbados 3-0 (2-0)
Goals: El-Masri (9), A.Rodrigues (37), Savona (55)
10.05.2010   Marvin Lee Stadium, Macoya:
            Trinidad and Tobago – Saint Lucia 6-1 (3-0)
Goals: Edwards (11, 23), Coroner (19, 52), Mollon (56), Shade (87) / Alphonse (60)
12.05.2010   Marvin Lee Stadium, Macoya: Saint Lucia – Guyana 0-8 (0-3)
Goals: El-Masri (9), A.Rodrigues (11, 54), Heydorn (15, 58, 64), Owen (47),
J.Rodrigues (63)
12.05.2010   Marvin Lee Stadium, Macoya:
            Trinidad and Tobago – Barbados 5-0 (2-0)
Goals: King (5, 11, 48), Herbert (72 og), Coroner (90)
14.05.2010   Marvin Lee Stadium, Macoya: Barbados – Saint Lucia 4-3 (2-0)
Goals: Stevenson (19), Brathwaite (35, 50, 55) / Henry (71, 86), Marquis (78)
14.05.2010   Marvin Lee Stadium, Macoya: Trinidad and Tobago – Guyana 3-0 (2-0)
Goals: Coroner (15, 65), Matthias (34)

Team	Pld	W	D	L	GF	GA	GD	Pts
Trinidad and Tobago	*3*	*3*	*0*	*0*	*14*	*1*	*+13*	*9*
Guyana	3	2	0	1	11	3	+8	6
Barbados	3	1	0	2	4	11	-7	3
Saint Lucia	3	0	0	3	4	18	-14	0

GROUP G

All matches played in Marabella, Trinidad and Tobago.

11.05.2010   Manny Ramjohn Stadium, Marabella: Cuba – Puerto Rico 4-3 (1-0)
Goals: Y.Martinez (37, 67), Z.Martinez (50), Cruz (56) / Tirelli (72, 75),
Hernandez (85)
11.05.2010   Manny Ramjohn Stadium, Marabella:
            Antigua and Barbuda – Haiti 1-4 (1-3)
Goals: London (36) / Louis (19), Batard (42), Aristide (43), Mathelier (49)
13.05.2010   Manny Ramjohn Stadium, Marabella: Haiti – Cuba 3-0 (0-0)
Goals: Charles (52), Boulos (75), Brand (86)

13.05.2010 Manny Ramjohn Stadium, Marabella:
Puerto Rico – Antigua and Barbuda 8-0 (5-0)
Goals: Felix (4, 16), Negron (18, 72), Soltero (35), C.Reyes (39), Tebosa (84),
Guerra (90)
15.05.2010 Manny Ramjohn Stadium, Marabella: Haiti – Puerto Rico 2-0 (1-0)
Goals: Saintilmond (15), Louis (87)
15.04.2010 Manny Ramjohn Stadium, Marabella:
Cuba – Antigua and Barbuda 6-1 (3-0)
Goals: Y.Martinez (8, 11, 64), González (35), Ellis (50), Torre (75) / Kai Jacobs (82)

Team	Pld	W	D	L	GF	GA	GD	Pts
Haiti	*3*	*3*	*0*	*0*	*9*	*1*	*+8*	*9*
Cuba	3	2	0	1	10	7	+3	6
Puerto Rico	3	1	0	2	11	6	+5	3
Antigua and Barbuda	3	0	0	3	2	18	-16	0

CARIBBEAN PLAY-OFF

26.06.2010 Estadio Pedro Marrero, Havana: Cuba – Guyana 1-0 (1-0)
Goal: Y.Martinez (21)
03.07.2010 Providence Stadium, Georgetown: Guyana – Cuba 3-1 (2-1)
Goals: A.Rodrigues (37 pen), B.Persaud (44), J.Rodrigues (48) / Y.Martinez (35)

Guyana advanced to the CONCACAF Women's World Cup Qualifying final
tournament.

**CONCACAF WOMEN'S WORLD CUP QUALIFYING FINAL
TOURNAMENT 2010**

The tournament finals were held in Cancún, Mexico and were played between 28
October and 8 November 2010.

United States, Canada and Mexico received byes into the final tournament after taking
the top three positions in the 2006 Gold Cup, while five other spots were determined
through regional qualification.

**GROUP STAGE
GROUP A**

29.10.2010 Estadio de Béisbol Beto Ávila, Cancún:
Trinidad and Tobago – Canada 0-1 (0-0)
Goal: Tancredi (63)
29.10.2010 Estadio de Béisbol Beto Ávila, Cancún: Mexico – Guyana 7-2 (4-2)
Goals: Garza (2, 45), Dominguez (24, 36 pen, 67, 79), Worbis (59) / El-Masri (34),
De Souza (39)
31.10.2010 Estadio de Béisbol Beto Ávila, Cancún: Canada – Guyana 8-0 (2-0)
Goals: Julien (15), Sinclair (34, 50, 63, 75), Filigno (46, 75), Lang (90)

149

31.10.2010   Estadio de Béisbol Beto Ávila, Cancún:
Mexico – Trinidad and Tobago 2-0 (1-0)
Goals: Dominguez (45), Lopez (58)
02.11.2010   Estadio de Béisbol Beto Ávila, Cancún:
Guyana – Trinidad and Tobago 1-4 (0-2)
Goals: El-Masri (60) / Cordner (11), Belgrave (25), Edwards (49), Mascall (65)
02.11.2010   Estadio de Béisbol Beto Ávila, Cancún: Mexico – Canada 0-3 (0-2)
Goals: Chapman (20), Belanger (45), Filigno (66)

Team	Pld	W	D	L	GF	GA	GD	Pts
Canada	3	3	0	0	12	0	+12	9
Mexico	3	2	0	1	9	5	+4	6
Trinidad and Tobago	3	1	0	2	4	4	0	3
Guyana	3	0	0	3	3	19	-16	0

GROUP B

28.10.2010   Estadio Quintana Roo, Cancún: Costa Rica – Guatemala 1-0 (0-0)
Goal: A.Venegas (51)
28.10.2010   Estadio Quintana Roo, Cancún: United States – Haiti 5-0 (4-0)
Goals: Buehler (9), Wambach (15, 45, 62), Rodriguez (40)
30.10.2010   Estadio Quintana Roo, Cancún: Haiti – Costa Rica 0-3 (0-2)
Goals: Cruz (35), Rodríguez (42, 52)
30.10.2010   Estadio Quintana Roo, Cancún: United States – Guatemala 9-0 (6-0)
Goals: Rodriguez (20, 45, 89), Rapinoe (22, 40), Wambach (29, 30), Morgan (49), Lloyd (58 pen)
01.11.2010   Estadio Quintana Roo, Cancún: Guatemala – Haiti 0-1 (0-1)
Goal: Saintilmond (22)
01.11.2010   Estadio Quintana Roo, Cancún: United States – Costa Rica 4-0 (1-0)
Goals: Wambach (32 pen), Cheney (69), Averbuch (73), Morgan (81)

Team	Pld	W	D	L	GF	GA	GD	Pts
United States	3	3	0	0	18	0	+18	9
Costa Rica	3	2	0	1	4	4	0	6
Haiti	3	1	0	2	1	8	-7	3
Guatemala	3	0	0	3	0	11	-11	0

KNOCKOUT STAGE
SEMI-FINALS

05.11.2010   Estadio de Béisbol Beto Ávila, Cancún: Canada – Costa Rica 4-0 (0-0)
Goals: Bélanger (62), Filigno (72), Sinclair (75), Cruz (90+3 og)
05.11.2010   Estadio de Béisbol Beto Ávila, Cancún:
United States – Mexico 1-2 (1-2)
Goals: Lloyd (25) / Domínguez (3), Pérez (26)

150

THIRD PLACE PLAY-OFF

08.11.2010   Estadio Quintana Roo, Cancún: Costa Rica – United States 0-3 (0-2)
Goals: Cheney (17), Wambach (33, 50)

FINAL

08.11.2010   Estadio Quintana Roo, Cancún: Canada – Mexico 1-0 (0-0)
Goal: Sinclair (53 pen)

Winner **Canada** and runner-up **Mexico** qualified for the FIFA Women's World Cup 2011. Third placed team United States had to play against the fifth placed team from UEFA in the UEFA-CONCACAF Play-Off 2010 for an additional World Cup berth.

OFC WOMEN'S CHAMPIONSHIP 2010

The OFC Women's Championship 2010 was held in Auckland, New Zealand between 29 September and 8 October 2010. Only the winner will qualify for the FIFA Women's World Cup 2011.

GROUP STAGE

GROUP A

29.09.2010   North Harbour Stadium, Auckland: New Zealand – Vanuatu 14-0 (7-0)
Goals: Hearn (10, 11, 18, 29, 90+1), Moorwood (25, 81), Wilkinson (42, 59, 73, 89), Erceg (45+2), White (54), Milne (68)
29.09.2010   North Harbour Stadium, Auckland: Cook Islands – Tahiti 1-0 (1-0)
Goal: Mustonen (15)
01.10.2010   North Harbour Stadium, Auckland: Tahiti – Vanuatu 5-1 (2-1)
Goals: Alvarez (14, 21, 83), White (81), Tokoragi (82) / Tougen (19)
01.10.2010   North Harbour Stadium, Auckland: Cook Islands – New Zealand 0-10 (0-6)
Goals: Hearn (9, 40, 64), Gregorius (16, 27, 56), Hoyle (21), Percival (45), Erceg (57), Jackman (80)
03-10-2010   North Harbour Stadium, Auckland: Tahiti – New Zealand 0-7 (0-1)
Goals: Armstrong (36), Hearn (59, 75), Green (76), Yallop (80), Gregorius (90), Percibal (90+2)
03.10.2010   North Harbour Stadium, Auckland: Vanuatu – Cook Islands 0-2 (0-0)
Goals: Napa (83), Henry (89)

Team	Pld	W	D	L	GF	GA	GD	Pts
New Zealand	*3*	*3*	*0*	*0*	*31*	*0*	*+31*	*9*
Cook Islands	*3*	*2*	*0*	*1*	*3*	*10*	*-7*	*6*
Tahiti	3	1	0	2	5	9	-4	3
Vanuatu	3	0	0	3	1	21	-20	0

GROUP B

30.09.2010   North Harbour Stadium, Auckland: Papua New Guinea – Fiji 3-0 (1-0)
Goals: Peninsa (8), Limbai (58), Morris (62)
30.09.2010   North Harbour Stadium, Auckland: Solomon Islands – Tonga 4-0 (2-0)
Goals: Pegi (12, 90+1), Misibini (37), Maenu'u (74 pen)
02.10.2010   North Harbour Stadium, Auckland: Tonga – Fiji 2-1 (0-1)
Goals: Siale (75), Feke (90) / Ratubalavu (13)
02.10.2010   North Harbour Stadium, Auckland:
Solomon Islands – Papua New Guinea 1-2 (0-1)
Goals: Saepio (84) / Limbai (29), Siniu (48)
04.10.2010   North Harbour Stadium, Auckland:
Tonga – Papua New Guinea 0-3 (0-1)
Goals: Limbai (28, 61), Likiliki (74 og)
04.10.2010   North Harbour Stadium, Auckland: Fiji – Solomon Islands 0-0

Team	Pld	W	D	L	GF	GA	GD	Pts
Papua New Guinea	*3*	*3*	*0*	*0*	*8*	*1*	*+7*	*9*
Solomon Islands	*3*	*1*	*1*	*1*	*5*	*2*	*+3*	*4*
Tonga	3	1	0	2	2	8	-6	3
Fiji	3	0	1	2	1	5	-4	1

KNOCKOUT STAGE
SEMI-FINALS

06.10.2010   North Harbour Stadium, Auckland:
New Zealand – Solomon Islands 8-0 (4-0)
Goals: White (7, 86), Percival (17), Moorwood (30), Hearn (36), Gregorius (52, 68),
Wilkinson (60)
06.10.2010   North Harbour Stadium, Auckland:
Papua New Guinea – Cook Islands 1-0 (0-0)
Goal: Limbai (62)

THIRD PLACE PLAY-OFF

08.10.2010   North Harbour Stadium, Auckland:
Solomon Islands – Cook Islands 0-2 (0-0)
Goals: Henry (70 pen), Mustonen (79)

FINAL

08.10.2010   North Harbour Stadium, Auckland:
New Zealand – Papua New Guinea 11-0 (6-0)
Goals: Riley (7, 15), Percival (18), Wilkinson (32, 36), White (38, 50, 56), Gregorius
(73), Hearn (79), Green (84)

The winner **New Zealand** qualified for the FIFA Women's World Cup 2011.

152

CONMEBOL SUDAMERICANO FEMENINO 2010

The tournament was held between 4 & 21 November 2010 in Ecuador, after originally being scheduled for 28 October to 14 November 2010.

FIRST STAGE
GROUP A

04.11.2010   Estadio La Cocha, Latacunga: Argentina – Bolivia 3-0 (2-0)
Goals: Ojeda (6, 39 pen), Banini (51)
04.11.2010   Estadio La Cocha, Latacunga: Ecuador – Chile 1-2 (1-2)
Goals: Quintero (42) / Quezada (2), Salgado (44)
06.11.2010   Estadio Bellavista, Ambato: Chile – Argentina 1-2 (0-1)
Goals: Lara (84 pen) / Pereyra (40, 70)
06.11.2010   Estadio Bellavista, Ambato: Ecuador – Peru 2-1 (1-1)
Goals: Quinteros (22), Palacios (78) / Tristàn (15)
08.11.2010   Estadio Olímpico, Riobamba: Chile – Bolivia 3-0 (2-0)
Goals: Lara (8), Zamora (40), Araya (55)
08.11.2010   Estadio Olímpico, Riobamba: Argentina – Peru 2-0 (0-0)
Goals: González (65), Blanco (68)
10.11.2010   Estadio Bellavista, Ambato: Peru – Chile 1-3 (1-1)
Goals: Chirinos (45) / Aedo (10), Araya (57, 90)
10.11.2010   Estadio Bellavista, Ambato: Bolivia – Ecuador 3-4 (1-1)
Goals: Loayza (30), Benavides (70), Padilla (87) / Sánchez (45+4, 53), Freire (68), Quinteros (73)
12.11.2010   Estadio La Cocha, Latacunga: Bolivia – Peru 2-1 (1-1)
Goals: Loayza (29, 61) / Chirinos (22)
12.11.2010   Estadio La Cocha, Latacunga: Ecuador – Argentina 1-0 (1-0)
Goal: Rodríguez (34)

Team	Pld	W	D	L	GF	GA	GD	Pts
Chile	*4*	*3*	*0*	*1*	*9*	*4*	*+5*	*9*
Argentina	*4*	*3*	*0*	*1*	*7*	*2*	*+5*	*9*
Ecuador	4	3	0	1	8	6	+2	9
Bolivia	4	1	0	3	5	11	-6	3
Peru	4	0	0	4	3	9	-6	0

GROUP B

05.11.2010   Estadio Federativo Reina del Cisne, Loja:
Paraguay – Colombia 0-3 (0-1)
Goals: Domínguez (18), Uzme (46), Rincón (70)
05.11.2010   Estadio Federativo Reina del Cisne, Loja: Brazil – Venezuela 4-0 (3-0)
Goals: Aline (26, 30), Cristiane (42), Renata Costa (60)
07.11.2010   Estadio Federativo Reina del Cisne, Loja:
Venezuela – Paraguay 0-4 (0-0)
Goals: Quintana (49), Villamayor (56, 59, 80)

07.11.2010   Estadio Federativo Reina del Cisne, Loja: Uruguay – Brazil 0-4 (0-3)
Goals: Cristiane (15 pen, 40), Marta (36, 57)
09.11.2010   Estadio Jorge Andrade, Azogues: Colombia – Venezuela 5-0 (2-0)
Goals: Arias (27), Rodallaega (45), Peralta (56), Rincón (58), Velásquez (73)
09.11.2010   Estadio Jorge Andrade, Azogues: Paraguay – Uruguay 4-0 (3-0)
Goals: Villamayor (29), Galeano (38), Quintana (42), Vásquez (89 pen)
11.11.2010   Estadio Alejandro Serrano Aguilar, Cuenca:
             Venezuela – Uruguay 5-2 (3-1)
Goals: Vizo (4, 17), Quintero (31), Torres (78), Altuber (83) / Viera (43),
Birizamberri (66)
11.11.2010   Estadio Alejandro Serrano Aguilar, Cuenca: Colombia – Brazil 1-2 (0-2)
Goals: Muñoz (57) / Cristiane (13), Marta (28)
13.11.2010   Estadio Alejandro Serrano Aguilar, Cuenca:
             Uruguay – Colombia 0-8 (0-3)
Goals: Uzme (35 pen), Rincón (41, 80), Castro (45, 84), Montoya (82), N.Arias (85),
Vidal (88)
13.11.2010   Estadio Alejandro Serrano Aguilar, Cuenca: Brazil – Paraguay 3-0 (2-0)
Goals: Cristiane (18, 36), Marta (57)

Team	Pld	W	D	L	GF	GA	GD	Pts
Brazil	*4*	*4*	*0*	*0*	*13*	*1*	*+12*	*12*
Colombia	*4*	*3*	*0*	*1*	*17*	*2*	*+15*	*9*
Paraguay	4	2	0	2	8	6	+2	6
Venezuela	4	1	0	3	5	15	-10	3
Uruguay	4	0	0	4	2	21	-19	0

SECOND STAGE

17.11.2010   Estadio La Cocha, Latacunga: Chile – Colombia 1-1 (0-1)
Goals: Lara (61) / Rincón (29)
17.11.2010   Estadio La Cocha, Latacunga: Brazil – Argentina 4-0 (2-0)
Goals: Grazielle (25), Dos Santos (37), Marta (63), Cristiane (77)
19.11.2010   Estadio La Cocha, Latacunga: Chile – Argentina 0-0
19.11.2010   Estadio La Cocha, Latacunga: Brazil – Colombia 5-0 (1-0)
Goals: Érika (23), Grazielle (48), Marta (69, 87), Cristiane (82)
21.11.2010   Estadio Olímpico Atahualpa, Quito: Colombia – Argentina 1-0 (0-0)
Goal: Betancourt (51)
21.11.2010   Estadio Olímpico Atahualpa, Quito: Chile – Brazil 1-3 (1-2)
Goals: Salgado (45) / Daniele (2), Marta (36, 83)

Team	Pld	W	D	L	GF	GA	GD	Pts
Brazil	*3*	*3*	*0*	*0*	*12*	*1*	*+11*	*9*
Colombia	*3*	*1*	*1*	*1*	*2*	*6*	*-4*	*4*
Chile	3	0	2	1	2	4	-2	2
Argentina	3	0	1	2	0	5	-5	1

The winner **Brazil** and the runner-up **Colombia** both qualified for the FIFA Women's
World Cup 2011.

20.11.2010   Stadio Euganeo, Padua: Italy – United States 0-1 (0-0)
Goal: Morgan (90+4)
27.11.2010   Toyota Park, Bridgeview: United States – Italy 1-0 (1-0)
Goal: Rodriguez (40)

The winner **United States** qualified for the FIFA Women's World Cup 2011.

FIFA WOMEN'S WORLD CUP FINAL TOURNAMENT IN GERMANY 2011

The Final Tournament was held in Germany between 26 June and 17 July 2011.

GROUP STAGE
GROUP A

26.06.2011   WIRSOL Rhein-Neckar-Arena, Sinsheim: Nigeria – France 0-1 (0-0)
Nigeria: Predious Uzoaru DEDE, Faith IKIDI (33 Josephine Chiwendu
CHUKWUNONYE), Onome EBI, Helen UKAONU, Osinachi Marvis OHALE, Rita
CHIKWELU, Glory IROKA, Perpetua Ijeoma NKWOCHA, Stella MBACHU, Ebere
ORJI (78 Uchechi Lopez SUNDAY), Ugochi Desire OPARANOZIE (66 Sarah
MICHAEL). (Coach: Ngozi UCHE).
France: Bérangère SAPOWICZ, Laura GEORGES, Wendie RENARD (69 Laure
Maud Yvette LEPAILLEUR), Sonia BOMPASTOR, Ophelie MEILLEROUX,
Camille ABILY, Louisa NECIB, Elise BUSSAGLIA, Sandrine SOUBEYRAND (46
Eugénie LE SOMMER), Marie Laure DELIE, Gaëtane THINEY (57 Elodie
THOMIS). (Coaches: Bruno BINI & Corinne DIACRE).
Goal: Marie Laure DELIE (56)
Referee: Kari SEITZ (United States)   Attendance: 25,475

26.06.2011   Olympiastadion Berlin, Berlin: Germany – Canada 2-1 (2-0)
Germany: Nadine ANGERER, Saskia BARTUSIAK, Babett PETER, Annike
KRAHN *(YC90)*, Kerstin GAREFREKES, Melanie BEHRINGER (70 Fatmire
ALUSHI), Linda BRESONIK, Simone LAUDEHR *(YC81)*, Kim KULIG, Birgit
PRINZ (56 Alexandra POPP), Célia SASIC (65 Inka GRINGS). (Coach: Silva NEID).
Canada: Erin McLEOD, Rhian WILKINSON, Candace Marie CHAPMAN, Emily
ZURRER, Marie Eve NAULT (46 Robyn GAYLE), Diana MATHESON, Sophie
SCHMIDT, Kaylyn KYLE (46 Kelly PARKER), Christine SINCLAIR, Melissa
TANCREDI (80 Brittany TIMKO), Jonelle FILIGNO. (Coach: Carolina MORACE).
Goals: Kerstin GAREFREKES (10), Célia SASIC (42) / Christine SINCLAIR (82)
Referee: Jacqui MELKSHAM (Australia)   Attendance: 73,680

30.06.2011 Vonovia Ruhrstadion, Bochum: Canada – France 0-4 (0-1)
Canada: Erin McLEOD, Rhian WILKINSON, Candace Marie CHAPMAN, Emily
ZURRER, Diana MATHESON *(YC52)*, Brittany TIMKO (77 Chelsea STEWART),
Sophie SCHMIDT, Kaylyn KYLE (60 Desiree SCOTT), Christine SINCLAIR,
Jonelle FILIGNO, Christina JULIEN (60 Melissa TANCREDI).
(Coach: Carolina MORACE).
France: Bérangère SAPOWICZ, Laura GEORGES, Laure Maud Yvette
LEPAILLEUR, Sonia BOMPASTOR *(YC37)*, Sabrina Marie-Christine VIGUIER,
Camille ABILY (82 Eugénie LE SOMMER), Louisa NECIB, Elise BUSSAGLIA,
Sandrine SOUBEYRAND, Marie Laure DELIE (74 Elodie THOMIS), Gaëtane
THINEY (79 Laure BOULLEAU). (Coaches: Bruno BINI & Corinne DIACRE).
Goals: Gaëtane THINEY (24, 60), Camille ABILY (67), Elodie THOMIS (83)
Referee: Etsuko FUKANO (Japan)   Attendance: 16,591

30.06.2011 Commerzbank-Arena, Frankfurt am Main: Germany – Nigeria 1-0 (0-0)
Germany: Nadine ANGERER, Saskia BARTUSIAK, Babett PETER, Annike
KRAHN, Kerstin GAREFREKES, Melanie BEHRINGER (31 Alexandra POPP),
Linda BRESONIK, Simone LAUDEHR, Kim KULIG *(YC74)*, Birgit PRINZ (52 Inka
GRINGS), Célia SASIC (87 Fatmire ALUSHI). (Coach: Silva NEID).
Nigeria: Predious Uzoaru DEDE, Faith IKIDI, Onome EBI, Helen UKAONU,
Osinachi Marvis OHALE *(YC50)*, Rita CHIKWELU, Perpetua Ijeoma NKWOCHA,
Stella MBACHU (85 Francisca ORDEGA), Sarah MICHAEL (70 Uchechi Lopez
SUNDAY), Ebere ORJI (62 Amenze AIGHEWI), Ugochi Desire OPARANOZIE.
(Coach: Ngozi UCHE).
Goal: Simone LAUDEHR (54)
Referee: CHA Sung-Mi (South Korea)   Attendance: 48,817

05.07.2011 Stadion im BORUSSIA-PARK, Mönchengladbach:
        France – Germany 2-4 (0-2)
France: Bérangère SAPOWICZ *(RC65)*, Laura GEORGES *(YC41)*, Laure Maud
Yvette LEPAILLEUR, Wendie RENARD *(YC59)*, Laure BOULLEAU, Louisa
NECIB (46 Camille ABILY), Elodie THOMIS (46 Marie Laure DELIE), Elise
BUSSAGLIA *(YC40)*, Sandrine SOUBEYRAND, Eugénie LE SOMMER (68 Céline
DEVILLE *goalkeeper*), Gaëtane THINEY.
(Coaches: Bruno BINI & Corinne DIACRE).
Germany: Nadine ANGERER, Saskia BARTUSIAK, Babett PETER, Annike
KRAHN (78 Alexandra POPP), Kerstin GAREFREKES, Fatmire ALUSHI *(YC82)*,
Simone LAUDEHR (46 Ariane HINGST), Lena GÖßLING *(YC17)*, Bianca
SCHMIDT, Inka GRINGS, Célia SASIC. (Coach: Silva NEID).
Goals: Marie Laure DELIE (56), Laura GEORGES (72) / Kerstin GAREFREKES
(25), Inka GRINGS (32, 68 pen), Célia SASIC (89)
Referee: Kirsi HEIKKINEN (Finland)   Attendance: 45,867

Sent-off: 65' Bérangère SAPOWICZ.

156

05.07.2011 DDV-Stadion, Dresden: Canada – Nigeria 0-1 (0-0)
Canada: Karina LeBLANC, Rhian WILKINSON, Candace Marie CHAPMAN, Emily ZURRER, Marie Eve NAULT, Diana MATHESON, Sophie SCHMIDT, Kaylyn KYLE (90 Desiree SCOTT), Christine SINCLAIR, Melissa TANCREDI (90+6 Jodi-Ann ROBINSON), Jonelle FILIGNO (56 Christina JULIEN).
(Coach: Carolina MORACE).
Nigeria: Predious Uzoaru DEDE, Faith IKIDI, Onome EBI *(YC59)*, Helen UKAONU, Osinachi Marvis OHALE, Rita CHIKWELU, Glory IROKA, Perpetua Ijeoma NKWOCHA, Stella MBACHU (82 Francisca ORDEGA), Ebere ORJI (54 Ogonna CHUKWUDI), Ugochi Desire OPARANOZIE (90+6 Uchechi Lopez SUNDAY).
(Coach: Ngozi UCHE).
Goal: Perpetua Ijeoma NKWOCHA (84)
Referee: Finau VULIVULI (Fiji)   Attendance: 13,638

Team	Pld	W	D	L	GF	GA	GD	Pts
Germany	*3*	*3*	*0*	*0*	*7*	*3*	*+4*	*9*
France	*3*	*2*	*0*	*1*	*7*	*4*	*+3*	*6*
Nigeria	3	1	0	2	1	2	-1	3
Canada	3	0	0	3	1	7	-6	0

GROUP B

27.06.2011 Vonovia Ruhrstadion, Bochum: Japan – New Zealand 2-1 (1-1)
Japan: Ayumi KAIHORI, Yukari KINGA, Azusa IWASHIMIZU, Aya SAMESHIMA, Saki KUMAGAI, Homare SAWA, Aya MIYAMA, Mizuho SAKAGUCHI, Kozue ANDO (90+1 Asuna TANAKA), Yuki NAGASATO (76 Karina MARUYAMA), Shinobu OHNO (55 Mana IWABUCHI).
(Coach: Norio SASAKI).
New Zealand: Jenny Lynn BINDON, Rebecca Katie SMITH *(YC67)*, Ria PERCIVAL (76 Annalie LONGO), Abby ERCEG, Alexandra RILEY, Anna GREEN, Katie BOWEN *(YC45)* (46 Hayley Rose MOORWOOD), Katie DUNCAN, Betsy HASSETT, Amber HEARN *(YC77)*, Sarah GREGORIUS (62 Hannah WILKINSON).
(Coach: John HERDMAN).
Goals: Yuki NAGASATO (6), Aya MIYAMA (68) / Amber HEARN (12)
Referee: Kirsi HEIKKINEN (Finland)   Attendance: 12,538

157

27.06.2011 VOLKSWAGEN ARENA, Wolfsburg: Mexico – England 1-1 (1-1)
Mexico: Cecilia SANTIAGO Cisneros, Alina Lisi GARCIAMENDEZ Rowold
(YC87), Rubí Marlene SANDOVAL Nungaray, Luz del Rosario SAUCEDO Soto,
Natalie Raquel VINTI Nuno-Vidarte, Nayeli RANGEL Hernandez, Sandra Stephany
MAYOR Gutierrez, Teresa Guadalupe (Lupita) WORBIS Aguilar, Dinora Lizeth
GARZA Rodríguez (85 Teresa NOYOLA Bayardo), Mónica OCAMPO Medina,
Maribel Guadalupe DOMÍNGUEZ Castelán (76 Juana Evelyn LOPEZ Luna).
(Coach: Leonardo CUÉLLAR Rivera).
England: Karen BARDSLEY, Alexandra SCOTT, Casey STONEY *(YC88)*, Faye
Deborah WHITE (83 Sophie Elizabeth BRADLEY), Rachel Elizabeth UNITT, Fara
WILLIAMS, Jill SCOTT, Karen CARNEY (72 Ellen WHITE), Eniola ALUKO,
Kelly SMITH, Rachel YANKEY. (Coach: Hope Patricia POWELL).
Goals: Mónica OCAMPO Medina (33) / Fara WILLIAMS (21)
Referee: Silvia Elizabeth REYES (Peru) Attendance: 18,702

01.07.2011 BayArena, Leverkusen: Japan – Mexico 4-0 (3-0)
Japan: Ayumi KAIHORI, Yukari KINGA, Azusa IWASHIMIZU, Aya
SAMESHIMA, Saki KUMAGAI, Homare SAWA (83 Rumi UTSUGI), Aya
MIYAMA, Mizuho SAKAGUCHI, Kozue ANDO (69 Mana IWABUCHI), Yuki
NAGASATO, Shinobu OHNO (69 Nahomi KAWASUMI). (Coach: Norio SASAKI).
Mexico: Cecilia SANTIAGO Cisneros, Alina Lisi GARCIAMENDEZ Rowold,
Natalie Ann GARCIA Mendez, Luz del Rosario SAUCEDO Soto, Natalie Raquel
VINTI Nuno-Vidarte, Nayeli RANGEL Hernandez (46 Liliana MERCADO Fuentes),
Sandra Stephany MAYOR Gutierrez, Dinora Lizeth GARZA Rodríguez, Veronica
Raquel PEREZ Murillo (79 Teresa NOYOLA Bayardo), Mónica OCAMPO Medina,
Maribel Guadalupe DOMÍNGUEZ Castelán (61 Kenti ROBLES Salas).
(Coach: Leonardo CUÉLLAR Rivera).
Goals: Homare SAWA (13, 39, 80), 15' Shinobu OHNO (15)
Referee: Christina Westrum PEDERSEN (Norway) Attendance: 22,291

01.07.2011 DDV-Stadion, Dresden: New Zealand – England 1-2 (1-0)
New Zealand: Jenny Lynn BINDON, Rebecca Katie SMITH, Ria PERCIVAL (71
Rosie WHITE), Abby ERCEG, Alexandra RILEY, Anna GREEN, Katie BOWEN (46
Hayley Rose MOORWOOD), Katie DUNCAN, Betsy HASSETT, Amber HEARN,
Sarah GREGORIUS (89 Hannah WILKINSON). (Coach: John HERDMAN).
England: Karen BARDSLEY, Alexandra SCOTT, Casey STONEY, Faye Deborah
WHITE (86 Sophie Elizabeth BRADLEY), Rachel Elizabeth UNITT, Fara
WILLIAMS, Jill SCOTT, Eniola ALUKO (46 Karen CARNEY), Kelly SMITH,
Rachel YANKEY (66 Jessica Anne CLARKE), Ellen WHITE.
(Coach: Hope Patricia POWELL).
Goals: Sarah GREGORIUS (18) / Jill SCOTT (63), Jessica Anne CLARKE (80)
Referee: Therese Raissa NEGUEL (Cameroon) Attendance: 19,110

05.07.2011   WWK Arena, Augsburg: England – Japan 2-0 (1-0)
England: Karen BARDSLEY, Alexandra SCOTT, Casey STONEY, Anita Amma
Ankyewah ASANTE, Rachel Elizabeth UNITT, Sophie Elizabeth BRADLEY, Jill
SCOTT, Karen CARNEY, Kelly SMITH (62 Eniola ALUKO), Jessica Anne
CLARKE (46 Rachel YANKEY), Ellen WHITE (90 Laura BASSETT).
(Coach: Hope Patricia POWELL).
Japan: Ayumi KAIHORI, Yukari KINGA, Azusa IWASHIMIZU, Aya
SAMESHIMA, Saki KUMAGAI, Homare SAWA, Aya MIYAMA, Mizuho
SAKAGUCHI (74 Mana IWABUCHI), Kozue ANDO (56 Karina MARUYAMA),
Yuki NAGASATO, Shinobu OHNO (82 Nahomi KAWASUMI).
(Coach: Norio SASAKI).
Goals: Ellen WHITE (15), Rachel YANKEY (66)
Referee: Carol Anne CHENARD (Canada)   Attendance: 20,777

05.07.2011   WIRSOL Rhein-Neckar-Arena, Sinsheim:
            New Zealand – Mexico 2-2 (0-2)
New Zealand: Jenny Lynn BINDON, Rebecca Katie SMITH, Abby ERCEG,
Alexandra RILEY, Anna GREEN, Katie DUNCAN, Hayley Rose MOORWOOD (60
Kristy YALLOP), Betsy HASSETT (79 Ria PERCIVAL), Rosie WHITE (YC33) (55
Hannah WILKINSON), Amber HEARN, Sarah GREGORIUS.
(Coach: John HERDMAN).
Mexico: Cecilia SANTIAGO Cisneros, Alina Lisi GARCIAMENDEZ Rowold, Kenti
ROBLES Salas (80 Luz del Rosario SAUCEDO Soto), Natalie Ann GARCIA
Mendez, Natalie Raquel VINTI Nuno-Vidarte, Nayeli RANGEL Hernandez (46
Dinora Lizeth GARZA Rodríguez), Sandra Stephany MAYOR Gutierrez (70
Verónica Charlyn CORRAL Ang), Teresa Guadalupe (Lupita) WORBIS Aguilar,
Veronica Raquel PEREZ Murillo, Mónica OCAMPO Medina, Maribel Guadalupe
DOMÍNGUEZ Castelán (YC90). (Coach: Leonardo CUÉLLAR Rivera).
Goals: Rebecca Katie SMITH (90), Hannah WILKINSON (90+3) / Sandra Stephany
MAYOR Gutierrez (2), Maribel Guadalupe DOMÍNGUEZ Castelán (30)
Referee: Jenny PALMQVIST (Sweden)   Attendance: 20,451

Team	Pld	W	D	L	GF	GA	GD	Pts
England	3	2	1	0	5	2	+3	7
Japan	3	2	0	1	6	3	+3	6
Mexico	3	0	2	1	3	7	-4	2
New Zealand	3	0	1	2	4	6	-2	1

GROUP C

28.06.2011   BayArena, Leverkusen: Colombia – Sweden 0-1 (0-0)
Colombia: Sandra Milena SEPÚLVEDA Lopera, Andrea Paola PERALTA Delgado
(79 Ingrid Yulieth VIDAL Isaza), Kelis Johana PEDUZINE Vargas, Katherine Nataly
ARIAS Peña, Natalia GAITÁN Laguado, Daniela MONTOYA Quiróz (66 Yulieth
Paola DOMÍNGUEZ Ochoa), Hazleydi Yoreli RINCÓN Torres, Lady Patricia
ANDRADE Rodríguez, Diana Carolina OSPINA García, Maria Catalina USME
Pineda (59 Katerin Fabiola CASTRO Muñoz), Carmen Elisa RODALLEGA.
(Coach: Ricardo ROZO Ocampo).
Sweden: Rut Hedvig LINDAHL, Annica SVENSSON, Sara Kristina THUNEBRO,
Sara LARSSON, Barbaro Charlotte ROHLIN, Lisa Karolina Viktoria DAHLKVIST,
Sara Caroline SEGER *(YC29)* (69 Nilla FISCHER), Kerstin Ingrid Therese
SJÖGRAN, Jessica LANDSTRÖM (81 Madeleine EDLUND), Linda FORSBERG
(54 Eva Sofia JAKOBSSON), Lotta Eva SCHELIN. (Coach: Thomas DENNERBY).
Goal: Jessica LANDSTRÖM (57)
Referee: Carol Anne CHENARD (Canada)   Attendance: 21,106

28.06.2011   DDV-Stadion, Dresden: United States – North Korea 2-0 (0-0)
United States: Hope Amelia SOLO, Christie PEARCE, Alexandra Blaire (Ali)
KRIEGER, Rachel VAN HOLLEBEKE, Amy LePEILBET, Shannon BOXX, Heather
O'REILLY (79 Megan RAPINOE), Carli LLOYD, Abby WAMBACH, Lauren
HOLIDAY, Amy RODRIGUEZ (75 Alexandra (Alex) MORGAN).
(Coach: Pia Mariane SUNDHAGE).
North Korea: HONG Myong-Hui, SONG Jong-Sun, RI Un-Hyang, JO Yun-Mi, RI
Ye-Gyong, JON Myong-Hwa (68 KIM Un-Ju), KIM Su-Gyong, JONG Pok-Sim,
YUN Hyon-Hi (48 PAEK Sol-Hui), RA Un-Sim, HO Un-Byol (81 KWON Song-
Hwa). (Coach: KIM Kwang-Min).
Goals: Lauren HOLIDAY (54), Rachel VAN HOLLEBEKE (76)
Referee: Bibiana STEINHAUS (Germany)   Attendance: 21,859

02.07.2011   WWK Arena, Augsburg: North Korea – Sweden 0-1 (0-0)
North Korea: HONG Myong-Hui, SONG Jong-Sun, RI Un-Hyang, JO Yun-Mi, RI
Ye-Gyong (82 KIM Chung-Sim), JON Myong-Hwa, KIM Su-Gyong (68 KIM Un-
Ju), JONG Pok-Sim, YUN Hyon-Hi (79 CHOE Mi-Gyong), RA Un-Sim, HO Un-
Byol. (Coach: KIM Kwang-Min).
Sweden: Rut Hedvig LINDAHL, Annica SVENSSON, Sara Kristina THUNEBRO,
Sara LARSSON, Barbaro Charlotte ROHLIN, Lisa Karolina Viktoria DAHLKVIST,
Sara Caroline SEGER *(YC60)*, Kerstin Ingrid Therese SJÖGRAN (87 Nilla
FISCHER), Jessica LANDSTRÖM (76 Josefine ÖQVIST), Linda FORSBERG, Lotta
Eva SCHELIN. (Coach: Thomas DENNERBY).
Goal: Lisa Karolina Viktoria DAHLKVIST (64)
Referee: Estela ÁLVAREZ (Argentina)   Attendance: 23,768

02.07.2011   WIRSOL Rhein-Neckar-Arena, Sinsheim:
United States – Colombia 3-0 (1-0)
United States: Hope Amelia SOLO, Christie PEARCE, Alexandra Blaire (Ali)
KRIEGER, Rachel VAN HOLLEBEKE, Amy LePEILBET (56 Stephanie COX), Lori
Ann LINDSEY, Heather O'REILLY (62 Tobin HEATH), Carli LLOYD, Abby
WAMBACH, Lauren HOLIDAY, Amy RODRIGUEZ (46 Megan RAPINOE).
(Coach: Pia Mariane SUNDHAGE).
Colombia: Sandra Milena SEPÚLVEDA Lopera, Yulieth Paola DOMÍNGUEZ
Ochoa, Kelis Johana PEDUZINE Vargas, Fátima MONTAÑO Rentería, Katherine
Nataly ARIAS Peña, Natalia GAITÁN Laguado, Liana Milena SALAZAR Vergara
(55 Hazleydi Yoreli RINCÓN Torres), Diana Carolina OSPINA García, Maria
Catalina USME Pineda (53 Oriánica VELÁSQUEZ Herrera), Carmen Elisa
RODALLEGA, Katerin Fabiola CASTRO Muñoz. (Coach: Ricardo ROZO Ocampo).
Goals: Heather O'REILLY (12), Megan RAPINOE (50), Carli LLOYD (57)
Referee: Dagmar DAMKOVA (Czech Republic)   Attendance: 25,475

06.07.2011   Vonovia Ruhrstadion, Bochum: North Korea – Colombia 0-0
North Korea: HONG Myong-Hui, YU Jong-Hee, PAEK Sol-Hui, RI Un-Hyang, JO
Yun-Mi, RI Ye-Gyong, KIM Un-Ju, JON Myong-Hwa, KIM Su-Gyong (48 KIM
Chung-Sim), RA Un-Sim (56 YUN Hyon-Hi, 76 CHOE Mi-Gyong), HO Un-Byol.
(Coach: KIM Kwang-Min).
Colombia: Sandra Milena SEPÚLVEDA Lopera, Yulieth Paola DOMÍNGUEZ
Ochoa, Kelis Johana PEDUZINE Vargas, Fátima MONTAÑO Rentería, Katherine
Nataly ARIAS Peña, Natalia GAITÁN Laguado, Daniele MONTOYA Quiróz (89
Liana Milena SALAZAR Vergara), Diana Carolina OSPINA García, Carmen Elisa
RODALLEGA, Oriánica VELÁSQUEZ Herrera, Katerin Fabiola CASTRO Muñoz
(88 Ingrid Yulieth VIDAL Isaza). (Coach: Ricardo ROZO Ocampo).
Referee: Christina Westrum PEDERSEN (Norway)   Attendance: 7,805

06.07.2011   VOLKSWAGEN ARENA, Wolfsburg:
Sweden – United States 2-1 (2-0)
Sweden: Rut Hedvig LINDAHL, Annica SVENSSON, Sara Kristina THUNEBRO,
Sara LARSSON, Barbaro Charlotte ROHLIN, Nilla FISCHER (YC60) (88 Linda
Brigitta SEMBRANT), Lisa Karolina Viktoria DAHLKVIST (77 Kristin
HAMMARSTRÖM), Kerstin Ingrid Therese SJÖGRAN (65 Antonia GÖRANSSON),
Linda FORSBERG, Josefine ÖQVIST, Lotta Eva SCHELIN.
(Coach: Thomas DENNERBY).
United States: Hope Amelia SOLO, Christie PEARCE, Alexandra Blaire (Ali)
KRIEGER, Rachel VAN HOLLEBEKE, Amy LePEILBET (YC14) (59 Stephanie
COX), Shannon BOXX, Carli LLOYD, Abby WAMBACH, Lauren HOLIDAY,
Megan RAPINOE (73 Kelly O'HARA), Amy RODRIGUEZ (46 Alexandra (Alex)
MORGAN). (Coach: Pia Mariane SUNDHAGE).
Goals: Lisa Karolina Viktoria DAHLKVIST (16 pen), Nilla FISCHER (35) /
Abby WAMBACH (67)
Referee: Etsuko FUKANO (Japan)   Attendance: 23,468

161

Team	Pld	W	D	L	GF	GA	GD	Pts
Sweden	*3*	*3*	*0*	*0*	*4*	*1*	*+3*	*9*
United States	*3*	*2*	*0*	*1*	*6*	*2*	*+4*	*6*
North Korea	3	0	1	2	0	3	-3	1
Colombia	3	0	1	2	0	4	-4	1

GROUP D

29.06.2011   WWK Arena, Augsburg: Norway – Equatorial Guinea 1-0 (0-0)
Norway: Ingrid HJELMSETH, Hedda Strand GARDSJORD, Nora Holstad BERGE, Trine RØNNING, Marita Skammelsrud LUND, Maren MJELDE *(YC63)*, Ingvild STENSLAND, Madeleine GISKE (46 Lene MYKJÅLAND, 70 Leni LARSEN KAURIN), Isabell HERLOVSEN (62 Cecilie PEDERSEN), Elise THORSNES *(YC90+2)*, Emilie HAAVI. (Coach: Eli LANDSEM).
Equatorial Guinea: MIRIAM Silva da Paixão, Carolina Conceição Martins de Pereira "CAROL CARIOCA", BRUNA Amarante da Silva, Dúlcia Maria Davi "DULCE", Ana Cristina da Silva "CRIS", DORINE Nina Chuigoue, Jumária Barbosa de Santana "JU" (52 Gloria CHINASA Okoro), Olive CHRISTELLE Ngo Nyepel (46 LAETITIA Chapeh Yimga), GENOVEVA AÑONMA, VANIA Cristina Martins, DIALA Blessing (65 ADRIANA Aparecida Costa). (Coach: MARCELO FRIGERIO).
Goal: Emilie HAAVI (84)
Referee: Quetzalli ALVARADO Godínez (Mexico)   Attendance: 12,928

29.06.2011   Stadion im BORUSSIA-PARK, Mönchengladbach:
Brazil – Australia 1-0 (0-0)
Brazil: ANDRÉIA Suntaque, ALINE Pellegrino, ÉRIKA Cristiano dos Santos, FABIANA da Silva Simões, DAIANE Menezes Ridrigues, ROSANA dos Santos Augusto, Miraildes Maciel Mota "FORMIGA" (84 FRANCIELLE Manoel Alberto), ESTER Aparecida dos Santos, MAURINE Dornelles Gonçalves, MARTA Vieira da Silva, CRISTIANE Rozeira de Souza Silva.
(Coaches: KLEITON Barbosa de Oliveira LIMA & JORGE BARCELLOS).
Australia: Melissa BARBIERI HUDSON, Emily VAN EGMOND (61 Sally SHIPARD), Kim CARROLL, Servet UZUNLAR, Heather GARRIOCK, Elise KELLOND, Tameka BUTT (86 Clare POLKINGHORNE), Collette McCALLUM, Lisa DE VANNA (79 Samantha KERR), Kyah SIMON, Caitlin FOORD.
(Coach: Tom SERMANNI).
Goal: ROSANA dos Santos Augusto (54)
Referee: Jenny PALMQVIST (Sweden)   Attendance: 27,258

03.07.2011 Vonovia Ruhrstadion, Bochum: Australia – Equatorial Guinea 3-2 (1-1)
Australia: Lydia WILLIAMS, Emily VAN EGMOND, Kim CARROLL, Servet
UZUNLAR, Heather GARRIOCK, Sally SHIPARD (46 Lisa DE VANNA *(YC72)*),
Lauren Elizabeth COLTHORPE, Elise KELLOND, Collette McCALLUM (78 Clare
POLKINGHORNE), Leena KHAMIS, Samantha KERR (69 Teigen ALLEN).
(Coach: Tom SERMANNI).
Equatorial Guinea: MIRIAM Silva da Paixão, Carolina Conceição Martins de Pereira
"CAROL CARIOCA", BRUNA Amarante da Silva (82 LAETITIA Chapeh Yimga),
Dúlcia Maria Davi "DULCE", Ana Cristina da Silva "CRIS" *(YC47)*, DORINE Nina
Chuigoue, Jumária Barbosa de Santana "JU" (65 SINFOROSA Eyang Nguema
Nchama *(YC79)*), Gloria CHINASA Okoro (57 ADRIANA Aparecida Costa),
GENOVEVA AÑONMA *(YC41)*, VANIA Cristina Martins, DIALA Blessing.
(Coach: MARCELO FRIGERIO).
Goals: Leena KHAMIS (8), Emily VAN EGMOND (48), Lisa DE VANNA (51) /
GENOVEVA AÑONMA (21, 83)
Referee: Gyöngyi Krisztina GAÁL (Hungary) Attendance: 15,640

03.07.2011 VOLKSWAGEN ARENA, Wolfsburg: Brazil – Norway 3-0 (1-0)
Brazil: ANDRÉIA Suntaque, ALINE Pellegrino, ÉRIKA Cristiano dos Santos,
FABIANA da Silva Simões (76 FRANCIELLE Manoel Alberto), DAIANE Menezes
Ridrigues *(YC19)* (84 Renata Aparecida da Costa "KÓKI"), ROSANA dos Santos
Augusto, Miraildes Maciel Mota "FORMIGA", ESTER Aparecida dos Santos (89
GRAZIELLE Pinheiro Nascimento), MAURINE Dornelles Gonçalves, MARTA
Vieira da Silva, CRISTIANE Rozeira de Souza Silva.
(Coaches: KLEITON Barbosa de Oliveira LIMA & JORGE BARCELLOS).
Norway: Ingrid HJELMSETH, Nora Holstad BERGE, Trine RØNNING, Marita
Skammelsrud LUND, Maren MJELDE, Ingvild STENSLAND (67 Gry Tofte IMS),
Leni LARSEN KAURIN (46 Elise THORSNES), Guro KNUTSEN Mienna,
Madeleine GISKE, Isabell HERLOVSEN, Emilie HAAVI (52 Cecilie PEDERSEN).
(Coach: Eli LANDSEM).
Goals: MARTA Vieira da Silva (22, 48), ROSANA dos Santos Augusto (46)
Referee: Kari SEITZ (United States) Attendance: 26,067

06.07.2011 BayArena, Leverkusen: Australia – Norway 2-1 (0-0)
Australia: Melissa BARBIERI HUDSON, Clare POLKINGHORNE, Kim CARROLL
(YC45+3), Servet UZUNLAR, Heather GARRIOCK *(YC68)*, Elise KELLOND,
Collette McCALLUM, Lisa DE VANNA, Samantha KERR (81 Laura ALLEWAY),
Kyah SIMON, Caitlin FOORD (90 Ellyse PERRY). (Coach: Tom SERMANNI).
Norway: Ingrid HJELMSETH (46 Erika Espeseth SKARBØ), Hedda Strand
GARDSJORD *(YC90+2)*, Trine RØNNING, Maren MJELDE, Ingvild STENSLAND,
Lene MYKJÅLAND, Guro KNUTSEN Mienna, Gry Tofte IMS (82 Isabell
HERLOVSEN), Elise THORSNES, Emilie HAAVI (46 Kristine MINDE), Cecilie
PEDERSEN. (Coach: Eli LANDSEM).
Goals: Kyah SIMON (57, 87) / Elise THORSNES (56)
Referee: Estela ÁLVAREZ (Argentina) Attendance: 18,474

163

06.07.2011 Commerzbank-Arena, Frankfurt am Main:
Equatorial Guinea – Brazil 0-3 (0-0)
Equatorial Guinea: MIRIAM Silva da Paixão, Carolina Conceição Martins de Pereira
"CAROL CARIOCA", BRUNA Amarante da Silva *(YC90+3)*, Dúlcia Maria Davi
"DULCE" *(YC9)*, LAETITIA Chapeh Yimga, Ana Cristina da Silva "CRIS" (71
SINFOROSA Eyang Nguema Nchama), DORINE Nina Chuigoue, Jumária Barbosa
de Santana "JU", GENOVEVA AÑONMA, VANIA Cristina Martins, DIALA
Blessing *(YC60)* (86 ADRIANA Aparecida Costa). (Coach: MARCELO FRIGERIO).
Brazil: ANDRÉIA Suntaque, ALINE Pellegrino, Renata Aparecida da Costa "KÓKI"
(YC77), ÉRIKA Cristiano dos Santos, FABIANA da Silva Simões (82 THAIS Duarte
GUEDES), ROSANA dos Santos Augusto (70 FRANCIELLE Manoel Alberto
(YC74)), Miraildes Maciel Mota "FORMIGA" (90 BEATRIZ Zaneratto João),
ESTER Aparecida dos Santos, MAURINE Dornelles Gonçalves, MARTA Vieira da
Silva, CRISTIANE Rozeira de Souza Silva.
(Coaches: KLEITON Barbosa de Oliveira LIMA & JORGE BARCELLOS).
Goals: ÉRIKA Cristiano dos Santos (49), CRISTIANE Rozeira de Souza Silva (54,
90+3 pen).
Referee: Bibiana STEINHAUS (Germany) Attendance: 35,859

Team	Pld	W	D	L	GF	GA	GD	Pts
Brazil	*3*	*3*	*0*	*0*	*7*	*0*	*+7*	*9*
Australia	*3*	*2*	*0*	*1*	*5*	*4*	*+1*	*6*
Norway	*3*	*1*	*0*	*2*	*2*	*5*	*-3*	*3*
Equatorial Guinea	*3*	*0*	*0*	*3*	*2*	*7*	*-5*	*0*

QUARTER FINALS

09.07.2011 BayArena, Leverkusen: England – France 1-1 (0-0,1-1) (a.e.t.)
England: Karen BARDSLEY *(YC87)*, Alexandra SCOTT (81 Stephanie
HOUGHTON), Casey STONEY, Faye Deborah WHITE, Rachel Elizabeth UNITT
(82' Claire RAFFERTY), Fara WILLIAMS *(YC5)*, Jill SCOTT *(YC90+3)*, Karen
CARNEY, Kelly SMITH, Rachel YANKEY (84 Anita Amma Ankyewah ASANTE),
Ellen WHITE *(YC77)*. (Coach: Hope Patricia POWELL).
France: Céline DEVILLE, Laura GEORGES, Laure Maud Yvette LEPAILLEUR,
Sonia BOMPASTOR, Sabrina Marie-Christine VIGUIER, Camille ABILY, Louisa
NECIB (79 Sandrine BRÉTIGNY, 106 Eugénie LE SOMMER), Elise BUSSAGLIA,
Sandrine SOUBEYRAND (67 Elodie THOMIS), Marie Laure DELIE, Gaëtane
THINEY. (Coaches: Bruno BINI & Corinne DIACRE).
Goals: Jill SCOTT (59) / Elise BUSSAGLIA (88)
Referee: Jenny PALMQVIST (Sweden) Attendance: 26,395

*Penalties: Camille ABILY missed, Kelly SMITH 0-1, Elise BUSSAGLIA 1-1, Karen
CARNEY 1-2, Gaëtane THINEY 2-2, Casey STONEY 2-3, Sonia
BOMPASTOR 3-3, Claire RAFFERTY missed, Eugénie LE SOMMER 3-4,
Faye Deborah WHITE missed.*

France won after extra time on penalties (4:3).

09.07.2011   VOLKSWAGEN ARENA, Wolfsburg:
Germany – Japan 0-1 (0-0,0-0) (a.e.t.)
Germany: Nadine ANGERER, Saskia BARTUSIAK, Babett PETER *(YC105)*, Annike KRAHN, Kerstin GAREFREKES, Melanie BEHRINGER, Linda BRESONIK (64 Lena GÖßLING), Simone LAUDEHR, Kim KULIG (8 Bianca SCHMIDT), Inka GRINGS (102 Alexandra POPP), Célia SASIC. (Coach: Silva NEID).
Japan: Ayumi KAIHORI, Yukari KINGA, Azusa IWASHIMIZU *(YC55)*, Aya SAMESHIMA, Saki KUMAGAI *(YC114)*, Homare SAWA *(YC87)*, Aya MIYAMA, Mizuho SAKAGUCHI *(YC72)*, Kozue ANDO, Yuki NAGASATO (46 Karina MARUYAMA), Shinobu OHNO (65 Mana IWABUCHI, 116 Rumi UTSUGI).
(Coach: Norio SASAKI).
Goal: Karina MARUYAMA (108)
Referee: Quetzalli ALVARADO Godínez (Mexico)   Attendance: 26,067

Japan won after extra time.

10.07.2011   WWK Arena, Augsburg: Sweden – Australia 3-1 (2-1)
Sweden: Rut Hedvig LINDAHL, Annica SVENSSON (90+2 Lina Therese NILSSON), Sara Kristina THUNEBRO, Sara LARSSON, Barbaro Charlotte ROHLIN, Lisa Karolina Viktoria DAHLKVIST, Sara Caroline SEGER, Kerstin Ingrid Therese SJÖGRAN *(YC67)*, Linda FORSBERG (67 Nilla FISCHER *(YC81)*), Josefine ÖQVIST (83 Madeleine EDLUND), Lotta Eva SCHELIN.
(Coach: Thomas DENNERBY).
Australia: Melissa BARBIERI HUDSON, Emily VAN EGMOND (58 Clare POLKINGHORNE), Kim CARROLL, Ellyse PERRY (59 Tameka BUTT), Servet UZUNLAR, Heather GARRIOCK *(YC80)*, Elise KELLOND, Collette McCALLUM (79 Sally SHIPARD), Lisa DE VANNA, Kyah SIMON *(YC23)*, Caitlin FOORD.
(Coach: Tom SERMANNI).
Goals: Kerstin Ingrid Therese SJÖGRAN (11), Lisa Karolina Viktoria DAHLKVIST (16), Lotta Eva SCHELIN (52) / Ellyse PERRY (40)
Referee: Silvia Elizabeth REYES (Peru)   Attendance: 24,605

165

10.07.2011 DDV-Stadion, Dresden: Brazil – United States 2-2 (0-1,1-1) (a.e.t.)
Brazil: ANDRÉIA Suntaque, ALINE Pellegrino (YC44), ÉRIKA Cristiano dos Santos
(YC117), FABIANA da Silva Simões, DAIANE Menezes Ridrigues, ROSANA dos
Santos Augusto (85 FRANCIELLE Manoel Alberto), Miraildes Maciel Mota
"FORMIGA" (113 Renata Aparecida da Costa "KÓKI"), ESTER Aparecida dos
Santos, MAURINE Dornelles Gonçalves (YC112), MARTA Vieira da Silva (YC45),
CRISTIANE Rozeira de Souza Silva.
(Coaches: KLEITON Barbosa de Oliveira LIMA & JORGE BARCELLOS).
United States: Hope Amelia SOLO (YC67), Christie PEARCE, Alexandra Blaire (Ali)
KRIEGER, Rachel VAN HOLLEBEKE (RC66), Amy LePEILBET, Shannon BOXX
(YC113), Heather O'REILLY (108 Tobin HEATH), Carli LLOYD (YC29), Abby
WAMBACH, Lauren HOLIDAY (55 Megan RAPINOE (YC90)), Amy RODRIGUEZ
(72 Alexandra (Alex) MORGAN). (Coach: Pia Mariane SUNDHAGE).
Goals: MARTA Vieira da Silva (68 pen, 92) / DAIANE Menezes Ridrigues (2 og),
Abby WAMBACH (120+2)
Referee: Jacqui MELKSHAM (Australia) Attendance: 25,598

Sent-off: 66' Rachel VAN HOLLEBEKE.

*Penalties: Shannon BOXX 1-0, CRISTIANE Rozeira de Souza Silva 1-1, Carli LLOYD
2-1, MARTA Vieira da Silva 2-2, Abby WAMBACH 3-2, DAIANE Menezes
Ridrigues missed, Megan RAPINOE 4-2, FRANCIELLE Manoel Alberto
4-3, Alexandra Blaire (Ali) KRIEGER 5-3.*

United States won after extra time on penalties (5:3).

SEMI-FINALS

13.07.2011 Stadion im BORUSSIA-PARK, Mönchengladbach:
          France – United States 1-3 (0-1)
France: Bérangère SAPOWICZ, Laura GEORGES, Laure Maud Yvette
LEPAILLEUR, Sonia BOMPASTOR, Ophelie MEILLEROUX, Camille ABILY,
Louisa NECIB, Elise BUSSAGLIA, Sandrine SOUBEYRAND (78 Elodie THOMIS
(YC90)), Marie Laure DELIE (46 Eugénie LE SOMMER), Gaëtane THINEY.
(Coaches: Bruno BINI & Corinne DIACRE).
United States: Hope Amelia SOLO, Christie PEARCE, Alexandra Blaire (Ali)
KRIEGER, Becky SAUERBRUNN, Amy LePEILBET, Shannon BOXX, Heather
O'REILLY (87 Tobin HEATH), Carli LLOYD (65 Megan RAPINOE), Abby
WAMBACH, Lauren HOLIDAY, Amy RODRIGUEZ (56 Alexandra (Alex)
MORGAN). (Coach: Pia Mariane SUNDHAGE).
Goals: Sonia BOMPASTOR (55) / Lauren HOLIDAY (9), Abby WAMBACH (79),
Alexandra (Alex) MORGAN (82)
Referee: Kirsi HEIKKINEN (Finland) Attendance: 25,676

13.07.2011   Commerzbank-Arena, Frankfurt am Main: Japan – Sweden 3-1 (1-1)
Japan: Ayumi KAIHORI, Yukari KINGA, Azusa IWASHIMIZU, Aya SAMESHIMA, Saki KUMAGAI, Homare SAWA, Aya MIYAMA (89 Megumi KAMIONOBE), Mizuho SAKAGUCHI, Kozue ANDO, Shinobu OHNO (86 Megumi TAKASE), Nahomi KAWASUMI (74 Yuki NAGASATO). (Coach: Norio SASAKI).
Sweden: Rut Hedvig LINDAHL, Annica SVENSSON (YC70), Sara Kristina THUNEBRO, Sara LARSSON, Barbaro Charlotte ROHLIN, Lisa Karolina Viktoria DAHLKVIST, Marie HAMMARSTRÖM (69 Jessica LANDSTRÖM), Kerstin Ingrid Therese SJÖGRAN, Linda FORSBERG (65 Eva Sofia JAKOBSSON), Josefine ÖQVIST (75 Antonia GÖRANSSON), Lotta Eva SCHELIN.
(Coach: Thomas DENNERBY).
Goals: Nahomi KAWASUMI (19, 64), Homare SAWA (60) / Josefine ÖQVIST (10)
Referee: Carol Anne CHENARD (Canada)   Attendance: 45,434

THIRD PLACE FINAL

16.07.2011   WIRSOL Rhein-Neckar-Arena, Sinsheim: Sweden – France 2-1 (1-0)
Sweden: Rut Hedvig LINDAHL, Annica SVENSSON, Sara Kristina THUNEBRO, Sara LARSSON, Barbaro Charlotte ROHLIN, Nilla FISCHER (73 Linda Brigitta SEMBRANT), Lisa Karolina Viktoria DAHLKVIST, Kerstin Ingrid Therese SJÖGRAN, Linda FORSBERG (62 Marie HAMMARSTRÖM), Josefine ÖQVIST (RC68), Lotta Eva SCHELIN. (Coach: Thomas DENNERBY).
France: Bérangère SAPOWICZ (32 Céline DEVILLE), Laura GEORGES, Wendie RENARD, Sonia BOMPASTOR, Corine PETIT-FRANCO (84 Caroline PIZZALA), Camille ABILY, Louisa NECIB (32 Elodie THOMIS), Elise BUSSAGLIA, Sandrine SOUBEYRAND, Eugénie LE SOMMER, Gaëtane THINEY.
(Coaches: Bruno BINI & Corinne DIACRE).
Goals: Lotta Eva SCHELIN (29), Marie HAMMARSTRÖM (82) /
Elodie THOMIS (56)
Referee: Kari SEITZ (United States)   Attendance: 25,475

Sent-off: 68' Josefine ÖQVIST.

FINAL

17.07.2011   Commerzbank-Arena, Frankfurt am Main:
Japan – United States 2-2 (0-0,1-1) (a.e.t.)

Japan: Ayumi KAIHORI, Yukari KINGA, Azusa IWASHIMIZU *(RC120+1)*, Aya
SAMESHIMA, Saki KUMAGAI, Homare SAWA, Aya MIYAMA *(YC97)*, Mizuho
SAKAGUCHI, Kozue ANDO (66 Yuki NAGASATO), Shinobu OHNO (66 Karina
MARUYAMA, 119 Mana IWABUCHI), Nahomi KAWASUMI.
(Coach: Norio SASAKI).

United States: Hope Amelia SOLO, Christie PEARCE, Alexandra Blaire (Ali)
KRIEGER, Rachel VAN HOLLEBEKE, Amy LePEILBET, Shannon BOXX, Heather
O'REILLY, Carli LLOYD, Abby WAMBACH, Lauren HOLIDAY (46 Alexandra
(Alex) MORGAN), Megan RAPINOE (114 Tobin HEATH).
(Coach: Pia Mariane SUNDHAGE).

Goals: Aya MIYAMA (81), Homare SAWA (117) / Alexandra (Alex) MORGAN
(68), Abby WAMBACH (104)
Referee: Bibiana STEINHAUS (Germany)   Attendance: 48,817

Sent-off: 120+1' Azusa IWASHIMIZU.

Penalties: Shannon BOXX missed, Aya MIYAMA 0-1, Carli LLOYD missed, Yuki
NAGASATO missed, Tobin HEATH missed, Mizuho SAKAGUCHI 0-2,
Abby WAMBACH 1-2, Saki KUMAGAI 1-3.

Japan won after extra time on penalties (3:1).

JAPAN BECAME WORLD CHAMPIONS

SEVENTH EDITION FIFA WOMEN'S WORLD CUP 2015

QUALIFYING TOURNAMENTS

CAF AFRICAN WOMEN'S CHAMPIONSHIP 2014

The African Women's Championship final tournament was held in Namibia between 11 & 25 October 2014.

FIRST ROUND

14.02.2014   Stade Omar Hamadi, Algiers: Algeria – Morocco 2-0 (1-0)
Goals: Bouhani (11, 56)
14.02.2014   Ethiopia – South Sudan   **Cancelled**
14.02.2014   Nigeria – Sierra Leone   **Cancelled**
14.02.2014   Guinea-Bissau – Senegal   **Cancelled**
14.02.2014   Mozambique – Comoros   **Cancelled**
14.02.2014   SSKB Stadium, Gaborone: Botswana – Zimbabwe 0-1 (0-1)
Goal: Bepete (43)
14.02.2014   Nkoloma Stadium, Lusaka: Zambia – Tanzania 2-1 (0-0)
Goals: Mubanga (78), Chisha (82) / Daniel (90)
15.02.2015   Stade Robert Champroux, Abidjan: Ivory Coast – Mali 4-0 (1-0)
Goals: Gnago (5 pen), Nahi (72), Nrehy (80), Elloh (85)
16.02.2014   Al Ahly Training Centre, 6th Ocober City: Egypt – Tunisia 0-3 (0-2)
Goals: Hidouri (23, Gonri (45), Maknoun (50)
16.02.2014   Stade du 4-Août, Ouagadougou: Burkina Faso – Ghana 0-3 (0-3)
Goals: Ibrahim (4, 19), Aduako (9)
16.02.2014   Stade Régional Nyamirambo, Kigali: Rwanda – Kenya 1-0 (1-0)
Goal: Niyoyita (29)
28.02.2014   South Sudan – Ethiopia   **Cancelled**
28.02.2014   Stade Modibo Keïta, Bamako: Mali – Ivory Coast 0-1 (0-0)
Goal: Nrehy (49)
28.02.2014   Sierra Leone – Nigeria   **Cancelled**
28.02.2014   Senegal – Guinea-Bissau   **Cancelled**
28.02.2014   Comoros – Mozambique   **Cancelled**
28.02.2014   Benjamin Mkapa National Stadium, Dar es Salaam:
                    Tanzania – Zambia 1-1 (1-0)
Goals: Rashid (39) / Banda (80)
01.03.2014   Stade 15 Octobre, Bizerte: Tunisia – Egypt 2-2 (1-1)
Goals: Houij (4 pen), Hidouri (61) / Tarek (18), Abdallah (77)
01.03.2014   Prince Moulay Abdellah Stadium, Rabat: Morocco – Algeria 0-0
01.03.2014   Accra sports Stadium, Accra: Ghana – Burkina Faso 3-0 (2-0)
Goals: Ibrahim (20), Aduako (26 pen, 72)
02.03.2014   Kenyatta Stadium, Machakos: Kenya – Rwanda 2-1 (2-1)
Goals: Ogolia (14), Amau (40) / Nyirahatashima (29)
Rwanda won on away goals

02.03.2014   Rufaro Stadium, Harare: Zimbabwe – Botswana 2-1 (2-0)
Goals: Makore (9), Nyaumwe (14) / Ngenda (90)

South Sudan withdrew, Ethiopia advanced.
Sierra Leone withdrew because of financial problems, Nigeria advanced.
Guinea Bissau withdrew, Senegal advanced.
Mozambique withdrew, Comoros advanced.

SECOND ROUND

23.05.2014   Stade Omar Hamadi, Algiers: Algeria – Tunisia 2-1 (2-1)
Goals: Laifa (1), Sekouane (45 pen) / Kaabachi (20)
23.05.2014   Stade Robert Champroux, Abidjan:
            Ivory Coast – Equatorial Guinea 1-1 (1-1)
Goals: Diakité (37 pen) / Añonma (32)
23.05.2014   Stade Said Mohamed Cheikh, Mitsamiouli:
            Comoros – South Africa 0-13 (0-5)
Goals: Portia (13, 19, 43, 49 pen), Smeda (25, 34, 54, 60), Ntsibande (64), Mollo (65, 68), Nogwanya (75 pen), Makhabane (85)
24.05.2014   Stade Régional Nyamirambo, Kigali: Rwanda – Nigeria 1-4 (0-2)
Goals: Mukamana (65) / Oshoala (35, 40), Sunday (48), Oparanozie (70 pen)
24.05.2014   Stade Aline Sitoe Diatta, Ziguinchor: Senegal – Cameroon 1-1 (0-0)
Goals: Sylla (76) / Njoya (58)
25.05.2014   Addis Ababa Stadium, Addis Ababa: Ethiopia – Ghana 0-2 (0-1)
Goals: Cudjoe (43), Suleman (55)
25.05.2014   Rufaro Stadium, Harare: Zimbabwe – Zambia 0-1 (0-0)
Goal: Mubanga (64)
07.05.2014   Estadio Internacional, Malabo:
            Equatorial Guinea – Ivory Coast 2-2 (1-1)
Goals: Jade (3), Chuigoué (89) / Guehai (35), N'Guessan (86)
Ivory Coast won on away goals
07.06.2014   Abuja Stadium, Abuja: Nigeria – Rwanda 8-0 (5-0)
Goals: Edoho (10), Oshoala (19, 61), Oparanozie (20, 30, 52), Sunday (41), Nku (89)
07.06.2014   South Africa – Comoros   **Cancelled**
08.06.2014   Stade 15 Octobre, Bizerte: Tunisia – Algeria 2-3 (2-2)
Goals: Kaabachi (13, 32) / Bouhani (8), Bekhedda (44 pen), Sekouane (81)
08.06.2014   Tamale Stadium, Tamale: Ghana – Ethiopia 3-0 (2-0)
Goals: Ibrahim (24 pen), Cudjoe (27), Kobblah (83)
08.06.2014   Stade Ahmadou Ahidjo, Yaoundé: Cameroon – Senegal 1-0 (0-0)
Goal: Edoa (67)
08.06.2014   Nkoloma Stadium, Lusaka: Zambia – Zimbabwe 1-0 (1-0)
Goal: Mubanga (36)

Comoros withdrew before the second leg, South Africa advanced.

GROUP STAGE

GROUP A

11.10.2014   Sam Nujoma Stadium, Windhoek: Namibia – Zambia 2-0 (2-0)
Goals: Williams (4), Adams (21)
11.10.2014   Sam Nujoma Stadium, Windhoek: Nigeria – Ivory Coast 4-2 (1-1)
Goals: Sunday (11), Diakité (54 og), Oparanozie (74, 86) / F.Coulibaly (21 pen),
Lohoues (75)
14.10.2014   Sam Nujoma Stadium, Windhoek: Zambia – Nigeria 0-6 (0-3)
Goals: Okobi (2), Ohale (6), Oparanozie (25 pen, 81), Oshoala (64), Nkwocha (84)
14.10.2014   Sam Nujoma Stadium, Windhoek: Ivory Coast – Namibia 3-1 (1-1)
Goals: Nahi (13), Nrehy (84, 90) / Coleman (20)
17.10.2014   Sam Nujoma Stadium, Windhoek: Namibia – Nigeria 0-2 (0-2)
Goals: Ofoegbu (36), Ordega (38)
17.10.2014   Independende Stadium, Windhoek: Zambia – Ivory Coast 1-1 (0-1)
Goals: Banda (58) / Nahi (3)

Team	Pld	W	D	L	GF	GA	GD	Pts
Nigeria	*3*	*3*	*0*	*0*	*12*	*2*	*+10*	*9*
Ivory Coast	*3*	*1*	*1*	*1*	*6*	*6*	*0*	*4*
Namibia	3	1	0	2	3	5	-2	3
Zambia	3	0	1	2	1	9	-8	1

GROUP B

12.10.2014   Independende Stadium, Windhoek: South Africa – Cameroon 0-1 (0-0)
Goal: Feudjio (86)
12.10.2014   Independende Stadium, Windhoek: Algeria – Ghana 1-0 (0-0)
Goal: Affak (87)
15.10.2014   Independende Stadium, Windhoek: Cameroon – Algeria 2-0 (1-0)
Goals: Enganamouit (17, 61 pen)
15.10.2014   Independende Stadium, Windhoek: Ghana – South Africa 1-1 (1-1)
Goals: Cudjoe (45) / Nongwanya (19)
18.10.2014   Independende Stadium, Windhoek: South Africa – Algeria 5-1 (2-0)
Goals: Dlamini (36), Modise (41, 87), Mollo (70), Makhabane (82) / Affak (90)
18.10.2014   Sam Nujoma Stadium, Windhoek: Cameroon – Ghana 0-1 (0-0)
Goal: Cudjoe (53)

Team	Pld	W	D	L	GF	GA	GD	Pts
Cameroon	*3*	*2*	*0*	*1*	*3*	*1*	*+2*	*6*
South Africa	*3*	*1*	*1*	*1*	*6*	*3*	*+3*	*4*
Ghana	3	1	1	1	2	2	0	4
Algeria	3	1	0	2	2	7	-5	3

KNOCKOUT STAGE
SEMI-FINALS

22.10.2014   Sam Nujoma Stadium, Windhoek: Nigeria – South Africa 2-1 (2-0)
Goals: Oshoala (38, 45) / Jane (67)
22.10.2014   Sam Nujoma Stadium, Windhoek:
                    Cameroon – Ivory Coast 2-1 (0-0,1-1) (a.e.t.)
Goals: Enganamouit (60, Manie (118) / Nrehy (65)
Cameroon won after extra time

THIRD PLACE PLAY-OFF

25.10.2014   Sam Nujoma Stadium, Windhoek: South Africa – Ivory Coast 0-1 (0-0)

FINAL

25.10.2014   Sam Nujoma Stadium, Windhoek: Nigeria – Cameroon 2-0 (2-0)
Goals: Oparanozie (12), Oshoala (43)

The winner **Nigeria**, the runner-up **Cameroon** and the third place team **Ivory Coast** qualified for the FIFA Women's World Cup 2015.

AFC WOMEN'S ASIAN CUP 2014

China PR, Australia, Japan and South Korea were automatically qualified for the Final Tournament which was held in Vietnam between 14 & 25 May 2014. North Korea was banned from the tournament due to the sanction on their doping cases in the FIFA Women's World Cup 2011.

QUALIFICATION

All four group winners will qualify for the Final Tournament.

GROUP A

All matches were played in Jordan.

05.06.2013   Amman International Stadium, Amman:
                    Uzbekistan – Kuwait 18-0 (11-0)
Goals: Juraeva (4, 14, 21, 35, 45+1, 51, 58, 73), Turdiboeva (6, 42), Riskieva (23), Sarikova (31), Turopova (34, 36, 65), Moiseeva (70), Bakhromova (72), Zarbieva (78)
05.06.2013   Amman International Stadium, Amman: Jordan – Lebanon 5-0 (3-0)
Goals: Al-Masri (21), Al-Naber (33, 40), Khraisat (53, 59)
07.06.2012   Amman International Stadium, Amman: Lebanon – Uzbekistan 0-4 (0-3)
Goals: Turdiboeva (2), Juraeva (41), Turopova (45+2), Ermatova (46)
07.06.2013   Amman International Stadium, Amman: Kuwait – Jordan 0-21 (0-12)
Goals: Jebreen (3, 70), Jbarah (16, 18, 19, 28, 32, 45+1, 53, 81), Al-Nabr (17, 35, 38, 72), Al-Nahar (20, 43, 56, 71, 84, 90+1), Al-Masri (78)

172

09.06.2013   Amman International Stadium, Amman: Lebanon – Kuwait 12-1 (6-0)
Goals: Dbouk (12), Assaf (19, 51), El Jaafil (27), Schtakleff (29, 77), Bahlawan (38, 90+3), Al Sayegh (45+1, 46), Hamadeh (56), Bakri (80) / Hajji (86)
09.06.2013   Amman International Stadium, Amman: Uzbekistan – Jordan 0-4 (0-0)
Goals: Khraisat (57, 80), Jebreen (59), Al-Naber (75)

Team	Pld	W	D	L	GF	GA	GD	Pts
Jordan	*3*	*3*	*0*	*0*	*30*	*0*	*+30*	*9*
Uzbekistan	3	2	0	1	22	4	+18	6
Lebanon	3	1	0	2	12	10	+2	3
Kuwait	3	0	0	3	1	51	-50	0

GROUP B

All matches were played in Bangladesh.

21.05.2013   Bangabandhu National Stadium, Dhaka: Iran – Phlippines 0-6 (0-5)
Goals: Cooke (1), Jurado (3), Shugg (4, 90+2), Kamangar (33 og), Houplin (40)
21.05.2013   Bangabandhu National Stadium, Dhaka:
             Thailand – Bangladesh 9-0 (4-0)
Goals: Rattikan (16), Naphat (18), Nisa (29, 45, 87, 90+3), Trishna (52 og), Sunisa (64), Boontan (79)
23.05.2013   Bangabandhu National Stadium, Dhaka: Philippines – Thailand 0-1 (0-1)
Goal: Nisa (37)
23.05.2013   Bangabandhu National Stadium, Dhaka: Bangladesh – Iran 0-2 (0-1)
Goals: Rahimi (26, 51)
25.05.2013   Bangabandhu National Stadium, Dhaka: Thailand – Iran 5-1 (0-0)
Goals: Nisa (46, 65, 85), Anootsara (70), Naphat (74) / Ghomi (79)
25.05.2013   Bangabandhu National Stadium, Dhaka:
             Philippines – Bangladesh 4-0 (2-0)
Goals: Park (19, 90+5), Delos Reyes (29), Barnekow (85)

Team	Pld	W	D	L	GF	GA	GD	Pts
Thailand	*3*	*3*	*0*	*0*	*15*	*1*	*+14*	*9*
Philippines	3	2	0	1	10	1	+9	6
Iran	3	1	0	2	3	11	-8	3
Bangladesh	3	0	0	3	0	15	-15	0

GROUP C

All matches were played in Bahrain.

22.05.2013   Bahrain National Stadium, Riffa: Vietnam – Bahrain 8-0 (5-0)
Goals: Minh Nguyet (3), Kim Hong (20), Thi Xuyen (22), Thi Muon (38, 58, 70), Thi Lieu (45), Kim Tien (65)
22.05.2013   Bahrain National Stadium, Riffa: Hong Kong – Kyrgyzstan 2-1 (1-0)
Goals: Cheung Wai Ki (41, 86) / Tynkova (59)

24.05.2013   Bahrain National Stadium, Riffa: Bahrain – Hong Kong 1-3 (1-0)
Goals: Al Hashmi (25) / Cheung Wa Ki (52), Fung Kam Mui (65, 69)
24.05.2013   Bahrain National Stadium, Riffa: Kyrgyzstan – Vietnam 0-12 (0-7)
Goals: Minh Nguyet (3, 12, 22), Ngoc Anh (5), Thi Xuyen (14), Thi Hoa (23, 71), Thi
Muon (35), Kim Tien (50), Kim Hong (65), Huynh Nhur (81, 88)
26.05.2013   Bahrain National Stadium, Riffa: Vietnam – Hong Kong 4-0 (3-0)
Goals: Minh Nguyet (5), Thi Hoa (7), Cheung Wai Ki (30 og), Kim Hong (57)
26.05.2013   Bahrain National Stadium, Riffa: Kyrgyzstan – Bahrain 1-4 (1-3)
Goals: Tynkova (31) / Abdelrahman (3, 33), Al Hashmi (20, 49)

Team	Pld	W	D	L	GF	GA	GD	Pts
Vietnam	*3*	*3*	*0*	*0*	*24*	*0*	*+24*	*9*
Hong Kong	3	2	0	1	5	6	-1	6
Bahrain	3	1	0	2	5	12	-7	3
Kyrgyzstan	3	0	0	3	2	18	-16	0

GROUP D

All matches were played in Palestine.

21.05.2013   Faisal Al-Husseini International Stadium, Al-Ram:
                     Chinese Taipei – Palestine 6-0 (4-0)
Goals: Lin Ya-han (5, 54, 80), Yu Hsiu-chin (40), Lai Li-chin (42),
Lin-Kai-ling (45+1)
21.05.2013   Faisal Al-Husseini International Stadium, Al-Ram:
                     Myanmar – India 2-0 (2-0)
Goals: Naw Ar Lo Wer Phaw (6), Khin Moe Wai (26)
23.05.2013   Faisal Al-Husseini International Stadium, Al-Ram:
                     Palestine – Myanmar 0-9 (0-3)
Goals: Yee Yee Oo (24, 74, 77, 80, 85, 88), Khin Moe Wai (17, 26),
Margret Marri (67)
23.05.2013   Faisal Al-Husseini International Stadium, Al-Ram:
                     India – Chinese Taipei 1-2 (0-1)
Goals: Sasmita (54) / Yu Hsiu-chin (42), Lai Li-chin (82)
25.05.2013   Faisal Al-Husseini International Stadium, Al-Ram:
                     Palestine – India 1-1 (0-1)
Goals: Sohgian (46 pen) / Sasmita (35)
25.05.2013   Faisal Al-Husseini International Stadium, Al-Ram:
                     Myanmar – Chinese Taipei 0-0

Team	Pld	W	D	L	GF	GA	GD	Pts
Myanmar	*3*	*2*	*1*	*0*	*11*	*0*	*+11*	*7*
Chinese Taipei	3	2	1	0	8	1	+7	7
India	3	0	1	2	2	5	-3	1
Palestine	3	0	1	2	1	16	-15	1

FINAL TOURNAMENT

The Final Tournament was held in Vietnam between 14 & 25 May 2014.

GROUP STAGE

The top two teams of each group advanced to the semi-finals and the two third-placed teams had to play a play-off match for the fifth place. The winner of the play-off match will qualify for the FIFA Women's World Cup 2015.

GROUP A

14.05.2014 Thong Nhat Stadium, Ho Chi Minh City: Vietnam – Jordan 3-1 (2-1)
Goals: Muon (18), Thanh Hurong (36, 84) / Jbarah (34)
14.05.2014 Thong Nhat Stadium, Ho Chi Minh City: Australia – Japan 2-2 (1-0)
Goals: Foord (21), De Vanna (64) / Polinghorne (71 og), Ogimi (84)
16.05.2014 Thong Nhat Stadium, Ho Chi Minh City: Jordan – Australia 1-3 (0-1)
Goals: Al-Naber (70) / Gill (35, 50), Gorry (66)
16.05.2014 Thong Nhat Stadium, Ho Chi Minh City: Japan – Vietnam 4-0 (1-0)
Goals: Kawasumi (44, 87), Kiryu (65), Ogimi (69)
18.05.2014 Thong Nhat Stadium, Ho Chi Minh City: Vietnam – Australia 0-2 (0-1)
Goals: Thurong (42 og), Gorry (90)
18.05.2014 Go Dau Stadium, Thu Dau Mot: Japan – Jordan 7-0 (2-0)
Goals: Kira (25, 90+3), Nakajima (45+1, 75), Sakaguchi (49, 81), Alhyasat (69 og)

Team	Pld	W	D	L	GF	GA	GD	Pts
Japan	*3*	*2*	*1*	*0*	*13*	*2*	*+11*	*7*
Australia	*3*	*2*	*1*	*0*	*7*	*3*	*+4*	*7*
Vietnam	3	1	0	2	3	7	-4	3
Jordan	3	0	0	3	2	13	-11	0

GROUP B

15.05.2014 Thong Nhat Stadium, Ho Chi Minh City:
        South Korea – Myanmar 12-0 (7-0)
Goals: Ji So-yun (4), Park Eun-sun (17 pen, 43), Park Hee-young (33), Jeon Ga-eul (36, 40 pen, 63), Cho So-hyun (45+3, 61, 82), Kwon Hah-nul (58), Yeo Min-ji (76)
15.05.2014 Thong Nhat Stadium, Ho Chi Minh City: China PR – Thailand 7-0 (4-0)
Goals: Li Dongna (6), Li Ying (8), Yang Li (16, 45+1, 64, 90+1), Xu Yanlu (75)
17.05.2014 Thong Nhat Stadium, Ho Chi Minh City: Myanmar – China PR 0-3 (0-1)
Goals: Ren Guixin (10), Ma Xiaoxu (60), Yang Yi (87)
17.05.2014 Thong Nhat Stadium, Ho Chi Minh City:
        Thailand – South Korea 0-4 (0-2)
Goals: Ji So-yun (11), Park Eun-sun (12, 47, 84)
19.05.2014 Thong Nhat Stadium, Ho Chi Minh City: South Korea – China PR 0-0
19.05.2014 Go Dau Stadium, Thu Dau Mot: Thailand – Myanmar 2-1 (1-1)
Goals: Sung-Ngoen (27 pen), Duangnapa (59) / Yee Yee Oo (45+1)

Team	Pld	W	D	L	GF	GA	GD	Pts
South Korea	*3*	*2*	*1*	*0*	*16*	*0*	*+16*	*7*
China PR	*3*	*2*	*1*	*0*	*10*	*0*	*+10*	*7*
Thailand	3	1	0	2	2	12	-10	3
Myanmar	3	0	0	3	1	17	-16	0

FIFTH PLACE PLAY-OFF

21.05.2014   Go Dau Stadium, Thu Dau Mot: Vietnam – Thailand 1-2 (0-0)
Goals: Tuyet Dung (86) / Sung-Ngoen (48, 65)

Thailand the winner of the play-off qualified for the FIFA Women's World Cup 2015.

KNOCKOUT STAGE

SEMI-FINALS

22.05.2014   Thong Nhat Stadium, Ho Chi Minh City:
              Japan – China PR 2-1 (0-0,1-1) (a.e.t.)
Goals: Sawa (51), Iwashimizu (120+2) / Li dongna (80 pen)
22.05.2014   Thong Nhat Stadium, Ho Chi Minh City:
              South Korea – Australia 1-2 (0-0)
Goals: Park Eun-sun (53 pen) / Gorry (47), Kellond-Knight (77)

THIRD PACE PLAY-OFF

25.05.2014   Thong Nhat Stadium, Ho Chi Minh City:
              China PR – South Korea 2-1 (1-0)
Goals: Park Eun-sun (3 og), Yang Li (90+3) / Yoo Young-a (80)

FINAL

25.05.2014   Thong Nhat Stadium, Ho Chi Minh City: Japan – Australia 1-0 (1-0)
Goal: Iwashimizu (28)

The winner **Japan**, **Australia**, **China PR**, **South Korea** and fifth placed **Thailand** all qualified for the FIFA Women'sWorld Cup 2015.

UEFA WOMEN'S WORLD CUP QUALIFICATION 2015

A record 46 UEFA teams entered qualification. The 8 lowest teams entered the tournament in the preliminary round and were drawn into 2 groups of four and played in single round-robin format between 4 & 9 April 2013 in Malta and Lithuania respectively. The winners and runners-up of each group advanced to the Group Stage.

PRELIMINARY ROUND
GROUP A

04.04.2013   Ta'Qali National Stadium, Ta'Qali: Albania – Malta 1-1 (0-0)
Goals: Curo (76) / Theuma (80)
04.04.2013   Ta'Qali National Stadium, Ta'Qali: Luxembourg – Latvia 0-0
06.04.2013   Ta'Qali National Stadium, Ta'Qali: Albania – Latvia 2-0 (2-0)
Goals: Memedov (17), Velaj (41)
06.04.2013   Ta'Qali National Stadium, Ta'Qali: Malta – Luxembourg 6-0 (4-0)
Goals: Carabott (12), Theuma (25 pen, 61), Cuschieri (28), Xeurreb (29),
Buttigieg (50)
09.04.2013   Ta'Qali National Stadium, Ta'Qali: Luxembourg – Albania 1-2 (1-1)
Goals: Maurer (45) / Jashari (16), Velaj (69)
09.04.2013   Ta'Qali National Stadium, Ta'Qali: Latvia – Malta 0-2 (0-1)
Goals: Theuma (45+1), Cuschieri (83)

Team	Pld	W	D	L	GF	GA	GD	Pts
Malta	*3*	*2*	*1*	*0*	*9*	*1*	*+8*	*7*
Albania	*3*	*2*	*1*	*0*	*5*	*2*	*+3*	*7*
Latvia	3	0	1	2	0	4	-4	1
Luxembourg	3	0	1	2	1	8	-7	1

GROUP B

04.04.2013   LFF Stadium, Vilnius: Faroe Islands – Montenegro 3-3 (0-1)
Goals: H.Sevdal (49, 76), Magnussen (51) / Vukcevic (18, 66), Kuc (59)
04.04.2013   LFF Stadium, Vilnius: Georgia – Lithuania 4-3 (2-2)
Goals: Pasikashvili (32, 85), Chkonia (39), Matveeva (60) / Vanagaité (9), Biozyté
(17), Mazukelyte (82)
06.04.2013   LFF Stadium, Vilnius: Georgia – Montenegro 0-2 (0-1)
Goals: Vukcevic (38, 90+4)
06.04.2013   LFF Stadium, Vilnius: Lithuania – Faroe Islands 0-1 (0-0)
Goal: Andreasen (61)
09.04.2013   LFF Stadium, Vilnius: Faroe Islands – Georgia 2-1 (1-0)
Goals: H.Sevdal (38, 73) / Chichinadze (47)
09.04.2013   LFF Stadium, Vilnius: Montenegro – Lithuania 1-1 (0-0)
Goals: Vukcevic (60) / Vanagaité (90+1)

Team	Pld	W	D	L	GF	GA	GD	Pts
Faroe Islands	*3*	*2*	*1*	*0*	*6*	*4*	*+2*	*7*
Montenegro	*3*	*1*	*2*	*0*	*6*	*4*	*+2*	*5*
Georgia	3	1	0	2	5	7	-2	3
Lithuania	3	0	1	2	4	6	-2	1

GROUP STAGE

Forty-two teams were drawn in 7 groups. All group matches were played between 20
September 2013 and 17 September 2014. The seven group winners advanced directly

to the FIFA Women's World Cup 2015. The four runners-up with the best record advanced to play-off matches for the remaining berth.

GROUP 1

21.09.2013   Stadion der Freundschaft, Cottbus: Germany – Russia 9-0 (4-0)
Goals: Sasic (22 pen), Keßler (25, 85), Marozsán (26, 37), Alushi (73), Leupolz (76), Goeßling (80),Schmidt (87)
22.09.2013   Tallaght Stadium, Dublin: Republic of Ireland – Slovakia 2-0 (0-0)
Goals: Russell (56), D.O'Sullivan (74)
26.09.2013   Gradski stadion, Sinj: Croatia – Republic of Ireland 1-1 (1-0)
Goals: Kolar (11) / Caldwell (90+4)
26.09.2013   NTC Senec, Senec: Slovakia – Slovenia 1-3 (0-2)
Goals: Skorvánková (77) / Rola (30), Nikl (45+1), Zver (89)
26.10.2013   Sv. Josip Radnik, Sesvete: Croatia – Slovakia 0-1 (0-1)
Goal: Bartovicová (33)
26.10.2013   Bonifika Stadium, Koper: Slovenia – Germany 0-13 (0-7)
Goals: Sasic (4 pen, 32, 66), Maier (10), Mittag (16, 20, 65), Krahn (19), Laudehr (42), Alushi (62), Goeßling (85, 87), Popp (90+3)
30.10.2013   Ob Jezeru City Stadium, Velenje:
                      Slovenia – Republic of Ireland 0-3 (0-2)
Goals: F.O'Sullivan (12), O'Gorman (42), D.O'Sullivan (46)
30.10.2013   Stadion am Bornheimer Hang, Frankfurt: Germany – Croatia 4-0 (0-0)
Goals: Sasic (52), Hercigonja-Moulton (56 og, 62 og), Wensing (80)
31.10.2013   NTC Senec, Senec: Slovakia – Russia 0-2 (0-0)
Goals: Kolenová (72 og), Morozova (74)
23.11.2013   Stadión pod Dubnom, Zilina: Slovakia – Germany 0-6 (0-1)
Goals: Keßler (8, 83), Mittag (57, 65), Popp (84), Marozsán (87)
27.11.2013   Stadion Gradski vrt, Osijek: Croatia – Germany 0-8 (0-3)
Goals: Marozsán (12, 22, 68, 80), Sasic (13), Mittag (53), Popp (72), Bartusiak (90+1)
05.04.2014   Rodina Stadium, Khimki: Russia – Slovenia 4-1 (2-1)
Goals: Orlova (31), Korovkina (36), Tsybutovich (53), Pantyukhina (87) / Jerina (12)
05.04.2014   Tallaght Stadium, Dublin: Republic of Ireland – Germany 2-3 (1-0)
Goals: Quinn (3), Roche (89) / Laudehr (65 pen), Lotzen (84), Leupolz (90+1)
09.04.2014   Rodina Stadium, Khimki: Russia – Croatia 1-0 (1-0)
Goal: Pantyukhina (9)
10.04.2014   Carl-Benz-Stadion, Mannheim: Germany – Slovenia 4-0 (2-0)
Goals: Leupolz (18), Mittag (21, 67), Lotzen (63)
07.05.2014   Tallaght Stadium, Dublin: Republic of Ireland – Russia 1-3 (1-3)
Goals: F.O'Sullivan (35) / Sochneva (7), Pantyukhina (12, 43)
08.05.2014   Stadion an der Bremer Brücke, Osnabrück:
                      Germany – Slovakia 9-1 (5-0)
Goals: Alushi (2, 35, 70), Mittag (24, 80), Keßler (39), Marozsán (40), Leupolz (73), Laudehr (76) / Biróová (85)
08.05.2014   Ptuj City Stadium, Ptuj: Slovenia – Croatia 0-3 (0-3)
Goals: Hercigonja-Moulton (7), Balog (10), Landeka (17 pen)
14.06.2014   Donzale Sports Park, Domzale: Slovenia – Russia 1-2 (0-2)
Goals: Jerina (59) / Tsybutocich (28), Grad (41 og)

178

14.06.2014   Tallaght Stadium, Dublin: Republic of Ireland – Croatia 1-0 (0-0)
Goal: D.O'Sullivan (90+3)
19.06.2014   Krasnoarmeysk Stadium, Krasnoameysk:
Russia – Republic of Ireland 0-0
19.06.2014   NTC Senec, Senec: Slovakia – Croatia 1-1 (1-1)
Goals: Susková (29) / Lojna (32)
20.08.2014   Tallaght Stadium, Dublin: Republic of Ireland – Slovenia 2-0 (1-0)
Goals: Russell (2), F.O'Sullivan (76)
21.08.2014   Metallurg Stadium, Samara: Russia – Slovakia 3-1 (0-1)
Goals: Sidorovskaya (58), Morozova (63), Pantyikhina (80) / Kolenová (25)
13.09.2014   Luzhniki sports Complex, Moscow: Russia – Germany 1-4 (1-3)
Goals: Tsybutovich (9 pen) / Laudehr (6), Sasic (19, 28, 72)
13.09.2014   Stadion Lucko, Zagreb: Croatia – Slovenia 1-0 (1-0)
Goal: Lojna (15)
13.09.2014   NTC Senec, Senec: Slovakia – Republic of Ireland 0-1 (0-0)
Goal: Roche (90+2)
17.09.2014   Dravograd Sports Centre, Dravograd: Slovenia – Slovakia 2-1 (0-0)
Goals: Nikl (47), Zver (76) / Ondrusová (74)
17.09.2014   Stadion NSC Stjepan Spajic, Zagreb: Croatia – Russia 1-3 (1-2)
Goals: Lojna (26) / Pantyukhina (11, 34), Terekhova (77)
17.09.2014   Voith-Arena, Heidenheim: Germany – Republic of Ireland 2-0 (2-0)
Goals: Behringer (28), Mittag (34)

Team	Pld	W	D	L	GF	GA	GD	Pts
Germany	*10*	*10*	*0*	*0*	*62*	*4*	*+58*	*30*
Russia	10	7	1	2	19	18	+1	22
Republic of Ireland	10	5	2	3	13	9	+4	17
Croatia	10	2	2	6	7	20	-13	8
Slovenia	10	2	0	8	7	34	-27	6
Slovakia	10	1	1	8	6	29	-23	4

GROUP 2

20.09.2013   Stadion Mladost, Strumica: Macedonia – Romania 1-9 (1-4)
Goals: Andonova (22 pen) / Dusa (4, 9, 21, 53), Sarghe (12), Rus (49, 59, 81), Vatafu (90+1)
20.09.2013   A. Le Coq Arena, Tallinn: Estonia – Italy 1-5 (0-0)
Goals: Loo (88) / Mauro (57), Gabbiadini (68, 72), Rosucci (70), Bonansea (77)
26.09.2013   Stadio Rino Mercante, Bassano del Grappa: Italy – Romania 1-0 (0-0)
Goal: Girelli (90+3)
26.10.2013   Stadion Mladost, Strumica: Macedonia – Czech Republic 1-3 (0-1)
Goals: Rochi (62) / Divisová (45+2), Vonková (60 pen, 73)
27.10.2013   Ciudad Deportiva, Collada Villalba: Spain – Estonia 6-0 (3-0)
Goals: Bermúdez (14, 58 pen), Torrejón (28), Hermoso (45), Natalia Pablos (72), Paredes (81)
30.10.2013   Stadion Mladost, Strumica: Macedonia – Estonia 0-2 (0-1)
Goals: Jekimova (8), Loo (58)
30.10.2013   Cluj Arena, Cluj-Napoca: Romania – Czech Republic 0-0

31.10.2013   Nuevo Matapiñonera, San Sebastián de los Reyes: Spain – Italy 2-0 (1-0)
Goals: Bermúdez (37), Natalia (56)
23.11.2013   Estadio El Deleite, Aranjuez: Spain – Romania 1-0 (1-0)
Goal: García (40)
27.11.2013   Estadio Fernando Torres, Fuenlabrada: Spain – Czech Republic 3-2 (2-0)
Goals: Bermúdez (15, 45+1), Corredera (78) / L.Martínková (80), Vonková (82)
13.02.2014   Stadio Silvio Piola, Novara: Italy – Czech Republic 6-1 (2-1)
Goals: Gabbiadini (26, 32), Manieri (49), Bonansea (61), Domenichetti (64), Panico
(71) / Divisová (44)
13.02.2014   Estadio Las Gaunas, Logroño: Spain – Macedonia 12-0 (4-0)
Goals: Boquete (4, 72), Bermúdez (11, 46), Hermoso (26, 70), Vicky (44), Natalia
(59, 64, 83, 90+3, 90+4)
05.04.2014   Stadio Romeo Menti, Vicenza: Italy – Spain 0-0
10.04.2014   FFM Training Centre, Skopje: Macedonia – Spain 0-10 (0-5)
Goals: Bermúdez (29, 30, 59), Torrejón (33), Pablos (45), Jenni (45+1, 65, 73),
Calderón (62, 64)
10.04.2014   Cluj Arena, Cluj-Napoca: Romania – Italy 1-2 (0-1)
Goals: Vatafu (80) / Panico (36), Gabbaidini (78)
26.04.2014   Stadion v Mestskych sadech, Opava: Czech Republic – Estonia 6-0 (5-0)
Goals: Kozarová (3), Cahynová (12), Krejciríková (24, 41), Svitková (26, 72)
07.05.2014   Mestsky fotbalovy stadion Miroslava Velenty, Uherské Hradiste:
            Czech Republic – Romania 0-0
08.05.2014   FFM Training Centre, Skopje: Macedonia – Italy 0-11 (0-7)
Goals: Panico (5), Girelli (9, 11, 39), Manieri (26), Gabbiadini (27, 43), Bonansea
(51), Carissimi (77), Brumana (83), Fuselli (90+4)
08.05.2014   A. Le Coq Arena, Tallinn: Estonia – Spain 0-5 (0-3)
Goals: Losada (21, 59), Natalia (32, 35), Hermoso (63)
14.06.2014   FK Viktoria Stadion, Prague: Czech Republic – Italy 0-4 (0-4)
Goals: Panico (13 pen, 18), Gabbiadini (20), Manieri (37)
15.06.2014   Haapsalu Iinnastaadion, Haapsalu: Estonia – Macedonia 1-1 (1-1)
Goals: Loo (3) / Andonova (39)
18.06.2014   FK Viktoria Stadion, Prague: Czech Republic – Macedonia 5-2 (1-0)
Goals: Cahynová (35), Pincová (47), Martínková (49, 80), Hloupá (90) /
Andonova (48, 72)
19.06.2014   Haapsalu Iinnastaadion, Haapsalu: Estonia – Romania 0-2 (0-2)
Goals: Dusa (29, 38)
20.08.2014   A. Le Coq Arena, Tallinn: Estonia – Czech Republic 1-4 (0-2)
Goals: Aarna (72) / Svitková (22, 27, 69), Raadik (81 og)
21.08.2014   Stadionul Mogosoaia, Mogosoaia: Romania – Macedonia 6-1 (2-0)
Goals: Voicu (12), Batea (42), Lunca (55, 63), Corduneanu (90+1), Spanu (90+4) /
Salihi (50)
13.09.2014   Stadionul Emil Alexandrescu, Iasi: Romania – Spain 0-2 (0-1)
Goals: Natalia (28, 59)
13.09.2014   Stadio Silvio Piola, Vercelli: Italy – Estonia 4-0 (3-0)
Goals: Bonansea (6), Zlidnis (8 og), Cernoia (27), Manieri (65)
17.09.2014   Spartak Pisek, Pisek: Czech Rupublic – Spain 0-1 (0-0)
Goal: Boquete (90+1)

180

17.09.2014   Stadionul Emil Alexandrescu, Iasi: Romania – Estonia 0-3 **Awarded**
Goals: Spanu (18, 38)
Estonia were awarded a 3-0 win after Romania fielded an ineligible player, Ioana
Bortan. The match originally ended 2-0 to Romania.
17.09.2014   Stadio Silvio Piola, Vercelli: Italy – Macedonia 15-0 (6-0)
Goals: Sabatino (14, 28, 45+1, 48, 51, 76), Camporese (22), Panico (23, 27), Tuttino
(61), Bonansea (62, 69, 85), Cernoia (64), D'Adda (72)

Team	Pld	W	D	L	GF	GA	GD	Pts
Spain	*10*	*9*	*1*	*0*	*42*	*2*	*+40*	*28*
Italy	10	8	1	1	48	5	+43	25
Czech Republic	10	4	2	4	21	18	+3	14
Romania	10	3	2	5	18	11	+7	11
Estonia	10	2	1	7	8	33	-25	7
Macedonia	10	0	1	9	6	74	-68	1

GROUP 3

21.09.2013   Centre sportif de Colovray Nyon, Nyon: Switzerland – Serbia 9-0 (4-0)
Goals: Bachmann (13, 83), Crnogorcevic (21, 61, 81, 87), Dickenmann (36 pen),
Wälti (38), Bürki (75)
26.09.2013   Laugardalsvöllur, Reykjavik: Iceland – Switzerland 0-2 (0-1)
Goals: Bachmann (9), Dickenmann (54 pen)
26.10.2013   Indjija Stadium, Indjija: Serbia – Denmark 1-1 (1-1)
Goals: Cubrilo (20) / Harder (19)
27.10.2013   Ramat Gan Stadium, Ramat Gan: Israel – Malta 2-0 (0-0)
Goals: Sofer (51), Shelina (60)
31.10.2013   FK Obilic Stadium, Belgrade: Serbia – Iceland 1-2 (0-2)
Goals: Ilic (68) / Vidarsdóttir (19), Ómarsdóttir (43)
31.10.2013   Vejle Stadion, Vejle: Denmark – Switzerland 0-1 (0-1)
Goal: Bachmann (26)
24.11.2013   Ta'Qali National Stadium, Ta'Qali: Malta – Denmark 0-5 (0-3)
Goals: S.Nielsen (7), Madim (26, 66), Harder (34), K.Nielsen (86)
24.11.2013   Ramat Gan Stadium, Ramat Gan: Israel – Serbia 3-1 (2-1)
Goals: Fridman (26), Falkon (38), Sofer (67) / Podovac (3 pen)
12.02.2014   HaMoshava Stadium, Petach-Tikva: Israel – Switzerland 0-5 (0-4)
Goals: Humm (6, 28, 36), Dickenmann (45 pen), Crnogorcevic (90+3)
13.02.2014   Ta'Qali National Stadium, Ta'Qali: Malta – Serbia 0-3 (0-2)
Goals: Damnjanovic (3), Cubrilo (38), Cankovic (84)
05.04.2014   Herti Alimend Stadion, Zug: Switzerland – Malta 11-0 (7-0)
Goals: Bachmann (4), Dickenmann (13, 45+4, 90+3), Moser (17, 62), Remund (31),
Abbé (39), Kiwic (41), Humm (59, 85)
05.04.2014   Ramat Gan Stadium, Ramat Gan: Israel – Iceland 0-1 (0-0)
Goal: Brynjarsdóttir (60)
10.04.2014   Ta'Qali National Stadium, Ta'Qali: Malta – Iceland 0-8 (0-4)
Goals: Thorsteinsdóttir (2, 23, 60), Lárusdóttir (15), Brynjarsdóttir (33, 90+4),
Fridriksdóttir (64), Óladóttir (87)

10.04.2014   Stadion Brügglifeld, Aarau: Switzerland – Denmark 1-1 (0-0)
Goals: Dickenmann (64 pen) / Røddik (51)
07.05.2014   Ta'Qali National Stadium, Ta'Qali: Malta – Israel 0-3 **Awarded**
Goals: M.Fridman (36), Lavi (60)
Israel were awarded a 3-0 win after Malta fielded an ineligible player, Dorianne
Theuma. The match originally ended 2-0 to Israel.
08.05.2014   Centre sportif de Colovray Nyon, Nyon: Switzerland – Iceland 3-0 (1-0)
Goals: Bernauer (33), Bürki (69), Dickenmann (80)
08.05.2014   Vejle Stadion, Vejle: Denmark – Serbia 3-1 (2-0)
Goals: Rasmussen (9 pen), Knudsen (10), Christiansen (83)
14.06.2014   Stadion Niedermatten, Wohlen: Switzerland – Israel 9-0 (5-0)
Goals: Humm (29), Kiwic (32), Bachmann (35, 39), Moser (37), Bürki (59, 84, 86),
Abbé (90+1)
14.06.2014   Indjija Stadium, Indjija: Serbia – Malta 5-0 (3-0)
Goals: Ilic (4), Cankovic (28), Savanovic (42), Krstic (67, 74)
15.06.2014   Vejle Stadion, Vejle: Denmark – Iceland 1-1 (1-1)
Goals: Rasmussen (35) / Lárusdóttir (28)
19.06.2014   Ramat Gan Stadium, Ramat Gan: Israel – Denmark 0-5 (0-1)
Goals: K.Nielsen (35, 86), Harder (48), Troelsgaard (56), Pedersen (90+3)
19.06.2014   Indjija Stadium, Indjija: Serbia – Switzerland 0-7 (0-2)
Goals: Bachmann (5), Dickenmann (21, 51), Moser (48), Crnogorcevic (60), Humm
(76), Betschart (81)
19.06.2014   Laugardalsvöllur, Reykjavik: Iceland – Malta 5-0 (3-0)
Goals: Magnúsdóttir (12), Jensen (20, 86), Lárusdóttir (40), Brynjarsdóttir (64)
21.08.2014   Sucaca Sportcenter, Pecinci: Serbia – Israel 3-0 (2-0)
Goals: Smiljkovic (31, 34), Bradic (82)
21.08.2014   Laugardalsvöllur, Reykjavik: Iceland – Denmark 0-1 (0-0)
Goal: Harder (58)
13.09.2014   Vejle Stadion, Vejle: Denmark – Malta 8-0 (5-0)
Goals: Røddik (5 pen, 89), Rasmussen (17, 50), Knudsen (27), Madim (28, 67),
Sørensen (45+1)
13.09.2014   Laugardalsvöllur, Reykjavik: Iceland – Israel 3-0 (2-0)
Goals: Brynjarsdóttir (2), Fridriksdóttir (26), Gunnarsdóttir (90+1)
17.09.2014   Victor Tedesco Stadium, Hamrun: Malta – Switzerland 0-5 (0-1)
Goals: Crnogorcevic (19, 84, 87 pen), Bürki (52, 68)
17.09.2014   Vejle Stadion, Vejle: Denmark – Israel 0-1 (0-1)
Goal: Falkon (10)
17.09.2014   Laugardalsvöllur, Reykjavik: Iceland – Serbia 9-1 (3-0)
Goals: Thorsteinsdóttir (7, 71), Viggósdóttir (10), Hönnudóttir (27, 72), Ásgrímsdóttir
(58), Brynjarsdóttir (63, 84), Helgadóttir (67 pen) / Cubrilo (60)

Team	Pld	W	D	L	GF	GA	GD	Pts
Switzerland	*10*	*9*	*1*	*0*	*53*	*1*	*+52*	*28*
Iceland	10	6	1	3	29	9	+20	19
Denmark	10	5	3	2	25	6	+19	18
Israel	10	4	0	6	9	27	-18	12
Serbia	10	3	1	6	16	34	-18	10
Malta	10	0	0	10	0	55	-55	0

GROUP 4

21.09.2013   Swedbank Stadion, Malmö: Sweden – Poland 2-0 (0-0)
Goals: Seger (52), Schelin (66)
22.09.2013   Tórsvøllur, Tórshavn: Faroe Islands – Scotland 2-7 (0-5)
Goals: Sevdal (82, 83) / Corsie (7), Evans (14), L.Ross (20, 29), J.Ross (21), Lappin (62), Malone (75)
26.09.2013   Stadion Oporowska, Wroclaw: Poland – Faroe Islands 6-0 (4-0)
Goals: Wisniewska (2, 27), Balcerzak (11), Winczo (31, 77), Pozerska (89)
26.09.2013   Fir Park, Motherwell: Scotland – Bosnia and Heregovina 7-0 (3-0)
Goals: Evans (8), L.Ross (13), Little (36), Corsie (48), J.Ross (55), Beattie (65), Lappin (90+1)
26.10.2013   Bilino Polje, Zenica: Bosnia and Herzegovina – Sweden 0-1 (0-1)
Goal: Schelin (34 pen)
26.10.2013   Fir Park, Motherwell: Scotland – Northern Ireland 2-0 (1-0)
Goals: J.Ross (3), Beattie (78)
30.10.2013   Mourneview Park, Lurgan:
             Northern Ireland – Bosnia and Herzegovina 0-0
31.10.2013   Dyskobolia Stadium, Grodzisk Wielkopolski:
             Poland – Scotland 0-4 (0-2)
Goals: J.Ross (23, 42, 46), Love (65)
31.01.2013   Gamla Ullevi, Gothenburg: Sweden – Faroe Islands 5-0 (4-0)
Goals: Schelin (12 pen, 30), Ilestedt (14), Asllani (18), Hjohlman (59)
23.11.2013   Mourneview Park, Lurgan: Northern Ireland – Poland 0-3 (0-2)
Goals: Pozerska (5, 29 pen), Szaj (88)
05.04.2014   Fir Park, Motherwell: Scotland – Poland 2-0 (0-0)
Goals: Evans (53), Crichton (82)
05.04.2014   Tórsvøllur, Tórshavn: Faroe Islands – Bosnia and Herzegovina 1-1 (0-1)
Goals: Klakstein (79) / Hasanbegovic (24)
05.04.2014   Goals: Klakstein (79) / Hasanbegovic (24)
05.04.2014   Shamrock Park, Portadown: Northern Ireland – Sweden 0-4 (0-2)
Goals: Asllani (8 pen), Schelin (18), Lundh (84), Nilsson (87)
10.04.2014   Bilino Polje, Zenica: Bosnia and Herzegovina – Scotland 1-3 (1-0)
Goals: M.Kulis (19) / J.Ross (62, 74, 86)
10.04.2014   Tórsvøllur, Tórshavn: Faroe Islands – Northern Ireland 0-0
08.05.2014   Svangaskard, Toftir: Faroe Islands – Poland 0-3 (0-2)
Goals: Siwinska (13), Pakulska (35 pen), Pajor (90)
08.05.2014   Myresjöhus Arena, Växjö: Sweden – Northern Ireland 3-0 (2-0)
Goals: Sjögran (12), Seger (28), Nilsson (74)
14.06.2014   Bilino Polje, Zenica:
             Bosnia and Herzegovina – Northern Ireland 1-0 (0-0)
Goal: L.Kulis (81)
14.06.2014   Fir Park, Motherwell: Scotland – Sweden 1-3 (1-2)
Goals: Little (19 pen) / Seger (13), Asllani (27, 52)
18.06.2014   Bilino Polje, Zenica: Bosnia and Herzegovina – Poland 1-1 (1-0)
Goals: Mika (45+3 og) / Pajor (63)
19.06.2014   Tórsvøllur, Tórshavn: Faroe Islands – Sweden 0-5 (0-3)
Goals: Seger (11), Schough (19), Schelin (35, 50), Lundh (84)

19.06.2014   Solitude, Belfast: Northern Ireland – Scotland 0-2 (0-1)
Goals: Little (44), J.Ross (77)
20.08.2014   Bilino Polje, Zenica: Bosnia and Herzegovina – Faroe Islands 2-0 (0-0)
Goals: Nikolic (46), Spahic (66)
21.08.2014   Stadion Kazimierza Deyny, Starogard Gdanski:
              Poland – Sweden 0-4 (0-1)
Goals: Schelin (8, 71), Asllani (56), Sembrant (89)
13.09.2014   Gamla Ullevi, Gothenburg: Sweden – Bosnia and Heregovina 3-0 (2-0)
Goals: Nilsson (5), Schelin (45+2, 73)
13.09.2014   MotoArena Torun, Torun: Poland – Northern Ireland 4-0 (3-0)
Goals: Sikora (33), Pajor (36, 68), Balcerzak (41)
13.09.2014   Fir Park, Motherwell: Scotland – Faroe Islands 9-0 (3-0)
Goals: Little (6), Weir (10), J.Ross (11, 46, 52), Corsie (57, 70), Crichton (59), Beattie
(90+2)
17.09.2014   Gamla Ullevi, Gothenburg: Sweden – Scotland 2-0 (1-0)
Goals: Sjögran (7), Schelin (76)
17.09.2014   OSiR Stadium, Wloclawek: Poland – Bosnia and Herzegovina 3-1 (3-1)
Goals: Pakulska (19 pen), Pajor (29), Kamczyk (33) / Ahmic (42)
17.09.2014   Mourneview Park, Lurgan: Northern Ireland – Faroe Islands 3-0 (1-0)
Goals: Furness (21 pen, 90+1), Jacobsen (52 og)

Team	Pld	W	D	L	GF	GA	GD	Pts
Sweden	*10*	*10*	*0*	*0*	*32*	*1*	*+31*	*30*
Scotland	10	8	0	2	37	8	+29	24
Poland	10	5	1	4	20	14	+6	16
Bosnia and Herzegovina	10	2	3	5	7	19	-12	9
Northern Ireland	10	1	2	7	3	19	-16	5
Faroe Islands	10	0	2	8	3	41	-38	2

GROUP 5

21.09.2013   King Baudouin Stadium, Brussels: Belgium – Albania 2-0 (1-0)
Goals: Philtjens (17), Zeler (53 pen)
25.09.2013   Ullevaal Stadion, Oslo: Norway – Belgium 4-1 (2-0)
Goals: Hansen (5), Hegland (35, 54, 66) / de Gernier (62)
26.09.2013   Fyli Municipal Stadium, Fyli: Greece – Portugal 1-5 (0-2)
Goals: Pelekouda (74) / Luis (6, 42), Xera (68 og), Fernandes (80), Silva (90+2)
26.09.2013   Qemal Stafa Stadium, Tirana: Albania – Netherlands 0-4 (0-2)
Goals: Melis (4, 8, 53), Slegers (90+1)
26.10.2013   Levadia Municipal Stadium, Livadia: Greece – Belgium 1-7 (1-3)
Goals: Kongouli (42) / Zeler (15, 27, 45+1 pen), Wullaert (58, 75), Coutereels (61
pen), van de Putte (74)
26.10.2013   Sarpsborg Stadion, Sarpsborg: Norway – Albania 7-0 (3-0)
Goals: Christensen (12), Thorsnes (29), Mjelde (45+2), Hansen (51, 70, 73),
Gulbrandsen (62)
26.10.2013   Estádio José de Carvalho, Maia: Portugal – Netherlands 0-7 (0-2)
Goals: Slegers (2, 35), Dekker (55), van den Berg (63) Miedema (78, 81, 90+4)

184

30.10.2013   Qemal Stafa Stadium, Tirana: Albania – Greece 1-0 (0-0)
Goal: Velaj (52)
30.10.2013   Kras Stadion, Volendam: Netherlands – Norway 1-2 (1-2)
Goals: Miedema (23) / Hansen (18), Stensland (37)
31.10.2013   Olympisch Stadion, Antwerp: Belgium – Portugal 4-1 (1-1)
Goals: Zeler (41 pen, 85), Wullaert (67, 87) / Costa (14)
23.11.2013   Stadion Woudestein, Rotterdam: Netherlands – Greece 7-0 (4-0)
Goals: Martens (9, 60), Miedema (23, 29, 64), Melis (37 pen), van den Berg (90)
12.02.2014   Oosterenkstadion, Zwolle: Netherlands – Belgium 1-1 (0-0)
Goals: Miedema (48) / Zeler (76)
12.02.2014   Estádio Municipal de Abrantes, Abrantes: Portugal – Albania 7-1 (3-0)
Goals: Mendes (19, 45+2, 69), Rodrigues (27, 90+2), Silva (61), Garcia (88) /
Serenaj (49)
13.02.2014   Komotini Municipal Stadium, Komotini: Greece – Norway 0-5 (0-1)
Goals: Hegland (45+1), Thorsnes (60, 75), Hegerberg (66), Bjånesøy (89)
05.04.2014   Niko Dovana Stadium, Durrës: Albania – Belgium 0-6 (0-1)
Goals: van de Putte (11), Wullaert (54), Mermans (65), Zeler (74, 84, 87)
05.04.2014   Pankritio Stadium, Heraklion: Greece – Netherlands 0-6 (0-3)
Goals: Melis (7), Middag (32), Miedema (40), van den Berg (47), Spitse (65),
Bakker (90)
09.04.2014   Dr. Marques Dos Santos, Sertã: Portugal – Greece 1-0 (0-00
Goal: Neto (78)
10.04.2014   Stadion De Braak, Helmond: Netherlands – Albania 10-1 (5-1)
Goals: van den Heiligenberg (4), Slegers (28, 31, 32, 79, 90+3), Gjini (45+4 og),
Martens (78, 82), Bakker (90+1) / Rrahmani (45+4)
10.04.2014   Den Dreef, Leuven: Belgium – Norway 1-2 (0-1)
Goals: Zeler (86) / Stensland (45) Hegerberg (51)
07.05.2014   Tønsberg Gressbane, Tønsberg: Norway – Portugal 2-0 (0-0)
Goals: Thorsnes (47), Herlovsen (89)
07.05.2014   Den Dreef, Leuven: Belgium – Netherlands 0-2 (0-2)
Goals: Miedema (9), Slegers (19)
14.06.2014   Brann Stadionm Bergen: Norway – Greece 6-0 (5-0)
Goals: Hegerberg (3), Hansen (25), Mjelde (27), Berge (32), Herlovsen (43),
Haavi (58)
14.06.2014   Loni Papuçiu Stadium, Fier: Albania – Portugal 0-3 (0-0)
Goals: Mendes (54), Malho (63), Pereira (66)
18.06.2014   Estádio Marcolino de Castr0, Santa Matia da Feira:
                     Portugal – Norway 0-2 (0-2)
Goals: Herlovsen (25), Mjelde (34)
13.09.2014   Niko Dovana Stadium, Durrës: Albania – Norway 0-11 (0-4)
Goals: Herlovsen (18, 45+2, 82), Mjelde (34, 66), Hansen (40, 89), Hegersberg (60,
63), Haavi (85), Engel (90+1)
13.09.2014   Den Dreef, Leuven: Belgium – Greece 11-0 (3-0)
Goals: De Caigny (16, 71), Zeler (34), Mermans (40, 50), Wullaert (46, 54, 69, 82),
Cayman (68), Van Gorp (73)
13.09.2014   De Koel, Venlo: Netherlands – Portugal 3-2 (1-0)
Goals: Miedema (28, 54, 68) / Silva (52), Luís (61)
17.09.2014   Veria Stadium, Veria: Greece – Albania 4-0 (2-0)
Goals: Franja (2 og), Kokoviadou (31), Kongouli (74), Panteliadou (90+2)

17.09.2014   Nadderud Stadion Bekkestua: Norway – Netherlands 0-2 (0-0)
Goals: Dekker (68), van de Donk (76)
17.09.2014   Estádio Municipal de Abrantes, Abrantes: Portugal – Belgium 0-1 (0-1)
Goals: Wullaert (18)

Team	Pld	W	D	L	GF	GA	GD	Pts
Norway	10	9	0	1	41	5	+36	27
Netherlands	10	8	1	1	43	6	+37	25
Belgium	10	6	1	3	34	11	+23	19
Portugal	10	4	0	6	19	21	-2	12
Greece	10	1	0	9	6	49	-43	3
Albania	10	1	0	9	3	54	-51	3

Greece scored more head-to-head goals than Albania

GROUP 6

21.09.2013   Dean Court, Bournemouth: England – Belarus 6-0 (4-0)
Goals: Carney (3, 26, 40), White (13), Dowie (60), Aluko (62)
26.09.2013   Cardiff City Stadium, Cardiff: Wales – Belarus 1-0 (0-0)
Goal: Ward (81)
26.09.2013   Fratton Park, Portsmouth: England – Turkey 8-0 (6-0)
Goals: Duggan (1, 2, 37), White (30, 39), Aluko (33, 49), Dowle (75)
26.10.2013   City Stadium, Molodechno: Belarus – Montenegro 3-1 (2-0)
Goals: Pilipenko (2), Kharlanova (45+1), Avkhimovich (84) / Vukcevic (69)
26.10.2013   The Den, London: England – Wales 2-0 (0-0)
Goals: Nobbs (48), Duggan (57)
31.10.2013   Gradski stadion, Niksic: Montenegro – Ukraine 1-4 (0-2)
Goals: Krivokapic (89) / Dyatel (31), Aloshycheva (43), Pomanenko (68), Pekur (82)
31.10.2013   Adana 5 Ocak Stadium, Adana: Turkey – England 0-4 (0-2)
Goals: Aluko (10), Williams (17 pen), Duggan (48), Nobbs (60)
23.11.2013   Gradski stadion, Niksic: Montenegro – Wales 0-3 (0-1)
Goals: Keryakoplis (31), Ward (70 pen, 79)
28.11.2013   Buca Arena, Izmir: Turkey – Montenegro 3-1 (1-0)
Goals: Çinar (11), Uraz (68), Topçu (75) / Vukcevic (90+3)
13.02.2014   Adana 5 Ocak Stadium, Adana: Turkey – Ukraine 0-1 (0-1)
Goal: Romanenko (39)
04.04.2014   Eskisehir Atatürk Stadium, Eskisehir: Turkey – Wales 1-5 (0-4)
Goals: Karabulut (90) / Fishlock (3, 25, 37), Wiltshire (32 pen), Harding (67)
05.04.2014   Falmer Stadium, Brighton and Hove: England – Montenegro 9-0 (4-0)
Goals: Duggan (2, 13, 71), Aluko (37), J.Scott (40), Carney (49), Sanderson (55),
Stokes (69), Dowie (84)
09.02.2014   Parc y Scarlets, Llanelli: Wales – Ukraine 1-1 (0-1)
Goals: Harding (78) / Boychenko (7)
10.04.2014   Gradski stadion, Niksic: Montenegro – Belarus 1-7 (1-1)
Goals: Krivokapic (24) / Pilipenko (37, 64), Borisenko (52), Miroshnichenko (71, 82,
87, 89)
07.05.2014   Spartak Stadium, Mogilev: Belarus – Turkey 1-2 (0-0)
Goals: Kozyupa (90+4) / Uraz (73), Kar (90+5)

186

08.05.2014   Nantporth, Bangor: Wales – Montenegro 4-0 (3-0)
Goals: Wiltshire (12), Fishlock (14,23, 50)
08.05.2014   New Meadow, Shrewsbury: England – Ukraine 4-0 (1-0)
Goals: Dowie (41, 53), Aluko (49, 63)
14.06.2014   Bridge Meadow Stadium, Haverfordwest: Wales – Turkey 1-0 (1-0)
Goal: Wiltshire (33)
14.06.2014   Traktor Stadium, Minsk: Belarus – England 0-3 (0-2)
Goals: Aluko (31), Houghton (36), Bronze (90+5)
14.06.2014   Arena Lviv, Lviv: Ukraine – Montenegro 7-0 (2-0)
Goals: Dyatel (31, 50), Yakovishyn (33), Apanaschenko (58), Boychenko (61), Mrkic
(76 og), Romanenko (79)
19.06.2014   Stadion Pod Malim Brdom, Petrovac: Montenegro – Turkey 2-3 (1-1)
Goals: Bulatovic (23, 49) / Duman (45+2), Uraz (58), Kara (80)
19.06.2014   Arena Lviv, Lviv: Ukraine – England 1-2 (0-2)
Goals: Ovdiychuk (63) / Stoney (11), Aluko (14)
19.06.2014   Traktor Stadium, Minsk: Belarus – Wales 0-3 (0-0)
Goals: Harding (79, 85, 90+4)
02.08.2014   FFU Training Complex, Kyiv: Ukraine – Belarus 8-0 (3-0)
Goals: Pekur (27, 82), Apanaschenko (34 pen), Ovdiychuk (38), Yakovishyn (58, 67),
Romanenko (61), Dyatel (64)
*Match was originally scheduled for 5 April 2014 but moved forward due to the
Ukrainian revolution.*
20.08.2014   Traktor Stadium, Minsk: Belarus – Ukraine 1-3 (0-1)
Goals: Pilipenko (61) / Yakovishyn (10), Apanaschenko (87), Dyatel (90+3)
21.08.2014   Cardiff City Stadium, Cardiff: Wales – England 0-4 (0-4)
Goals: Carney (16), Aluko (39), Bassett (44), Sanderson (45)
13.09.2014   Arena Lviv, Lviv: Ukraine – Turkey 8-0 (3-0)
Goals: Romanenko (33), Boychenko (44, 45, 53), Yakovishyn (67, 69, 77),
Dyatel (80)
17.09.2014   Minareliçavus Spor Tesisleri, Bursa: Turkey – Belarus 3-0 (1-0)
Goals: Kara (40), Uraz (60, 69)
17.09.2014   Arena Lviv, Lviv: Ukraine – Wales 1-0 (0-0)
Goal: Romanenko (61)
17.09.2014   Stadion Pod Malin Brdom, Petrovac: Montenegro – England 0-10 (0-4)
Goals: Aluko (8, 31, 64), Carney (22, 51), Bronze (27), Duggan (56, 90+4),
Greenwood (90), Potter (90+3)

Team	Pld	W	D	L	GF	GA	GD	Pts
England	*10*	*10*	*0*	*0*	*52*	*1*	*+51*	*30*
Ukraine	10	7	1	2	34	9	+25	22
Wales	10	6	1	3	18	9	+9	19
Turkey	10	4	0	6	12	31	-19	12
Belarus	10	2	0	8	12	31	-19	6
Montenegro	10	0	0	10	6	53	-47	0

GROUP 7

21.09.2013   Kazhimukan Munaitpasov Stadium Astana:
Kazakhstan – Finland 0-2 (0-0)
Goals: Kukkonen (69), Talonen (85)
21.09.2013   Voralpenstadion, Vöcklabruck: Austria – Bulgaria 4-0 (1-0)
Goals: Burger (33), Feiersinger (81), Boycheva (90 og), Pöltl (90+1)
25.09.2013   Kazhimukan Munaitpasov Stadium Astana:
Kazakhstan – France 0-4 (0-4)
Goals: Delie (15), Thiney (17, 37), Delannoy (21)
25.09.2013   Veritas Stadion, Turku: Finland – Austria 2-1 (1-0)
Goals: Engman (42), Alanen (86) / Burger (79)
26.10.2013   Lovech Stadium, Lovech: Bulgaria – Kazakhstan 1-1 (1-1)
Goals: Kireva (43) / Radoyska (26 og)
26.10.2013   Bozsik Stadion, Budapest: Hungary – Austria 0-3 (0-2)
Goals: Wenninger (7), Demeter (35 og), Makas (55)
31.10.2013   Bozsik Stadion, Budapest: Hungary – Bulgaria 4-0 (2-0)
Goals: B.Szabó (4), Vágó (40 pen), Sipos (70), Zeller (76)
31.10.2013   Sonera Stadium, Helsinki: Finland – Kazakhstan 1-0 (1-0)
Goal: Sjölund (40)
31.10.2013   Sonnensee Stadion, Ritzing: Austria – France 1-3 (0-2)
Goals: Wenninger (65) / Nécib (16), Henry (18), Renard (61)
23.11.2013   ETO Park, Györ: Hungary – Kazakhstan 4-1 (0-1)
Goals: Jakabfi (50), Kaján (54), Zeller (56), Vágó (64) / Kirgizbaeva (36)
23.11.2013   Lovech Stadium, Lovech: Bulgaria – France 0-10 (0-6)
Goals: Delie (2, 6, 10), Thiney (9, 75, 80), Renard (19, 34), Bussaglia (73),
Le Sommer (81)
27.11.2013   MMArena, Le Mans: Francce – Bulgaria 14-0 (10-0)
Goals: Thiney (1, 4, 11, 41, 83), Le Sommer (3, 24, 45+1, 90), Nécib (6), Renard (21,
37), Abily (48), Georges (57)
05.04.2014   Lovech Stadium, Lovech: Bulgaria – Austria 1-6 (0-4)
Goals: Radoyska (66) / Burger (4), Pöltl (8, 41), Puntigam (43), Aschauer (51),
Makas (56)
05.04.2014   ETO Park, Györ: Hungary – Finland 0-4 (0-2)
Goals: Talonen (10, 64, 90+2), Westerlund (15)
05.04.2014   Jean-Bouin Stadium, Angers: France – Kazakhstan 7-0 (5-0)
Goals: Delie (9, 12), Thomis (14), Abily (21, 24), Thiney (54, 88)
09.04.2014   MMArena, Le Mans: France – Austria 3-1 (3-0)
Goals: Bussaglia (31 pen), Delie (36), Thomis (39) / Puntigam (58)
10.04.2014   Sonera Stadium, Helsinki: Finland – Hungary 4-0 (2-0)
Goals: Talonen (20, 84), Kemppi (40), Engman (67)
07.05.2014   Astana Arena, Astana: Kazakhstan – Bulgaria 4-1 (3-1)
Goals: Zhanatayeva (9), Kirgizbaeva (21, 34), Yalova (70) / Kireva (43)
07.05.2014   Stade Léo Lagrange, Besançon: France – Hungary 4-0 (1-0)
Goals: Thomis (35), Abily (52), Thiney (61), Majri (89)
14.06.2014   Tsentralny, Almaty: Kazakhstan – Hungary 1-2 (0-0)
Goals: Kirgizbaeva (58) / Vágó (49), Padár (53)
14.06.2014   Stadion Wiener Neustadt, Wiener Neustadt: Austria – Finland 3-1 (2-0)
Goals: Makas (31), Saari (41 og), Prohaska (80) / Alanen (79)

18.06.2014   Sonera Stadium, Helsinki: Finland – Bulgaria 4-0 (1-0)
Goals: Alanen (20), Talonen (78), Hyyrynen (85), Saarinen (88)
19.06.2014   Tsentralny, Almata: Kazakhstan – Austria 0-3 (0-1)
Goals: Billa (4, 78), Burger (62)
20.08.2014   Bozsik Stadion, Budapest: Hungary – France 0-4 (0-3)
Goals: Le Sommer (10, 25), Smuczer (39 og), Delie (73)
21.08.2014   Lovech Stadium, Lovech: Bulgaria – Finland 0-8 (0-5)
Goals: Sjölund (6), Saarinen (9), Saari (14), Talonen (38, 49, 53), Alanen (41),
Ruutu (75)
13.09.2014   ISS Stadion, Vantaa: Finland – France 0-2 (0-1)
Goals: Nécib (24), Thiney (58)
13.09.2014   NV Arena, Sankt Pölten: Austria – Hungary 4-3 (3-2)
Goals: Tóth (14 og), Makas (12, 20), Burger (67) / Zeller (27), Sipos (42), Rácz (51)
17.09.2014   Lovech Stadium, Lovech: Bulgaria – Hungary 0-7 (0-2)
Goals: Csiszár (30), Sipos (39, 90), Vágó (51, 64, 67, 71)
17.09.2014   Stade de l'Épopée, Calais: France – Finland 3-1 (1-1)
Goals: Bussaglia (44), Nécib (66), Delie (71) / Kemppi (19)
17.09.2014   Waldstadion, Pasching: Austria – Kazakhstan 5-1 (2-0)
Goals: Makas (4, 81), Burger (40), Puntigam (57), Billa (76) / Yalova (51)

Team	Pld	W	D	L	GF	GA	GD	Pts
France	*10*	*10*	*0*	*0*	*54*	*3*	*+51*	*30*
Austria	10	7	0	3	31	14	+17	21
Finland	10	7	0	3	27	9	+18	21
Hungary	10	4	0	6	20	25	-5	12
Kazakhstan	10	1	1	8	8	30	-22	4
Bulgaria	10	0	1	9	3	62	-59	1

Austria scored more head-to-head goals than Finland

The seven group winners **Germany**, **Spain**, **Switzerland**, **Sweden**, **Norway**, **England** and **France** qualified for the FIFA Women's World Cup 2015.

RANKING OF SECOND-PLACED TEAMS

Matches againstthe sixth-placed team in each group are not included in this ranking. As a result, eight matches played by each team counted for the purposes of the second-placed table.

Pos	Grp	Team	Pld	W	D	L	GF	GA	GD	Pts
1	*5*	*Netherlands*	*8*	*6*	*1*	*1*	*29*	*5*	*+24*	*19*
2	*2*	*Italy*	*8*	*6*	*1*	*1*	*22*	*5*	*+17*	*19*
3	*4*	*Scotland*	*8*	*6*	*0*	*2*	*21*	*6*	*+15*	*18*
4	*6*	*Ukraine*	*8*	*5*	*1*	*2*	*23*	*8*	*+15*	*16*
5	1	Russia	8	5	1	2	14	17	-3	16
6	7	Austria	8	5	0	3	21	13	+8	15
7	3	Iceland	8	4	1	3	16	9	+7	13

Netherlands, Italy, Scotland ans Ukraine qualified for the UEFA Play-offs.

189

UEFA PLAY-OFFS

SEMI-FINALS

25.10.2014   Stadio Centro d'Italia, Rieti: Italy – Ukraine 2-1 (2-1)
Goals: Cernoia (1), Gabbiadini (45+1) / Apanaschenko (34)
25.10.2014   Tynecastle Stadium, Edinburgh: Scotland – Netherlands 1-2 (0-2)
Goals: Little (49 pen) / Martens (10), Melis (23 pen)
29.10.2014   Arena Lviv, Lviv: Ukraine – Italy 2-2 (1-0)
Goals: Dyatel (26, 47) / Gabbiadini (55), Panico (79)
30.10.2014   Sparta Stadion, Rotterdam: Netherlands – Scotland 2-0 (0-0)
GoalsL Martens (51), Melis (77)

FINALS

22.11.2014   Kyocera Stadion, The Hague: Netherlands – Italy 1-1 (0-1)
Goals: Miedema (54) / Gabbiadini (19)
27.11.2014   Stadio Marc'Antonio Bentegodi, Verona: Italy – Netherlands 1-2 (0-2)
Goals: van der Gragt (53 og) / Miedema (9, 43)

Netherlands qualified for the FIFA Women's World Cup 2015

CONCACAF WOMEN'S CHAMPIONSHIP 2014

QUALIFYING NORTH AMERICA

As host, **Canada** automatically qualified for the FIFA Women's World Cup 2015 and did not participate in either the CONCACAF Women's Championship Final Tournament of the CONCACAF Women's Championship Qualification. The United States and Mexico received byes directly to the CONCACAF Women's Championship Final Tournament.

QUALIFYING CENTRAL AMERICA

Only the group winners will qualify for the CONCACAF Women's Championship Final Tournament. The qualifying tournament was hosted in Guatemala.

GROUP 1

20.05.2014   Estadio Mateo Flores, Guatemala City: Honduras – Belize 8-0 (7-0)
Goals: Alarcón (2, 34, 45, 58), Rodriguez (13), Amaya (25), Umanzor (28), Castellón (36)
20.05.2014   Estadio Mateo Flores, Guatemala City: Guatemala – Panama 1-0 (1-0)
Goal: M.Monterroso (24)
22.05.2014   Estadio Mateo Flores, Guatemala City: Belize – Panama 1-13 (1-4)
Goals: Pollard (17) / Johnson (6), Gamboa (7 og), Mills (31), Cox (38, 55, 71, 82), Sotillo (59), De Mera (69, 90, 90+2), Dow (73), Vernon (77)
22.05.2014   Estadio Mateo Flores, Guatemala City: Guatemala – Honduras 3-2 (2-0)
Goals: C.Monterroso (8), M.Monterroso (45+1), Barrera (77) / Alarcón (61), Hall (85)

24.05.2015   Estadio Mateo Flores, Guatemala City: Panama – Honduras 4-1 (2-0)
Goals: Mills (18), De Mera (22, 66, 72) / Amaya (90+3 pen)
24.05.2014   Estadio Mateo Flores, Guatemala City: Guatemala – Belize 5-0 (2-0)
Goals: Barrera (10, 32), Recinos (55), Ramírez (72 og), Martínez (77)

Team	Pld	W	D	L	GF	GA	GD	Pts
Guatemala	*3*	*3*	*0*	*0*	*9*	*2*	*+7*	*9*
Panama	3	2	0	1	17	3	+14	6
Honduras	3	1	0	2	11	7	+4	3
Belize	3	0	0	3	1	26	-25	0

GROUP 2

20.05.2014   Estadio Mateo Flores, Guatemala City:
             Nicaragua – El Salvador 0-2 (0-0)
Goals: González (67), Quélez (86)
22.05.2014   Estadio Mateo Flores, Guatemala City:
             El Salvador – Costa Rica 0-4 (0-2)
Goals: Acosta (15), R.Rodríguez (43), Alvarado (50), L.Rodríguez (51)
24.05.2014   Estadio Mateo Flores, Guatemala City: Costa Rica – Nicaragua 3-0 (2-0)
Goals: R.Rodríguez (14), Alvarado (19), G.Villalobos (72)

Team	Pld	W	D	L	GF	GA	GD	Pts
Costa Rica	*2*	*2*	*0*	*0*	*7*	*0*	*+7*	*6*
El Salvador	2	1	0	1	2	4	-2	3
Nicaragua	2	0	0	2	0	5	-5	0

Guatemala and Costa Rica qualified for the CONCACAF Women's Championship
Final Tournament.

CFU WOMEN'S CARIBBEAN CUP 2014

FIRST ROUND

The five group winners will qualify for the Final Round.

GROUP 1

Hosted in Antigua and Barbuda.

23.05.2014   Antigua Recreation Ground, St. John's:
             Aruba – Saint Vincent and the Grenadines 0-2 (0-2)
Goals: Franklyn (19, 38)
23.05.2014   Antigua Recreation Ground, St. John's:
             Antigua and Barbuda – U.S. Virgin Islands 1-0 (0-0)
Goal: Hughes (49)
25.05.2014   Antigua Recreation Ground, St. John's:
             Saint Vincent and the Grenadines – U.S. Virgin Islands 0-0

25.05.2014 Antigua Recreation Ground, St. John's:
Antigua and Barbuda – Aruba 1-0 (1-0)
Goal: Green (21)
27.05.2014 Antigua Recreation Ground, St. John's:
U.S. Virgin Islands – Aruba 1-0 (1-0)
Goal: Adams (7)
27.05.2014 Antigua Recreation Ground, St. John's:
Antigua and Barbuda – Saint Vincent and the Grenadines 1-0 (1-0)
Goal: Buckley (38)

Team	Pld	W	D	L	GF	GA	GD	Pts
Antigua and Barbuda	*3*	*3*	*0*	*0*	*3*	*0*	*+3*	*9*
Saint Vincent and the Grenadines	3	1	1	1	2	1	+1	4
U.S. Virgin Islands	3	1	1	1	1	1	0	4
Aruba	3	0	0	3	0	4	-4	0

GROUP 2

Hosted in Puerto Rico.

23.05.2014 Juan Ramón Loubriel Stadium, Bayamón:
Martinique – Barbados 3-1 (2-1)
Goals: ?? (3), ?? (44), ?? (47) / ?? (7)
25.05.2014 Juan Ramón Loubriel Stadium, Bayamón:
Puerto Rico – Barbados 1-0 (0-0)
Goal: Socarrás (69)
27.05.2014 Juan Ramón Loubriel Stadium, Bayamón:
Puerto Rico – Martinique 1-1 (1-1)
Goals: Guerra (9) / Carin (36)

Team	Pld	W	D	L	GF	GA	GD	Pts
Martinique	*2*	*1*	*1*	*0*	*4*	*2*	*+2*	*4*
Puerto Rico	2	1	1	0	2	1	+1	4
Barbados	2	0	0	2	1	4	-3	0
Dominica	0	0	0	0	0	0	0	0

Dominica withdrew before the tournament due to some members not receiving visas.

GROUP 3

Hosted in Turks and Caicos Islands.

Bermuda was added to the group after the group stage draw.

23.05.2014 TCIFA National Academy, Providenciales:
Cayman Islands – Saint Kitts and Nevis 0-5 (0-3)
Goals: Browne (12, 26, 90), Powell (39), Harris (81)

23.05.2014   TCIFA National Academy, Providenciales:
                Turks and Caicos Islands – Bermuda 0-5 (0-3)
Goals: Todd (14, 17), Bell (27, 64), Nolan (54)
25.05.2014   TCIFA National Academy, Providenciales:
                Bermuda – Cayman Islands 2-2 (1-0)
Goals: Todd (32), Bell (55) / Gall (74), Ebanks (88)
25.05.2014   TCIFA National Academy, Providenciales:
                Turks and Caicos Islands – Saint Kitts and Nevis 0-4 (0-2)
Goals: Browne (5, 24), Springer (48), Francis (62)
27.05.2014   TCIFA National Academy, Providenciales:
                Saint Kitts and Nevis – Bermuda 1-3 (1-2)
Goals: Browne (31) / Furbert (14), Todd (17 pen), Richardson (70)
27.05.2014   TCIFA National Academy, Providenciales:
                Turks and Caicos Islands – Cayman Islands 0-3 (0-1)
Goals: Gall (45, 68), Frederick (89)

Team	Pld	W	D	L	GF	GA	GD	Pts
Bermuda	*3*	*2*	*1*	*0*	*9*	*3*	*+7*	*7*
Saint Kitts and Nevis	3	2	0	1	10	3	+7	6
Cayman Islands	3	1	1	1	5	7	-2	4
Turks and Caicos Islands	3	0	0	3	0	12	-12	0

GROUP 4

Hosted in Haiti.

30.05.2014   Parc Bayas, Mirebalais: Cuba – Suriname 2-0 (0-0)
Goals: Pelaez (62 pen), Calderon (83)
01.06.2014   Parc Bayas, Mirebalais: Haiti – Suriname 3-0 (1-0)
Goals: Brand (34), Dolce (75 pen), Louis (83)
03.06.2014   Parc Bayas, Mirebalais: Haiti – Cuba 1-0 (0-0)
Goal: Mesa (85 og)

Team	Pld	W	D	L	GF	GA	GD	Pts
Haiti	*2*	*2*	*0*	*0*	*4*	*0*	*+4*	*6*
Cuba	2	1	0	1	2	1	+1	3
Suriname	2	0	0	2	0	5	-5	0
Guadeloupe	0	0	0	0	0	0	0	0

Guadeloupe withdrew before the tournament due to outbreak of chikungunya virus.

GROUP 5

Hosted in Dominican Republic.

18.06.2014   Estadio Panamericano, San Cristóbal:
                Dominican Republic – Saint Lucia 7-0 (2-0)
Goals: Ubri (24, 62), Nuñez (26, 54, 84, 90+2), Peña (47)

20.06.2014   Estadio Panamericano, San Cristóbal: Saint Lucia – Jamaica 0-14 (0-5)
Goals: Davis (2), Campbell (28), Duncan (37, 55, 56, 61), Henry (45+2), Marquis (45+6 og), Allen (67, 74, 86), Reid (79), Loughran (88), Forrester (90)
22.06.2014   Estadio Panamericano, San Cristóbal:
           Dominican Republic – Jamaica 0-7 (0-4)
Goals: Duncan (3, 23, 64, 77), Davis (31, 90+1), Henry (42)

Team	Pld	W	D	L	GF	GA	GD	Pts
Jamaica	*2*	*2*	*0*	*0*	*21*	*0*	*+21*	*6*
Dominican Republic	2	1	0	1	7	7	0	3
Saint Lucia	2	0	0	2	0	21	-21	0
Anguilla	0	0	0	0	0	0	0	0

Anguilla withdrew before the tournament due to outbreak of chikungunya virus.

RANKING OF SECOND PLACED TEAMS

The two runners-up with the best records against the 1st and 3rd placed teams in their respective groups also qualified for the Final Round.

Pos	Grp	Team	Pld	W	D	L	GF	GA	GD	Pts
1	*2*	*Puerto Rico*	*2*	*1*	*1*	*0*	*2*	*1*	*+1*	*4*
2	3	Saint Kitts and Nevis	2	1	0	1	6	3	+3	3
3	4	Cuba	2	1	0	1	2	1	+1	3
4	5	Dominican Republic	2	1	0	1	7	7	0	3
5	1	Saint Vincent and the Grenadines	2	0	1	1	0	1	-1	1

FINAL ROUND

The Final Round was hosted in Trinidad and Tobago. The top two teams and the two runners-up of each group will qualify for the CONCACAF Women's Championship Final Tournament.

GROUP A

19.08.2014   Ato Boldan Stadium, Couva: Jamaica – Puerto Rico 4-1 (2-1)
Goals: Henry (6 pen), Duncan (34, 51), Campbell-Green (47) / Suarez (25)
19.08.2014   Ato Boldan Stadium, Couva: Haiti – Bermuda 5-1 (3-0)
Goals: Jean-Pierre (8, 40), Zullo (38), Dolce (86), Charles (89) / Todd (88)
21.08.2014   Ato Boldan Stadium, Couva: Bermuda – Jamaica 1-9 (0-5)
Goals: Todd (70) / Henry (5, 90+2), Dill (23 og), Wilson (28), Duncan (32, 45, 47, 76), Reid (79)
21.08.2014   Ato Boldan Stadium, Couva: Puerto Rico – Haiti 0-4 (0-2)
Goals: Gervil (9), Marseille (45+2), Brand (75), Jean-Pierre (79)
23.08.2014   Ato Boldan Stadium, Couva: Bermuda – Puerto Rico 1-5 (1-3)
Goals: Garcia (16 og) / Socarrás (13, 76), Fantauzzi (15), Benson (45), Aquino (82 pen)

23.08.2014   Ato Boldan Stadium, Couva: Haiti – Jamaica 0-2 (0-1)
Goals: McGregor (8), Henry (81)

Team	Pld	W	D	L	GF	GA	GD	Pts
Jamaica	*3*	*3*	*0*	*0*	*15*	*2*	*+13*	*9*
Haiti	*3*	*2*	*0*	*1*	*9*	*3*	*+6*	*6*
Puerto Rico	3	1	0	2	6	9	-3	3
Bermuda	3	0	0	3	3	19	-16	0

GROUP B

20.08.2014   Hasely Crawford Stadium, Port of Spain:
             Antigua and Barbuda – Martinique 0-2 (0-1)
Goals: Carin (12, 64)
20.08.2014   Hasely Crawford Stadium, Port of Spain:
             Trinidad and Tobago – Saint Kitts and Nevis 10-0 (7-0)
Goals: Cordner (3, 7), St. Louis (6, 10 pen, 22), Johnson (12), Shade (44), François
(55, 59), Mascall (68)
22.08.2014   Hasely Crawford Stadium, Port of Spain:
             Saint Kitts and Nevis – Martinique 0-1 (0-0)
Goal: Rouge (52)
22.08.2014   Hasely Crawford Stadium, Port of Spain:
             Trinidad and Tobago – Antigua and Barbuda 3-0 (1-0)
Goals: Shade (35, 53), St. Louis (64)
24.08.2014   Hasely Crawford Stadium, Port of Spain:
             Antigua and Barbuda – Saint Kitts and Nevis 1-2 (1-0)
Goals: Humphreys (5) / Powell (70), Browne (90)
24.08.2014   Hasely Crawford Stadium, Port of Spain:
             Trinidad and Tobago – Martinique 7-0 (4-0)
Goals: Cordner (1), St. Louis (4, 9, 45), Shade (48, 62), Mascall (69)

Team	Pld	W	D	L	GF	GA	GD	Pts
Trinidad and Tobago	*3*	*3*	*0*	*0*	*20*	*0*	*+20*	*9*
Martinique	*3*	*2*	*0*	*1*	*3*	*7*	*-4*	*6*
Saint Kitts and Nevis	3	1	0	2	2	12	-10	3
Antigua and Barbuda	3	0	0	3	1	7	-6	0

THIRD PLACE PLAY-OFF

26.08.2014   Hasely Crawford Stadium, Port of Spain: Haiti – Martinique 5-1 (2-0)
Goals: Bobo (15, 47, 72), Wisline Dolce (45), Pierre-Louis (70) / Brena (64)

FINAL

26.08.2014   Hasely Crawford Stadium, Port of Spain:
             Jamaica – Trinidad and Tobago 0-1 (0-1)
Goal: Shade (8)

Trinidad and Tobago, Jamaica, Martinique and Haiti qualified for the CONCACAF Women's Championship Final Tournament.

CONCACAF WOMEN'S CHAMPIONSHIP FINAL TOURNAMENT

The tournament was held in the United States between 15 & 26 October 2014. The top three teams will qualify directly for the FIFA Women's World Cup 2015.

The United States and Mexico received byes into this tournament. A total of 30 teams entered qualifying, with Martinique and Guadeloupe not eligible for World Cup qualification as they are only members of CONCACAF and not FIFA. Therefore, a total of 28 teams were in contention for the three direct places plus the play-off against CONMEBOL Copa América Femenina 2014 third placed team.

GROUP STAGE
GROUP A

15.10.2014   Sporting Park, Kansas City: Guatemala – Haiti 0-1 (0-0)
Goal: Zullo (69)
15.10.2014   Sporting Park, Kansas City:
            United States – Trinidad and Tobago 1-0 (0-0)
Goal: Wambach (55)
17.10.2014   Toyota Park, Bridgeview: Haiti – Trinidad and Tobago 0-1 (0-1)
Goal: Cordner (37)
17.10.2014   Toyota Park, Bridgeview: United States – Guatemala 5-0 (1-0)
Goals: Heath (7, 57), Lloyd (46), Engen (58), Rapinoe (66)
20.10.2014   RFK Stadium, Washington: Trinidad and Tobago – Guatemala 2-1 (0-0)
Goals: Cordner (74), Johnson (83 pen) / M.Monterroso (90)
20.10.2014   RFK Stadium, Washington: Haiti – United States 0-6 (0-2)
Goals: Lloyd (15), Wambach (39, 61), Klingenberg (57), Press (65), Brian (82)

Team	Pld	W	D	L	GF	GA	GD	Pts
United States	*3*	*3*	*0*	*0*	*12*	*0*	*+12*	*9*
Trinidad and Tobago	*3*	*2*	*0*	*1*	*3*	*2*	*+1*	*6*
Haiti	3	1	0	2	1	7	-6	3
Guatemala	3	0	0	3	1	8	-7	0

GROUP B

16.10.2014   Sporting Park, Kansas City: Jamaica – Martinique 6-0 (3-0)
Goals: Murray (2, 74), Duncan (6), Henry (22, 77), Allen (71)
16.10.2014   Sporting Park, Kansas City: Costa Rica – Mexico 1-0 (1-0)
Goal: Venegas (8)
18.10.2014   Toyota Park, Bridgeview: Costa Rica – Jamaica 2-1 (0-0)
Goals: Cruz Traña (76), Cedeño (86) / Duncan (77)
18.10.2014   Toyota Park, Bridgeview: Martinique – Mexico 0-10 (0-5)
Goals: Samarzich (6), Duarte (28, 49), Mayor (34), Guillou (36 og), Garciamendez (40), Garza (58), Ocampo (75, 87), Noyola (90+2)

21.10.2014   RFK Stadium, Washington: Martinique – Costa Rica 1-6 (0-3)
Goals: Carin (62) / Sanchez (7), Venegas (25, 90), Acosta (32), Cedeño (81, 83)
21.10.2014   RFK Stadium, Washington: Mexico – Jamaica 3-1 (1-1)
Goals: Mayor (29), Corral (59, 76) / Henry (14)

Team	Pld	W	D	L	GF	GA	GD	Pts
Costa Rica	3	3	0	0	9	2	+5	9
Mexico	3	2	0	1	13	2	+11	6
Jamaica	3	1	0	2	8	5	+3	3
Martinique	3	0	0	3	1	22	-21	0

KNOCKOUT STAGE
SEMI-FINALS

24.10.2014   PPL Park, Chester:
          Costa Rica – Trinidad and Tobago 1-1 (1-0,1-1) (a.e.t.)
Goals: Venegas (19) / Hutchinson (73)
Costa Rica won after extra time on penalties (3:0)
24.10.2014   PPL Park, Chester: United States – Mexico 3-0 (2-0)
Goals: Lloyd (6, 30 pen), Press (56)

THIRD PLACE PLAY-OFF

26.10.2014   PPL Park, Chester: Trinidad and Tobago – Mexico 2-4 (0-1,2-2) (a.e.t.)
Goals: Cordner (57), Shade (78) / Mayor (24), Ocampo (79), Corral (104, 106)
Mexico won after extra time

FINAL

26.10.2014   PPL Park, Chester: Costa Rica – United States 0-6 (0-4)
Goals: Wambach (4, 35, 41, 71), Lloyd (18), Leroux (73)

The winner **United States**, the runner-up **Costa Rica** and the third placed team
Mexico qualified for the FIFA Women's World Cup 2015. The fourth placed team
Trinidad and Tobago advanced to the CONCACAF-CONMEBOL Play-off 2014.

OFC WOMEN'S NATIONS CUP 2014

The OFC Women's Nations Cup 2014 was held in Papua New Guinea between 25 &
29 October 2014. Only the winner will qualify for the FIFA Women's World Cup
2015.

GROUP STAGE

All eleven OFC members were eligible to participate but only four entered the
tournament.

197

25.10.2014   Kalabond Oval, Kokopo: New Zealand – Tonga 16-0 (7-0)
Goals: Cleverley (1, 18), Gregorius (8 pen, 50, 70), Hassett (17), Collins (20, 69, 76),
White (26, 29), Longo (67, 77), Hearn (86, 90+7), Percival (90+2)
25.10.2014   Kalabond Oval, Kokopo: Papue New Guinea – Cook Islands 4-1 (3-0)
Goals: Birum (16), M.Gunemba (26, 36, 84) / Maoate-Cox (90)
27.10.2014   Kalabond Oval, Kokopo: Tonga – Cook Islands 1-1 (0-0)
Goals: Loto'aniu (90+5) / Toka (83)
27.10.2014   Kalabond Oval, Kokopo: Papua New Guinea – New Zealand 0-3 (0-0)
Goals: Stott (59), Hearn (70), Longo (90+2)
29.10.2014   Kalabond Oval, Kokopo: Cook Islands – New Zealand 0-11 (0-6)
Goals: Collins (12, 20), Erceg (14), Hearn (19, 47, 56, 86), Percival (43), White
(45+4), Stott (54), Hassett (75)
29.10.2014   Kalabond Oval, Kokopo: Tonga – Papua New Guinea 0-3 (0-2)
Goals: M.Gunemba (25), Kaipu (32, 62)

Team	Pld	W	D	L	GF	GA	GD	Pts
New Zealand	*3*	*3*	*0*	*0*	*30*	*0*	*+30*	*9*
Papua New Guinea	3	2	0	1	7	4	+3	6
Cook Islands	3	0	1	2	2	16	-14	1
Tonga	3	0	1	2	1	20	-19	1

The winner **New Zealand** qualified for the FIFA Women's World Cup 2015.

CONMEBOL COPA AMÉRICA FEMENINO 2014

The tournament was held between 11 & 28 September 2014 in Ecuador.

FIRST STAGE
GROUP A

11.09.2014   Estadio Olímpico de Riobamba, Riobamba:
             Uruguay – Venezuela 1-3 (1-2)
Goals: Viana (42) / Ascanio (9), García (23), Rodríguez (71)
11.09.2014   Estadio Olímpico de Riobamba, Riobamba: Ecuador – Peru 1-0 (0-0)
Goal: Barre (84)
13.09.2014   Estadio Bellavista, Ambato: Colombia – Uruguay 4-0 (1-0)
Goals: Andrade (6), N.Arias (58), Santos (69), Ospina (90)
13.09.2014   Estadio Bellavista, Ambato: Ecuador – Venezuela 1-0 (1-0)
Goal: Vázquez (30)
15.09.2014   Estadio Olímpico de Riobamba, Riobamba:
             Colombia – Venezuela 4-1 (2-0)
Goals: Rincón (15), Ortiz (40), Velasquez (65), Cosme (90+1) / García (78)
15.09.2014   Estadio Olímpico de Riobamba, Riobamba: Uruguay – Peru 2-1 (1-1)
Goals: Pion (30), P.González (90+2) / Flores (14)
17.09.2014   Estadio Bellavista, Ambato: Venezuela – Peru 0-0
17.09.2014   Estadio Bellavista, Ambato: Ecuador – Colombia 0-1 (0-0)
Goal: Ariza (60)

19.09.2014   Estadio La Cocha, Latacunga: Colombia – Peru 1-0 (1-0)
Goal: Rincón (39)
19.09.2014   Estadio La Cocha, Latacunga: Ecuador – Uruguay 1-2 (0-1)
Goals: Lattanzio (87) / P.González (7), Badell (56)

Team	Pld	W	D	L	GF	GA	GD	Pts
Colombia	4	4	0	0	10	1	+9	12
Ecuador	4	2	0	2	3	3	0	6
Uruguay	4	2	0	2	5	9	-4	6
Venezuela	4	1	1	2	4	6	-2	4
Peru	4	0	1	3	1	4	-3	1

GROUP B

12.09.2014   Estadio Federativo Reina del Cisne, Loja: Argentina – Chile 0-1 (0-0)
Goal: Lara (47)
12.09.2014   Estadio Federativo Reina del Cisne, Loja: Brazil – Bolivia 6-0 (2-0)
Goal: Formiga (19, 73), Andressa Alves (30), Darlene (51), Thaisa (84),
Fabiana (90+2)
14.09.2014   Estadio Bellavista, Ambato: Bolivia – Argentina 0-6 (0-0)
Goals: Vallejos (50, 72), Bonsegundo (54), Larroquette (62, 77, 87)
14.09.2014   Estadio Bellavista, Ambato: Paraguay – Brazil 1-4 (1-2)
Goals: Fleitas (9) / Andressa Alves (35), Cristiane (45+5, 56), Fabiana (57)
16.09.2014   Estadio Alejandro Serrano Aguilar, Cuenca: Chile – Bolivia 3-0 (1-0)
Goals: Lara (26 pen), Guerrero (61), Zamora (90+2)
16.09.2014   Estadio Alejandro Serrano Aguilar, Cuenca:
         Argentina – Paraguay 1-0 (1-0)
Goal: Cabrera (9)
18.09.2014   Estadio Alejandro Serrano Aguilar, Cuenca:
         Bolivia – Paraguay 2-10 (1-3)
Goals: Morón (43, 85) / Fernández (10, 77, 81, 90+1), Riveros (35), Ortiz (44, 89),
Quintana (65), Martinez (75, 84)
18.09.2014   Estadio Alejandro Serrano Aguilar, Cuenca: Chile – Brazil 0-2 (0-1)
Goals: Maurine (22), Cristiane (49)
20.09.2014   Estadio Jorge Andrade, Azogues: Paraguay – Chile 3-2 (1-0)
Goals: Ortiz (15), Quintana (78), Martinez (85) / Lara (47), Araya (72)
20.09.2014   Estadio Jorge Andrade, Azogues: Brazil – Argentina 0-2 (0-1)
Goals: Cometti (23), Banini (73 pen)

Team	Pld	W	D	L	GF	GA	GD	Pts
Brazil	4	3	0	1	12	3	+9	9
Argentina	4	3	0	1	9	1	+8	9
Paraguay	4	2	0	2	14	9	+5	6
Chile	4	2	0	2	6	5	+1	6
Bolivia	4	0	0	4	2	25	-23	0

FINAL STAGE

24.09.2014 Estadio Chillogallo, Quito: Colombia – Argentina 0-0
24.09.2014 Estadio Chillogallo, Quito: Brazil – Ecuador 4-0 (3-0)
Goals: Cristiane (14, 17), Maurine (37), Raquel (87)
26.09.2014 Estadio Rumiñahui, Sangolquí: Colombia – Ecuador 2-1 (1-0)
Goals: Echeverry (12), Rincón (55) / Lattanzio (86)
26.09.2014 Estadio Rumiñahui, Sangolquí: Brazil – Argentina 6-0 (2-0)
Goals: Cristiane (32), Andressa Alves (36), Maurine (58), Tayla (66), Tamires (71),
Raquel (84)
28.09.2014 Estadio Olímpico Atahualpa, Quito: Argentina – Ecuador 2-3 (2-1)
Goals: Banini (25), Bonsegundo (30) / Caicedo (36), Rodríguez (60), Lattanzio (77)
28-09-2014 Estadio Olímpico Atahualpa, Quito: Colombia – Brazil 0-0

Team	Pld	W	D	L	GF	GA	GD	Pts
Brazil	*3*	*2*	*1*	*0*	*10*	*0*	*+10*	*7*
Colombia	*3*	*1*	*2*	*0*	*2*	*1*	*+1*	*5*
Ecuador	3	1	0	2	4	8	-4	3
Argentina	3	0	1	2	2	9	-7	1

The winner **Brazil** and runner-up **Colombia** both qualified for the FIFA Women's
World Cup 2015. Ecuador advanced to the CONCACAF-CONMEBOL Play-off
2014.

CONCACAF-CONMEBOL PLAY-OFF 2014

08.11.2014 Estadio Olímpico Atahualpa, Quito: Ecuador – Trinidad and Tobago 0-0
02.12.2014 Hasely Crawford Stadium, Port of Spain:
             Trinidad and Tobago – Ecuador 0-1 (0-0)
Goal: Quinteros (90+1)

Ecuador qualified for the FIFA Women's World Cup 2015.

FIFA WOMEN'S WORLD CUP FINAL TOURNAMENT IN CANADA 2015

GROUP STAGE

GROUP A

06.06.2015 Commonwealth Stadium, Edmonton: Canada – China PR 1-0 (0-0)
Canada: Erin McLEOD, Lauren SESSELMANN, Josee BELANGER, Allysha
CHAPMAN, Kadiesha BUCHANAN, Sophie SCHMIDT, Ashley LAWRENCE,
Desiree SCOTT *(YC22)* (71 Jessie FLEMING), Christine SINCLAIR, Melissa
TANCREDI (77 Adriana LEON), Jonelle FILIGNO (61 Kaylyn KYLE).
(Coach: John HERDMAN).
China PR: WANG Fei, LI Dongna, WU Haiyan, LIU Shanshan, WANG Shanshan,
REN Guixin, TAN Ruyin, WANG Lisi (42 HAN Peng), GU Yasha (87 MA Jun), LI
Ying (62 ZHANG Rui), ZHAO Rong. (Coach: HAO Wei).
Goal: Christine SINCLAIR (90+2)
Referee: Kateryna MONZUL (Ukraine)   Attendance: 53,058

06.06.2015   Commonwealth Stadium, Edmonton:
           New Zealand – Netherlands 0-1 (0-1)
New Zealand: Erin NAYLER, Ria PERCIVAL, Abby ERCEG, Alexandra RILEY,
Katie BOWEN (72 Betsy HASSETT), Rebekah STOTT, Katie DUNCAN, Annalie
LONGO, Amber HEARN, Hannah WILKINSON, Sarah GREGORIUS (67 Jasmine
PEREIRA). (Coach: Tony READINGS).
Netherlands: Loes GEURTS, Mandy VAN DEN BERG, Petra HOGEWONING,
Stephanie VAN DER GRAGT, Anouk DEKKER (84 Tessel MIDDAG), Sherida
SPITSE, Danielle VAN DE DONK *(YC32)*, Desiree VAN LUNTEREN, Lieke
MARTENS *(YC64)* (90+2 Kirsten VAN DE VEN), Manon MELIS, Vivianne
MIEDEMA (81 Shanice VAN DE SANDEN). (Coach: Roger REIJNERS).
Goal: Lieke MARTENS (33)
Referee: Quetzalli ALVARADO Godínez (Mexico)   Attendance: 53,058

11.06.2015   Commonwealth Stadium, Edmonton: China PR – Netherlands 1-0 (0-0)
China PR: WANG Fei, LI Dongna, WU Haiyan, LIU Shanshan, WANG Shanshan (57
WANG Shuang), TANG Jiali (86 LOU Jiahui), HAN Peng, REN Guixin (71 MA
Jun), TAN Ruyin, WANG Lisi, ZHAO Rong. (Coach: HAO Wei).
Netherlands: Sari VAN VEENENDAAL, Mandy VAN DEN BERG, Petra
HOGEWONING (59 Merel VAN DONGEN), Stephanie VAN DER GRAGT,
Sherida SPITSE, Danielle VAN DE DONK, Desiree VAN LUNTEREN, Lieke
MARTENS, Tessel MIDDAG (70 Anouk DEKKER), Manon MELIS, Vivianne
MIEDEMA. (Coach: Roger REIJNERS).
Goal: WANG Lisi (90+1)
Referee: Yeimi Lucero MARTÍNEZ Valverde (Colombia)   Attendance: 35,544

11.06.2015   Commonwealth Stadium, Edmonton: Canada – New Zealand 0-0
Canada: Erin McLEOD, Lauren SESSELMANN (68 Carmelina MOSCATO), Josee
BELANGER, Allysha CHAPMAN *(YC31)*, Kadiesha BUCHANAN, Sophie
SCHMIDT, Ashley LAWRENCE, Desiree SCOTT (73 Adriana LEON), Christine
SINCLAIR, Melissa TANCREDI, Jonelle FILIGNO (63 Kaylyn KYLE).
(Coach: John HERDMAN).
New Zealand: Erin NAYLER, Ria PERCIVAL *(YC52)*, Abby ERCEG, Alexandra
RILEY, Rebekah STOTT, Katie DUNCAN, Annalie LONGO, Betsy HASSETT (77
Katie BOWEN), Amber HEARN, Hannah WILKINSON (89 Jasmine PEREIRA),
Sarah GREGORIUS *(YC71)* (80 Rosie WHITE). (Coach: Tony READINGS).
Referee: Bibiana STEINHAUS (Germany)   Attendance: 35,544

Amber HEARN missed a penalty kick (32).

15.06.2015   Stade Olympique, Montréal: Netherlands – Canada 1-1 (0-1)
Netherlands: Loes GEURTS, Mandy VAN DEN BERG, Stephanie VAN DER
GRAGT *(YC73)*, Merel VAN DONGEN, Anouk DEKKER, Sherida SPITSE,
Danielle VAN DE DONK (72 Kirsten VAN DE VEN), Desiree VAN LUNTEREN
(13 Dominique JANSSEN), Lieke MARTENS, Manon MELIS, Vivianne
MIEDEMA. (Coach: Roger REIJNERS).
Canada: Erin McLEOD, Carmelina MOSCATO, Josee BELANGER *(YC72)*, Allysha
CHAPMAN, Kadiesha BUCHANAN, Sophie SCHMIDT (81 Rhian WILKINSON),
Kaylyn KYLE (61 Melissa TANCREDI), Ashley LAWRENCE, Jessie FLEMING (61
Desiree SCOTT), Christine SINCLAIR, Adriana LEON. (Coach: John HERDMAN).
Goals: Kirsten VAN DE VEN (87) / Ashley LAWRENCE (10)
Referee: OK Ri-Hyang (North Korea)   Attendance: 45,420

15.06.2015   Investors Group Field, Winnipeg: China PR – New Zealand 2-2 (1-1)
China PR: WANG Fei, LI Dongna, WU Haiyan, LIU Shanshan *(YC75)*, WANG
Shanshan, TANG Jiali (72 WANG Shuang *(YC86)*), HAN Peng (84 LOU Jiahui),
REN Guixin, TAN Ruyin, WANG Lisi (90+3 LI Ying), ZHAO Rong.
(Coach: HAO Wei).
New Zealand: Erin NAYLER, Ria PERCIVAL, Abby ERCEG *(YC83)*, Alexandra
RILEY, Rebekah STOTT, Katie DUNCAN *(YC86)*, Annalie LONGO, Betsy
HASSETT (46 Katie BOWEN), Amber HEARN, Hannah WILKINSON, Sarah
GREGORIUS (46 Rosie WHITE, 89 Kirsty YALLOP). (Coach: Tony READINGS).
Goals: WANG Lisi (41 pen), WANG Shanshan (60) / Rebekah STOTT (28), Hannah
WILKINSON (64)
Referee: Katalin KULCSAR (Hungary)   Attendance: 26,191

Team	Pld	W	D	L	GF	GA	GD	Pts
Canada	*3*	*1*	*2*	*0*	*2*	*1*	*+1*	*5*
China PR	*3*	*1*	*1*	*1*	*3*	*3*	*0*	*4*
Netherlands	*3*	*1*	*1*	*1*	*2*	*2*	*0*	*4*
New Zealand	3	0	2	1	2	3	-1	2

GROUP B

07.06.2015   TD Place Stadiu, Ottawa: Norway – Thailand 4-0 (3-0)
Norway: Ingrid HJELMSETH, Nora Holstad BERGE (46 Marita Skammelsrud
LUND), Trine RØNNING (63 Elise THORSNES), Maren MJELDE, Ingrid Moe
WOLD, Lene MYKJÅLAND, Gry Tofte IMS, Solveig GULBRANDSEN (69 Emilie
HAAVI), Kristine MINDE, Isabell HERLOVSEN, Ada Stolsmo HEGERBERG.
(Coach: Even Jostein PELLERUD).
Thailand: Warapom BOONSING, Sunisa SRANGTHAISONG, Duangnapa
SRITALA *(YC74)*, Natthakam CHINWONG, Warunee PHETWISET *(YC51)*, Pikul
KHUEANPET, Naphat SEESRAUM (59 Orathai SRIMANEE), Anootsara
MAIJAREM (90 Thanatta CHAWONG), Kanjana SUNGNGOEN, Silawan
INTAMEE, Rattikan THONGSOMBUT. (Coach: Nuengrutai SRATHONGVIAN).
Goals: Trine RØNNING (15), Isabell HERLOVSEN (29, 34), Ada Stolsmo
HEGERBERG (68)
Referee: Anna-Marie KEIGHLEY (New Zealand)   Attendance: 20,953

Maren MJELDE missed a penalty kick (75).

07.06.2015   TD Place Stadiu, Ottawa: Germany – Côte d'Ivoire 10-0 (5-0)
Germany: Nadine ANGERER, Saskia BARTUSIAK, Annike KRAHN, Tabea
KEMME, Leonie MAIER, Simone LAUDEHR (73 Lena PETERMANN), Lena
GÖßLING, Melanie LEUPOLZ (17 Melanie BEHRINGER), Anja MITTAG, Célia
SASIC (46 Sara DÄBRITZ), Alexandra POPP. (Coach: Silva NEID).
Côte d'Ivoire: Dominique THIAMALE *(YC40)*, Fatou COULIBALY *(YC70)*, Nina
KPAHO (38 Fernande TCHETCHE), Sophie AGUIE *(YC58)*, Raymonde KACOU,
Ida Rebecca GUEHAI, Rita AKAFFOU *(YC36)*, Binta DIAKITÉ, Josee NAHI
(YC86), Nadege ESSOH (51 Ines NREHY), Rebecca ELLOH *(YC66)* (72 Ange
N'GUESSAN). (Coach: Clementine TOURE).
Goals: Célia SASIC (3, 14, 31), Anja MITTAG (29, 35, 64), Simone LAUDEHR (71),
Sara DÄBRITZ (75), Melanie BEHRINGER (79), Alexandra POPP (85)
Referee: Carol Anne CHENARD (Canada)   Attendance: 20,953

11.06.2015   TD Place Stadiu, Ottawa: Germany – Norway 1-1 (1-0)
Germany: Nadine ANGERER, Saskia BARTUSIAK *(YC59)*, Annike KRAHN, Tabea
KEMME, Leonie MAIER, Simone LAUDEHR (66 Lena LOTZEN), Lena GÖßLING,
Dzsenifer MAROZSAN, Anja MITTAG (80 Pauline BREMER), Célia SASIC,
Alexandra POPP (70 Sara DÄBRITZ). (Coach: Silva NEID).
Norway: Ingrid HJELMSETH, Marita Skammelsrud LUND, Maren MJELDE, Ingrid
Moe WOLD, Maria THORISDOTTIR, Lene MYKJÅLAND, Gry Tofte IMS (46
Solveig GULBRANDSEN), Ingrid SCHJELDERUP, Kristine MINDE (60 Elise
THORSNES), Isabell HERLOVSEN (90+1 Emilie HAAVI), Ada Stolsmo
HEGERBERG. (Coach: Even Jostein PELLERUD).
Goals: Anja MITTAG (6) / Maren MJELDE (61)
Referee: Teodora ALBON (Romania)   Attendance: 18,987

11.06.2015   TD Place Stadiu, Ottawa: Côte d'Ivoire – Thailand 2-3 (1-2)
Côte d'Ivoire: Dominique THIAMALE, Fatou COULIBALY, Djelika COULIBALY,
Fernande TCHETCHE, Raymonde KACOU, Ida Rebecca GUEHAI (81 Jessica ABY
(YC90+4)), Rita AKAFFOU (46 Rebecca ELLOH), Christine LOHOUES, Binta
DIAKITÉ (34 Josee NAHI), Ines NREHY, Ange N'GUESSAN.
(Coach: Clementine TOURE).
Thailand: Warapom BOONSING, Sunisa SRANGTHAISONG, Duangnapa
SRITALA, Natthakam CHINWONG (90+7 Darut CHANGPLOOK), Warunee
PHETWISET, Pikul KHUEANPET, Anootsara MAIJAREM, Kanjana
SUNGNGOEN, Silawan INTAMEE, Nisa ROMYEN (43 Rattikan
THONGSOMBUT), Orathai SRIMANEE (73 Thanatta CHAWONG).
(Coach: Nuengrutai SRATHONGVIAN).
Goals: Ange N'GUESSAN (4), Josee NAHI (88) / Orathai SRIMANEE (26, 45+3),
Thanatta CHAWONG (75)
Referee: Margaret DOMKA (United States)   Attendance: 18,987

15.06.2015   Investors Group Field, Winnipeg: Thailand – Germany 0-4 (0-1)
Thailand: Warapom BOONSING, Sunisa SRANGTHAISONG, Duangnapa
SRITALA, Natthakam CHINWONG, Warunee PHETWISET, Pikul KHUEANPET,
Anootsara MAIJAREM (YC82) (87 Alisa RUKPINIJ), Kanjana SUNGNGOEN,
Silawan INTAMEE, Rattikan THONGSOMBUT (89 Darut CHANGPLOOK),
Orathai SRIMANEE (79 Wilaiporn BOOTHDUANG).
(Coach: Nuengrutai SRATHONGVIAN).
Germany: Nadine ANGERER, Babett PETER, Annike KRAHN (61 Josephine
HENNING), Melanie BEHRINGER, Bianca SCHMIDT, Dzsenifer MAROZSAN (46
Lena PETERMANN), Jennifer CRAMER, Melanie LEUPOLZ, Sara DÄBRITZ,
Célia SASIC (46 Anja MITTAG), Lena LOTZEN. (Coach: Silva NEID).
Goals: Melanie LEUPOLZ (24), Lena PETERMANN (56, 58), Sara DÄBRITZ (73)
Referee: Gladys LENGWE (Zambia)   Attendance: 26,191

15.06.2015   Moncton Stadium, Moncton: Côte d'Ivoire – Norway 1-3 (0-1)
Côte d'Ivoire: Cynthia DJOHORE, Fatou COULIBALY (YC25), Djelika
COULIBALY, Fernande TCHETCHE, Ida Rebecca GUEHAI, Christine LOHOUES
(90+4 Rita AKAFFOU), Josee NAHI, Ines NREHY, Ange N'GUESSAN, Rebecca
ELLOH, Nadège CISSÉ (68 Binta DIAKITÉ, 90+3 Nadege ESSOH).
(Coach: Clementine TOURE).
Norway: Ingrid HJELMSETH (80 Silje VESTERBEKKMO), Marita Skammelsrud
LUND, Maria THORISDOTTIR, Lene MYKJÅLAND, Solveig GULBRANDSEN,
Ingrid SCHJELDERUP, Kristine MINDE (46 Ingrid Moe WOLD), Elise
THORSNES, Emilie HAAVI (YC52), Lisa-Marie UTLAND (64 Maren MJELDE),
Ada Stolsmo HEGERBERG. (Coach: Even Jostein PELLERUD).
Goals: Ange N'GUESSAN (71) / Ada Stolsmo HEGERBERG (6, 62), Solveig
GULBRANDSEN (67)
Referee: Jessica Salome DI IORIO (Argentina)   Attendance: 7,147

Team	Pld	W	D	L	GF	GA	GD	Pts
Germany	*3*	*2*	*1*	*0*	*15*	*1*	*+14*	*7*
Norway	*3*	*2*	*1*	*0*	*8*	*2*	*+6*	*7*
Thailand	3	1	0	2	3	10	-7	3
Côte d'Ivoire	3	0	0	3	3	16	-13	0

GROUP C

08.06.2015   BC Place Stadium, Vancouver: Cameroon – Ecuador 6-0 (3-0)
Cameroon: Annette NGO, Yvonne LEUKO, Christine MANIE, Claudine Falonne
MEFFOMETOU Tcheno, Cathy Bou NDJOUH, Raissa FEUDJIO Tchuanyo,
Geneviève NGO MBELECK (61 Francine ZOUGA), Madeleine NGONO (74 Najara
CHOUT), Gabrielle ONGUENE (83 Henriette AKABA), Gaelle ENGANAMOUIT,
Jeannette YANGO *(YC38)*. (Coach: Carl ENOW NGACHU).
Ecuador: Shirley Viviana BERRUZ Aguilar, Nancy Lorena AGUILAR Murillo,
Angie Paola PONCE Baque, Ligia Elena MOREIRA Burgos *(RC66)*, Mayra Fabiola
OLVERA Reyes, Madelin Stefania RIERA Bajana, Kerlly Lizeth REAL Carranza
(YC43), Mabel VELARDE Coba (45 Ingrid Roxana RODRIGUEZ Alvarado
(YC45+2)), Ambar Gillians TORRES Laz (54 Giannina Maria LATTANZIO Flores),
Monica Rebeca QUINTEROS Cabeza (72 Katherine Solange ORTIZ Simisterra
(YC70)), Denise Andrea PESANTES Tenorio. (Coach: Vanessa ARAUZ).
Goals: Madeleine NGONO (34), Gaelle ENGANAMOUIT (36, 73, 90+4 pen),
Christine MANIE (44 pen), Gabrielle ONGUENE (79 pen),
Referee: Katalin KULCSAR (Hungary)   Attendance: 25,942

Sent-off: 66' Ligia Elena MOREIRA Burgos.

08.06.2015   BC Place Stadium, Vancouver: Japan – Switzerland 1-0 (1-0)
Japan: Erina YAMANE, Azusa IWASHIMIZU, Saki KUMAGAI, Saori ARIYOSHI,
Homare SAWA (57 Yuri KAWAMURA), Aya MIYAMA, Mizuho SAKAGUCHI,
Rumi UTSUGI, Kozue ANDO (32 Yuika SUGASAWA), Yuki NAGASATO,
Shinobu OHNO (90 Nahomi KAWASUMI). (Coach: Norio SASAKI).
Switzerland: Gaëlle THALMANN *(YC28)*, Ana-Maria CRNOGORCEVIC, Rachel
RINAST, Caroline ABBÉ *(YC90+3)*, Noelle MARITZ, Martina MOSER (81 Cinzia
ZEHNDER), Lara DICKENMANN, Vanessa BERNAUER, Fabienne HUMM (46
Eseosa AIGBOGUN), Lia WÄLTI, Ramona BACHMANN *(YC22)*.
(Coach: Martina VOSS-TECKLENBURG).
Goal: Aya MIYAMA (29 pen).
Referee: Lucila VENEGAS Montes (Mexico)   Attendance: 25,942

12.06.2015   BC Place Stadium, Vancouver: Switzerland – Ecuador 10-1 (2-0)
Switzerland: Gaëlle THALMANN, Ana-Maria CRNOGORCEVIC, Rachel RINAST,
Caroline ABBÉ (51 Cinzia ZEHNDER), Rahel KIWIC (72 Selina KUSTER), Noelle
MARITZ (57 Nicole REMUND), Martina MOSER, Fabienne HUMM, Lia WÄLTI,
Ramona BACHMANN, Eseosa AIGBOGUN.
(Coach: Martina VOSS-TECKLENBURG).
Ecuador: Shirley Viviana BERRUZ Aguilar, Katherine Solange ORTIZ Simisterra (46
Alexandra Lucia Jean SALVADOR Duthie), Nancy Lorena AGUILAR Murillo,
Angie Paola PONCE Baque, Ingrid Roxana RODRIGUEZ Alvarado, Mayra Fabiola
OLVERA Reyes, Ana Valeria PALACIOS Mendoza (69 Adriana Margarita BARRE
Cusme), Kerlly Lizeth REAL Carranza, Mabel VELARDE Coba (79 Erika Paola
VASQUEZ Valencia), Monica Rebeca QUINTEROS Cabeza, Denise Andrea
PESANTES Tenorio (YC72). (Coach: Vanessa ARAUZ).
Goals: Angie Paola PONCE Baque (24 og, 71 og), Eseosa AIGBOGUN (45+2),
Fabienne HUMM (47, 49, 52), Ramona BACHMANN (60 pen, 61, 81), Martina
MOSER (76) / Angie Paola PONCE Baque (64 pen)
Referee: Rita Binti GANI (Malaysia)   Attendance: 31,441

12.06.2015   BC Place Stadium, Vancouver: Japan – Cameroon 2-1 (2-0)
Japan: Ayumi KAIHORI, Yukari KINGA, Azusa IWASHIMIZU, Aya
SAMESHIMA, Saki KUMAGAI, Aya MIYAMA, Mizuho SAKAGUCHI (64
Homare SAWA), Rumi UTSUGI, Yuki NAGASATO, Nahomi KAWASUMI (55
Shinobu OHNO), Yuika SUGASAWA (85 Megumi KAMIONOBE).
(Coach: Norio SASAKI).
Cameroon: Annette NGO, Yvonne LEUKO, Christine MANIE, Claudine Falonne
MEFFOMETOU Tcheno, Cathy Bou NDJOUH, Raissa FEUDJIO Tchuanyo,
Geneviève NGO MBELECK (YC43) (46 Francine ZOUGA), Madeleine NGONO (62
Ajara NCHOUT), Gabrielle ONGUENE (72 Augustin EJANGUE), Gaelle
ENGANAMOUIT, Jeannette YANGO. (Coach: Carl ENOW NGACHU).
Goals: Aya SAMESHIMA (6), Yuika SUGASAWA (17) / Ajara NCHOUT (90)
Referee: Pernilla LARSSON (Sweden)   Attendance: 31,441

16.06.2015   Investors Group Field, Winnipeg: Ecuador – Japan 0-1 (0-1)
Ecuador: Shirley Viviana BERRUZ Aguilar, Katherine Solange ORTIZ Simisterra,
Nancy Lorena AGUILAR Murillo (YC52), Angie Paola PONCE Baque, Ingrid
Roxana RODRIGUEZ Alvarado, Ligia Elena MOREIRA Burgos, Mayra Fabiola
OLVERA Reyes, Erika Paola VASQUEZ Valencia (YC39) (90 Madelin Stefania
RIERA Bajana), Kerlly Lizeth REAL Carranza, Monica Rebeca QUINTEROS
Cabeza (83 Carina Elizabeth CAICEDO Caicedo), Denise Andrea PESANTES
Tenorio. (Coach: Vanessa ARAUZ).
Japan: Miho FUKUMOTO, Aya SAMESHIMA, Asuna TANAKA, Saori
ARIYOSHI, Yuri KAWAMURA, Kana KITAHARA (46 Megumi KAMIONOBE),
Homare SAWA, Aya MIYAMA, Yuki NAGASATO, Shinobu OHNO (YC17) (75
Asano NAGASATO), Yuika SUGASAWA (80 Mana IWABUCHI).
(Coach: Norio SASAKI).
Goal: 5' Yuki NAGASATO 0-1.
Referee: Melissa BORJAS (Honduras)   Attendance: 14,522

16.06.2015 Commonwealth Stadium, Edmonton: Switzerland – Cameroon 1-2 (1-0)
Switzerland: Gaëlle THALMANN, Ana-Maria CRNOGORCEVIC, Rachel RINAST,
Selina KUSTER, Rahel KIWIC (65 Vanessa BERNAUER), Noelle MARITZ,
Martina MOSER, Lara DICKENMANN (80 Nicole REMUND), Fabienne HUMM
(69 Eseosa AIGBOGUN), Lia WÄLTI *(YC82)*, Ramona BACHMANN.
(Coach: Martina VOSS-TECKLENBURG).
Cameroon: Annette NGO, Marie Aurelle AWONA, Augustin EJANGUE, Christine
MANIE, Claudine Falonne MEFFOMETOU Tcheno *(YC68)*, Raissa FEUDJIO
Tchuanyo *(YC19)*, Ajara NCHOUT *(YC35)* (57 Madeleine NGONO), Francine
ZOUGA (87 Agathe NGANI), Gabrielle ONGUENE (90+2 Henriette AKABA),
Gaelle ENGANAMOUIT *(YC90+2)*, Jeannette YANGO.
(Coach: Carl ENOW NGACHU).
Goals: Ana-Maria CRNOGORCEVIC (24) / Gabrielle ONGUENE (47),
Madeleine NGONO (62)
Referee: Claudia Inés UMPIÉRREZ Rodríguez (Uruguay) Attendance: 10,177

Team	Pld	W	D	L	GF	GA	GD	Pts
Japan	*3*	*3*	*0*	*0*	*4*	*1*	*+3*	*9*
Cameroon	*3*	*2*	*0*	*1*	*9*	*3*	*+6*	*6*
Switzerland	*3*	*1*	*0*	*2*	*11*	*4*	*+7*	*3*
Ecuador	3	0	0	3	1	17	-16	0

GROUP D

08.06.2015 Investors Group Field, Winnipeg: Sweden – Nigeria 3-3 (2-0)
Sweden: Rut Hedvig LINDAHL, Emma Sofia BERGLUND (73 Amanda
ILESTADT), Nilla FISCHER, Lina Therese NILSSON, Lisa Karolina Viktoria
DAHLKVIST (57 Linda Brigitta SEMBRANT), Sara Caroline SEGER, Kerstin
Ingrid Therese SJÖGRAN, Elin Ingrid Johanna RUBENSSON, Kosovare ASLLANI
(46 Olivia Alma Charlotta SCHOUGH), Eva Sofia JAKOBSSON, Lotta Eva
SCHELIN. (Coach: Pia Mariane SUNDHAGE).
Nigeria: Predious Uzoaru DEDE, Onome EBI, Ngozi EBERE, Osinachi Marvis
OHALE, Josephine Chiwendu CHUKWUNONYE, Ngozi Sonia OKOBI, Halimatu
Ibrahim AYINDE, Evelyn Chiedu NWABUOKU, Ugochi Desire OPARANOZIE,
Francisca ORDEGA, Asisat Lamina OSHOALA. (Coach: Edwin OKON).
Goals: Ugochi Desire OPARANOZIE (20 og), Nilla FISCHER (31), Linda Brigitta
SEMBRANT (60) / Ngozi Sonia OKOBI (50), Asisat Lamina OSHOALA (53),
Francisca ORDEGA (87)
Referee: OK Ri-Hyang (North Korea) Attendance: 31,148

08.06.2015   Investors Group Field, Winnipeg: United States – Australia 3-1 (1-1)
United States: Hope Amelia SOLO, Alexandra Blaire (Ali) KRIEGER, Becky
SAUERBRUNN, Meghan KLINGENBERG, Julie ERTZ, Carli LLOYD, Abby
WAMBACH, Lauren HOLIDAY *(YC56)*, Megan RAPINOE *(YC64)* (87 Morgan
BRIAN), Sydney LEROUX (79 Alexandra (Alex) MORGAN), Christen PRESS (68
Tobin HEATH). (Coach: Jillian ELLIS).
Australia: Melissa BARBIERI HUDSON, Emily VAN EGMOND, Laura ALLEWAY
(83 Ashleigh SYKES), Steph CATLEY, Servet UZUNLAR, Elise KELLOND,
Katrina GORRY (80 Alanna KENNEDY), Lisa DE VANNA, Samantha KERR,
Michelle HEYMAN (69 Kyah SIMON), Caitlin FOORD. (Coach: Alen STAJCIC).
Goals: Megan RAPINOE (12, 78), Christen PRESS (61) / Lisa DE VANNA (27)
Referee: Claudia Inés UMPIÉRREZ Rodríguez (Uruguay)   Attendance: 31,148

12.06.2015   Investors Group Field, Winnipeg: Australia – Nigeria 2-0 (1-0)
Australia: Lydia WILLIAMS, Emily VAN EGMOND, Laura ALLEWAY, Steph
CATLEY, Alanna KENNEDY, Elise KELLOND, Katrina GORRY (62 Tameka
BUTT), Lisa DE VANNA, Samantha KERR, Kyah SIMON (87 Michelle HEYMAN),
Caitlin FOORD. (Coach: Alen STAJCIC).
Nigeria: Predious Uzoaru DEDE, Onome EBI, Ngozi EBERE, Osinachi Marvis
OHALE (52 Ugo NJOKU), Josephine Chiwendu CHUKWUNONYE *(YC60)*, Ngozi
Sonia OKOBI, Halimatu Ibrahim AYINDE, Evelyn Chiedu NWABUOKU *(YC42)*,
Ugochi Desire OPARANOZIE (54 Perpetua Ijeoma NKWOCHA), Francisca
ORDEGA, Asisat Lamina OSHOALA (84 Courtney Ozioma DIKE).
(Coach: Edwin OKON).
Goals: Kyah SIMON (29, 68)
Referee: Stéphanie FRAPPART (France)   Attendance: 32,716

12.06.2015   Investors Group Field, Winnipeg: United States – Sweden 0-0
United States: Hope Amelia SOLO, Alexandra Blaire (Ali) KRIEGER, Becky
SAUERBRUNN, Meghan KLINGENBERG, Julie ERTZ, Morgan BRIAN (58 Amy
RODRIGUEZ), Carli LLOYD, Lauren HOLIDAY, Megan RAPINOE, Sydney
LEROUX (78 Alexandra (Alex) MORGAN), Christen PRESS (67 Abby
WAMBACH). (Coach: Jillian ELLIS).
Sweden: Rut Hedvig LINDAHL, Nilla FISCHER, Lina Therese NILSSON (70 Linda
Brigitta SEMBRANT), Amanda ILESTADT, Jessica Marie SAMUELSSON, Lisa
Karolina Viktoria DAHLKVIST, Sara Caroline SEGER, Kerstin Ingrid Therese
SJÖGRAN (75 Emilia APPELQVIST), Elin Ingrid Johanna RUBENSSON, Eva Sofia
JAKOBSSON, Lotta Eva SCHELIN. (Coach: Pia Mariane SUNDHAGE).
Referee: Sachiko YAMAGISHI (Japan)   Attendance: 32,716

16.06.2015 Commonwealth Stadium, Edmonton: Australia – Sweden 1-1 (1-1)
Australia: Lydia WILLIAMS, Emily VAN EGMOND, Laura ALLEWAY, Steph CATLEY, Alanna KENNEDY, Elise KELLOND, Katrina GORRY (85 Tameka BUTT), Lisa DE VANNA (63 Larissa CRUMMER), Samantha KERR, Kyah SIMON (72 Michelle HEYMAN), Caitlin FOORD. (Coach: Alen STAJCIC).
Sweden: Rut Hedvig LINDAHL, Nilla FISCHER, Lina Therese NILSSON (74 Kosovare ASLLANI), Amanda ILESTADT, Jessica Marie SAMUELSSON, Lisa Karolina Viktoria DAHLKVIST, Sara Caroline SEGER, Kerstin Ingrid Therese SJÖGRAN, Elin Ingrid Johanna RUBENSSON (76 Sara Kristina THUNEBRO), Eva Sofia JAKOBSSON, Lotta Eva SCHELIN. (Coach: Pia Mariane SUNDHAGE).
Goals: Lisa DE VANNA (5) / Eva Sofia JAKOBSSON (15)
Referee: Lucila VENEGAS Montes (Mexico) Attendance: 10,177

16.06.2015 BC Place Stadium, Vancouver: Nigeria – United States 0-1 (0-1)
Nigeria: Predious Uzoaru DEDE, Onome EBI *(YC43)*, Ngozi EBERE, Sarah Ihechiluru Amaka NNODIM *(YC38,YC69)*, Josephine Chiwendu CHUKWUNONYE *(YC59)*, Ngozi Sonia OKOBI *(YC68)*, Chiedu NWABUOKU, Ukpong Esther SUNDAY (50 Halimatu Ibrahim AYINDE), Francisca ORDEGA (77 Cecilia Ngibo NKU), Asisat Lamina OSHOALA, Courtney Ozioma DIKE (50 Ugochi Desire OPARANOZIE). (Coach: Edwin OKON).
United States: Hope Amelia SOLO, Alexandra Blaire (Ali) KRIEGER, Becky SAUERBRUNN, Meghan KLINGENBERG, Julie ERTZ, Tobin HEATH (80 Christie PEARCE), Carli LLOYD, Abby WAMBACH, Lauren HOLIDAY, Megan RAPINOE (74 Shannon BOXX), Alexandra (Alex) MORGAN (66 Sydney LEROUX). (Coach: Jillian ELLIS).
Goal: Abby WAMBACH (45)
Referee: Kateryna MONZUL (Ukraine) Attendance: 52,193

Sent-off: 69' Sarah Ihechiluru Amaka NNODIM.

Team	Pld	W	D	L	GF	GA	GD	Pts
United States	*3*	*2*	*1*	*0*	*4*	*1*	*+3*	*7*
Australia	*3*	*1*	*1*	*1*	*4*	*4*	*0*	*4*
Sweden	*3*	*0*	*3*	*0*	*4*	*4*	*0*	*3*
Nigeria	*3*	*0*	*1*	*2*	*3*	*6*	*-3*	*1*

GROUP E

09.06.2015   Stade Olympique, Montréal: Spain – Costa Rica 1-1 (1-1)
Spain: AINHOA TIRAPU de Goñi, MARTA TORREJÓN Moya, LEIRE LANDA
Iroz, IRENE PAREDES Hernandez, CELIA JIMÉNEZ Delgado *(YC44)* (63 RUTH
GARCÍA García), María VICTORIA LOSADA Gómez, ALÈXIA PUTELLAS
Segura, SONIA BERMÚDEZ Tribano (72 MARTA CORREDERA Rueda),
VERÓNICA (Vero) BOQUETE Giadans, NATALIA Teresa de PABLOS Sanchón,
JENIFER HERMOSO Fuentes (84 PRISCILA BORJA Moreno).
(Coach: IGNACIO QUEREDA Laviña).
Costa Rica: Dinnia Cecilia DIAZ Artavia, Carol SANCHEZ Cruz, Lixy
RODRIGUEZ Zamora, Diana Carolina SAENZ Brown, Shirley CRUZ Traña,
Katherine Maria ALVARADO Aguilar, Raquel (Rocky) RODRÍGUEZ Cedeño,
Carolina Paola VENEGAS Morales (80 Cristin Yorleny GRANADOS Gomez),
Wendy Patricia Salas ACOSTA, Maria Fernanda BARRANTES Rojas (74 Karla
Gabriela VILLALOBOS Duran), Melissa HERRERA Monge (88 Gabriela GUILLEN
Alvarez). (Coach: Amelia VALVERDE Villalobos).
Goals: María VICTORIA LOSADA Gómez (13) / Raquel (Rocky) RODRÍGUEZ
Cedeño (14)
Referee: Jessica Salome DI IORIO (Argentina)   Attendance: 10,175

09.06.2015   Stade Olympique, Montréal: Brazil – South Korea 2-0 (1-0)
Brazil: LUCIANA Maria Dionizio, MÔNICA Hickmann Alves, FABIANA da Silva
Simões, RAFAELLE Leone Carvalho Souza (82 GESSICA do Nascimento),
TAMIRES Cassia Dias Gomes, Miraildes Maciel Mota "FORMIGA", ANDRESSA
Cavalari Machry (81 RAQUEL Fernandes dos Santos), MARTA Vieira da Silva,
CRISTIANE Rozeira de Souza Silva, ANDRESSA ALVES da Silva (90+1 Rafaela de
Miranda Travalao "RAFINHA"), Thaysa de Moraes Rosa Moreno "ISA".
(Coach: Oswaldo Fumeiro Alvarez "VADÃO").
South Korea: KIM Jung-Mi, LEE Eun-Mi, KIM Do-Yeon, KIM Hye-Ri, SIM Seo-
Yeon, JEON Ga-Eul, JI So-Yeon, KWON Hah-Nul (77 LEE So-Dam), CHO So-Hyun
(YC53), KANG Yu-Mi (90+1 PARK Hee-Young), YOO Young-A (67 JUNG Seol-
Bin). (Coach: YOON Deuk-Yeo).
Goals: Miraildes Maciel Mota "FORMIGA" (33), MARTA Vieira da Silva (53 pen)
Referee: Esther STAUBLI (Switzerland)   Attendance: 10,175

13.06.2015　Stade Olympique, Montréal: Brazil – Spain 1-0 (1-0)
Brazil: LUCIANA Maria Dionizio, MÔNICA Hickmann Alves, FABIANA da Silva Simões (77 POLIANA Barbosa Medeiros), RAFAELLE Leone Carvalho Souza, TAMIRES Cassia Dias Gomes, Miraildes Maciel Mota "FORMIGA", ANDRESSA Cavalari Machry, MARTA Vieira da Silva, CRISTIANE Rozeira de Souza Silva (89 RAQUEL Fernandes dos Santos *(YC90+3)*), ANDRESSA ALVES da Silva, Thaysa de Moraes Rosa Moreno "ISA" (60 DARLENE de Souza Reguera).
(Coach: Oswaldo Fumeiro Alvarez "VADÃO").
Spain: AINHOA TIRAPU de Goñi, MARTA TORREJÓN Moya, LEIRE LANDA Iroz *(YC23)*, IRENE PAREDES Hernandez, CELIA JIMÉNEZ Delgado, María VICTORIA LOSADA Gómez, ALÈXIA PUTELLAS Segura, VIRGINIA TORRECILLA Reyes (77 SONIA BERMÚDEZ Tribano), VERÓNICA (Vero) BOQUETE Giadans, NATALIA Teresa de PABLOS Sanchón (71 Silvia Meseguer Bellido "MESI"), MARTA CORREDERA Rueda (70 PRISCILA BORJA Moreno).
(Coach: IGNACIO QUEREDA Laviña).
Goal: ANDRESSA ALVES da Silva (44)
Referee: Carol Anne CHENARD (Canada)　Attendance: 28,623

13.06.2015　Stade Olympique, Montréal: South Korea – Costa Rica 2-2 (2-1)
South Korea: KIM Jung-Mi, LEE Eun-Mi, KIM Hye-Ri *(YC70)* (84 LIM Seon-Joo), HWANG Bo-Ram *(YC86)*, SIM Seo-Yeon, JEON Ga-Eul, JI So-Yeon, KWON Hah-Nul, CHO So-Hyun, KANG Yu-Mi (63 JUNG Seol-Bin), YOO Young-A (77 LEE Geum-Min *(YC81)*). (Coach: YOON Deuk-Yeo).
Costa Rica: Dinnia Cecilia DIAZ Artavia, Carol SANCHEZ Cruz, Lixy RODRIGUEZ Zamora, Diana Carolina SAENZ Brown, Shirley CRUZ Traña, Katherine Maria ALVARADO Aguilar, Raquel (Rocky) RODRÍGUEZ Cedeño, Cristin Yorleny GRANADOS Gomez, Wendy Patricia Salas ACOSTA, Maria Fernanda BARRANTES Rojas (76 Karla Gabriela VILLALOBOS Duran), Melissa HERRERA Monge. (Coach: Amelia VALVERDE Villalobos).
Goals: JI So-Yeon (21 pen), JEON Ga-Eul (25) / Melissa HERRERA Monge (17), Karla Gabriela VILLALOBOS Duran (89)
Referee: Carina Susanna VITULANO (Italy)　Attendance: 28,623

17.06.2015   Moncton Stadium, Moncton: Costa Rica – Brazil 0-1 (0-0)
Costa Rica: Dinnia Cecilia DIAZ Artavia, Carol SANCHEZ Cruz, Lixy
RODRIGUEZ Zamora, Diana Carolina SAENZ Brown, Shirley CRUZ Traña,
Katherine Maria ALVARADO Aguilar (86 Fabiola Maria SANCHEZ Jimenez),
Raquel (Rocky) RODRÍGUEZ Cedeño, Cristin Yorleny GRANADOS Gomez (57
Carolina Paola VENEGAS Morales), Wendy Patricia Salas ACOSTA, Maria
Fernanda BARRANTES Rojas (72 Karla Gabriela VILLALOBOS Duran), Melissa
HERRERA Monge. (Coach: Amelia VALVERDE Villalobos).
Brazil: LUCIANA Maria Dionizio, MÔNICA Hickmann Alves (66 GESSICA do
Nascimento), RAFAELLE Leone Carvalho Souza, POLIANA Barbosa Medeiros,
TAMIRES Cassia Dias Gomes, ROSANA dos Santos Augusto, MAURINE Dornelles
Gonçalves, ANDRESSA Cavalari Machry, DARLENE de Souza Reguera (59
BEATRIZ Zaneratto João), GABRIELA Maria Zanotti Demoner (78 Rafaela de
Miranda Travalao "RAFINHA"), RAQUEL Fernandes dos Santos.
(Coach: Oswaldo Fumeiro Alvarez "VADÃO").
Goal: RAQUEL Fernandes dos Santos (83)
Referee: Thalia MITSI (Greece)   Attendance: 9,543

17.06.2015   TD Place Stadium, Ottawa: South Korea – Spain 2-1 (0-1)
South Korea: KIM Jung-Mi, LEE Eun-Mi, KIM Hye-Ri (46 KIM Soo-Yun),
HWANG Bo-Ram (YC69), SIM Seo-Yeon, JEON Ga-Eul, JI So-Yeon, KWON Hah-
Nul, CHO So-Hyun, KANG Yu-Mi (77 PARK Hee-Young), PARK Eun-Sun (59
YOO Young-A). (Coach: YOON Deuk-Yeo).
Spain: AINHOA TIRAPU de Goñi, MARTA TORREJÓN Moya, LEIRE LANDA
Iroz, IRENE PAREDES Hernandez, CELIA JIMÉNEZ Delgado, María VICTORIA
LOSADA Gómez (57 Silvia Meseguer Bellido "MESI"), ALÈXIA PUTELLAS
Segura, VIRGINIA TORRECILLA Reyes (YC57), VERÓNICA (Vero) BOQUETE
Giadans, NATALIA Teresa de PABLOS Sanchón (64 SONIA BERMÚDEZ
Tribano), MARTA CORREDERA Rueda (75 ERIKA VÁZQUEZ Morales).
(Coach: IGNACIO QUEREDA Laviña).
Goals: CHO So-Hyun (53), KIM Soo-Yun (78) / VERÓNICA (Vero) BOQUETE
Giadans (29)
Referee: Anna-Marie KEIGHLEY (New Zealand)   Attendance: 21,562

Team	Pld	W	D	L	GF	GA	GD	Pts
Brazil	*3*	*3*	*0*	*0*	*4*	*0*	*+4*	*9*
South Korea	*3*	*1*	*1*	*1*	*4*	*5*	*-1*	*4*
Costa Rica	3	0	2	1	3	4	-1	2
Spain	3	0	1	2	2	4	-2	1

212

GROUP F

09.06.2015   Moncton Stadium, Moncton: France – England 1-0 (1-0)
France: Sarah BOUHADDI, Laura GEORGES, Wendie RENARD, Jessica
HOUARA, Laure BOULLEAU, Camille ABILY, Amandine HENRY, Louisa NECIB
(87 Claire LAVOGEZ), Elodie THOMIS (71 Kenza DALI), Eugénie LE SOMMER
(81 Elise BUSSAGLIA), Gaëtane THINEY.
(Coaches: Corinne DIACRE & Philippe BERGEROO).
England: Karen BARDSLEY, Alexandra SCOTT (68 Francesca KIRBY), Stephanie
HOUGHTON, Laura BASSETT, Claire RAFFERTY, Lucy BRONZE, Katie
CHAPMAN *(YC66)* (76 Jade MOORE), Fara WILLIAMS, Jill SCOTT, Eniola
ALUKO, Ellen WHITE (60 Toni DUGGAN). (Coach: Mark SAMPSON).
Goal: Eugénie LE SOMMER (29)
Referee: Thalia MITSI (Greece)   Attendance: 11,686

09.06.2015   Moncton Stadium, Moncton: Colombia – Mexico 1-1 (0-1)
Colombia: Derly Stefany CASTAÑO Cardozo, Carolina ARIAS Vidal, Katherine
Nataly ARIAS Peña, Angela Corina CLAVIJO Silva, Natalia GAITÁN Laguado
(YC25), Daniele MONTOYA Quiróz *(YC55)*, Hazleydi Yoreli RINCÓN Torres, Lady
Patricia ANDRADE Rodríguez (77 Tatiana ARIZA Díaz), Diana Carolina OSPINA
García (87 Yisela CUESTA Bejarano), Maria Catalina USME Pineda (78 Ingrid
Yulieth VIDAL Isaza), Oriánica VELÁSQUEZ Herrera *(YC34)*.
(Coach: Fabián Felipe TABORDA).
Mexico: Cecilia SANTIAGO Cisneros *(YC18)*, Alina Lisi GARCIAMENDEZ
Rowold, Valeria Aurora MIRANDA Rodriguez, Christina MURILLO Ruiz, Kenti
ROBLES Salas, Nayeli RANGEL Hernandez, Sandra Stephany MAYOR Gutierrez,
Veronica Raquel PEREZ Murillo, Verónica Charlyn CORRAL Ang, Renae Nicole
CUÉLLAR Cuéllar (79 Jennifer Marie RUIZ Brown), Mónica OCAMPO Medina (87
Claudia Fabiola IBARRA Muro). (Coach: Leonardo CUÉLLAR Rivera).
Goals: Daniele MONTOYA Quiróz (82) / Veronica Raquel PEREZ Murillo (35)
Referee: Therese Raissa NEGUEL (Cameroon)   Attendance: 11,686

13.06.2015   Moncton Stadium, Moncton: France – Colombia 0-2 (0-1)
France: Sarah BOUHADDI, Laura GEORGES, Wendie RENARD, Jessica
HOUARA, Laure BOULLEAU, Camille ABILY, Louisa NECIB (63 Claire
LAVOGEZ), Elise BUSSAGLIA (63 Amandine HENRY), Kenza DALI (77 Marie
Laure DELIE), Eugénie LE SOMMER, Gaëtane THINEY.
(Coaches: Corinne DIACRE & Philippe BERGEROO).
Colombia: Sandra Milena SEPÚLVEDA Lopera *(YC69)*, Carolina ARIAS Vidal,
Katherine Nataly ARIAS Peña, Angela Corina CLAVIJO Silva, Natalia GAITÁN
Laguado, Daniele MONTOYA Quiróz, Hazleydi Yoreli RINCÓN Torres (87 Isabella
ECHEVERRI Restrepo), Lady Patricia ANDRADE Rodríguez (90+2 Tatiana ARIZA
Díaz), Diana Carolina OSPINA García *(YC79)*, Oriánica VELÁSQUEZ Herrera,
Ingrid Yulieth VIDAL Isaza (55 Maria Catalina USME Pineda).
(Coach: Fabián Felipe TABORDA).
Goals: Lady Patricia ANDRADE Rodríguez (19), Maria Catalina USME Pineda
(90+3)
Referee: QIN Liang (China PR)   Attendance: 13,138

13.06.2015 Moncton Stadium, Moncton: England – Mexico 2-1 (0-0)
England: Karen BARDSLEY, Stephanie HOUGHTON, Laura BASSETT, Claire RAFFERTY (53 Alex GREENWOOD), Lucy BRONZE (85 Alexandra SCOTT), Fara WILLIAMS, Jill SCOTT (66 Karen CARNEY *(YC90+2)*), Jade MOORE, Eniola ALUKO, Toni DUGGAN, Francesca KIRBY. (Coach: Mark SAMPSON).
Mexico: Cecilia SANTIAGO Cisneros, Alina Lisi GARCIAMENDEZ Rowold *(YC64)*, Bianca Elissa SIERRA Garcia (46 Valeria Aurora MIRANDA Rodriguez), Kenti ROBLES Salas, Nayeli RANGEL Hernandez, Sandra Stephany MAYOR Gutierrez, Veronica Raquel PEREZ Murillo, Jennifer Marie RUIZ Brown, Verónica Charlyn CORRAL Ang, Renae Nicole CUÉLLAR Cuéllar (77 Maria Guadalupe SANCHEZ Morales), Mónica OCAMPO Medina (89 Claudia Fabiola IBARRA Muro). (Coach: Leonardo CUÉLLAR Rivera).
Goals: Francesca KIRBY (70), Karen CARNEY (82) / Claudia Fabiola IBARRA Muro (90+1)
Referee: Anna-Marie KEIGHLEY (New Zealand)   Attendance: 13,138

17.06.2015   TD Place Stadium, Ottawa: Mexico – France 0-5 (0-4)
Mexico: Cecilia SANTIAGO Cisneros, Alina Lisi GARCIAMENDEZ Rowold, Valeria Aurora MIRANDA Rodriguez *(YC62)*, Kenti ROBLES Salas, Greta Alejandra ESPINOZA Casas, Nayeli RANGEL Hernandez (83 Christina MURILLO Ruiz), Sandra Stephany MAYOR Gutierrez (46 Arianna Jeanette ROMERO Tellez), Veronica Raquel PEREZ Murillo *(YC87)*, Jennifer Marie RUIZ Brown, Verónica Charlyn CORRAL Ang (46 Renae Nicole CUÉLLAR Cuéllar), Mónica OCAMPO Medina. (Coach: Leonardo CUÉLLAR Rivera).
France: Sarah BOUHADDI, Laura GEORGES, Wendie RENARD, Jessica HOUARA, Laure BOULLEAU (78 Sabrina DELANNOY), Camille ABILY (70 Elise BUSSAGLIA), Amandine HENRY, Amel MAJRI, Elodie THOMIS, Eugénie LE SOMMER (63 Gaëtane THINEY), Marie Laure DELIE.
(Coaches: Corinne DIACRE & Philippe BERGEROO).
Goals: Marie Laure DELIE (1), Jennifer Marie RUIZ Brown (9 og), Eugénie LE SOMMER (13, 36), Amandine HENRY (80)
Referee: Sachiko YAMAGISHI (Japan)   Attendance: 21,562

17.06.2015   Stade Olympique, Montréal: England – Colombia 2-1 (2-0)
England: Karen BARDSLEY, Alexandra SCOTT *(YC65)*, Casey STONEY, Stephanie HOUGHTON, Alex GREENWOOD, Fara WILLIAMS, Jade MOORE, Jordan NOBBS, Karen CARNEY (56 Lianne SANDERSON), Toni DUGGAN (81 Jodie TAYLOR), Francesca KIRBY (66 Josanne POTTER). (Coach: Mark SAMPSON).
Colombia: Sandra Milena SEPÚLVEDA Lopera *(YC85)*, Carolina ARIAS Vidal *(YC37)*, Katherine Nataly ARIAS Peña, Angela Corina CLAVIJO Silva, Natalia GAITÁN Laguado, Daniele MONTOYA Quiróz, Hazleydi Yoreli RINCÓN Torres (74 Tatiana ARIZA Díaz), Lady Patricia ANDRADE Rodríguez, Diana Carolina OSPINA García (83 Leicy Maria SANTOS Herrera), Maria Catalina USME Pineda *(YC36)* (58 Ingrid Yulieth VIDAL Isaza), Oriánica VELÁSQUEZ Herrera.
(Coach: Fabián Felipe TABORDA).
Goals: Karen CARNEY (15), Fara WILLIAMS 2-0 (38 pen), / Lady Patricia ANDRADE Rodríguez (90+4)
Referee: Carol Anne CHENARD (Canada)   Attendance: 13,862

Team	Pld	W	D	L	GF	GA	GD	Pts
France	*3*	*2*	*0*	*1*	*6*	*2*	*+4*	*6*
England	*3*	*2*	*0*	*1*	*4*	*3*	*+1*	*6*
Colombia	3	1	1	1	4	3	+1	4
Mexico	3	0	1	2	2	8	-6	1

ROUND OF 16

20.06.2015   TD Place Stadium, Ottawa: Germany – Sweden 4-1 (2-0)
Germany: Nadine ANGERER, Saskia BARTUSIAK *(YC28)*, Annike KRAHN, Tabea
KEMME (77 Jennifer CRAMER), Leonie MAIER, Simone LAUDEHR, Lena
GÖßLING, Melanie LEUPOLZ (46 Dzsenifer MAROZSAN), Anja MITTAG, Célia
SASIC, Alexandra POPP (89 Lena LOTZEN). (Coach: Silva NEID).
Sweden: Rut Hedvig LINDAHL, Emma Sofia BERGLUND (80 Jenny Josefina
HJOHLMAN), Linda Brigitta SEMBRANT, Nilla FISCHER, Amanda ILESTADT
(YC35), Jessica Marie SAMUELSSON (46 Lina Therese NILSSON), Sara Caroline
SEGER, Kerstin Ingrid Therese SJÖGRAN, Elin Ingrid Johanna RUBENSSON (67
Kosovare ASLLANI), Eva Sofia JAKOBSSON, Lotta Eva SCHELIN (YC68).
(Coach: Pia Mariane SUNDHAGE).
Goals: Anja MITTAG (24), Célia SASIC (35 pen, 78), Dzsenifer MAROZSAN (88) /
Linda Brigitta SEMBRANT (82)
Referee: OK Ri-Hyang (North Korea)   Attendance: 22,486

20.06.2015   Commonwealth Stadium, Edmonton: China PR – Cameroon 1-0 (1-0)
China PR: WANG Fei, LI Dongna, WU Haiyan, LIU Shanshan, WANG Shanshan
(90+1 GU Yasha), TANG Jiali (40 WANG Shuang), HAN Peng, REN Guixin, TAN
Ruyin, WANG Lisi (72 LOU Jiahui), ZHAO Rong. (Coach: HAO Wei).
Cameroon: Annette NGO, Yvonne LEUKO, Marie Aurelle AWONA, Christine
MANIE, Claudine Falonne MEFFOMETOU Tcheno *(YC90+3)*, Raissa FEUDJIO
Tchuanyo, Madeleine NGONO (74 Henriette AKABA), Francine ZOUGA (64 Ajara
NCHOUT), Gabrielle ONGUENE, Gaelle ENGANAMOUIT, Jeannette YANGO.
(Coach: Carl ENOW NGACHU).
Goal: WANG Shanshan (12)
Referee: Bibiana STEINHAUS (Germany)   Attendance: 15,958

21.06.2015   Moncton Stadium, Moncton: Brazil – Australia 0-1 (0-0)
Brazil: LUCIANA Maria Dionizio, MÔNICA Hickmann Alves, FABIANA da Silva
Simões *(YC14)*, RAFAELLE Leone Carvalho Souza, TAMIRES Cassia Dias Gomes
(83 RAQUEL Fernandes dos Santos), Miraildes Maciel Mota "FORMIGA",
ANDRESSA Cavalari Machry, MARTA Vieira da Silva *(YC81)*, CRISTIANE
Rozeira de Souza Silva, ANDRESSA ALVES da Silva, Thaysa de Moraes Rosa
Moreno "ISA" (83 BEATRIZ Zaneratto João).
(Coach: Oswaldo Fumeiro Alvarez "VADÃO").
Australia: Lydia WILLIAMS, Emily VAN EGMOND, Laura ALLEWAY, Steph
CATLEY, Alanna KENNEDY, Elise KELLOND, Tameka BUTT (72 Katrina
GORRY), Lisa DE VANNA, Samantha KERR, Michelle HEYMAN (64 Kyah
SIMON), Caitlin FOORD. (Coach: Alen STAJCIC).
Goal: Kyah SIMON (80)
Referee: Teodora ALBON (Romania)   Attendance: 12,054

21.06.2015   Stade Olympique, Montréal: France – South Korea 3-0 (2-0)
France: Sarah BOUHADDI, Laura GEORGES, Wendie RENARD, Jessica
HOUARA, Laure BOULLEAU, Camille ABILY (77 Kheira HAMRAOUI *(YC80)*),
Amandine HENRY, Louisa NECIB, Elodie THOMIS, Eugénie LE SOMMER (74
Gaëtane THINEY), Marie Laure DELIE (84 Kadidiatou DIANI).
(Coaches: Corinne DIACRE & Philippe BERGEROO).
South Korea: KIM Jung-Mi, LEE Eun-Mi *(YC33)*, KIM Do-Yeon, KIM Soo-Yun,
SIM Seo-Yeon, JEON Ga-Eul, KWON Hah-Nul (60 LEE So-Dam), CHO So-Hyun,
KANG Yu-Mi (78 PARK Hee-Young), LEE Geum-Min *(YC85)*, PARK Eun-Sun (55
YOO Young-A). (Coach: YOON Deuk-Yeo).
Goals: Marie Laure DELIE (4), Elodie THOMIS (8), Marie Laure DELIE (47)
Referee: Jessica Salome DI IORIO (Argentina)   Attendance: 15,518

21.06.2015   BC Place Stadium, Vancouver: Canada – Switzerland 1-0 (0-0)
Canada: Erin McLEOD, Rhian WILKINSON (88 Marie Eve NAULT), Lauren
SESSELMANN, Ashley LAWRENCE (76 Kaylyn KYLE), Josee BELANGER,
Allysha CHAPMAN, Kadiesha BUCHANAN *(YC74)*, Sophie SCHMIDT, Desiree
SCOTT, Christine SINCLAIR *(YC14)*, Melissa TANCREDI (69 Jonelle FILIGNO).
(Coach: John HERDMAN).
Switzerland: Gaëlle THALMANN, Ana-Maria CRNOGORCEVIC, Rachel RINAST
(80 Rahel KIWIC), Selina KUSTER *(YC46)* (61 Vanessa BÜRKI), Caroline ABBÉ,
Noelle MARITZ, Martina MOSER (72 Fabienne HUMM), Lara DICKENMANN,
Vanessa BERNAUER, Lia WÄLTI, Ramona BACHMANN.
(Coach: Martina VOSS-TECKLENBURG).
Goal: Josee BELANGER (52)
Referee: Anna-Marie KEIGHLEY (New Zealand)   Attendance: 53,855

22.06.2015   TD Place Stadium, Ottawa: Norway – England 1-2 (0-0)
Norway: Ingrid HJELMSETH, Trine RØNNING (46 Maria THORISDOTTIR),
Marita Skammelsrud LUND, Maren MJELDE, Ingrid Moe WOLD (87 Lisa-Marie
UTLAND), Lene MYKJÅLAND, Gry Tofte IMS, Solveig GULBRANDSEN,
Kristine MINDE (70 Elise THORSNES), Isabell HERLOVSEN, Ada Stolsmo
HEGERBERG. (Coach: Even Jostein PELLERUD).
England: Karen BARDSLEY, Stephanie HOUGHTON, Laura BASSETT, Claire
RAFFERTY, Lucy BRONZE, Katie CHAPMAN, Fara WILLIAMS, Jade MOORE,
Karen CARNEY, Toni DUGGAN (63 Jodie TAYLOR), Francesca KIRBY (54 Jill
SCOTT). (Coach: Mark SAMPSON).
Goals: Solveig GULBRANDSEN (54) / Stephanie HOUGHTON (61),
Lucy BRONZE (76)
Referee: Esther STAUBLI (Switzerland)   Attendance: 19,829

22.06.2015   Commonwealth Stadium, Edmonton: United States – Colombia 2-0 (0-0)
United States: Hope Amelia SOLO, Alexandra Blaire (Ali) KRIEGER (81 Lori
CHALUPNY), Becky SAUERBRUNN, Meghan KLINGENBERG, Julie ERTZ,
Tobin HEATH, Carli LLOYD, Abby WAMBACH (69 Morgan BRIAN), Lauren
HOLIDAY *(YC17)*, Megan RAPINOE *(YC41)* (75 Christen PRESS), Alexandra
(Alex) MORGAN. (Coach: Jillian ELLIS).
Colombia: Catalina PÉREZ Jaramillo *(RC47)*, Carolina ARIAS Vidal, Katherine
Nataly ARIAS Peña, Angela Corina CLAVIJO Silva *(YC65)*, Natalia GAITÁN
Laguado, Daniele MONTOYA Quiróz (85 Leicy Maria SANTOS Herrera), Hazleydi
Yoreli RINCÓN Torres (72 Maria Catalina USME Pineda), Lady Patricia ANDRADE
Rodríguez, Diana Carolina OSPINA García, Oriánica VELÁSQUEZ Herrera, Ingrid
Yulieth VIDAL Isaza (49 Derly Stefany CASTAÑO Cardozo).
(Coach: Fabián Felipe TABORDA).
Goals: 53' Alexandra (Alex) MORGAN (53), Carli LLOYD (66 pen)
Referee: Stéphanie FRAPPART (France)   Attendance: 19,412

Abby WAMBACH missed a penalty kick (49).

Sent-off: 47' Catalina PÉREZ Jaramillo.

23.06.2015   BC Place Stadium, Vancouver: Japan – Netherlands 2-1 (1-0)
Japan: Ayumi KAIHORI, Azusa IWASHIMIZU, Aya SAMESHIMA, Saori
ARIYOSHI *(YC51)*, Aya MIYAMA, Mizuho SAKAGUCHI, Rumi UTSUGI, Saki
KUMAGAI, Yuki NAGASATO, Shinobu OHNO (86 Mana IWABUCHI), Nahomi
KAWASUMI (80 Homare SAWA). (Coach: Norio SASAKI).
Netherlands: Loes GEURTS, Mandy VAN DEN BERG, Stephanie VAN DER
GRAGT, Merel VAN DONGEN (86 Tessel MIDDAG), Anouk DEKKER, Sherida
SPITSE, Danielle VAN DE DONK (53 Kirsten VAN DE VEN), Desiree VAN
LUNTEREN, Lieke MARTENS, Manon MELIS, Vivianne MIEDEMA.
(Coach: Roger REIJNERS).
Goals: Saori ARIYOSHI (10), Mizuho SAKAGUCHI (78) /
Kirsten VAN DE VEN (90+2)
Referee: Lucila VENEGAS Montes (Mexico)   Attendance: 28,717

QUARTER FINALS

26.06.2015   Stade Olympique, Montréal: Germany – France 1-1 (0-0,1-1) (a.e.t.)
Germany: Nadine ANGERER, Babett PETER, Annike KRAHN, Tabea KEMME, Leonie MAIER, Simone LAUDEHR, Lena GÖßLING *(YC68)* (79 Melanie BEHRINGER), Melanie LEUPOLZ *(YC91)*, Anja MITTAG *(YC37)* (46 Dzsenifer MAROZSAN *(YC68)*), Célia SASIC, Alexandra POPP (70 Sara DÄBRITZ). (Coach: Silva NEID).
France: Sarah BOUHADDI, Laura GEORGES *(YC57)*, Wendie RENARD, Jessica HOUARA, Camille ABILY, Amandine HENRY, Louisa NECIB, Amel MAJRI, Elodie THOMIS (69 Claire LAVOGEZ), Eugénie LE SOMMER (90 Gaëtane THINEY), Marie Laure DELIE *(YC55)* (101 Kheira HAMRAOUI). (Coaches: Corinne DIACRE & Philippe BERGEROOO).
Goals: Célia SASIC (84 pen) / Louisa NECIB (64)
Referee: Carol Anne CHENARD (Canada)   Attendance: 24,859

Penalties: Melanie BEHRINGER 1-0, Gaëtane THINEY 1-1, Simone LAUDEHR 2-1, Camille ABILY 2-2, Babett PETER 3-2, Louisa NECIB 3-3, Dzsenifer MAROZSAN 4-3, Wendie RENARD 4-4, Célia SASIC 5-4, Claire LAVOGEZ missed.

Germany won after extra time on penalties (5:4).

26.06.2015   TD Place Stadium, Ottawa: China PR – United States 0-1 (0-0)
China PR: WANG Fei, LI Dongna, WU Haiyan *(YC50)*, LIU Shanshan, WANG Shanshan, HAN Peng (75 TANG Jiali), REN Guixin, TAN Ruyin (58 PANG Fengyue), WANG Lisi, LOU Jiahui (35 WANG Shuang), ZHAO Rong. (Coach: HAO Wei).
United States: Hope Amelia SOLO, Alexandra Blaire (Ali) KRIEGER, Becky SAUERBRUNN, Meghan KLINGENBERG, Julie ERTZ, Tobin HEATH, Morgan BRIAN, Carli LLOYD, Kelley O'HARA (61 Christen PRESS), Alexandra (Alex) MORGAN (81 Heather O'REILLY), Amy RODRIGUEZ (86 Abby WAMBACH). (Coach: Jillian ELLIS).
Goal: Carli LLOYD (51)
Referee: Carina Susanna VITULANO (Italy)   Attendance: 24,141

27.06.2015   Commonwealth Stadium, Edmonton: Australia – Japan 0-1 (0-0)
Australia: Lydia WILLIAMS, Emily VAN EGMOND, Laura ALLEWAY, Steph CATLEY, Alanna KENNEDY, Elise KELLOND, Katrina GORRY (76 Michelle HEYMAN), Lisa DE VANNA (67 Larissa CRUMMER), Samantha KERR, Kyah SIMON (89 Ashleigh SYKES), Caitlin FOORD. (Coach: Alen STAJCIC).
Japan: Ayumi KAIHORI, Azusa IWASHIMIZU *(YC27)*, Aya SAMESHIMA, Saori ARIYOSHI, Aya MIYAMA, Mizuho SAKAGUCHI (90 Homare SAWA), Rumi UTSUGI, Saki KUMAGAI, Yuki NAGASATO, Shinobu OHNO (72 Mana IWABUCHI), Nahomi KAWASUMI. (Coach: Norio SASAKI).
Goal: Mana IWABUCHI (87)
Referee: Kateryna MONZUL (Ukraine)   Attendance: 19,814

27.06.2015   BC Place Stadium, Vancouver: England – Canada 2-1 (2-1)
England: Karen BARDSLEY (52 Siobhan CHAMBERLAIN), Stephanie
HOUGHTON, Laura BASSETT, Claire RAFFERTY, Lucy BRONZE, Katie
CHAPMAN, Fara WILLIAMS (79 Ellen WHITE), Jill SCOTT, Jade MOORE
(YC63), Karen CARNEY (90+3 Casey STONEY), Jodie TAYLOR.
(Coach: Mark SAMPSON).
Canada: Erin McLEOD, Rhian WILKINSON (62 Diana MATHESON), Lauren
SESSELMANN *(YC90+3)*, Ashley LAWRENCE, Josee BELANGER, Allysha
CHAPMAN, Kadiesha BUCHANAN, Sophie SCHMIDT, Desiree SCOTT (77
Kaylyn KYLE), Christine SINCLAIR, Melissa TANCREDI (71 Adriana LEON).
(Coach: John HERDMAN).
Goals: Jodie TAYLOR (11), Lucy BRONZE (14) / Christine SINCLAIR (42)
Referee: Claudia Inés UMPIÉRREZ Rodríguez (Uruguay)   Attendance: 54,027

SEMI-FINALS

30.06.2015   Stade Olympique, Montréal: United States – Germany 2-0 (0-0)
United States: Hope Amelia SOLO, Alexandra Blaire (Ali) KRIEGER, Becky
SAUERBRUNN *(YC38)*, Meghan KLINGENBERG, Julie ERTZ *(YC59)*, Tobin
HEATH (75 Kelley O'HARA), Morgan BRIAN, Carli LLOYD, Lauren HOLIDAY,
Megan RAPINOE (80 Abby WAMBACH), Alexandra (Alex) MORGAN (90+3
Sydney LEROUX). (Coach: Jillian ELLIS).
Germany: Nadine ANGERER, Saskia BARTUSIAK, Annike KRAHN *(YC67)*, Tabea
KEMME, Leonie MAIER *(YC34)*, Simone LAUDEHR, Lena GÖßLING, Melanie
LEUPOLZ, Anja MITTAG (78 Dzsenifer MAROZSAN), Célia SASIC, Alexandra
POPP. (Coach: Silva NEID).
Goals: Carli LLOYD (69 pen), Kelley O'HARA (84)
Referee: Teodora ALBON (Romania)   Attendance: 51,176

Célia SASIC missed a penalty kick (60).

01.07.2015   Commonwealth Stadium, Edmonton: Japan – England 2-1 (1-1)
Japan: Ayumi KAIHORI, Azusa IWASHIMIZU, Aya SAMESHIMA, Saori
ARIYOSHI, Aya MIYAMA, Mizuho SAKAGUCHI, Rumi UTSUGI, Saki
KUMAGAI, Yuki NAGASATO *(YC90)*, Shinobu OHNO (70 Mana IWABUCHI),
Nahomi KAWASUMI. (Coach: Norio SASAKI).
England: Karen BARDSLEY, Stephanie HOUGHTON, Laura BASSETT, Claire
RAFFERTY *(YC31)*, Lucy BRONZE (75 Alexandra SCOTT), Katie CHAPMAN,
Fara WILLIAMS (85 Karen CARNEY), Jill SCOTT, Jade MOORE, Toni DUGGAN,
Jodie TAYLOR (60 Ellen WHITE). (Coach: Mark SAMPSON).
Goals: Aya MIYAMA (32 pen), Laura BASSETT (90+2 og) /
Fara WILLIAMS (40 pen)
Referee: Anna-Marie KEIGHLEY (New Zealand)   Attendance: 31,467

THIRD PLACE PLAY-OFF

04.07.2015   Commonwealth Stadium, Edmonton:
    Germany – England 0-1 (0-0,0-0) (a.e.t.)
Germany: Nadine ANGERER, Saskia BARTUSIAK, Babett PETER, Tabea
KEMME, Melanie BEHRINGER (46 Melanie LEUPOLZ), Simone LAUDEHR, Lena
GÖßLING (101 Alexandra POPP), Bianca SCHMIDT, Sara DÄBRITZ, Célia SASIC
(73 Anja MITTAG), Lena PETERMANN. (Coach: Silva NEID).
England: Karen BARDSLEY *(YC83)*, Stephanie HOUGHTON, Laura BASSETT
(YC92), Lucy BRONZE, Alex GREENWOOD, Katie CHAPMAN *(YC77)* (80 Lianne
SANDERSON), Fara WILLIAMS (112 Casey STONEY), Jill SCOTT, Josanne
POTTER, Karen CARNEY, Ellen WHITE (61 Eniola ALUKO).
(Coach: Mark SAMPSON).
Goal: Fara WILLIAMS (108)
Referee: OK Ri-Hyang (North Korea)   Attendance: 21,483

FINAL

05.07.2015   BC Place Stadium, Vancouver: United States – Japan 5-2 (4-1)
United States: Hope Amelia SOLO, Alexandra Blaire (Ali) KRIEGER, Becky
SAUERBRUNN, Meghan KLINGENBERG, Julie ERTZ, Tobin HEATH (79 Abby
WAMBACH), Morgan BRIAN, Carli LLOYD, Lauren HOLIDAY, Megan
RAPINOE (61 Kelley O'HARA), Alexandra (Alex) MORGAN (86 Christie
PEARCE). (Coach: Jillian ELLIS).
Japan: Ayumi KAIHORI, Azusa IWASHIMIZU (33 Homare SAWA *(YC82)*), Aya
SAMESHIMA, Saori ARIYOSHI, Aya MIYAMA, Mizuho SAKAGUCHI, Rumi
UTSUGI, Saki KUMAGAI, Yuki NAGASATO, Shinobu OHNO (60 Mana
IWABUCHI *(YC85)*), Nahomi KAWASUMI (39 Yuika SUGASAWA).
(Coach: Norio SASAKI).
Goals: Carli LLOYD (3, 5, 16), Lauren HOLIDAY (14), Tobin HEATH (54) / Yuki
NAGASATO (27), Julie ERTZ (52 og)
Referee: Kateryna MONZUL (Ukraine)   Attendance: 53,341

UNITED STATES BECAME WORLD CHAMPIONS

EIGHT EDITION FIFA WOMEN'S WORLD CUP 2019

QUALIFYING TOURNAMENTS

CAF AFRICA WOMEN CUP OF NATIONS 2018

QUALIFICATION

The first round was originally scheduled for 26 February – 6 March 2018, and the second round for 2-10 April 2018, but these dates were moved due to a clash with the CAF Women's Symposium in early March. The qualification rounds were now played between 4 April and 9 June 2018. The seven winners of the Second Round qualified for the Final Tournament to join the hosts Ghana who qualified automatically.

FIRST ROUND

04.04.2018   Stade Al Djigo, Dakar: Senegal – Algeria 2-1 (2-1)
Goals: Diédhiou (6 pen), Diop (10) / Benlazar (38)
04.04.2018   Petro Sport Stadium, Cairo: Libya – Ethiopia 0-8 (0-6)
Goals: Zergaw (4, 20, 61), Abera (18, 23), Feleke (32), Tadesse (44), Kefyalew (47)
Libya played their home match outside Libya due to security concerns from the ongoing civil war.
04.04.2018   Stade Alphonse Massemba-Débat, Brazzaville:
　　　　　　　Congo – Central African Republic 2-0 (2-0)
Goals: Kokolo (40 pen), Dembélé (44)
04.04.2018   Kenyatta Stadium, Machakos: Kenya – Uganda 1-0 (0-0)
Goal: Adera (53)
04.04.2018   National Stadium, Dar es Salaam: Tanzania – Zambia 3-3 (2-1)
Goals: Abdallah (1), Rashid (22, 47) / Banda (25, 78), Zulu (46)
05.04.2018   Sam Nujoma Stadium, Windhoek: Namibia – Zimbabwe 0-2 (0-1)
Goals: Nyaumwe (21), Chirandu (89)
06.04.2018   Complexe Moulay El Hassan, Rabat: Morocco – Ivory Coast 1-1 (0-0)
Goals: Chebbak (76) / Fatou Coulibaly (52 pen)
06.04.2018   Setsoto Stadium, Maseru: Lesotho – Eswatini 1-0 (1-0)
Goal: Maloro (18)
Eswatini was former known as Swaziland.
07.04.2018   Sierra Leone – Mali   **Cancelled**
07.04.2018   Stade du 4 Août, Ouagadougou: Burkina Faso – Gambia 2-1 (1-1)
Goals: S.Simporé (27, 80) / Ad.Tamba (23)
08.04.2018   Barthélemy Boganda Stadium, Bangui:
　　　　　　　Central African Republic – Congo 1-1 (0-1)
Goals: Demba (71) / Dembélé (18)
08.04.2018   Phillip Omondi Stadium, Kampala: Uganda – Kenya 0-0
08.04.2018   Nkoloma Stadium, Lusaka: Zambia – Tanzania 1-1 (1-0)
Goals: Kundananji (2) / Minja (71)
Zambia won on away goals.

08.04.2018 Rufaro Stadium, Harare: Zimbabwe – Namibia 2-0 (0-0)
Goals: Msipa (73), Chirandu (84)
10.04.2018 20 August Stadium, Algiers: Algeria – Senegal 2-0 (1-0)
Goals: Sekouane (24 pen), Benaichouche (90+3)
10.04.2018 Addis Ababa Stadium, Addis Ababa: Ethiopia – Libya 7-0 (3-0)
Goals: Buwli (13), Abera (27, 51, 82, 87), Zergaw (45), Boyzo (74)
10.04.2018 Stade Félix Houphouët-Boigny, Abidjan: Ivory Coast – Morocco 0-0
Ivory Coast won on away goals.
10.04.2018 Stade Mamadou Konaté, Bamako: Mali – Sierra Leone **Cancelled**
10.04.2018 Independence Stadium, Bakau: Gambia – Burkina Faso 2-1 (2-0)
Goals: Ad.Tamba (19), Kouanda (20 og) / S.Simporé (53)
Gambia won on penalties (5:3).
10.04.2018 Somhlolo National Stadium, Lobamba: Eswatini – Lesotho 1-2 (0-1)
Goals: Dlamini (88) / Kheme (30), Lebakeng (65)

Sierra Leone withdrew, Mali advanced.

SECOND ROUND

06.06.2018 5 July Stadium, Algiers: Algeria – Ethiopia 3-1 (2-1)
Goals: Ramdani (19), Sidhoum (32), Sekouane (68) / Biza (16)
06.06.2018 Stade Félix Houphouët-Boigny, Abidjan: Ivory Coast – Mali 2-2 (1-1)
Goals: Elloh (37 pen), N'Guessan (90) / Tangara (7), Touré (47)
06.06.2018 Independence Stadium, Bakau: Gambia – Nigeria 0-1 (0-1)
Goal: Okoronkwo (19)
06.06.2018 Stade Alphonse Massemba-Débat, Brazzaville:
              Congo – Cameroon 0-5 (0-3)
Goals: Abena (2), Nchout (27), Mani (29), Yango (61 pen), Onguéné (64)
06.06.2018 Kenyatta Stadium, Machakos: Kenya – Equarotial Guinea 2-1 (1-1)
Goals: Engesha (41), Akida (82) / Boho (39)
06.06.2018 Setsoto Stadium, Maseru: Lesotho – South Africa 0-1 (0-1)
Goal: Seoposenwe (9)
06.06.2018 Nkoloma Stadium, Lusaka: Zambia – Zimbabwe 0-1 (0-1)
Goal: Nyaumwe (18)
09.06.2018 Stade Ahmadou Ahidjo, Yaoundé: Cameroon – Congo 5-0 (2-0)
Goals: Nchout (19), Abena (22), Onguéné (51, 53), Akaba (84)
09.06.2018 Nuevo Estadio de Malabo, Malabo: Equatorial Guinea – Kenya 2-0 (0-0)
Goals: Chinasa (61), Nke (63)
*Equatorial Guinea won 3-2 on aggregate. On 17 October 2018, Kenya were awarded
the tie after Equatorial Guinea were disqualified for fielding an ineligible player.
However, on 7 November 2018, the decision was overturned on appeal.*
10.06.2018 Addis Ababa Stadium, Addis Ababa: Ethiopia – Algeria 2-3 (0-2)
Goals: Abera (63, 72) / Bouhani (18), Sekouane (45+2), Benlazar (53)
10.06.2018 Stade mamadou Konaté, Bamako: Mali – Ivory Coast 0-0
Mali won on away goals.

10.06.2018   Dr. Petrus Molemela Stadium, Bloemfontein:
South Africa – Lesotho 6-0 (2-0)
Goals: Seoposenwe (2, 60, 83), Esau (5, 51), Magaia (79)
10.06.2018   Rufaro Stadium, Harare: Zimbabwe – Zambia 1-2 (1-0)
Goals: Jeke (45) / Chanda (53), Banda (86)
Zambia won on away goals.
11.06.2018   Agege Stadium, Lagos: Nigeria – Gambia 6-0 (2-0)
Goals: Oparanozie (3 pen, 49, 69, 83), Oshoala (44, 74)

FINAL TOURNAMENT

The Final Tournament was held in Ghana between 17 November to 1 December 2018.

GROUP STAGE

GROUP A

17.11.2018   Accra Sports Stadium, Accra: Ghana – Algeria 1-0 (1-0)
Goal: Amfobea (13)
17.11.2018   Accra Sports Stadium, Accra: Mali – Cameroon 1-2 (0-0)
Goals: A.Traoré (56) / Meffometou (71), Nchout (73)
20.11.2018   Accra Sports Stadium, Accra: Ghana – Mali 1-2 (0-1)
Goals: Addo (71 pen) / Touré (24 pen, 75)
20.11.2018   Accra Sports Stadium, Accra: Cameroon – Algeria 3-0 (1-0)
Goals: Onguéné (13), Enganamouit (54), Nchout (60)
23.11.2018   Accra Sports Stadium, Accra: Cameroon – Ghana 1-1 (1-1)
Goals: Manie (41 pen) / Boakye (31)
23.11.2018   Cape Coast Sports Stadium, Cape Coast: Algeria – Mali 2-3 (1-0)
Goals: Belkacemi (37), Merrouche (63 pen) / F.Diarra (58, 90+4 pen), Diadhiou (83)

Team	Pld	W	D	L	GF	GA	GD	Pts
Cameroon	*3*	*2*	*1*	*0*	*6*	*2*	*+4*	*7*
Mali	*3*	*2*	*0*	*1*	*6*	*5*	*+1*	*6*
Ghana	3	1	1	1	3	3	0	4
Algeria	3	0	0	3	2	7	-5	0

GROUP B

18.11.2018   Cape Coast Sports Stadium, Cape Coast:
Nigeria – South Africa 0-1 (0-0)
Goal: Kgatlana (85)
18.11.2018   Cape Coast Sports Stadium, Cape Coast:
Zambia – Equatorial Guinea 5-0 (2-0)
Goals: G.Chanda (7), Lungu (43), Kundananji (57, 87), Mwakapila (66 pen)
21.11.2018   Cape Coast Sports Stadium, Cape Coast: Nigeria – Zambia 4-0 (1-0)
Goals: Oparanozie (41), Ordega (69), Ajibade (75), Okoronkwo (90+4)

223

21.11.2018 Cape Coast Sports Stadium, Cape Coast: Equatorial Guinea – South Africa 1-7 (1-2)
Goals: E.Obono (45+1) / Motlhalo (19 pen), Nyandeni (21), Jane (56), Kgatlana (60, 63), Mthandi (76), Seoposenwe (79)
24.11.2018 Cape Coast Sports Stadium, Cape Coast:
Equatorial Guinea – Nigeria 0-6 (0-4)
Goals: Ordega (10), Oshoala (13, 22, 33), Oparanozia (48), Chikwelu (63)
24.11.2018 Accra Sports Stadium, Accra: South Africa – Zambia 1-1 (1-1)
Goals: Kgatlana (8) / Kundananji (10)

Team	Pld	W	D	L	GF	GA	GD	Pts
Soth Africa	3	2	1	0	9	2	+7	7
Nigeria	3	2	0	1	10	1	+9	6
Zambia	3	1	1	1	6	5	+1	4
Equatorial Guinea	3	0	0	3	1	18	-17	0

KNOCKOUT STAGE
SEMI-FINALS

27.11.2018 Accra Sports Stadium, Accra: Cameroon – Nigeria 0-0 (a.e.t.)
Nigeria won after extra time on penalties (4:2).
27.11.2018 Cape Coast Sports Stadium, Cape Coast: South Africa – Mali 2-0 (1-0)
Goals: Kgatlana (31), Ramalepe (81)

THIRD PLACE PLAY-OFF

30.11.2018 Cape Coast Sports Stadium, Cape Coast: Cameroon – Mali 4-2 (2-1)
Goals: Abena (32, 40), Onguéné (62), Manie (90+2) / F.Diarra (44), Awona (56 og)

FINAL

01.12.2018 Accra Sports Stadium, Accra: Nigeria – South Africa 0-0 (a.e.t.)
Nigeria won after extra time on penalties (4:3).

Winner **Nigeria**, runner-up **South Africa** and third-place winner **Cameroon** qualified for the FIFA Women's World Cup 2019.

AFC WOMEN'S ASIAN CUP 2018

The Final Tournament was originally scheduled to be held in Jordan between 7 & 22 April 2018, but was later changed to 6 & 20 April 2018.

QUALIFICATION

Of the 47 AFC member associations, a total of 24 teams entered the competition, with Japan, Australia and China PR automatically qualified for the Final Tournament. Jordan als automatically qualified for the Final Tournament as hosts, but decided to participate in the qualifying competition.

GROUP A

All matches were played in Tajikistan.

03.04.2017 <u>Pamir Stadium, Dushanbe</u>: Bahrain – Jordan 0-6 (0-4)
Goals: Jebreen (9), Jbarah (22, 30, 43), Al-Naber 986), Al-Masri (90)
03.04.2017 <u>Pamir Stadium, Dushanbe</u>: Iraq – Tajikistan 0-1 (0-0)
Goal: Halimova (87)
03.04.2017 <u>Pamir Stadium, Dushanbe</u>: Philippines – United Arab Emirates 4-0 (2-0)
Goals: Madarang (14, 45+1), Navaja (49), S.Castañeda (54)
05.04.2017 <u>Pamir Stadium, Dushanbe</u>: Philippines – Iraq 4-0 (4-0)
Goals: Madarang (21), Long (44), S.Castañeda (45+1), Dolino (45+3)
05.04.2017 <u>Pamir Stadium, Dushanbe</u>: Bahrain – Tajikistan 4-0 (2-0)
Goals: Al-Hashmi (17, 20, 78), Al-Dossary (46)
05.04.2017 <u>Pamir Stadium, Dushanbe</u>: Jordan – United Arab Emirates 6-0 (3-0)
Goals: Jbarah (3, 40, 77, 81), Al-Naber (44, 80)
07.04.2017 <u>Pamir Stadium, Dushanbe</u>: United Arab Emirates – Bahrain 1-1 (0-0)
Goals: Jaseem (50) / Abdulrahman (84)
07.04.2017 <u>Pamir Stadium, Dushanbe</u>: Tajikistan – Philippines 0-8 (0-3)
Goals: Madarang (17), A.Castañeda (34, 85), Long (38, 59, 84), S.Castañeda (48), Duran (90)
07.04.2017 <u>Pamir Stadium, Dushanbe</u>: Jordan – Iraq 10-0 (4-0)
Goals: Jebreen (1), Al-Masri (20), Al-Naber (27 pen, 61 pen, 81), Jbarah (45+5, 65, 79, 84), Breesam (77 og)
10.04.2017 <u>Pamir Stadium, Dushanbe</u>: Iraq – United Arab Emirates 0-3 (0-1)
Goals: Taheri (17), Faleh (78), Rashid (87)
10-04-2017 <u>Pamir Stadium, Dushanbe</u>: Tajikistan – Jordan 2-10 (1-7)
Goals: Iskandari (21), Sotnikova (76) / Al-Naber (4 pen, 63), Jebreen (8, 15, 23, 45+3), Sweilem (34, 45+2), Al-Kousheh (69), Al-Nahar (81)
10.04.2017 <u>Pamir Stadium, Dushanbe</u>: Philippines – Bahrain 1-1 (0-0)
Goals: S.Castañeda (82) / Al-Dossary (55)
12.04.2017 <u>Pamir Stadium, Dushanbe</u>: Jordan – Philippines 5-1 (3-0)
Goals: Al-Masri (15, 48), Jbarah (29, 37), Al-Naber (67) / Del Campo (90+1)
12.04.2017 <u>Pamir Stadium, Dushanbe</u>: United Arab Emirates – Tajikistan 1-0 (0-0)
Goal: Rashid (90+3)
12.04.2017 <u>Pamir Stadium, Dushanbe</u>: Bahrain – Iraq 4-0 (2-0)
Goals: Al-Hashmi (31), Abdulrahman (41, 71), Tobellah (80 pen)

Team	Pld	W	D	L	GF	GA	GD	Pts
Jordan	5	5	0	0	37	3	+34	15
Philippines	5	3	1	1	18	6	+12	10
Bahrain	5	2	2	1	10	8	+2	8
United Arab Emirates	5	2	1	2	5	11	-6	7
Tajikistan	5	1	0	4	3	23	-20	3
Iraq	5	0	0	5	0	22	-22	0

Jordan, as final tournament hosts, automatically qualified regardless of qualification results.

225

GROUP B

All matches were played in North Korea.

03.04.2017   Kim Il-sung Stadium, Pyongyang: North Korea – India 8-0 (4-0)
Goals: Ri Un-yong (7), Ri Kyong-hyang (13), R Hyang-sim (21), Kim Pgyong-hwa (45+1, 78), Wi Jong-sim (48, 64 pen), Sung Hyang-sim (80)
03.04.2017   Kim Il-sung Stadium, Pyongyang: Hong Kong – Uzbekistan 1-2 (0-1)
Goals: Cheung Wai Ki (80) / Karachik (16), Nozimova (90+4)
05.04.2017   Kim Il-sung Stadium, Pyongyang: North Korea – Hong Kong 5-0 (4-0)
Goals: Ri Un-yong (12), Kim Yun-mi (28, 39), Ho Wan Tung (45+1 og), Choe Un-ju (77)
05.04.2017   Kim Il-sung Stadium, Pyongyang: India – South Korea 0-10 (0-5)
Goals: Kang Yu-mi (12), Lee Min-a (19), Lee Geum-mim (29, 36, 67), Lee Eun-mi (45+1), Yoo Young-a (65), Ji So-yun (68, 90+1), Lee So-dam (69)
07.04.2017   Kim Il-sung Stadium, Pyongyang: South Korea – North Korea 1-1 (0-1)
Goals: Jang Sel-gi (76) / Sung Hyang-sim (45+3)
07.04.2017   Kim Il-sung Stadium, Pyongyang: Uzbekistan – India 7-1 (5-1)
Goals: Karachik (3, 6), Sarikova (11, 44), Zoirova (19), Narbekova (63), Trudiboeva (90+2 pen) / Bala Devi (22)
09.04.2017   Kim Il-sung Stadium, Pyongyang: Uzbekistan – North Korea 0-4 (0-1)
Goals: Kim Yun-mi (28, 90+2), Sung Hyang-sim (54, 65)
09.04.2017   Kim Il-sung Stadium, Pyongyang: Hong Kong – South Korea 0-6 (0-1)
Goals: Cho So-hyun (44 pen, 71 pen), Yoo Young-a (63), Kwon Eun-som (74), Lee Geum-min (83), Jang Sel-gi (88)
11.04.2017   Kim Il-sung Stadium, Pyongyang: India – Hong Kong 2-0 (0-0)
Goals: Malik (68 pen), Ratanbala Devi (70)
11.04.2017   Kim Il-sung Stadium, Pyongyang: South Korea – Uzbekistan 4-0 (3-0)
Goals: Yoo Young-a (21), Ji So-yun (23, 53), Cho So-hyun (42)

Team	Pld	W	D	L	GF	GA	GD	Pts
South Korea	4	3	1	0	21	1	+20	10
North Korea	4	3	1	0	18	1	+17	10
Uzbekistan	4	2	0	2	9	10	-1	6
India	4	1	0	3	3	25	-22	3
Hong Kong	4	0	0	4	1	15	-14	0

GROUP C

All matches were played in Palestine.

03.04.2017   Faisal Al-Husseini International Stadium, Al-Ram:
    Palestine – Thailand 0-6 (0-3)
Goals: Kanjana (7), Al-Sarras (19 og), Taneekarn (26), Suchawadee (64), Orathai (73), Rattikan (76)
05.04.2017   Faisal Al-Husseini International Stadium, Al-Ram:
    Chinese Taipei – Palestine 5-0 (3-0)
Goals: Pao (2, 14), Yu Hsiu-chin (6, 66, 70 pen)

226

07.04.2017 Faisal Al-Husseini International Stadium, Al-Ram:
Thailand – Chinese Taipei 1-0 (1-0)
Goal: Suchawadee (3)

Team	Pld	W	D	L	GF	GA	GD	Pts
Thailand	2	2	0	0	7	0	+7	6
Chinese Taipei	2	1	0	1	5	1	+4	3
Palestine	2	0	0	2	0	11	-11	0
Lebanon	0	0	0	0	0	0	0	0
Guam	0	0	0	0	0	0	0	0

Lebanon and Guam withdrew before the start of the qualification.

GROUP D

All matches were played in Vietnam.

03.04.2017 Vietnam YFT Center Field no.3, Hanoi: Iran – Myanmar 0-2 (0-2)
Goals: July Kyaw (4), Win Theingi Tun (45+3)
03.04.2017 Vietnam YFT Center Field no.3, Hanoi: Singapore – Syria 1-0 (0-0)
Goal: Lim (81)
05.04.2017 Vietnam YFT Center Field no.3, Hanoi: Singapore – Iran 0-6 (0-2)
Goals: Ghanbari (14), Ghomi (15, 52), Ghasemi (84), Mouri (87, 90)
05.04.2017 Vietnam YFT Center Field no.3, Hanoi: Syria – Vietnam 0-11 (0-8)
Goals: Lieu (1, 45+1), Yen (6, 24), Dung (13 pen, 38), Nguyet (17), Thi Hoa (20, 90), Muon (71), Hang (76)
07.04.2017 Vietnam YFT Center Field no.3, Hanoi: Myanmar – Syria 14-0 (6-0)
Goals: Naw Ar Lo Wer Phaw (7, 41, 90+6), Yee Yee Oo (19, 45+2, 76, 82), Win Theingi Tun (25 pen, 38, 39, 53, 60), Wai Wai Aung (67), Phu Pwint Khaing (87)
07.04.2017 Vietnam YFT Center Field no.3, Hanoi: Vietnam – Singapore 8-0 (4-0)
Goals: Pang (8 og), Huynh Nhu (21 pen, 52, 63), Vu Nhung (36), Trang (45+1), Thy (67 pen), Nguyet (81)
09.04.2017 Vietnam YFT Center Field no.3, Hanoi: Myanmar – Singapore 6-0 (2-0)
Goals: Hla Yin Win (22), Wai Wai Aung (41, 76), Win Theingi Tun (56, 85), Yee Yee Oo (72)
09.04.2017 Vietnam YFT Center Field no.3, Hanoi: Iran – Vietnam 1-6 (1-2)
Goals: Ghanbari (8) / Dung (15), Yen (25, 79), Huyn Nhur (61, 82), Thi Hoa (74)
11.04.2017 Vietnam YFT Center Field no.3, Hanoi: Syria – Iran 0-12 (0-6)
Goals: Ghanbari (4, 35, 66, 88), Zohrabinia (13, 27, 45+1, 54, 87), Rouzbahan (16), Ghasemi (63), Ghomi (90+2)
11.04.2017 Vietnam YFT Center Field no.3, Hanoi: Vietnam – Myanmar 2-0 (0-0)
Goals: Dung (55), Huynh Nhu (82)

Team	Pld	W	D	L	GF	GA	GD	Pts
Vietnam	4	4	0	0	27	1	+26	12
Myanmar	4	3	0	1	22	2	+20	9
Iran	4	2	0	2	19	8	+11	6
Singapore	4	1	0	3	1	20	-19	3
Syria	4	0	0	4	0	38	-38	0

FINAL TOURNAMENT

The Final Tournament was held in Jordan between 6 & 20 April 2018.

GROUP STAGE

The top two teams of each group qualified for the FIFA Women's World Cup 2019 as well as the semi-finals. The third-placed team of each group entered the fifth-placed play-off.

GROUP A

06.04.2018   Amman International Stadium, Amman: China PR – Thailand 4-0 (0-0)
Goals: Song Duan (56, 77), Wang Shuang (63), Li Ying (67)
06.04.2018   Amman International Stadium, Amman: Jordan – Philippines 1-2 (1-0)
Goals: Jbarah (15) / Khair (51 og), Bolden (76)
09.04.2018   King Abdullah II Stadium, Amman: Phlippines – China PR 0-3 (0-2)
Goals: Li Ying (17, 57), Ma Jun (31)
09.04.2018   King Abdullah II Stadium, Amman: Thailand – Jordan 6-1 (4-1)
Goals: Suchawadee (1, 69), Taneekam (6), Silawan (39), Kanjana (41), Pitsamai (90) / Jebreen (43)
12.04.2018   Amman International Stadium, Amman: Jordan – China PR 1-8 (1-2)
Goals: Sabbah (17) / Wang Shuang (14, 53, 84), Khair (41 og), Song Duan (51), Li Ying (60, 72 pen), Tang Jiali (86)
12.04.2018   King Abdullah II Stadium, Amman: Thailand – Philippines 3-1 (1-0)
Goals: Kanjana (28 pen, 53), Silawan (62) / Shugg (90+3)

Team	Pld	W	D	L	GF	GA	GD	Pts
China PR	3	3	0	0	15	1	+14	9
Thailand	3	2	0	1	9	6	+3	6
Phlippines	3	1	0	2	3	7	-4	3
Jordan	3	0	0	3	3	16	-13	0

GROUP B

07.04.2018   King Abdullah II Stadium, Amman: Japan – Vietnam 4-0 (2-0)
Goals: Yokoyama (3), Nakajima (17), Iwabichi (57), Tanaka (66)
07.04.2018   King Abdullah II Stadium, Amman: Australia – South Korea 0-0
10.04.2018   Amman International Stadium, Amman: South Korea – Japan 0-0
10.04.2018   Amman International Stadium, Amman: Vietnam – Australia 0-8 (0-5)
Goals: Simon (8), Kennedy (18), Logarzo (21), van Egmond (28), Kerr (44, 51), Tuyet Dung (71 og), Raso (75)
13.04.2018   Amman International Stadium, Amman: Japan – Australia 1-1 (0-0)
Goals: Sakaguchi (63) / Kerr (86)
13.04.2018   King Abdullah II Stadium, Amman: South Korea – Vietnam 4-0 (2-0)
Goals: Cho So-hyun (14), Lee Geum-min (38), Lee Min-a (49, 73)

Team	Pld	W	D	L	GF	GA	GD	Pts
Australia	*3*	*1*	*2*	*0*	*9*	*1*	+8	*5*
Japan	*3*	*1*	*2*	*0*	*5*	*1*	+4	*5*
South Korea	3	1	2	0	4	0	+4	5
Vietnam	3	0	0	3	0	16	-16	0

South Korea are ranked on head-to-head goals scored. Australia and Japan are tied on their own head-to head result, and are ranked on total goal difference.

KNOCKOUT STAGE

FIFTH PLACE PLAY-OFF

16.04.2018   Amman International Stadium, Amman:
Philippines – South Korea 0-5 (0-2)
Goals: Jang Sel-gi (34), Lee Min-a (45+3), Lim Seon-joo (56), Cho So-hyun (66, 84 pen)

Winner of the Fifth Place Play-off **South Korea** qualified for FIFA Women's World Cup 2019.

SEMI-FINALS

17.04.2018   King Abdullah II Stadium, Amman:
Australia – Thailand 2-2 (1-1,2-2) (a.e.t.)
Goals: Kanjanaporn (17 og), Kennedy (90+1) / Kanjana (20), Rattikan (63)
Australia won after extra time on penalties (3:1)
17.04.2018   King Abdullah II Stadium, Amman: China PR – Japan 1-3 (0-1)
Goals: Li Ying (90 pen) / Iwabuchi (39), Yokoyama (85, 88 pen)

THIRD PLACE PLAY-OFF

20.04.2018   Amman International Stadium, Amman: China PR – Thailand 3-1 (0-0)
Goals: Li Ying (51), Wang Shanshan (56), Song Duan (61) / Rattikan (81)

FINAL

20.04.2018   Amman International Stadium, Amman: Japan – Australia 1-0 (0-0)
Goal: Yokoyama (84)

The winner **Japan**, runner-up **Australia** and both semi-finals losers **China PR** and **Thailand** qualified for the FIFA Women's World Cup 2019.

UEFA WOMEN'S WORLD CUP QUALIFICATION 2018

PRELIMINARY ROUND

The four group winners and the best runner-up (not counting results against the fourth-place team) advanced to the qualifying group stage to join the 30 direct entrants.

GROUP 1

All matches in this group were played in Georgia.

06.04.2017   Mikheil Meskhi Stadium-2, Tbilisi: Estonia – Latvia 0-4 (0-2)
Goals: Fjodorova (37), Spruntule (44), Voltāne (62), Sevcova (68)
06.04.2017   Mikheil Meskhi Stadium, Tbilisi: Kazakhstan – Georgia 1-0 (1-0)
Goal: Nikolayenko (34)
08.04.2017   Mikheil Meskhi Stadium-2, Tbilisi: Kazakhstan – Latvia 2-2 (0-1)
Goals: Myasnikova (75, 85) / Fjodorova (37), Fedotova (64)
08.04.2017   Mikheil Meskhi Stadium, Tbilisi: Georgia – Estonia 2-1 (2-0)
Goals: Tchkonia (16), Gabelia (22) / Aarna (59)
11.04.2017   Mikheil Meskhi Stadium-2, Tbilisi: Estonia – Kazakhstan 0-1 (0-0)
Goal: Nikolayenko (62)
11.04.2017   Mikheil Meskhi Stadium, Tbilisi: Latvia – Georgia 1-1 (1-1)
Goals: Miksone (45) / Danelia (19)

Team	Pld	W	D	L	GF	GA	GD	Pts
Kazakhstan	3	2	1	0	4	2	+2	7
Latvia	3	1	2	0	7	3	+4	5
Georgia	3	1	1	1	3	3	0	4
Estonia	3	0	0	3	1	7	-6	0

GROUP 2

All matches in this group were played in Albania.

06.04.2017   Elbasan Arena, Elbasan: Albania – Kosovo 3-2 (1-1)
Goals: Bajraktari (17), Belaj (75), Musa (90+6 og) / Rexha (35, 59)
06.04.2017   Selman Stërmasi Stadium, Tirana: Greece – Malta 1-0 (1-0)
Goal: Papadopoulou (18)
08.04.2017   Selman Stërmasi Stadium, Tirana: Greece – Kosovo 6-0 (2-0)
Goals: Markou (33), Chatzigiannidou (39), Kakambouki (51), Nati (57), Kongouli (76), Sidira (82)
08.04.2017   Elbasan Arena, Elbasan: Malta – Albania 0-0
11.04.2017   Elbasan Arena, Elbasan: Albania – Greece 2-1 (1-1)
Goals: Doci (16), Velaj (90) / Nati (18)
11.04.2017   Selman Stërmasi Stadium, Tirana: Kosovo – Malta 1-3 (0-3)
Goals: Shala (80) / Cuschieri (12), Flask (27), Theuma (38)

Team	Pld	W	D	L	GF	GA	GD	Pts
Albania	*3*	*2*	*1*	*0*	*5*	*3*	*+2*	*7*
Greece	3	2	0	1	8	2	+6	6
Malta	3	1	1	1	3	2	+1	4
Kosovo	3	0	0	3	3	12	-9	0

GROUP 3

All matches in this group were played in Lithuania.

06.04.2017   LFF Stadium, Vilnius: Moldova – Andorra 4-0 (3-0)
Goals: Chiper (9), Cerescu (41), Munteanu (45 pen), Colesnicenco (71)
06.04.2017   LFF Stadium, Vilnius: Israel – Lithuania 2-0 (0-0)
Goals: Awad (77), Falkon (90)
08.04.2017   LFF Stadium, Vilnius: Lithuania – Moldova 0-2 (0-0)
Goals: Mikutaité (90+2 og), Tabur (90+3)
08.04.2017   LFF Stadium, Vilnius: Israel – Andorra 7-0 (5-0)
Goals: Shahaf (15, 37), Tizón (29 og), Rogers (34), D.Sofer (45+1 pen, 47),
Sendel (62 pen)
11.04.2017   LFF Stadium, Vilnius: Moldova – Israel 0-0
11.04.2017   National Football Academy Stadium, Kaunas:
        Andorra – Lithuania 0-2 (0-0)
Goals: Kyzaité (49), Vaiciulaityté (90+2)

Team	Pld	W	D	L	GF	GA	GD	Pts
Israel	*3*	*2*	*1*	*0*	*9*	*0*	*+9*	*7*
Moldova	3	2	1	0	6	0	+6	7
Lithuania	3	1	0	2	2	4	-2	3
Andorra	3	0	0	3	0	13	-13	0

GROUP 4

All matches in this group were played in Faroe Islands.

06.04.2017   Tórsvøllur, Tórshavn: Turkey – Montenegro 3-0 (3-0)
Goals: Topçu (15, 39), Altunkulak (28)
06.04.2017   Tórsvøllur, Tórshavn: Faroe Islands – Luxembourg 5-1 (3-0)
Goals: H.Sevdal (7, 64), Klakstein (18), Á.Johannesen (37), Arge (54) / Birkel (88)
08.04.2017   Tórsvøllur, Tórshavn: Montenegro – Faroe Islands 1-2 (0-0)
Goals: Kuc (65) / Klakstein (78), Nielsen (80)
08.04.2017   Tórsvøllur, Tórshavn: Turkey – Luxembourg 9-1 (3-0)
Goals: Topçu (10), Pekel (17, 51, 70), Elias (40 og), Altunkulak (57, 75, 86),
Karagenç (90+3) / De Lemos (58)
11.04.2017   Tórsvøllur, Tórshavn: Faroe Islands – Turkey 2-1 (1-1)
Goals: Andreasen (36), Simonsen (64) / Pekel (17)

11.04.2017   Gundadalur, Tórshavn: Luxembourg – Montenegro 1-7 (0-4)
Goals: De Lemos (80) / Bulatovic (5, 27), Djokovic (35, 45+5), Pavicevic (48),
Kuc (50, 56)

Team	Pld	W	D	L	GF	GA	GD	Pts
Faroe Islands	*3*	*3*	*0*	*0*	*9*	*3*	*+6*	*9*
Turkey	3	2	0	1	13	3	+10	6
Montenegro	3	1	0	2	8	6	+2	3
Luxembourg	3	0	0	3	3	21	-18	0

RANKING OF SECOND-PLACED TEAMS

To determine the best second-placed teams from the preliminary round which
advanced to the qualifying group stage, only the results of the second-placed teams
against the first and third-placed teams in their group are taken into account, while
results against the fourth-placed team are not included.

Pos	Grp	Team	Pld	W	D	L	GF	GA	GD	Pts
1	*3*	*Moldova*	*2*	*1*	*1*	*0*	*2*	*0*	*+2*	*4*
2	4	Turkey	2	1	0	1	4	2	+2	3
3	2	Greece	2	1	0	1	2	2	0	3
4	1	Latvia	2	0	2	0	3	3	0	2

Kazakhstan, Albania, Israel and the Faroe Islands advanced as group winners, and
Moldova advanced as the best runner-up.

QUALIFYING GROUP STAGE

The group winners qualified directly for the FIFA Women's World Cup 2019, while
the runners-up advanced to the Play-offs if they were one of the four best runners-up
among all seven groups (not counting results against the fifth-placed team).

GROUP 1

17.09.2017   Astana Arena, Astana: Kazakhstan – Wales 0-1 (0-0)
Goal: Fishlock (54)
19.09.2017   Prenton Park, Birkenhead: England – Russia 6-0 (4-0)
Goals: Parris (11), Taylor (14), Nobbs (36), Bronze (44), Duggan (57, 84)
21.10.2017   Astana Arena, Astana: Kazakhstan – Bosnia and Herzegovina 0-2 (0-1)
Goals: Kameric (2), Nikolic (63)
24.10.2017   Minor Sport Arena Petrovsky, St. Petersburg: Russia – Wales 0-0
24.11.2017   Cardiff City Stadium, Cardiff: Wales – Kazakhstan 1-0 (0-0)
Goal: Ladd (83)
24.11.2017   Bescot Stadium, Walsall: England – Bosnia and Herzegovina 4-0 (1-0)
Goals: Houghton (19, 54), Parris (46), Kirby (83 pen)
28.11.2017   Bosnia and Herzegovina FA Training Centre, Zenica:
                Bosnia and Herzegovina – Wales 0-1 (0-0)
Goal: Green (58)

28.11.2017   Colchester Community Stadium, Colchester:
England – Kazakhstan 5-0 (1-0)
Goals: Lawley (15), Kirby (64 pen), Parris (69, 75), Christiansen (76)
05.04.2018   Bosnia and Herzegovina FA Training Centre, Zenica:
Bosnia and Herzegovina – Russia 1-6 (1-2)
Goals: Todua (5 og) / Danilova (26, 81), Galay (39), Morozova (53 pen),
Smirnova (58, 90+2)
06.04.2018   St Mary's Stadium, Southampton: England – Wales 0-0
09.04.2018   Astana Arena, Astana: Kazakhstan – Russia 0-3 (0-0)
Goals: Danilova (59), Smirnova (70, 90)
10.04.2018   Bosnia and Herzegovina FA Training Centre, Zenica:
Bosnia and Herzegovina – England 0-2 (0-0)
Goals: Duggan (56), Taylor (90+3 pen)
07.06.2018   Liberty Stadium, Swansea: Wales – Bosnia and Herzegovina 1-0 (0-0)
Goal: Green (62)
08.06.2018   Sapsan Arena, Moscow: Russia – England 1-3 (1-3)
Goals: Danilova (31) / Parris (22), Scott (27, 38)
12.06.2018   Bosnia and Herzegovina FA Training Centre, Zenica:
Bosnia and Herzegovina – Kazakhstan 0-2 (0-1)
Goals: Spahic (33 og), Babshuk (74)
12.06.2018   Newport Stadium, Newport: Wales – Russia 3-0 (0-0)
Goals: Green (48, 62), Harding (68)
30.08.2018   Sapsan Arena, Moscow: Russia – Kazakhstan 3-0 (2-0)
Goals: Fedorova (4), Smirnova (44, 56)
31.08.2018   Rodney Parade, Newport: Wales – England 0-3 (0-0)
Goals: Duggan (57), Scott (60), Parris (69)
04.09.2018   Sapsan Arena, Moscow: Russia – Bosnia and Herzegovina 3-0 (3-0)
Goals: Danilova (13, 18 pen), Kozhnikova (45)
04.09.2018   Pavlodar Central Stadium, Pavlodar: Kazakhstan – England 0-6 (0-2)
Goals: Mead (9 pen, 82), Daly (35), Christansen (54), Staniforth (66), Bronze (87)

Team	Pld	W	D	L	GF	GA	GD	Pts
England	*8*	*7*	*1*	*0*	*29*	*1*	*+28*	*22*
Wales	8	5	2	1	7	3	+4	17
Russia	8	4	1	3	16	13	+3	13
Bosnia and Herzegovina	8	1	0	7	3	19	-16	3
Kazakhstan	8	1	0	7	2	21	-19	3

GROUP 2

15.09.2017   Elbasan Arena, Elbasan: Albania – Switzerland 1-4 (0-3)
Goals: Begolli (81) / Brunner (23), Bachmann (39), Crnogorcevic (41 pen),
Dickenmann (67)
15.09.2017   Stadion Górnika Leczna, Leczna: Poland – Belarus 4-1 (3-1)
Goals: Tarczynska (14), Kamczyk (37), Pajor (42, 59) / Shcherbachenia (44)
19.09.2017   FC Minsk Stadium, Minsk: Belarus – Albania 1-0 (0-0)
Goal: Shuppo (48)

19.09.2017   Tissot Arena, Biel/Bienne: Switzerland – Poland 2-1 (2-1)
Goals: Bernauer (20), Dickenmann (39) / Pajor (34)
19.10.2017   FC Minsk Stadium, Minsk: Belarus – Scotland 1-2 (1-1)
Goals: Kharlanova (25) / Ross (28), Kozyupa (62 og)
24.10.2017   St Mirren Park, Paisley: Scotland – Albania 5-0 (2-0)
Goals: Begolli (21 og), Brown (33), Ross (54), Emslie (56), Evans (82)
24.11.2017   Loro Boriçi Stadium, Shkodër: Albania – Poland 1-4 (0-3)
Goals: Doci (78) / Sikora (5), Gusciora (13), Winczo (37, 66)
24.11.2017   LIPO Park, Schaffhausen: Switzerland – Belarus 3-0 (2-0)
Goals: Calligaris (17), Wälti (18), Reuteler (56)
28.11.2017   Tissot Arena, Biel/Bienne: Switzerland – Albania 5-1 (2-1)
Goals: Ismaili (8, 87), Bachmann (35), Kiwic (73), Calligaris (80) / Krasniqi (29)
05.04.2018   LIPO Park, Schaffhausen: Switzerland – Scotland 1-0 (1-0)
Goal: Dickenmann (32)
06.04.2018   Osrodek Stortu I Rekreacji, Wloclawek: Poland – Albania 1-1 (1-0)
Goals: Daleszczyk (2) / Morina (74)
10.04.2018   Elbasan Arena, Elbasan: Albania – Belarus 1-0 (0-0)
Goal: Gjini (88)
10.04.2018   St Mirren Park, Paisley: Scotland – Poland 3-0 (0-0)
Goals: Ness (79), Emslie (86), Cuthbert (90+1)
07.06.2018   Falkirk Stadium, Falkirk: Scotland – Belarus 2-1 (1-1)
Goals: Cuthbert (45+2, 65) / Olkhovik (27)
12.06.2018   Kielce City Stadium, Kielce: Poland – Scotland 2-3 (1-0)
Goals: Jaszek (6), Howard (66 og) / Little (78), Ross (80), Evans (90)
12.06.2018   FC Minsk Stadium, Minsk: Belarus – Switzerland 0-5 (0-3)
Goals: Crnogorcevic (5 pen), Dickenmann (18, 55), Karachun (34 og), Calligaris (76)
30.08.2018   St Mirren Park, Paisley: Scotland – Switzerland 2-1 (2-1)
Goals: Cuthbert (2), Little (6) / Dickenmann (7)
31.08.2018   Traktor Stadium, Minsk: Belarus – Poland 1-4 (0-1)
Goals: Shlapakova (53) / Winczo (44), Pajor (47, 86), Kamczyk (56)
04.09.2018   Stadion Stali Mielec, Mielec: Poland – Switzerland 0-0
04.09.2018   Loro Boriçi Stadium, Shkodër: Albania – Scotland 1-2 (1-1)
Goals: Doci (45) / Little (9), Ross (68)

Team	Pld	W	D	L	GF	GA	GD	Pts
Scotland	*8*	*7*	*0*	*1*	*19*	*7*	*+12*	*21*
Switzerland	8	6	1	1	21	5	+16	19
Poland	8	3	2	3	16	12	+4	11
Albania	8	1	1	6	6	22	-16	4
Belarus	8	1	0	7	5	21	-16	3

GROUP 3

15.09.2017   Fredrikstad Stadion, Fredrikstad: Norway – Northern Ireland 4-1 (2-0)
Goals: Reiten (15, 90+2), Graham Hansen (45+2 pen), Utland (52) / Milligan (89)
19.09.2017   Sarpsborg Stadion, Sarpsborg: Norway – Slovakia 6-1 (6-0)
Goals: Utland (3), Thorsnes (9), Reiten (21), Graham Hansen (27, 42 pen),
Mjelde (37 pen) / Fabová (55)

19.09.2017   Mourneview Park, Lurgan:
            Northern Ireland – Republic of Ireland 0-2 (0-1)
Goals: Furness (45+1 og), Campbell (69)
24.10.2017   NTC Senec, Senec: Slovakia – Republic of Ireland 0-2 (0-2)
Goals: O'Sullivan (11), Vojteková (33 og)
24.10.2017   Euroborg, Groningen: Netherlands – Norway 1-0 (0-0)
Goal: Miedema (90+3)
24.11.2017   NTC Senec, Senec: Slovakia – Netherlands 0-5 (0-3)
Goals: van der Gragt (8, 90+1), Spitse (42), Miedema (45+1, 46)
28.11.2017   Stadión pod Dubnom, Zilina: Slovakia – Northern Ireland 1-3 (1-1)
Goals: Vojteková (20) / Nelson (34), Furness (52), Milligan (61)
28.11.2017   Stadion de Goffert, Nijmegen: Netherlands – Republic of Ireland 0-0
06.04.2018   Tallaght Stadium, Dublin: Republic of Ireland – Slovakia 2-1 (0-0)
Goals: Kiernan (69), Barrett (87) / Hourihan (73 og)
06.04.2018   Philips Stadion, Eindhoven: Netherlands – Northern Ireland 7-0 (4-0)
Goals: Martens (9, 17), Miedema (27), Spitse (42 pen, 76), van de Sanden (63),
Simpson (90+3 og)
10.04.2018   Tallaght Stadium, Dublin: Republic of Ireland – Netherlands 0-2 (0-2)
Goals: Beerensteyn (11), Spitse (23 pen)
10.04.2018   Shamrock Park, Portadown: Northern Ireland – Norway 0-3 (0-0)
Goals: Graham Hansen (61, 87), Herlovsen (90+3)
08.06.2018   Tallaght Stadium, Dublin: Republic of Ireland – Norway 0-2 (0-1)
Goals: Utland (21, 61)
08.06.2018   Shamrock Park, Portadown: Northern Ireland – Netherlands 0-5 (0-1)
Goals: Beerensteyn (37), van de Donk (61), van de Sanden (65), Spitse (75 pen),
Groenen (89)
12.06.2018   Viking Stadion, Stavanger: Norway – Republic of Ireland 1-0 (1-0)
Goal: Graham Hansen (25 pen)
12.06.2018   Abe Lenstra Stadion, Heerenveen: Netherlands – Slovakia 1-0 (0-0)
Goal: Martens (90+2)
31.08.2018   Tallaght Stadium, Dublin:
            Republic of Ireland – Northern Ireland 4-0 (3-0)
Goals: Kiernan (4, 27), McCabe (12, 58 pen)
31.08.2018   NTC Senec, Senec: Slovakia – Norway 0-4 (0-3)
Goals: Utland (11, 26, 87), Reiten (22)
04.09.2018   Intility Arena, Oslo: Norway – Netherlands 2-1 (2-1)
Goals: Engen (5), Herlovsen (6) / Miedema (31)
04.09.2018   Shamrock Park, Portadown: Northern Ireland – Slovakia 0-1 (0-1)
Goal: Skorvánková (36)

Team	Pld	W	D	L	GF	GA	GD	Pts
Norway	8	7	0	1	22	4	+18	21
Netherlands	8	6	1	1	22	2	+20	19
Republic of Ireland	8	4	1	3	10	6	+4	13
Northern Ireland	8	1	0	7	4	27	-23	3
Slovakia	8	1	0	7	4	23	-19	3

GROUP 4

15.09.2017   Arena Lviv, Lviv: Ukraine – Croatie 1-1 (0-0)
Goals: Apanaschenko (75 pen) / Rudelic (90+1)
19.09.2017   Ménfői úti Stadion, Győr: Hungary – Denmark 1-6 (1-2)
Goals: Jakabfi (41 pen) / Nadim (28 pen), Troelsgaard (44, 67, 74), Harder (55),
Sørensen (88)
19.09.2017   Stadion Andjelko Herjavec, Varazdin: Croatia – Sweden 0-2 (0-0)
Goals: Hurtig (62), Asllani (90+2)
19.09.2017   Ménfői úti Stadion, Győr: Hungary – Croatia 2-2 (0-0)
Goals: Csiszár (75, 90+4) / Zigic (79), Dujmenovic (90+1)
20.09.2017   Gamla Ullevi, Gothenburg: Sweden – Denmark 3-0   **Awarded**
*The match was cancelled because of a disagreement between the Danish team and
their federation. UEFA opened disciplinary proceedings against Denmark for refusal
to play and on 16 November 2017 UEFA announced that the result was awarded 3-0
to Sweden.*
24.10.2017   Stadion SRC Zapresic, Zapresic: Croatia – Denmark 0-4 (0-2)
Goals: Harder (7, 27), Christiansen (89), Bruun (90+4)
24.10.2017   Borås Arena, Borås: Sweden – Hungary 5-0 (4-0)
Goals: Hurtig (14), Fischer (20), Asllani (42, 50), Seger (43)
24.11.2017   Balmazújvárosi Városi Sportpálya, Balmazújváros:
             Hungary – Ukraine 0-1 (0-0)
Goal: Apanashchenko (90+4)
05.04.2018   Stadion Stanovi, Zadar: Croatia – Ukraine 0-3 (0-3)
Goals: Bosnjak (25 og), Koryrenko (41, 45+3)
05.04.2018   Haladás Sportkomplexum, Szombathely: Hungary – Sweden 1-4 (0-2)
Goals: Vágó (63) / Seger (17), Jakobsson (25), Blackstenius (87'), Larsson (90+3)
09.04.2018   Stadion Stanovi, Zadar: Croatia – Hungary 1-3 (0-1)
Goals: Zigic (90+4) / Vágó (43, 84), Jakabfi (72)
09.04.2018   Viborg Stadium, Viborg: Denmark – Ukraine 1-0 (0-0)
Goal: Troelsgaard (78)
07.06.2018   Gamla Ullevi, Gothenburg: Sweden – Croatia 4-0 (1-0)
Goals: Blackstenius (16, 67), Rubensson (63), Folkesson (90)
08.06.2018   Arena Lviv, Lviv: Ukraine – Denmark 1-5 (0-2)
Goals: Ovdiychuk (90+3) / Nadim (6, 52 pen), Harder (33), Troelsgaard (81, 90+4)
12.06.2018   Viborg Stadium, Viborg: Denmark – Hungaria 5-1 (2-1)
Goals: Nadim (44, 45+1), Boye (47), Nielsen (57), Harder (90+4) / Jakabfi (24)
12.06.2018   Arena Lviv, Lviv: Ukraine – Sweden 1-0 (1-0)
Goal: Apanashchenko (41)
30.08.2018   Gamla Ullevi, Gothenburg: Sweden – Ukraine 3-0 (2-0)
Goals: Rubensson (34), Eriksson (38), Asllani (51)
30.08.2018   Viborg Stadium, Viborg: Denmark – Croatia 1-1 (0-0)
Goals: Nadim (90+2) / Lojna (60)
04.09.2018   Viborg Stadium, Viborg: Denmark – Sweden 0-1 (0-0)
Goal: Jakobsson (46)
04.09.2018   Ternopilsky Msiky Stadion, Ternopil: Ukraine – Hungary 2-0 (2-0)
Goals: Kravets (26), Apanashchenko (31)

Team	Pld	W	D	L	GF	GA	GD	Pts
Sweden	8	7	0	1	22	2	+20	21
Denmark	8	5	1	2	22	8	+14	16
Ukraine	8	4	1	3	9	10	-1	13
Hungary	8	1	1	6	8	26	-18	4
Croatia	8	0	3	5	5	20	-15	3

GROUP 5

14.09.2017 Tórsvøllur, Thórshavn: Faroe Islands – Czech Republic 0-8 (0-6)
Goals: Svitková (8, 44), Bartonová (25), Kozárová (27, 40, 68), Divisová (39), Vonková (70)
16.09.2017 Audi Sportpark, Ingolstadt: Germany – Slovenia 6-0 (4-0)
Goals: Huth (15), Marozsán (18 pen), Hendrich (35), Kemme (45+2, 80), Demann (88)
18.09.2017 Laugardalsvöllur, Reykjavík: Iceland – Faroe Islands 8-0 (4-0)
Goals: Jensen (3, 26), Jónsdóttir (17, 47), S.Gunnarsdóttir (39), Fridriksdóttir (66, 90+1), Thorvaldsdóttir (90)
19.09.2017 Mestsky stadion, Ústí nad Labem: Czech Republic – Germany 0-1 (0-0)
Goal: Bartonová (51 og)
20.10.2017 BRITA-Arena, Wiesbaden: Germany – Iceland 2-3 (1-1)
Goals: Popp (42), Schüller (88) / Brynjarsdóttir (15, 58), Jensen (47)
20.10.2017 Domzale Sports Park, Domzale: Slovenia – Czech Republic 0-4 (0-2)
Goals: Divisová (9, 32), Kozárová (72), Vonková (76)
24.10.2017 Mechatronik Arena, Aspach: Germany – Faroe Islands 11-0 (6-0)
Goals: Popp (12, 45+1), Kemme (15, 27), Peter (30), Hendrich (33), Magull (48), Kayikçi (63, 76, 83, 89)
24.10.2017 Mestsky stadion, Znojmo: Czech Republic – Iceland 1-1 (0-1)
Goals: Bartonová (63) / Brynjarsdóttir (44)
24.11.2017 Ajdovscina Stadium, Ajdovscina: Slovenia – Faroe Islands 5-0 (4-0)
Goals: Prasnikar (7, 36, 87), Agrez (29), Rozmaric (41)
06.04.2018 Lendava Sports Park, Lenvada: Slovenia – Iceland 0-2 (0-2)
Goals: Jónsdóttir (15), Hönnudóttir (37)
07.04.2018 Erdgas Sportpark, Halle: Germany – Czech Republic 4-0 (2-0)
Goals: Schüller (5, 31, 68, 79)
10.04.2018 Domzale Sports Park, Domzale: Slovenia – Germany 0-4 (0-2)
Goals: Magull (10), Golob (43 og), Popp (53), Dallmann (61)
10.04.2018 Tórsvøllur, Thórshavn: Faroe Islands – Iceland 0-5 (0-1)
Goals: Jónsdóttir (37), Hönnudóttir (48), Thorsteinsdóttir (58), Albertsdóttir (89), Fridriksdóttir (90+4)
07.06.2018 Tórsvøllur, Thórshavn: Faroe Islands – Slovenia 0-4 (0-2)
Goals: Ivanusa (10), Zver (21 pen, 65), Prasnikar (88)
11.06.2018 Laugardalsvöllur, Reykjavík: Iceland – Slovenia 2-0 (0-0)
Goals: Viggósdóttir (54, 68)
12.06.2018 Letni stadion, Chomutov: Czech Republic – Faroe Islands 4-1 (1-0)
Goals: Svitková (14), Martinková (52), Vonková (63), Stárová (75) / Simonsen (89)

31.08.2018   Stadion Strelnice, Jablonec nad Nisou:
Czech Republic – Slovenia 2-0 (1-0)
Goals: Svitková (12), Divisová (63)
01.09.2018   Laugardalsvöllur, Reykjavík: Iceland – Germany 0-2 (0-1)
Goals: Huth (42, 74)
04.09.2018   Laugardalsvöllur, Reykjavík: Iceland – Czech Republic 1-1 (0-1)
Goals: Viggósdóttir (87) / Szewieczková (12)
04.09.2018   Tórsvøllur, Thórshavn: Faroe Islands – Germany 0-8 (0-3)
Goals: Schüller (3), Magull (25, 68), Maier (27), Simon (58, 73), Popp (71, 90+2)

Team	Pld	W	D	L	GF	GA	GD	Pts
Germany	8	7	0	1	38	3	+35	21
Iceland	8	5	2	1	22	6	+16	17
Czech Republic	8	4	2	2	20	8	+12	14
Slovenia	8	2	0	6	9	20	-11	6
Faroe Islands	8	0	0	8	1	53	-52	0

GROUP 6

15.09.2017   Stadio Alberto Picco, La Spezia: Italy – Moldova 5-0 (4-0)
Goals: Sabatino (9), Bonansea (22), Girelli (33, 60), Bergamaschi (38)
19.09.2017   Stadionul Dr. Constantin Radulescu, Cluj-Napoca:
Romania – Italy 0-1 (0-0)
Goal: Corduneanu (77 og)
19.09.2017   Den Dreef, Leuven: Belgium – Moldova 12-0 (5-0)
Goals: Cayman (3, 55, 60 pen, 70), Wullaert (26, 29, 38), Philtjens (35), Deloose (62),
Vanmechelen (65), De Caigny (69), Colesnicenco (84 og)
20.10.2017   Den Dreef, Leuven: Belgium – Romania 3-2 (2-1)
Goals: Cayman (30, 37), Wullaert (87) / Dusa (38), Rus (53)
24.10.2017   Stadio Teofilo Patini, Cstel di Sangro: Italy – Romania 3-0 (0-0)
Goals: Girelli (51, 76), Bonansea (78)
24.10.2017   Estádio Municipal 25 de Abril, Penafiel: Portugal – Belgium 0-1 (0-0)
Goal: De Caigny (47)
24.11.2017   Estádio do Bonfim, Setúbal: Portugal – Moldova 8-0 (2-0)
Goals: Mendes (19), Cusinova (32 og), Costa (47, 83), Diana Silva (63), Dolores Silva
(72 pen), Malho (79, 90+2)
28.11.2017   Stadionul Mogosoaia, Mogosoaia: Romania – Moldova 3-1 (1-0)
Goals: Voicu (27, 52), Miron (59 og) / Miron (51)
28.11.2017   Estádio António Coimbra da Mota, Estoril: Portugal – Italy 0-1 (0-1)
Goal: Sabatino (37)
06.04.2018   Stadionul CPSM, Vadul lui Voda: Moldova – Italy 1-3 (1-2)
Goals: Toma (43) / Tucceri Cimini (8), Colesnicenco (30 og), Giacinti (76)
06.04.2018   Den Dreef, Leuven: Belgium – Portugal 1-1 (0-0)
Goals: De Caigny (90+1) / Dolores Silva (90+3 pen)
10.04.2018   Stadio Paolo Mazza, Ferrara: Italy – Belgium 2-1 (1-1)
Goals: Rosucci (42), Girelli (80) / Cayman (37 pen)
10.04.2018   Zimbru Stadium, Chisinau: Moldova – Romania 0-0

238

08.06.2018   Stadio Artemio Franchi, Florence: Italy – Portugal 3-0 (2-0)
Goals: Girelli (4), Salvai (13) / Bonansea (90+1)
10.06.2018   Zimbru Stadium, Chisinau: Moldova – Belgium 0-7 (0-1)
Goals: Cayman (45, 88), Velde (49), Zeler (65), Biesmans (77), Colesnicenco (80 og),
Wullaert (83 pen)
12.06.2018   Stadionul Municipal, Botosina: Romania – Portugal 1-1 (1-1)
Goals: Mihail (34) / Norton (39)
30.08.2018   Zimbru Stadium, Chisinau: Moldova – Portugal 0-7 (0-4)
Goals: Mendes (21), Norton (35), Malho (39, 41), Diana Silva (85, 88), Pinto (90+1)
31.08.2018   Stadionul Municipal, Botosina: Romania – Belgium 0-1 (0-0)
Goal: Van Kerkhoven (84)
04.09.2018   Den Dreef, Leuven: Belgium – Italy 2-1 (2-1)
Goals: Vanmechelen (6, 35) / Girelli (30 pen)
04.09.2018   Estádio Dr. Machado de Matos, Felgueiras:
            Portugal – Romania 5-1 (2-1)
Goals: Leite (30, 53), Nagy (42 og), Diana Silva (59, 90) / Batea (3)

Team	Pld	W	D	L	GF	GA	GD	Pts
Italy	*8*	*7*	*0*	*1*	*19*	*4*	*+15*	*21*
Belgium	8	6	1	1	28	6	+22	19
Portugal	8	3	2	3	22	8	+14	11
Romania	8	1	2	5	7	15	-8	5
Moldova	8	0	1	7	2	45	-43	1

GROUP 7

19.09.2017   Mladost Stadium, Krusevac: Serbia – Austria 0-4 (0-3)
Goals: Burger (15, 37, 90+2), Billa (18)
19.10.2017   Cukaricki Stadium, Belgrade: Serbia – Israel 2-0 (2-0)
Goals: Filipovic (8), Damjanovic (13)
22.10.2017   Telia 5G -areena, Helsinki: Finland – Serbia 1-0 (0-0)
Goal: Tenkov (79 og)
23.10.2017   Ramat Gan Stadium, Ramat Gan: Israel – Spain 0-6 (0-2)
Goals: Paredes (37, 57), Hermoso (43, 84), Latorre (73), Sampedro (90+1)
23.11.2017   Bundesstadion Südstadt, Maria Enzersdorf: Austria – Israel 2-0 (1-0)
Goals: Puntigam (12), Burger (57)
24.11.2017   Vozdovac Stadium, Belgrade: Serbia – Spain 1-2 (0-1)
Goals: Damjanovic (78) / Hermoso (13), Guijarro (90+1)
26.11.2017   Telia 5G -areena, Helsinki: Finland – Israel 4-0 (2-0)
Goals: Collin (40), Sällström (43, 55), Alanen (52)
28.11.2017   Son Moix, Palma: Spain – Austria 4-0 (3-0)
Goals: Putellas (3), Guijarro (16), Paredes (43), Torrecilla (57)
22.01.2018   Ramat Gan Stadium, Ramat Gan: Israel – Finland 0-0
05.04.2018   Bundesstadion Südstadt, Maria Enzersdorf: Austria – Serbia 1-1 (1-1)
Goals: Lazarevic (32 og) / Radojicic (5)
06.04.2018   Telia 5G -areena, Helsinki: Finland – Spain 0-2 (0-1)
Goals: Paredes (11), O.García (50)

239

10.04.2018 Ramat Gan Stadium, Ramat Gan: Israel – Serbia 0-1 (0-0)
Goal: Stankovic (65)
10.04.2018 Bundesstadion Südstadt, Maria Enzersdorf: Austria – Spain 0-1 (0-0)
Goal: Hermoso (59)
07.06.2018 La Condomina, Murcia: Spain – Israel 2-0 (0-0)
Goals: Vilas (51), Putellas (88 pen)
08.06.2018 Telia 5G -areena, Helsinki: Finland – Austria 0-2 (0-1)
Goals: Koivisto (6 og), Schiechtl (72)
12.06.2018 Zemun Stadium, Zemun: Serbia – Finland 0-2 (0-1)
Goals: Hyyrynen (17), Kostic (82 og)
12.06.2018 Ramat Gan Stadium, Ramat Gan: Israel – Austria 0-6 (0-2)
Goals: Schiechtl (5), Wenninger (19), Billa (49), Puntigam (56 pen), Aschauer (69), Feiersinger (88)
31.08.2018 El Sardinero, Santander: Spain – Finland 5-1 (3-1)
Goals: Corredera (28, 45), Hermoso (38), Meriluoto (65 og), N.García (69) / Sällström (33)
04.09.2018 Stadion Wiener Neustadt, Wiener Neustadt: Austria – Finland 4-1 (2-1)
Goals: Billa (13, 68), Zadrazil (34), Pinther (49) / Sällström (45)
04.09.2018 Las Gaunas, Logroño: Spain – Serbia 3-0 (2-0)
Goals: Hermoso (3 pen, 75), Sampedro (35)

Team	Pld	W	D	L	GF	GA	GD	Pts
Spain	8	8	0	0	25	2	+23	24
Austria	8	5	1	2	19	7	+12	16
Finland	8	3	1	4	9	13	-4	10
Serbia	8	2	1	5	5	13	-8	7
Israel	8	0	1	7	0	23	-23	1

RANKING OF SECOND-PLACED TEAMS

To determine the four best second-placed teams from the qualifying round which advanced to the Play-off round, only the results of the second-placed teams against the first, third and fourth-placed teams in their group are taken into account, while results against the fifth-placed team are not included.

Pos	Grp	Team	Pld	W	D	L	GF	GA	GD	Pts
1	3	Netherlands	6	4	1	1	16	2	+14	13
2	2	Switzerland	6	4	1	1	13	5	+8	13
3	6	Belgium	6	4	1	1	9	6	+3	13
4	4	Denmark	6	4	0	2	17	7	+10	12
5	5	Iceland	6	3	2	1	9	6	+3	11
6	1	Wales	6	3	2	1	5	3	+2	11
7	7	Austria	6	3	1	2	11	7	+4	10

Netherlands, Switzerland, Belgium and Denmark advanced to the Play-off round.

PLAY-OFF ROUND

PLAY-OFF SEMI-FINALS

05.10.2018   Rat Verlegh Stadion, Breda: Netherlands – Denmark 2-0 (2-0)
Goals: Beerensteyn (21), van de Sanden (42)
05.10.2018   Den Dreef, Leuven: Belgium – Switzerland 2-2 (1-0)
Goals: Cayman (5), De Neve (60) / Lehmann (55, 87)
09.10.2018   Viborg Stadium, Viborg: Denmark – Netherlands 1-2 (1-1)
Goals: Nadim (5 pen) / Beerensteyn (7, 90+2)
09.10.2018   Tissot Arena, Biel/Bienne: Switzerland – Belgium 1-1 (1-0)
Goals: Reuteler (23) / De Caigny (77)
Switzerland won on away goals.

PLAY-OFF FINAL

09.11.2018   Stadion Galgenwaard, Utrecht: Netherlands – Switzerland 3-0 (0-0)
Goals: Spitse (49), Martens (71), Miedema (80)
13.11.2018   LIPO Park, Schaffhausen: Switzerland – Netherlands 1-1 (0-0)
Goals: Sow (71) / Miedema (52)

The seven group winners **England, Scotland, Norway, Sweden, Germany, Italy** and **Spain** qualified for the FIFA Women's World Cup 2019. The winner of the Play-off round **Netherlands** also qualified for the FIFA Women's World Cup 2019.

CONCACAF WOMEN'S CHAMPIONSHIP 2018

QUALIFYING NORTH AMERICAN ZONE

In the North American Zone (NAFU) were no qualifying matches played. Canada, Mexico and United States were automatically qualified for the Final Tournament.

QUALIFYING CENTRAL AMERICAN ZONE
In the Central American Zone (UNCAF) the top two teams of the group qualify for the Final Tournament. The qualifying competition was originally scheduled to take place in Nicaragua, but a new host was selected due to security concerns caused by civil unrest in Nicaragua. In July 2018, CONCACAF announced that all matches would be played at the IMG Academy in Bradenton, Florida, United States between 27 & 31 August 2018.

Guatemala was suspended by FIFA in October 2016, and therefore was ineligible after missing the entry deadline of 30 March 2018.

GROUP STAGE

27.08.2018   IMG Academy Field 6, Bradenton: Panama – Nicaragua 4-0 (1-0)
Goals: Riley (9, 68), Pinzón (49), Cedeño (90+4)
27.08.2018   IMG Academy Field 11, Bradenton: Costa Rica – El Salvador 11-0 (7-0)
Goals: Herrera (5, 45+1, 55), Alvarado (9), Cruz (19, 21), G.Villalobos (30),
Rodríguez (36), Granados (64), F.Villalobos (82), Salas (84)
29.08.2018   IMG Academy Field 6, Bradenton: Costa Rica – Nicaragua 4-1 (1-0)
Goals: Sánchez (3), Rodríguez (61), Barrabtes (67), Acosta (84) / Aguilar (71)
29.08.2018   IMG Academy Field 11, Bradenton: El Salvador – Panama 2-6 (2-2)
Goals: Quelez (38), Cerén (45+1 pen) / Mills (41), Riley (42), Rangel (58, 69, 90+1),
Cedeño (80)
31.08.2018   IMG Academy Field 6, Bradenton: El Salvador – Nicaragua 2-2 (1-0)
Goals: Ramirez (18), Tamacas (55) / Silva (76, 79)
31.08.2018   IMG Academy Field 11, Bradenton: Costa Rica – Panama 3-1 (2-0)
Goals: Rodríguez (14, 25), Granados (86) / Hernández (74)

Team	Pld	W	D	L	GF	GA	GD	Pts
Costa Rica	3	3	0	0	18	2	+16	9
Panama	3	2	0	1	11	5	+6	6
Nicaragua	3	0	1	2	3	10	-7	1
El Salvador	3	0	1	2	4	19	-15	1

Costa Rica and Panama qualified for the Final Tournament.

QUALIFYING CARIBBEAN ZONE

In the Caribbean Zone (CFU), 23 member national teams entered the qualifying
competition, consisting of two stages. All teams entered the First Round. The winners
of each First Round group advanced to the Final Round. The top three teams of the
Final Round qualify for the Final Tournament.

FIRST ROUND
GROUP A

Hosted in the Dominican Republic.

05.05.2018   Estadio Panamericano, San Cristóbal: Puerto Rico – Anguilla 10-0 (5-0)
Goals: Socarrás (10), Pagán (12, 38, 83), Castain (20, 62, 65), Suárez (23), López
(46), Robinson (85)
05.05.2018   Estadio Panamericano, San Cristóbal:
          Dominican Republic – Cuba 1-5 (1-3)
Goals: Oviedo (15) / Peláez (10, 63), L.Pérez (19), M.Pérez (36), Mengana (73)
07.05.2018   Estadio Panamericano, San Cristóbal: Cuba – Aruba 11-0 (5-0)
Goals: M.Pérez (4, 38, 58), Sablón (20), Mengana (29), Carbonell (33, 88), Maceo
(61), Arrebato (65), Rodríguez (67), Fuentes (90)
07.05.2018   Estadio Panamericano, San Cristóbal:
          Puerto Rico – Dominican Republic 0-0

09.05.2018   Estadio Panamericano, San Cristóbal: Anguilla – Aruba 1-2 (0-1)
Goals: Johnson (71) / Saladin (44), Florance (51)
09.05.2018   Estadio Panamericano, San Cristóbal: Cuba – Puerto Rico 2-2 (0-2)
Goals: Peláez (71), L.Pérez (82) / Socarrás (15), Blankenship (22)
11.05.2018   Estadio Panamericano, San Cristóbal: Aruba – Puerto Rico 0-5 (0-3)
Goals: Castain (3, 90), Tirado (25), Maduro (38 og), Pagán (87)
11.05.2018   Estadio Panamericano, San Cristóbal:
                Dominican Republic – Anguilla 3-0 (1-0)
Goals: Oviedo (1, 60), Romney (50 og)
13.05.2018   Estadio Panamericano, San Cristóbal: Anguilla – Cuba 0-4 (0-2)
Goals: Peláez (18, 73), M.Pérez (33), Riquelme (54)
13.05.2018   Estadio Panamericano, San Cristóbal:
                Aruba – Dominican Republic 0-3 (0-3)
Goals: Vargas (4 pen, 36 pen), Rivas (45)

Team	Pld	W	D	L	GF	GA	GD	Pts
Cuba	4	3	1	0	22	3	+19	10
Puerto Rico	4	2	2	0	17	2	+15	8
Dominican Republic	4	2	1	1	7	5	+2	7
Aruba	4	1	0	3	2	20	-18	3
Anguilla	4	0	0	4	1	19	-18	0

GROUP B
Hosted in Haiti.

09.05.2018   Stade Sylvio Cator, Port-au-Prince: Jamaica – Guadeloupe 13-0 (7-0)
Goals: Shaw (4, 37, 42, 45, 62, 73), Blackwood (23), Plummer (32), Bond-Flasza (43,
71), Washington (61, 79), Reid (83)
09.05.2018   Stade Sylvio Cator, Port-au-Prince: Haiti – Martinique 2-0 (2-0)
Goals: Salomon-Ali (3), Louis (15)
11.05.2018   Stade Sylvio Cator, Port-au-Prince: Martinique – Jamaica 0-3 (0-0)
Goals: Asher (60), Carter (70), Shaw (75)
11.05.2018   Stade Sylvio Cator, Port-au-Prince: Guadeloupe – Haiti 0-11 (0-8)
Goals: Eloissaint (3, 12, 14), Saint Felix (31, 34, 45+2, 45+3, 51), Louis (38), Shelsie
(75), Jeudy (90)
13.05.2018   Stade Sylvio Cator, Port-au-Prince: Guadeloupe – Martinique 0-3 (0-1)
Goals: Carin (5), Guillou (53), Paulin (58)
13.05.2018   Stade Sylvio Cator, Port-au-Prince: Jamaica – Haiti 2-2 (1-2)
Goals: Carter (44), Shaw 66 pen) / Dumornay (24), Jeudy (43)

Team	Pld	W	D	L	GF	GA	GD	Pts
Jamaica	3	2	1	0	18	2	+16	7
Haiti	3	2	1	0	15	2	+13	7
Martinique	3	1	0	2	3	5	-2	3
Guadeloupe	3	0	0	3	0	27	-27	0
Turks and Caicos Islands	0	0	0	0	0	0	0	0

Turks And Caicos Islands withdrew.

243

GROUP C

Hosted in Trinidad and Tobago.

19.05.2018   Ato Boldon Stadium, Couva: Dominica – Saint Kitts and Nevis 1-2 (1-2)
Goals: Phillip (10) / Lawrence (8, 11)
19.05.2018   Ato Boldon Stadium, Couva:
            Trinidad and Tobago – U.S. Virgin Islands 10-0 (6-0)
Goals: Superville (15), Shade (20, 40, 81, 90), Forbes (37), St.Louis (39),
Cunningham (45), Johnson (60), Wiater (73 og)
21.05.2018   Ato Boldon Stadium, Couva: U.S. Virgin Islands – Grenada 3-0 (0-0)
Goals: Wright (74), Canizio (89), Aguillar (90+2)
21.05.2018   Ato Boldon Stadium, Couva: Dominica – Trinidad and Tobago 0-3 (0-2)
Goals: Cunningham (5), Belgrave (37), Forbes (54)
23.05.2018   Ato Boldon Stadium, Couva: Saint Kitts and Nevis – Grenada 10-0 (4-0)
Goals: Uddenberg (6, 19, 71), Browne (9, 52), Lawrence (40, 73, 85), Bailey-
Williams (86), Wilkinson (89)
23.05.2018   Ato Boldon Stadium, Couva: U.S. Virgin Islands – Dominica 0-3 (0-1)
Goals: Francis (23), Phillip (49, 88)
25.05.2018   Ato Boldon Stadium, Couva: Grenada – Dominica 1-1 (0-1)
Goals: George (64) / Phillip (29)
25.05.2018   Ato Boldon Stadium, Couva:
            Trinidad and Tobago – Saint Kitts and Nevis 1-1 (0-1)
Goals: St.Louis (79) / Browne (3 pen)
27.05.2018   Ato Boldon Stadium, Couva:
            Saint Kitss and Nevis – U.S. Virgin Islands 7-0 (2-0)
Goals: Browne (27, 38, 52), Fernandez (46), Francis (57), Springer (70),
Uddenberg (83)
27.05.2018   Ato Boldon Stadium, Couva: Grenada – Trinidad and Tobago 0-13 (0-6)
Goals: Johnson (10), Cunningham (13), Shade (33, 82), St.Louis (42, 90+2), Prince
(43, 88, 90), Cato (45, 54), François (51, 80)

Team	Pld	W	D	L	GF	GA	GD	Pts
Trinidad and Tobago	4	3	1	0	27	1	+26	10
Saint Kitts and Nevis	4	3	1	0	20	2	+18	10
Dominica	4	1	1	2	5	6	-1	4
U.S. Virgin Islands	4	1	0	3	3	20	-17	3
Grenada	4	0	1	3	1	27	-26	1

GROUP D

Hosted in Antigua and Barbuda.

23.05.2018   Antigua Recreation Ground, St. John's: Saint Lucia – Curaçao 2-1 (1-0)
Goals: Marquis (30), Lionel (58) / Statia (55)
23.05.2018   Antigua Recreation Ground, St. John's:
            Antigua and Barbuda – Saint Vincent and the Grenadines 1-0 (0-0)
Goal: James (69)

25.05.2018   Antigua Recreation Ground, St. John's:
             Saint Vincent and the Grenadines – Saint Lucia 1-2 (0-1)
Goals: Duncan (74) / Willie (5), Cox (88)
25.05.2018   Antigua Recreation Ground, St. John's:
             Curaçao – Antigua and Barbuda 0-3 (0-0)
Goals: Jarvis (49), Simon-Ponte (60), Humphreys (79)
27.05.2018   Antigua Recreation Ground, St. John's:
             Curaçao – Saint Vincent and the Grenadines 1-0 (0-0)
Goal: Tokaay (52)
27.05.2018   Antigua Recreation Ground, St. John's:
             Saint Lucia – Antigua and Barbuda 0-1 (0-1)
Goal: Edwards (2)

Team	Pld	W	D	L	GF	GA	GD	Pts
Antigua and Barbuda	3	3	0	0	5	0	+5	9
Saint Lucia	3	2	0	1	4	3	+1	6
Curaçao	3	1	0	2	2	5	-3	3
Saint Vincent and the Grenadines	3	0	0	3	1	4	-3	0

GROUP E

Hosted in Guyana.

23.05.2018   Synthetic Track and Field Facility, Leonora:
             Barbados – Suriname 2-1 (2-1)
Goals: Padmore (2), Jarvis (40) / Hoogdorp (20)
23.05.2018   Synthetic Track and Field Facility, Leonora:
             Guyana – Bermuda 2-2 (1-2)
Goals: Desa (7), Hazelwood (58) / Lindo (5, 16)
25.05.2018   Synthetic Track and Field Facility, Leonora:
             Bermuda – Barbados 3-2 (1-1)
Goals: Furbert (17), Lindo (68), Darrell (74) / Jarvis (32), Padmore (89)
25.05.2018   Synthetic Track and Field Facility, Leonora:
             Suriname – Guyana 1-6 (1-2)
Goals: Rigters (38) / Persaud (40, 67), Desa (45), Copland (58), Cummings (65),
Smith (88)
27.05.2018   Synthetic Track and Field Facility, Leonora:
             Suriname – Bermuda 0-1 (0-1)
Goal: Furbert (41)
27.05.2018   Synthetic Track and Field Facility, Leonora: Barbados – Guyana 0-0

Team	Pld	W	D	L	GF	GA	GD	Pts
Bermuda	3	2	1	0	6	4	+2	7
Guyana	3	1	2	0	8	3	+5	5
Barbados	3	1	1	1	4	4	0	4
Suriname	3	0	0	3	2	9	-7	0

FINAL ROUND

Hosted in Jamaica.

25.08.2018   National Stadium, Kingston: Cuba – Trinidad and Tobago 2-3 (1-1)
Goals: Ramos (23), Mengana (83) / Taylor (20, 51, 55)
25.08.2018   National Stadium, Kingston: Jamaica – Antigua and Barbuda 9-0 (4-0)
Goals: Chang (2 pen), Carter (6), Shaw (9, 48, 53), Blackwood (27), Shim (65),
Sweatman (68, 73)
27.08.2018   National Stadium, Kingston: Antigua and Barbuda – Cuba 0-7 (0-2)
Goals: M.Pérez (8, 56), L.Pérez (25, 64), Peláez (67, 78), Carbonell (90+1)
27.08.2018   National Stadium, Kingston: Bermuda – Jamaica 0-4 (0-2)
Goals: Carter (17), Plummer (32), Shaw (61), Washington (90+1)
29.08.2018   National Stadium, Kingston: Trinidad and Tobago – Antigua and
Barbuda 5-0 (4-0)
Goals: François (4), Taylor (16, 39), St.Louis (30 pen), Cordner (65)
29.08.2018   National Stadium, Kingston: Cuba – Bermuda 2-0 (1-0)
Goals: L.Pérez (31), M.Pérez (52)
31.08.2018   National Stadium, Kingston: Antigua and Barbuda – Bermuda 0-5 (0-2)
Goals: Furbert (14), Christopher (44), Darrell (76, 81 pen), Lindo (87)
31.08.2018   National Stadium, Kingston: Trinidad and Tobago – Jamaica 1-4 (1-0)
Goals: Taylor (10) / Washington (70), Shaw (79, 89), Brown (90+2)
02.09.2018   National Stadium, Kingston: Bermuda – Trinidad and Tobago 0-3 (0-1)
Goals: Taylor (12), Cordner (57, 87)
02.09.2018   National Stadium, Kingston: Jamaica – Cuba 6-1 (5-0)
Goals: Asher (19, 70), Shaw (20, 38), Silver (32), Brown (34 pen) / M.Pérez (90+3)

Team	Pld	W	D	L	GF	GA	GD	Pts
Jamaica	4	4	0	0	23	2	+21	12
Trinidad and Tobago	4	3	0	1	12	6	+6	9
Cuba	4	2	0	2	12	9	+3	6
Bermuda	4	1	0	3	5	9	-4	3
Antigua and Barbuda	4	0	0	4	0	26	-26	0

Jamaica, Trinidad and Tobago and Cuba qualified for the Final Tournament.

FINAL TOURNAMENT

The Final Tournament was held in the United States between 4 & 17 October 2018.

GROUP STAGE

The top two of each group advanced to the semi-finals.

246

GROUP A

04.10.2018   Sahlen's Stadium, Cary: Trinidad and Tobago – Panama 0-3 (0-1)
Goals: Cox (12), Rangel (68), Hernández (89)
04.10.2018   Sahlen's Stadium, Cary: United States – Mexico 6-0 (1-0)
Goals: Rapinoe (3, 71), Ertz (47), Morgan (57, 80), Heath (61)
07.10.2018   Sahlen's Stadium, Cary: Panama – United States 0-5 (0-4)
Goals: Mewis (6), Lloyd (23, 29, 48), Press (32)
07.10.2018   Sahlen's Stadium, Cary: Mexico – Trinidad and Tobago 4-1 (1-0)
Goals: Corral (33, 62), Johnson (55), Sánchez (71) / Cato (50 pen)
10.10.2018   Sahlen's Stadium, Cary: Panama – Mexico 2-0 (0-0)
Goals: Riley (47), Cedeño (85)
10.10.2018   Sahlen's Stadium, Cary: Trinidad and Tobago – United States 0-7 (0-4)
Goals: Morgan (9, 50), Lavelle (41, 43), Dunn (45), Horan (49), Heath (58)

Team	Pld	W	D	L	GF	GA	GD	Pts
United States	3	3	0	0	18	0	+18	9
Panama	3	2	0	1	5	5	0	6
Mexico	3	1	0	2	4	9	-5	3
Trinidad and Tobago	3	0	0	3	1	14	-13	0

GROUP B

05.10.2018   H-E-B Park, Edinburg: Costa Rica – Cuba 8-0 (6-0)
Goals: Herrera (4), Chinchilla (5, 45+1), F.Sánchez (19), S.Cruz (33, 38), Barrantes (82 pen, 90+2)
05.10.2018   H-E-B Park, Edinburg: Canada – Jamaica 2-0 (1-0)
Goals: Prince (33, 80)
08.10.2018   H-E-B Park, Edinburg: Jamaica – Costa Rica 1-0 (0-0)
Goal: Shaw (46)
08.10.2018   H-E-B Park, Edinburg: Cuba – Canada 0-12 (0-5)
Goals: Leon (11, 23, 55, 59), Huitema (13, 37, 52, 71), Rose (25), Quinn (56), Sinclair (63), Matheson (72)
11.10.2018   H-E-B Park, Edinburg: Cuba – Jamaica 0-9 (0-4)
Goals: Shaw (2), Brown (26, 38, 72), Campbell (30, 75), Blackwood (50 pen), Chang 64), Sweatman (82)
11.10.2018   H-E-B Park, Edinburg: Costa Rica – Canada 1-3 (0-2)
Goals: G.Villalobos (73) / Beckie (25), Prince (40), Sinclair (57)

Team	Pld	W	D	L	GF	GA	GD	Pts
Canada	3	3	0	0	17	1	+16	9
Jamaica	3	2	0	1	10	2	+8	6
Costa Rica	3	1	0	2	9	4	+5	3
Cuba	3	0	0	3	0	29	-29	0

KNOCKOUT STAGE
SEMI-FINALS

14.10.2018   Toyota Stadium, Frisco: Panama – Canada 0-7 (0-1)
Goals: Sinclair (44, 49), Fleming (47), Beckie (58), Quinn (63), Leon (76, 78)
14.10.2018   Toyota Stadium, Frisco: United States – Jamaica 6-0 (5-0)
Goals: Heath (2, 29), Rapinoe (15), Ertz (21), Morgan (33, 84 pen)

THIRD PLACE PLAY-OFF

17.10.2018   Toyota Stadium, Frisco: Panama – Jamaica 2-2 (0-1, 1-1) (a.e.t.)
Goals: Mills (74), Cedeño (115) / Shaw (14), Brown (95)
Jamaica won after extra time on penalties (2:4).

FINAL

17.10.2018   Toyota Stadium, Frisco: Canada – United States 0-2 (0-1)
Goals: Lavelle (2), Morgan (89)

The winner **United States**, the runner-up **Canada** and the **third place** winner Jamaica qualfied for the FIFA Women's World Cup 2019. The tourth-placed team Panama advanced to a play-off against the third-placed team from the South American Confederation in the CONCACAF-CONMEBOL Play-off 2018.

OFC WOMEN'S NATIONS CUP 2018

The OFC Women's Nations Cup 2018 was held in New Caledonia between 18 November – 1 December 2018. Only the winner will qualify for the FIFA Women's World Cup 2019.

QUALIFICATION

The OFC Women's Nations Cup Qualification was held in Lautoka, Fiji between 24 & 30 August 2018 to determine the final women's national team which joined the seven automatically qualified teams in the Final Tournament in New Caledonia. The tournament was originally scheduled to be held in Pago Pago, American Samoa from 27 August to 4 September 2018, but in March 2018 the venue was changed to Fiji.

24.08.2018   Churchill Park, Lautoka: American Samoa – Solomon Islands 0-2 (0-1)
Goals: Samani (39, 90+4)
24.08.2018   Churchill Park, Lautoka: Vanuatu – Fiji 1-5 (0-2)
Goals: Gere (75) / Tamanitoakula (6), David (41, 54, 55), Nasau (57)
27.08.2018   Churchill Park, Lautoka: Vanuatu – American Samoa 1-0 (1-0)
Goal: Wakeret (44)
27.08.2018   Churchill Park, Lautoka: Fiji – Solomon Islands 0-0
30.08.2018   Churchill Park, Lautoka: Solomon Islands – Vanuatu 0-1 (0-1)
Goal: Solomon (5)

30.08.2018   Churchill Park, Lautoka: Fiji – American Samoa 2-0 (2-0)
Goals: Davis (40), Nasau (45)

Team	Pld	W	D	L	GF	GA	GD	Pts
Fiji	*3*	*2*	*1*	*0*	*7*	*1*	*+6*	*7*
Vanuatu	3	2	0	1	3	5	-2	6
Solomon Islands	3	1	1	1	2	1	+1	4
American Samoa	3	0	0	3	0	5	-5	0

Fiji qualified for the Final Tournament.

FINAL TOURNAMENT

The final Tournament was held in New Caledonia between 18 November and 1 December 2018. Only the winner qualified for the FIFA Women's World Cup 2019.

GROUP STAGE
GROUP A

18.11.2018   Stade Yoshida, Koné: Samoa – Papua New Guinea 0-5 (0-3)
Goals: M.Guenemba (17, 22, 53), Gabong (27), Bauelua (90+2)
18.11.2018   Stade Yoshida, Koné: Tahiti – New Caledonia 2-4 (2-3)
Goals: Tamarii (27), Hioe (45) / Xowie (19), Pahoa (22, 25), Lalie (81)
21.11.2018   Stade Yoshida, Koné: Tahiti – Samoa 5-5 (4-3)
Goals: Teotahi (3, 7, 50), Taumaa (10), Hioe (45+4) / Sataraka (1, 79, 89), Kimitete (4 og), Malo (21)
21.11.2018 Stade Yoshida, Koné: New Caledonia – Papua New Guinea 2-6 (0-3)
Goals: Maguire (48), Gatha (90+3) / Kaipu (20, 31, 46, 60, 81), Padio (36)
24.11.2018   Stade Yoshida, Koné: Papua New Guinea – Tahiti 3-1 (1-1)
Goals: Unamba (31), Padio (74, 84 pen) / Taumaa (6)
24.11.2018   Stade Yoshida, Koné: New Caledonia – Samoa 2-0 (0-0)
Goals: Ajapuhnya (50), Xowie (67)

Team	Pld	W	D	L	GF	GA	GD	Pts
Papua New Guinea	*3*	*3*	*0*	*0*	*14*	*3*	*+11*	*9*
New Caledonia	*3*	*2*	*0*	*1*	*8*	*8*	*0*	*6*
Tahiti	3	0	1	2	8	12	-4	1
Samoa	3	0	1	2	4	12	-7	1

GROUP B

19.11.2018   Stade Numa-Daly Magenta, Nouméa: New Zealand – Tonga 11-0 (8-0)
Goals: White (8, 15), Longo (9, 13), Hassett (34, 35), Gregorius (37, 39, 52), Percival (67), Jale (88)
19.11.2018   Stade Numa-Daly Magenta, Nouméa: Cook Islands – Fiji 0-3 (0-2)
Goals: Nasau (34), Davis (36), Tamanitoakula (57)

249

22.11.2018 Stade Numa-Daly Magenta, Nouméa: Tonga – Fiji 0-12 (0-9)
Goals: Tamanitoakula (6, 11, 24, 36), Nasau (13, 43, 51), Davis (20, 81),
Diyalowai (22, 30, 90)
22.11.2018 Stade Numa-Daly Magenta, Nouméa:
         New Zealand – Cook Islands 6-0 (3-0)
Goals: Longo (13), Rolston (15, 45), Rood (68), Morton (90+1), Jale (90+2)
25.11.2018 Stade Numa-Daly Magenta, Nouméa: Tonga – Cook Islands 1-0 (1-0)
Goal: Vaka (3)
25.11.2018 Stade Numa-Daly Magenta, Nouméa: Fiji – New Zealand 0-10 (0-4)
Goals: Longo (8, 38), Gregorius (16, 24, 88), Moore (54), Rood (58, 79),
Tora (70 og), Rolston (85)

Team	Pld	W	D	L	GF	GA	GD	Pts
New Zealand	3	3	0	0	27	0	+27	9
Fiji	3	2	0	1	15	10	+5	6
Tonga	3	1	0	2	1	23	-22	3
Cook Islands	3	0	0	3	0	10	-10	0

KNOCKOUT STAGE

SEMI-FINALS

28.11.2018 Stade de la Roche, Maré: Papua New Guinea – Fiji 1-5 (1-2)
Goals: M.Gunemba (12) / Davis (24, 65), Tamanitoakula (27), Nasau (72),
Diyalowai (87)
28.11.2018 Stade de Hnassé, Lifou: New Zealand – New Caledonia 8-0 (7-0)
Goals: Hassett (1), Rolston (7, 20, 43), Bowen (26), Satchell (31), White (38, 68)

THIRD PLACE PLAY-OFF

01.12.2018 Stade Numa-Daly Magenta, Nouméa: Papua New Guinea – New
Caledonia 7-1 (3-0)
Goals: N.Gunemba (5, 36, 54, 82), Gabong (41), Unamba (52), Birum (84) /
Pahoa (60)

FINAL

01-12-2018 Stade Numa-Daly Magenta, Nouméa: Fiji – New Zealand 0-8 (0-4)
Goals: White (2, 90+1), Gregorius (6 pen, 75), Hassett (38, 55), Moore (45+2),
Rood (48)

Winner **New Zealand** qualified for the FIFA Women's World Cup 2019.

CONMEBOL COPA AMÉRICA FEMENINA 2018

The tournament was held between 4 & 22 april 2018 in Chile.

FIRST STAGE

The top two teams of each group advanced to the Final Stage.

GROUP A

04.04.2018 Estadio La Portada, La Serena: Colombia – Uruguay 7-0 (4-0)
Goals: Usme (2, 45+1, 57, 90+2), Montoya (17), Rincón (43), Echeverri (58)
04.04.2018 Estadio La Portada, La Serena: Chile – Paraguay 1-1 (0-0)
Goals: Aedo (62) / Villamayor (53)
06.04.2018 Estadio La Portada, La Serena: Paraguay – Peru 3-0 (0-0)
Goals: Peña (70), J.Martínez (84), Peralta (90+3)
06.04.2018 Estadio La Portada, La Serena: Chile – Colombia 1-1 (0-0)
Goals: Sáez (79) / Usme (49)
08.04.2018 Estadio La Portada, La Serena: Uruguay – Peru 1-1 (0-1)
Goals: Badell (58) / Martínez (37)
08.04.2018 Estadio La Portada, La Serena: Colombia – Paraguay 5-1 (1-0)
Goals: Usme (41, 56, 65), Ospina (70), Santos (81) / Cortaza (90+2)
10.04.2018 Estadio La Portada, La Serena: Colombia – Peru 3-0 (1-0)
Goals: Usme (23), Santos (54), Echeverri (83)
10.04.2018 Estadio La Portada, La Serena: Chile – Uruguay 1-0 (0-0)
Goal: Rojas (79)
12.04.2018 Estadio La Portada, La Serena: Paraguay – Uruguay 2-1 (1-1)
Goals: J.Martínez (36), Peralta (90+2) / Ramírez (1)
12.04.2018 Estadio La Portada, La Serena: Peru – Chile 0-5 (0-2)
Goals: Aedo (28, 65), López (38), Lara (62), Rojas (85)

Team	Pld	W	D	L	GF	GA	GD	Pts
Colombia	4	3	1	0	16	2	+14	10
Chile	4	2	2	0	8	2	+6	8
Paraguay	4	2	1	1	7	7	0	7
Uruguay	4	0	1	3	2	11	-9	1
Peru	4	0	1	3	1	12	-11	1

GROUP B

05.04.2018 Estadio Municipal Francisco Sánchez Rumoroso, Coquimbo:
Ecuador – Venezuela 0-1 (0-0)
Goal: Castellanos (85)
05.04.2018 Estadio Municipal Francisco Sánchez Rumoroso, Coquimbo:
Brazil – Argentina 3-1 (1-0)
Goals: Bia Zaneratto (17), Cristiane (57 pen), Debinha (90) / Banini (54)

07.04.2018   Estadio Municipal Francisco Sánchez Rumoroso, Coquimbo:
           Argentina – Bolivia 3-0 (2-0)
Goals: Jaimes (33 pen, 39), Larroquette (71)
07.04.2018   Estadio Municipal Francisco Sánchez Rumoroso, Coquimbo:
           Brazil – Ecuador 8-0 (2-0)
Goals: Cristiane (10, 90+2), Bia Zaneratto (21, 81), Andressinha (48), Formiga (65), Rafaelle (70), Debinha (86)
09.04.2018   Estadio Municipal Francisco Sánchez Rumoroso, Coquimbo:
           Venezuela – Bolivia 8-0 (1-0)
Goals: Castellanos (23, 49, 55, 90+3 pen), Viso (63, 65, 89), Altuve (74)
09.04.2018   Estadio Municipal Francisco Sánchez Rumoroso, Coquimbo:
           Ecuador – Argentina 3-6 (2-5)
Goals: Vásquez (20), Rodríguez (37 pen), Fajardo (76) / Banini (2), Larroquetto (8), Bravo (10), Jaimes (41), Bonsegundo (45 pen, 85)
11.04.2018   Estadio Municipal Francisco Sánchez Rumoroso, Coquimbo:
           Ecuador – Bolivia 0-1 (0-0)
Goal: Morón (68 pen)
11.04.2018   Estadio Municipal Francisco Sánchez Rumoroso, Coquimbo:
           Brazil – Venezuela 4-0 (2-0)
Goals: Mônica (10), Bia Zaneratto (38, 72), Marta (82)
13.04.2018   Estadio Municipal Francisco Sánchez Rumoroso, Coquimbo:
           Argentina – Venezuela 2-0 (1-0)
Goals: Jaimes (44 pen), Banini (61 pen)
13.04.2018   Estadio Municipal Francisco Sánchez Rumoroso, Coquimbo:
           Bolivia – Brazil 0-7 (0-3)
Goals: Érika (3, 65), Andressinha (17, 54), Andressa Alves (41), Millene (80), aline Milene (82)

Team	Pld	W	D	L	GF	GA	GD	Pts
Brazil	4	4	0	0	22	1	+21	12
Argentina	4	3	0	1	12	6	+6	9
Venezuela	4	2	0	2	9	6	+3	6
Bolivia	4	1	0	3	1	18	-17	3
Ecuador	4	0	0	4	3	16	-13	0

FINAL STAGE

16.04.2018   Estadio La Portada, La Serena: Colombia – Argentina 1-3 (1-0)
Goals: Salazar (31) / Bonsegundo (50), Jaimes (66), Coronel (70)
16.04.2018   Estadio La Portada, La Serena: Brazil – Chile 3-1 (3-0)
Goals: Mônica (21), Bia Zaneratto (25), Thaís (34) / López (63)
19.04.2018   Estadio La Portada, La Serena: Brazil – Argentina 3-0 (0-0)
Goals: Cristiane (47), Thaisa (52), Debinha (78)
19.04.2018   Estadio La Portada, La Serena: Colombia – Chile 0-0
22.04.2018   Estadio La Portada, La Serena: Chile – Argentina 4-0 (3-0)
Goals: Sáez (8), Hernández (24), Barroso (40 og), Lara (90+2)
22.04.2018   Estadio La Portada, La Serena: Brazil – Colombia 3-0 (2-0)
Goals: Mônica (29, 71), Clavijo (45+2 og)

Team	Pld	W	D	L	GF	GA	GD	Pts
Brazil	3	3	0	0	9	1	+8	9
Chile	3	1	1	1	5	3	+2	4
Argentina	3	1	0	2	3	8	-5	3
Colombia	3	0	1	2	1	6	-5	1
Ecuador	4	0	0	4	3	16	-13	0

Winner **Brazil** and runner-up **Chile** qualified for the FIFA Women's World Cup 2019. Third-placed team Argentina qualified for the CONCACAF-CONMEBOL Play-off 2018.

CONCACAF-CONMEBOL PLAY-OFF 2018

08.11.2018   Estadio Julio Humberto Grondona, Sarandi:
        Argentina – Panama 4-0 (2-0)
Goals: Larroquetto (20), Stabile (26, 90+7 pen), Rodríguez (90+4)
13.11.2018   Estadio Rommel Fernández, Panama City: Panama – Argentina 1-1 (1-0)
Goals: Mills (37) / Bonsegundo (65)

Winner **Argentina** qualified for the FIFA Women's World cup 2019.

FIFA WOMEN'S WORLD CUP FINAL TOURNAMENT IN FRANCE 2019

GROUP STAGE
GROUP A

07.06.2019 Parc des Princes, Paris: France – South Korea 4-0 (3-0)
France: Sarah BOUHADDI, Wendie RENARD, Marion TORRENT, Griedge
MBOCK Bathy, Amandine HENRY, Élise BUSSAGLIA, Amel MAJRI (74 Ève
PERISSET), Eugénie LE SOMMER, Gaëtane THINEY (86 Graca GEYORO),
Kadidiatou DIANI, Delphine CASCARINO (70 Valérie GAUVIN).
(Coach: Corinne DIACRE).
South Korea: KIM Min-Jeong, KIM Do-Yeon, KIM Hye-Ri, JANG Sel-Gi, HWANG
Bo-Ram, JI So-Yun, CHO So-Hyun, LEE Young-Ju (69 LEE Mi-Na), KANG Yu-Mi
(52 KANG Chae-Rim), JUNG Seol-Bin (86 YEO Min-Ji), LEE Geum-Min.
(Coach: YOON Deuk-Yeo).
Goals: Eugénie LE SOMMER (9), Wendie RENARD (35, 45+2), Amandine HENRY
(85).
Referee: Claudia UMPIÉRREZ (Uruguay)   Attendance: 45,261.

08.06.2019 Stade Auguste-Delaune II, Reims: Norway – Nigeria 3-0 (3-0)
Norway: Ingrid HJELMSETH, Ingrid WOLD, Maria THORISDOTTIR, Maren
MJELDE, Kristine HEGLAND-MINDE, Caroline Graham HANSEN, Vilde Bøe
RISA (84 Frida LEONHARDSEN MAANUM), Ingrid ENGEN, Isabell
HERLOVSEN, Lisa-Marie KARLSENG UTLAND (80 Elise THORSNES), Guro
REITEN (90+1 Elilie HAAVI). (Coach: Martin SJÖGREN).
Nigeria: Tochukwu OLUEHI, Faith MICHAEL (54 Chidinma OKEKE), Onome EBI,
Ngozi EBERE, Osinachi OHALE, Rita CHIKWELU, Ngozi OKOBI, Halimatu
AYINDE (51 Chinaza UCHENDU), Desire OPARANOZIE *(YC13)* (71 Uchenna
KANU), Francisca ORDEGA *(YC45+1)*, Asisat OSHOALA.
(Coach: Thomas DENNERBY).
Goals: Guro REITEN (17), Lisa-Marie KARLSENG UTLAND (34), Osinachi
OHALE (37 og).
Referee: Kate JACEWICZ (Australia)   Attendance: 11,058.

12.06.2019 Stade des Alpes, Grenoble: Nigeria – South Korea 2-0 (1-0)
Nigeria: Chiamaka NNADOZIE, Onome EBI, Ngozi EBERE, Osinachi OHALE,
Chidinma OKEKE, Rita CHIKWELU *(YC61)*, Ngozi OKOBI, Chinaza UCHENDU
(65 Halimatu AYINDE), Desire OPARANOZIE, Francisca ORDEGA (80 Anam
IMO), Asisat OSHOALA (83 Uchenna KANU). (Coach: Thomas DENNERBY).
South Korea: KIM Min-Jeong, KIM Do-Yeon, KIM Hye-Ri, JANG Sel-Gi, HWANG
Bo-Ram *(YC71)*, JI So-Yun *(YC49)*, CHO So-Hyun, LEE Mi-Na (56 MOON Mi-Ra),
JUNG Seol-Bin (56 YEO Min-Ji), KANG Chae-Rim (76 LEE So-Dam), LEE Geum-
Min. (Coach: YOON Deuk-Yeo).
Goals: KIM Do-Yeon (29 og), Asisat OSHOALA (75).
Referee: Anastasia PUSTOVOITOVA (Russia)   Attendance: 11,252.

12.06.2019   Allianz Riviera, Nice: France – Norway 2-1 (0-0)
France: Sarah BOUHADDI, Wendie RENARD, Marion TORRENT, Griedge
MBOCK Bathy, Amandine HENRY, Élise BUSSAGLIA, Amel MAJRI, Eugénie LE
SOMMER *(YC56)*, Gaëtane THINEY (82 Charlotte BILBAULT), Kadidiatou DIANI,
Valérie GAUVIN (85 Delphine CASCARINO). (Coach: Corinne DIACRE).
Norway: Ingrid HJELMSETH, Ingrid WOLD (86 Synne Skinnes HANSEN), Maria
THORISDOTTIR, Maren MJELDE, Kristine HEGLAND-MINDE, Caroline Graham
HANSEN, Vilde Bøe RISA (90+1 Frida LEONHARDSEN MAANUM), Karina
SÆVIK (76 Lisa-Marie KARLSENG UTLAND), Ingrid ENGEN *(YC71)*, Isabell
HERLOVSEN, Guro REITEN. (Coach: Martin SJÖGREN).
Goals: Valérie GAUVIN (46), Eugénie LE SOMMER (72 pen) / Wendie RENARD
(54 og).
Referee: Bibiana STEINHAUS (Germany)   Attendance: 34,872.

17.06.2019   Roazhon Park, Rennes: Nigeria – France 0-1 (0-0)
Nigeria: Chiamaka NNADOZIE *(YC78)*, Onome EBI, Ngozi EBERE *(YC28,YC75)*,
Osinachi OHALE, Chidinma OKEKE, Rita CHIKWELU *(YC90+9)*, Ngozi OKOBI,
Halimatu AYINDE, Desire OPARANOZIE (90+1 Uchenna KANU), Francisca
ORDEGA (85 Evelyn NWABUOKU), Asisat OSHOALA (85 Anam IMO).
(Coach: Thomas DENNERBY).
France: Sarah BOUHADDI, Wendie RENARD, Griedge MBOCK Bathy, Ève
PERISSET, Amandine HENRY, Charlotte BILBAULT, Amel MAJRI, Gaëtane
THINEY (89 Grace GEYORO), Viviane ASSEYI, Delphine CASCARINO (62
Eugénie LE SOMMER), Valérie GAUVIN *(YC45+1)* (63 Kadidiatou DIANI).
(Coach: Corinne DIACRE).
Goal: Wendie RENARD (79 pen).
Referee: Melissa Paola BORJAS Pastrana (Honduras)   Attendance: 28,267.

17.06.2019   Stade Auguste-Delaune II, Reims: South Korea – Norway 1-2 (0-1)
South Korea: KIM Min-Jeong, LEE Eun-Mi (79 JEONG Yeong-Ah), KIM Do-Yeon,
JANG Sel-Gi, SHIN Dam-Yeong, JI So-Yun, CHO So-Hyun *(YC4)*, MOON Mi-Ra
(82 KANG Yu-Mi), KANG Chae-Rim (66 LEE Mi-Na), YEO Min-Ji *(YC85)*, LEE
Geum-Min. (Coach: YOON Deuk-Yeo).
Norway: Ingrid HJELMSETH, Ingrid WOLD, Maria THORISDOTTIR, Maren
MJELDE, Kristine HEGLAND-MINDE, Caroline Graham HANSEN (54 Frida
LEONHARDSEN MAANUM), Vilde Bøe RISA, Ingrid ENGEN, Isabell
HERLOVSEN (69 Elise THORSNES), Lisa-Marie KARLSENG UTLAND (46
Karina SÆVIK), Guro REITEN. (Coach: Martin SJÖGREN).
Goals: YEO Min-Ji (78) / Caroline Graham HANSEN (4 pen), Isabell HERLOVSEN
(50 pen).
Referee: Marie-Soleil BEAUDOIN (Canada)   Attendance: 13,034.

Team	Pld	W	D	L	GF	GA	GD	Pts
France	3	3	0	0	7	1	+6	9
Norway	3	2	0	1	6	3	+3	6
Nigeria	3	1	0	2	2	4	-2	3
South Korea	3	0	0	3	1	8	-7	0

255

GROUP B

08.06.2019 Roazhon Park, Rennes: Germany – China PR 1-0 (0-0)
Germany: Almuth SCHULT, Marina HEGERING, Sara DOORSOUN-KHAJEH, Kathrin HENDRICH, Carolin SIMON (46 Lena OBERDORF *(YC82)*), Dzsenifer MAROZSÁN, Melanie LEUPOLZ (63 Lina MAGULL), Sara DÄBRITZ, Giulia GWINN, Svenja HUTH (86 Lea SCHÜLLER), Alexandra POPP.
(Coach: Martina VOSS-TECKLENBURG).
China PR: PENG Shimeng, WU Haiyan, LIU Shanshan *(YC50)*, LIN Yuping, WANG Shanshan *(YC12)*, ZHANG Rui, HAN Peng, GU Yasha, LOU Jiahui (33 TAN Ruyin), WEI Yao (46 WANG Shuang *(YC71)*), YANG Li *(YC44)* (69 SONG Duan).
(Coach: JIA Xiuquan).
Goal: Giulia GWINN (66).
Referee: Marie-Soleil BEAUDOIN (Canada) Attendance: 15,283.

08.06.2019 Stade Océane, Le Havre: Spain – South Africa 3-1 (0-1)
Spain: SANDRA PAÑOS García-Villamil, MARTA TORREJÓN Moya, María Pilar "MAPI" LEÓN Cebrián, IRENE Paredes HERNANDEZ, María Victoria "VICKY" LOSADA Gómez (46 AITANA BONMATI Conca), AMANDA SAMPEDRO Bustos (46 LUCÍA GARCÍA Córdoba), ALEXIA PUTELLAS Segura (73 NAHIKARI GARCÍA Pérez), VIRGINIA TORRECILLA Reyes, MARTA CORREDERA Rueda *(YC90+4)*, JENNIFER HERMOSO Fuentes, MARIONA Caldentey Oliver.
(Coach: JORGE VILDA Rodríguez).
South Africa: Andile DLAMINI, Nothando VILAKAZI *(YC60,YC82)*, Janine VAN WYK *(YC69)*, Lebohang RAMALEPE, Refiloe JANE, Linda MOTLHALO (52 Busisiwe NDIMENI), Kholosa BIYANA *(YC77)*, Noko MATLOU, Thembi KGATLANA, Ode FULUTUDILU (77 Leandra SMEDA), Amanda MTHANDI (56 Jermaine SEOPOSENWE). (Coach: Desiree ELLIS).
Goals: JENNIFER HERMOSO Fuentes (69 pen, 82 pen), LUCÍA GARCÍA Córdoba (89) / Thembi KGATLANA (25)
Referee: María Belén CARVAJAL Peña (Chile) Attendance: 12,044.

12.06.2019 Stade du Hainaut, Valenciennes: Germany – Spain 1-0 (1-0)
Germany: Almuth SCHULT, Marina HEGERING, Verena SCHWEERS *(YC63)*, Sara DOORSOUN-KHAJEH, Kathrin HENDRICH (46 Klara BÜHL), Lena GÖßLING (80 Melanie LEUPOLZ), Sara DÄBRITZ, Giulia GWINN, Lena OBERDORF (65 Lina MAGULL), Svenja HUTH, Alexandra POPP.
(Coach: Martina VOSS-TECKLENBURG).
Spain: SANDRA PAÑOS García-Villamil, MARTA TORREJÓN Moya, María Pilar "MAPI" LEÓN Cebrián, IRENE Paredes HERNANDEZ, SILVIA MESEGUER Bellido (66 Patricia "PATRI" GUIJARRO Gutiérrez), ALEXIA PUTELLAS Segura (77 AITANA BONMATI Conca), VIRGINIA TORRECILLA Reyes, MARTA CORREDERA Rueda, JENNIFER HERMOSO Fuentes, MARIONA Caldentey Oliver (59 LUCÍA GARCÍA Córdoba), NAHIKARI GARCÍA Pérez.
(Coach: JORGE VILDA Rodríguez).
Goal: Sara DÄBRITZ (42).
Referee: Kateryna MONZUL (Ukraine) Attendance: 20,761.

13.06.2019 Parc de Princes, Paris: South Africa – China PR 0-1 (0-1)
South Africa: Kaylin SWART, Janine VAN WYK, Lebohang RAMALEPE, Bambanani MBANE, Refiloe JANE (82 Linda MOTLHALO), Mamello MAKHABANE, Kholosa BIYANA, Sibulele HOLWENI (72 Leandra SMEDA), Noko MATLOU *(YC83)*, Thembi KGATLANA, Ode FULUTUDILU (60 Jermaine SEOPOSENWE). (Coach: Desiree ELLIS).
China PR: PENG Shimeng, WU Haiyan, LIU Shanshan, LIN Yuping, WANG Shanshan, WANG Yan (81 YANG Li), ZHANG Rui, WANG Shuang, HAN Peng, GU Yasha (65 LOU Jiahui), LI Ying (78 WEI Yao). (Coach: JIA Xiuquan).
Goal: LI Ying (40)
Referee: Katalin Anna KULCSÁR (Hungary) Attendance: 20,011.

17.06.2019 Stade de la Mosson, Montpellier: South Africa – Germany 0-4 (0-3)
South Africa: Andile DLAMINI, Nothando VILAKAZI *(YC58)*, Janine VAN WYK, Lebohang RAMALEPE *(YC53)*, Refiloe JANE, Mamello MAKHABANE, Kholosa BIYANA (89 Leandra SMEDA), Busisiwe NDIMENI, Noko MATLOU, Ode FULUTUDILU (46 Rhoda MULAUDZI *(YC66)*), Amanda MTHANDI (46 Thembi KGATLANA). (Coach: Desiree ELLIS).
Germany: Almuth SCHULT, Marina HEGERING, Verena SCHWEERS (46 Carolin SIMON), Sara DOORSOUN-KHAJEH, Lina MAGULL *(YC54)*, Melanie LEUPOLZ, Sara DÄBRITZ, Giulia GWINN, Svenja HUTH (59' Linda DALLMANN), Alexandra POPP, Klara BÜHL (66 Lea SCHÜLLER).
(Coach: Martina VOSS-TECKLENBURG).
Goals: Melanie LEUPOLZ (14), Sara DÄBRITZ (29), Alexandra POPP (40), Lina MAGULL (58).
Referee: SANDRA BRAZ Bastos (Portugal) Attendance: 15,502.

17.06.2019 Stade Océane, Le Havre: China PR – Spain 0-0
China PR: PENG Shimeng, WU Haiyan, LIU Shanshan, LIN Yuping, WANG Shanshan (46 YANG Li), WANG Yan, ZHANG Rui, WANG Shuang (56 LI Wen *(YC63)*), HAN Peng, GU Yasha (87 WEI Yao), LI Ying. (Coach: JIA Xiuquan).
Spain: SANDRA PAÑOS García-Villamil, LEILA OUAHABI El Ouahabi, María Pilar "MAPI" LEÓN Cebrián, IRENE Paredes HERNANDEZ, VIRGINIA TORRECILLA Reyes, Patricia "PATRI" GUIJARRO Gutiérrez, MARTA CORREDERA Rueda, JENNIFER HERMOSO Fuentes, MARIONA Caldentey Oliver (46 ANDREA Sánchez FALCÓN), NAHIKARI GARCÍA Pérez (67 ALEXIA PUTELLAS Segura), LUCÍA GARCÍA Córdoba (86 CELIA JIMÉNEZ Delgado). (Coach: JORGE VILDA Rodríguez).
Referee: Edina ALVES BATISTA (Brazil) Attendance: 11,814.

Team	Pld	W	D	L	GF	GA	GD	Pts
Germany	3	3	0	0	6	0	+6	9
Spain	3	1	1	1	3	2	+1	4
China PR	3	1	1	1	1	1	0	4
South Africa	3	0	0	3	1	8	-7	0

GROUP C

09.06.2019 Stade du Hainaut, Valenciennes: Australia – Italy 1-2 (1-0)
Australia: Lydia WILLIAMS, Clare POLKINGHORNE, Stephanie CATLEY, Alanna KENNEDY, Ellie CARPENTER, Tameka BUTT-YALLOP (83 Elise KELLOND-KNIGHT), Emily VAN EGMOND, Chloe LOGARZO (61 Lisa DE VANNA (YC76)), Samantha KERR, Caitlin FOORD, Hayley RASO (69 Katrina GORRY). (Coach: Ante MILICIC).
Italy: Laura GIULIANI, Sara GAMA (YC21), Alia GUAGNI, Elena LINARI, Valentina CERNOIA (YC69), Aurora GALLI (46 Elisa BARTOLI), Manuela GIUGLIANO, Ilaria MAURO (58 Daniela SABATINO), Cristiana GIRELLI (YC63), Barbara BONANSEA, Valentina BERGAMASCHI (77 Valentina GIACINTI). (Coach: Milena BERTOLINI).
Goals: Samantha KERR (22) / Barbara BONANSEA (56, 90+5).
Referee: Melissa Paola BORJAS Pastrana (Honduras) Attendance: 15,380.

Samantha KERR missed a penalty kick (22).

09.06.2019 Stade des Alpes, Grenoble: Brazil – Jamaica 3-0 (1-0)
Brazil: BÁRBARA Micheline do Monte Barbosa, MÔNICA Hickmann Alves, TAMIRES Cassia Dias Gomes, LETÍCIA SANTOS de Oliveira, KATHELLEN SOUSA Feitoza (76 DAIANE Limeira Santos Silva (YC82)), Miraildes Maciel Mota "FORMIGA" (YC58), Débora Cristiane de Oliveira "DÉBINHA", BEATRIZ Zaneratto João (65 GEYSE da Silva Ferreira), Thaysa de Moraes Rosa Moreno "ISA", CRISTIANE Rozeira de Souza Silva (65 LUDMILA da Silva), ANDRESSA ALVES da Silva. (Coach: Oswaldo Fumeiro Alvarez "VADÃO").
Jamaica: Sydney SCHNEIDER, Allyson SWABY, Dominique BOND-FLASZA, Chantelle SWABY, Trudi CARTER (79 Tiffany CAMERON), Havana SOLAUN (72 Chinyelu ASHER), Deneisha BLACKWOOD, Khadija SHAW, Marlo SWEATMAN, Konya PLUMMER (YC17), Cheyna MATTHEWS (62 Jody BROWN). (Coach: Hue MENZIES).
Goals: CRISTIANE Rozeira de Souza Silva (15, 50, 64).
Referee: Riem HUSSEIN (Germany) Attendance: 17,668.

ANDRESSA ALVES da Silva missed a penalty kick (38).

13.06.2019 Stade de la Mosson, Montpellier: Australia – Brazil 3-2 (1-2)
Australia: Lydia WILLIAMS, Stephanie CATLEY, Alanna KENNEDY, Ellie
CARPENTER, Elise KELLOND-KNIGHT, Tameka BUTT-YALLOP, Emily VAN
EGMOND, Chloe LOGARZO, Samantha KERR, Emily GIELNIK (72 Hayley
RASO), Caitlin FOORD (90+5 Karly ROESTBAKKEN). (Coach: Ante MILICIC).
Brazil: BÁRBARA Micheline do Monte Barbosa, MÔNICA Hickmann Alves,
TAMIRES Cassia Dias Gomes, LETÍCIA SANTOS de Oliveira, KATHELLEN
SOUSA Feitoza, Miraildes Maciel Mota "FORMIGA" *(YC14)* (46 LUANA
Bertolucci Paixão *(YC87)*), Débora Cristiane de Oliveira "DÉBINHA", Thaysa de
Moraes Rosa Moreno "ISA", MARTA Vieira da Silva (46' LUDMILA da Silva),
CRISTIANE Rozeira de Souza Silva (75 BEATRIZ Zaneratto João), ANDRESSA
ALVES da Silva *(YC85)*. (Coach: Oswaldo Fumeiro Alvarez "VADÃO").
Goals: Caitlin FOORD (45+1), Chloe LOGARZO (58), MÔNICA Hickmann Alves
(66 og) / MARTA Vieira da Silva (27 pen), CRISTIANE Rozeira de Souza Silva (38)
Referee: Esther STAUBLI (Switzerland) Attendance: 17,032.

14.06.2019 Stade Auguste-Delaune II, Reims: Jamaica – Italy 0-5 (0-2)
Jamaica: Sydney SCHNEIDER *(YC12)*, Allyson SWABY, Chantelle SWABY (46
Marlo SWEATMAN), Havana SOLAUN, Deneisha BLACKWOOD, Khadija SHAW
(YC59), Chinyelu ASHER, Konya PLUMMER, Sashana CAMPBELL, Olufolasade
ADAMOLEKUN (76 Lauren SILVER), Mireya GREY (66 Jody BROWN).
(Coach: Hue MENZIES).
Italy: Laura GIULIANI, Sara GAMA, Alia GUAGNI (57 Lisa BOATTIN), Elisa
BARTOLI, Elena LINARI, Valentina CERNOIA, Manuela GIUGLIANO, Daniela
SABATINO, Cristiana GIRELLI (72 Valentina GIACINTI), Barbara BONANSEA,
Valentina BERGAMASCHI (65 Aurora GALLI). (Coach: Milena BERTOLINI).
Goals: Cristiana GIRELLI (12 pen, 25, 46), Aurora GALLI (71, 81).
Referee: Anna-Marie KEIGHLEY (New Zealand) Attendance: 12,016.

Cristiana GIRELLI missed a penalty kick (11).

18.06.2019 Stade des Alpes, Grenoble: Jamaica – Australia 1-4 (0-2)
Jamaica: Nicole McCLURE, Toriana PATTERSON, Allyson SWABY, Chantelle
SWABY, Deneisha BLACKWOOD, Khadija SHAW, Konya PLUMMER *(YC71)*,
Sashana CAMPBELL, Tiffany CAMERON (46 Havana SOLAUN), Cheyna
MATTHEWS (59 Trudi CARTER), Mireya GREY (72 Jody BROWN).
(Coach: Hue MENZIES).
Australia: Lydia WILLIAMS, Stephanie CATLEY, Alanna KENNEDY, Ellie
CARPENTER, Emily VAN EGMOND *(YC76)*, Katrina GORRY (87 Aivi LUIK),
Chloe LOGARZO, Karly ROESTBAKKEN, Lisa DE VANNA (63 Hayley RASO),
Samantha KERR, Emily GIELNIK (59 Caitlin FOORD). (Coach: Ante MILICIC).
Goals: Havana SOLAUN (49) / Samantha KERR (11, 42, 69, 83)
Referee: Katalin KULCSÁR (Hungary) Attendance: 17,402.

259

18.06.2019 Stade du Hainaut, Valenciennes: Italy- Brazil 0-1 (0-0)
Italy: Laura GIULIANI, Sara GAMA, Alia GUAGNI, Elisa BARTOLI *(YC15)* (71 Lisa BOATTIN), Elena LINARI, Valentina CERNOIA, Aurora GALLI, Manuela GIUGLIANO, Cristiana GIRELLI (78 Ilaria MAURO), Barbara BONANSEA, Valentina GIACINTI (63 Valentina BERGAMASCHI).
(Coach: Milena BERTOLINI).
Brazil: BÁRBARA Micheline do Monte Barbosa, MÔNICA Hickmann Alves, TAMIRES Cassia Dias Gomes, LETÍCIA SANTOS de Oliveira *(YC12)* (76 POLIANA Barbosa Medeiros), KATHELLEN SOUSA Feitoza *(YC90+4)*, Débora Cristiane de Oliveira "DÉBINHA", Andressa Cavalari Machry "ANDRESSINHA", Thaysa de Moraes Rosa Moreno "ISA", MARTA Vieira da Silva (84 LUANA Bertolucci Paixão), CRISTIANE Rozeira de Souza Silva (65 BEATRIZ Zaneratto João), LUDMILA da Silva. (Coach: Oswaldo Fumeiro Alvarez "VADÃO").
Goal: MARTA Vieira da Silva (74' pen).
Referee: Lucila VENEGAS Montes (Mexico)   Attendance: 21,669.

Team	Pld	W	D	L	GF	GA	GD	Pts
Italy	3	2	0	1	7	2	+5	6
Australia	3	2	0	1	8	5	+3	6
Brazil	3	2	0	1	6	3	+3	6
Jamaica	3	0	0	3	1	12	-11	0

GROUP D

09.06.2019 Allianz Riviera, Nice: England – Scotland 2-1 (2-0)
England: Karen BARDSLEY, Steph HOUGHTON, Lucy BRONZE, Alex GREENWOOD, Millie BRIGHT (55 Abbie McMANUS), Jill SCOTT, Keira WALSH, Ellen WHITE, Nikita PARRIS, Bethany MEAD (71 Karen CARNEY), Francesca KIRBY (82 Georgia STANWAY). (Coach: Philip NEVILLE).
Scotland: Lee ALEXANDER, Jennifer BEATTIE *(YC43)*, Sophie HOWARD (75 Chloe ARTHUR), Rachel CORSIE, Kim LITTLE, Nicola DOCHERTY *(YC47)* (55 Kirsty SMITH), Christie MURRAY (87 Elizabeth ARNOT), Claire EMSLIE, Lisa EVANS, Caroline WEIR, Erin CUTHBERT. (Coach: Michelle KERR).
Goals: Nikita PARRIS (14 pen), Ellen WHITE (40) / Claire EMSLIE (79).
Referee: Jana ADÁMKOVÁ (Czech Republic)   Attendance: 13,188.

10.06.2019 Parc des Princes, Paris: Argentina – Japan 0-0
Argentina: Vanina CORREA, Agustina BARROSO Basualdo, Aldana COMETTI, Eliana STÁBILE, Ruth BRAVO (64 Vanesa SANTANA), Florencia BONSEGUNDO (77 Mariana LARROQUETTE), Estefanía BANINI Ruiz, Miriam MAYORGA, Virginia GÓMEZ, Lorena BENÍTEZ (79 Mariela CORONEL), Sole JAIMES.
(Coach: José Carlos BORRELLO).
Japan: Ayaka YAMASHITA, Aya SAMESHIMA, Risa SHIMIZU *(YC38)*, Moeka MINAMI, Saki KUMAGAI, Emi NAKAJIMA (74 Jun ENDO), Hina SUGITA *(YC45+1)*, Yui HASEGAWA, Narumi MIURA, Yuika SUGASAWA (90 Saori TAKARADA), Kumi YOKOYAMA (57 Mana IWABUCHI *(YC85)*).
(Coach: Asako TAKAKURA).
Referee: Stéphanie FRAPPART (France)   Attendance: 25,055.

14.06.2019 Roazhon Park, Rennes: Japan – Scotland 2-1 (2-0)
Japan: Ayaka YAMASHITA, Aya SAMESHIMA *(YC19)*, Risa SHIMIZU, Nana
ICHISE, Saki KUMAGAI, Emi NAKAJIMA, Hina SUGITA, Narumi MIURA, Yuika
SUGASAWA, Mana IWABUCHI (82 Yui HASEGAWA), Jun ENDO (66 Rikako
KOBAYASHI). (Coach: Asako TAKAKURA).
Scotland: Lee ALEXANDER, Jennifer BEATTIE, Rachel CORSIE *(YC36)*, Kirsty
SMITH, Kim LITTLE, Jane ROSS (76 Lana CLELLAND), Hayley LAUDER, Lisa
EVANS (85 Fiona BROWN), Caroline WEIR, Elizabeth ARNOT (60 Claire
EMSLIE), Erin CUTHBERT. (Coach: Michelle KERR).
Goals: Mana IWABUCHI (23), Yuika SUGASAWA (37 pen) / Lana CLELLAND
(88).
Referee: Lidya TAFESSE ABEBE (Ethiopia) Attendance: 13,201.

14.06.2019 Stade Océane, Le Havre: England – Argentina 1-0 (0-0)
England: Carly TELFORD, Steph HOUGHTON, Lucy BRONZE, Alex
GREENWOOD, Abbie McMANUS, Jill SCOTT, Jade MOORE *(YC45+2)*, Nikita
PARRIS (87 Rachel DALY), Jodie TAYLOR, Bethany MEAD (81 Georgia
STANWAY), Francesca KIRBY (89 Karen CARNEY). (Coach: Philip NEVILLE).
Argentina: Vanina CORREA, Agustina BARROSO Basualdo *(YC69)*, Adriana
SACHS, Aldana COMETTI *(YC39)*, Eliana STÁBILE, Ruth BRAVO, Florencia
BONSEGUNDO, Estefanía BANINI Ruiz (68 Mariana LARROQUETTE), Miriam
MAYORGA, Lorena BENÍTEZ (77 Vanesa SANTANA), Sole JAIMES (90 Yael
OVIEDO). (Coach: José Carlos BORRELLO).
Goal: Jodie TAYLOR (62).
Referee: QIN Liang (China PR) Attendance: 20,294.

Nikita PARRIS missed a penalty kick (28).

19.06.2019 Allianz Riviera, Nice: Japan – England 0-2 (0-1)
Japan: Ayaka YAMASHITA, Aya SAMESHIMA, Risa SHIMIZU, Nana ICHISE,
Saki KUMAGAI, Emi NAKAJIMA, Hina SUGITA, Mana IWABUCHI, Kumi
YOKOYAMA (61 Yuika SUGASAWA), Rikako KOBAYASHI (62 Narumi
MIURA), Jun ENDO (85 Saori TAKARADA). (Coach: Asako TAKAKURA).
England: Karen BARDSLEY, Steph HOUGHTON, Demi STOKES, Lucy BRONZE,
Millie BRIGHT, Jill SCOTT, Keira WALSH (72 Jade MOORE), Ellen WHITE, Toni
DUGGAN (83 Nikita PARRIS), Rachel DALY, Georgia STANWAY (74 Karen
CARNEY). (Coach: Philip NEVILLE).
Goals: Ellen WHITE (14, 84)
Referee: Claudia Inés UMPIÉRREZ Rodríguez (Uruguay) Attendance: 14,319.

19.06.2019 Parc des Princes, Paris: Scotland – Argentina 3-3 (1-0)
Scotland: Lee ALEXANDER *(YC90+3)*, Jennifer BEATTIE, Rachel CORSIE, Kirsty SMITH (86 Sophie HOWARD), Kim LITTLE, Nicola DOCHERTY, Leanne CRICHTON, Claire EMSLIE, Lisa EVANS (86 Fiona BROWN), Caroline WEIR *(YC85)*, Erin CUTHBERT *(YC85)*. (Coach: Michelle KERR).
Argentina: Vanina CORREA, Agustina BARROSO Basualdo, Aldana COMETTI, Eliana STÁBILE, Ruth BRAVO, Florencia BONSEGUNDO, Estefanía BANINI Ruiz (60 Milagros MENÉNDEZ), Vanesa SANTANA (82 Miriam MAYORGA), Lorena BENÍTEZ, Mariana LARROQUETTE *(YC75)*, Sole JAIMES (70 Dalila IPPÓLITO). (Coach: José Carlos BORRELLO).
Goals: Kim LITTLE (19), Jennifer BEATTIE (49), Erin CUTHBERT (69) / Milagros MENÉNDEZ (74), Lee ALEXANDER (79 og), Florencia BONSEGUNDO (90+4 pen).
Referee: RI Hyanh-ok (North Korea) Attendance: 28,205.

Team	Pld	W	D	L	GF	GA	GD	Pts
England	3	3	0	0	5	1	+4	9
Japan	3	1	1	1	2	3	-1	4
Argentina	3	0	2	1	3	4	-1	2
Scotland	3	0	1	2	5	7	-2	1

GROUP E

10.06.2019 Stade de la Mosson, Montpellier: Canada – Cameroon 1-0 (1-0)
Canada: Stephanie LABBÉ, Shelina ZADORSKY, Allysha CHAPMAN, Kadeisha BUCHANAN, Sophie SCHMIDT, Ashley LAWRENCE, Desiree SCOTT, Jessie FLEMING, Christine SINCLAIR, Nichelle PRINCE (75' Deanne ROSE), Janine BECKIE. (Coach: Kenneth HEINER-MØLLER).
Cameroon: Annette NGO NDOM, Yvonne LEUKO, Estelle JOHNSON, Aurelle AWONA, Christine MANIE, Claudine MEFFOMETOU, Marlyse NGO NDOUMBOUK *(YC37)* (68 Gaëlle ENGANAMOUIT *(YC74)*), Raissa FEUDJIO, Jeannette YANGO (82 Charlène MEYONG), Ajara NCHOUT (67 Henriette AKABA), Gabrielle ABOUDI ONGUÉNÉ. (Coach: Alain DJEUMFA Defrasne).
Goal: Kadeisha BUCHANAN (45).
Referee: RI Hyang-ok (North Korea) Attendance: 10,710.

11.06.2019 Stade Océane, Le Havre: New Zealand – Netherlands 0-1 (0-0)
New Zealand: Erin NAYLER, Ria PERCIVAL, Abby ERCEG, Ali RILEY, Rebekah STOTT, Catherine BOTT, Betsy HASSETT (67 Annalie LONGO), Olivia CHANCE, Katie BOWEN, Rosie WHITE (74 Hannah WILKINSON), Sarah GREGORIUS (74 Paige SATCHELL). (Coach: Tom SERMANNI).
Netherlands: Sari VAN VEENENDAAL, Kika VAN ES (71 Merel VAN DONGEN), Stefanie VAN DER GRAGT, Sherida SPITSE, Daniëlle VAN DE DONK, Desiree VAN LUNTEREN, Jackie GROENEN (76 Jill ROORD), Dominique BLOODWORTH, Shanice VAN DE SANDEN (87' Lineth BEERENSTEYN), Lieke MARTENS, Vivianne MIEDEMA. (Coach: Sarina WIEGMAN).
Goal: Jill ROORD (90+2).
Referee: Edina ALVES BATISTA (BRA) Attendance: 10,654.

15.06.2019   Stade du Hainaut, Valenciennes: Netherlands – Cameroon 3-1 (1-1)
Netherlands: Sari VAN VEENENDAAL, Kika VAN ES (86' Merel VAN DONGEN),
Anouk DEKKER, Sherida SPITSE, Daniëlle VAN DE DONK (71 Jill ROORD),
Desiree VAN LUNTEREN, Jackie GROENEN, Dominique BLOODWORTH,
Shanice VAN DE SANDEN (66 Lineth BEERENSTEYN), Lieke MARTENS,
Vivianne MIEDEMA. (Coach: Sarina WIEGMAN).
Cameroon: Annette NGO NDOM, Yvonne LEUKO, Estelle JOHNSON, Christine
MANIE (YC14), Claudine MEFFOMETOU, Raissa FEUDJIO (YC68), Jeannette
YANGO, Genevieve NGO MBELECK (YC37) (66 Charlène MEYONG), Gabrielle
ABOUDI ONGUÉNÉ, Gaëlle ENGANAMOUIT (75 Henriette AKABA), Michaela
ABAM (60 Ajara NCHOUT). (Coach: Alain DJEUMFA Defrasne).
Goals: Vivianne MIEDEMA (41, 85), Dominique BLOODWORTH (48) / Gabrielle
ABOUDI ONGUÉNÉ (43).
Referee: Casey REIBELT (Australia)   Attendance: 22,423.

15.06.2019   Stade des Alpes, Grenoble: Canada – New Zealand 2-0 (0-0)
Canada: Stephanie LABBÉ, Shelina ZADORSKY, Kadeisha BUCHANAN, Sophie
SCHMIDT, Ashley LAWRENCE, Desiree SCOTT, Jessie FLEMING, Christine
SINCLAIR, Nichelle PRINCE (84 Adriana LEON), Janine BECKIE (83 Rebecca
QUINN), Jayde RIVIERE (75 Allysha CHAPMAN).
(Coach: Kenneth HEINER-MØLLER).
New Zealand: Erin NAYLER, Ria PERCIVAL, Abby ERCEG, Ali RILEY, Rebekah
STOTT, Catherine BOTT (18 Annalie LONGO), Betsy HASSETT (85 Emma KETE),
Olivia CHANCE, Katie BOWEN, Rosie WHITE, Sarah GREGORIUS (62 Anna
GREEN). (Coach: Tom SERMANNI).
Goals: Jessie FLEMING (49), Nichelle PRINCE (79).
Referee: Yoshimi YAMASHITA (Japan)   Attendance: 14,856.

20.06.2019   Stade Auguste-Delaune II, Reims: Netherlands – Canada 2-1 (0-0)
Netherlands: Sari VAN VEENENDAAL, Merel VAN DONGEN, Anouk DEKKER
(YC23), Sherida SPITSE (70 Jill ROORD), Daniëlle VAN DE DONK (87 Renate
JANSEN), Desiree VAN LUNTEREN, Jackie GROENEN, Dominique
BLOODWORTH, Shanice VAN DE SANDEN, Lieke MARTENS (70 Lineth
BEERENSTEYN), Vivianne MIEDEMA. (Coach: Sarina WIEGMAN).
Canada: Stephanie LABBÉ, Shelina ZADORSKY, Allysha CHAPMAN (69 Jayde
RIVIERE), Kadeisha BUCHANAN (YC38), Sophie SCHMIDT, Ashley
LAWRENCE, Desiree SCOTT (79 Rebecca QUINN), Jessie FLEMING, Christine
SINCLAIR (69 Adriana LEON), Janine BECKIE, Jordyn HUITEMA. (Coach:
Kenneth HEINER-MØLLER).
Goals: Anouk DEKKER (54), Lineth BEERENSTEYN (75) / Christine SINCLAIR
(60).
Referee: Stéphanie FRAPPART (France)   Attendance: 19,277.

20.06.2019 Stade de la Mosson, Montpellier: Cameroon – New Zealand 2-1 (0-0)
Cameroon: Annette NGO NDOM, Yvonne LEUKO, Estelle JOHNSON, Aurelle AWONA, Augustine EJANGUE, Raissa FEUDJIO, Jeannette YANGO (84' Ninon ABENA), Ajara NCHOUT, Gabrielle ABOUDI ONGUÉNÉ, Gaëlle ENGANAMOUIT (54' Alexandra TAKOUNDA *(YC69)*), Michaela ABAM. (Coach: Alain DJEUMFA Defrasne).
New Zealand: Erin NAYLER, Ria PERCIVAL, Abby ERCEG, Ali RILEY, Anna GREEN *(YC68)* (68 Betsy HASSETT), Rebekah STOTT, Katie DUNCAN (68 Hannah WILKINSON), Olivia CHANCE (88 Annalie LONGO), Katie BOWEN, Rosie WHITE, Sarah GREGORIUS. (Coach: Tom SERMANNI).
Goals: Ajara NCHOUT (57, 90+5) / Aurelle AWONA (80 og).
Referee: Kateryna MONZUL (Ukraine)   Attendance: 8,009.

Team	Pld	W	D	L	GF	GA	GD	Pts
Netherlands	3	3	0	0	6	2	+4	9
Canada	3	2	0	1	4	2	+2	6
Cameroon	3	1	0	2	3	5	-2	3
New Zealand	3	0	0	3	1	5	-4	0

GROUP F

11.06.2019 Roazhon Park, Rennes: Chile – Sweden 0-2 (0-0)
Chile: Claudia Christiane ENDLER Mutinelli, Camila Alejandra SÁEZ Oyaneder, Su Helen Ignacia GALAZ Espinoza, Carla Valentina GUERRERO Puelle *(YC78)*, Javiera Paz TORO Ibarra, Yanara Katherine Nicole AEDO Muñoz (84 Rocío Andrea SOTO Collao), María José URRUTIA Sánchez (59 Yesenia Andrea LÓPEZ López *(YC90+6)*), Francisca Alejandra LARA Lara, Karen Andrea ARAYA Ponce, Daniela Paz ZAMORA Mancilla, Rosario Francisca María BALMACEDA Holley. (Coach: José Antonio LETELIER Henríquez).
Sweden: Hedvig LINDAHL, Linda SEMBRANT, Nilla FISCHER, Magdalena ERICSSON *(YC67)*, Hanna GLAS, Kosovare ASSLANI, Caroline SEGER, Elin RUBENSSON (81 Madelen JANOGY), Sofia JAKOBSSON, Fridolina ROLFÖ (65 Lina HURTIG), Stina BLACKSTENIUS (65 Anna ANVEGÅRD). (Coach: Peter GERHARDSSON).
Goals: Kosovare ASSLANI (83), Madelen JANOGY (90+4).
Referee: Lucila VENEGAS Montes (Mexico)   Attendance: 15,875.

11.06.2019   Stade Auguste-Delaune II, Reims: United States – Thailand 13-0 (3-0)
United States: Alyssa NAEHER, Crystal DUNN, Abby DAHLKEMPER, Kelley
O'HARA, Samantha MEWIS, Lindsey HORAN, Julie ERTZ (69 Mallory PUGH),
Rose LAVELLE (57 Carli LLOYD), Tobin HEATH (57 Christen PRESS), Megan
RAPINOE, Alex MORGAN. (Coach: Jill ELLIS).
Thailand: Sukanya Chor CHAROENYING, Sunisa SRANGTHAISONG, Natthakarn
CHINWONG, Warunee PHETWISET (71 Orathai SRIMANEE), Ainon PHANCHA,
Kanjanapom SAENKHUN, Wilaiporn BOOTHDUANG (35 Pikul KHUEANPET),
Kanjana SUNGNGOEN, Silawan INTAMEE, Rattikan THONGSOMBUT (65
Taneekarn DANGDA (YC72)), Suchawadee NILDHAMRONG.
(Coach: Nuengrutai SRATHONGVIAN).
Goals: Alex MORGAN (12, 53, 74, 81, 87), Rose LAVELLE (20, 56), Lindsey
HORAN (32), Samantha MEWIS (50, 54) Megan RAPINOE (79), Mallory PUGH
(85), Carli LLOYD (90+2).
Referee: María Laura FORTUNATO (Argentina)   Attendance: 18,591.

16.06.2019   Allianz Riviera, Nice: Sweden – Thailand 5-1 (3-0)
Sweden: Hedvig LINDAHL, Linda SEMBRANT, Nilla FISCHER, Magdalena
ERICSSON, Hanna GLAS, Kosovare ASSLANI, Caroline SEGER (69 Olivia
SCHOUGH), Elin RUBENSSON, Anna ANVEGÅRD (77 Mimmi LARSSON),
Fridolina ROLFÖ (46 Madelen JANOGY), Lina HURTIG.
(Coach: Peter GERHARDSSON).
Thailand: Waraporn BOONSING, Sunisa SRANGTHAISONG, Natthakarn
CHINWONG (YC90+5), Ainon PHANCHA, Pikul KHUEANPET, Kanjana
SUNGNGOEN, Silawan INTAMEE (89' Sudarat CHUCHUEN), Rattikan
THONGSOMBUT (56 Orathai SRIMANEE, 81 Orapin WAENNGOEN), Pitsamai
SORNSAI, Taneekarn DANGDA (YC45), Suchawadee NILDHAMRONG.
(Coach: Nuengrutai SRATHONGVIAN).
Goals: Linda SEMBRANT (6), Kosovare ASSLANI (19), Fridolina ROLFÖ (42),
Lina HURTIG (81), Elin RUBENSSON (90+6 pen) / Kanjana SUNGNGOEN (90+1).
Referee: Salima MUKANSANGA (Rwanda)   Attendance: 9,354.

16.06.2019   Parc des Princes, Paris: United States – Chile 3-0 (3-0)
United States: Alyssa NAEHER, Ali KRIEGER, Becky SAUERBRUNN, Abby
DAHLKEMPER (82 Emily SONNETT), Tierna DAVIDSON, Morgan BRIAN,
Lindsey HORAN (YC23) (59' Allie LONG (YC88)), Julie ERTZ (46 Jessica
McDONALD), Carli LLOYD, Christen PRESS, Mallory PUGH. (Coach: Jill ELLIS).
Chile: Claudia Christiane ENDLER Mutinelli, Camila Alejandra SÁEZ Oyaneder, Su
Helen Ignacia GALAZ Espinoza (YC90+4), Carla Valentina GUERRERO Puelle,
Javiera Paz TORO Ibarra, María José URRUTIA Sánchez (68 Yessenia Estefani
HUENTEO Cheuqueman (YC80)), Claudia Paola SOTO Figueroa (46 Yesenia Andrea
LÓPEZ López), Francisca Alejandra LARA Lara (YC76) (89 Daniela Andrea PARDO
Moreno), Karen Andrea ARAYA Ponce, Daniela Paz ZAMORA Mancilla, Rosario
Francisca María BALMACEDA Holley.
(Coach: José Antonio LETELIER Henríquez).
Goals: Carli LLOYD (11, 35), Julie ERTZ (26).
Referee: Riem HUSSEIN (GER)   Attendance: 45,594.

Carli LLOYD missed a penalty kick (81).

20.06.2019   Stade Océane, Le Havre: Sweden – United States 0-2 (0-1)
Sweden: Hedvig LINDAHL, Linda SEMBRANT, Jonna ANDERSSON, Amanda
ILESTEDT, Nathalie BJÖRN, Kosovare ASSLANI (79 Lina HURTIG), Caroline
SEGER (64 Hanna GLAS), Sofia JAKOBSSON *(YC86)*, Olivia SCHOUGH (57'
Fridolina ROLFÖ), Julia ZIGIOTTI-OLME, Stina BLACKSTENIUS.
(Coach: Peter GERHARDSSON).
United States: Alyssa NAEHER, Becky SAUERBRUNN, Crystal DUNN, Abby
DAHLKEMPER, Kelley O'HARA *(YC59)*, Samantha MEWIS, Lindsey HORAN,
Rose LAVELLE (63 Christen PRESS), Tobin HEATH, Megan RAPINOE (83
Mallory PUGH), Alex MORGAN (46 Carli LLOYD). (Coach: Jill ELLIS).
Goals: Lindsey HORAN (3), Jonna ANDERSSON (50 og).
Referee: Anastasia PUSTOVOITOVA (Russia)   Attendance: 22,418.

20.06.2019   Roazhon Park, Rennes: Thailand – Chile 0-2 (0-0)
Thailand: Waraporn BOONSING *(YC85)*, Sunisa SRANGTHAISONG, Natthakarn
CHINWONG, Warunee PHETWISET (90+1 Kanjanaporn SAENGKOON), Ainon
PHANCHA, Pikul KHUEANPET, Kanjana SUNGNGOEN, Silawan INTAMEE (73
Sudarat CHUCHUEN), Rattikan THONGSOMBUT (58 Orapin WAENNGOEN),
Pitsamai SORNSAI *(YC59)*, Suchawadee NILDHAMRONG.
(Coach: Nuengrutai SRATHONGVIAN).
Chile: Claudia Christiane ENDLER Mutinelli, Camila Alejandra SÁEZ Oyaneder,
Carla Valentina GUERRERO Puelle, Yanara Katherine Nicole AEDO Muñoz, María
José URRUTIA Sánchez, Rocío Andrea SOTO Collao, Francisca Alejandra LARA
Lara, Yesenia Andrea LÓPEZ López, Karen Andrea ARAYA Ponce (46 Javiera
GREZ Valenzuela, 87' María José Alondra ROJAS Pino), Daniela Paz ZAMORA
Mancilla, Rosario Francisca María BALMACEDA Holley.
(Coach: José Antonio LETELIER Henríquez).
Goals: Waraporn BOONSING (48 og), María José URRUTIA Sánchez (80).
Referee: Anna-Marie KEIGHLEY (New Zealand)   Attendance: 13,567.

Francisca Alejandra LARA Lara missed a penalty kick (86).

Team	Pld	W	D	L	GF	GA	GD	Pts
United States	3	3	0	0	18	0	+18	9
Sweden	3	2	0	1	7	3	+4	6
Chile	3	1	0	2	2	5	-3	3
Thailand	3	0	0	3	1	20	-19	0

Ranking of third-placed teams

Team	Pld	W	D	L	GF	GA	GD	Pts
Brazil	3	2	0	1	6	3	+3	6
China PR	3	1	1	1	1	1	0	4
Cameroon	3	1	0	2	3	5	-2	3
Nigeria	3	1	0	2	2	4	-2	3
Chile	3	1	0	2	2	5	-3	3
Argentina	3	0	2	1	3	4	-1	2

266

KNOCKOUT STAGE

ROUND OF 16

22.06.2019 Stade des Alpes, Grenoble: Germany – Nigeria 3-0 (2-0)
Germany: Almuth SCHULT, Marina HEGERING, Verena SCHWEERS (46 Carolin
SIMON), Sara DOORSOUN-KHAJEH, Lina MAGULL (69 Lena OBERDORF),
Melanie LEUPOLZ (46 Klara BÜHL), Sara DÄBRITZ, Giulia GWINN, Svenja
HUTH *(YC57)*, Alexandra POPP *(YC32)*, Lea SCHÜLLER.
(Coach: Martina VOSS-TECKLENBURG).
Nigeria: Chiamaka NNADOZIE, Onome EBI, Osinachi OHALE, Chidinma OKEKE,
Ngozi OKOBI, Halimatu AYINDE, Evelyn NWABUOKU *(YC26)* (46 Rasheedat
AJIBADE *(YC82)*), Desire OPARANOZIE *(YC61)*, Francisca ORDEGA, Chinwendu
IHEZUO (75 Chinaza UCHENDU), Uchenna KANU (84 Alice Oya OGEBE).
(Coach: Thomas DENNERBY).
Goals: Alexandra POPP (20), Sara DÄBRITZ (27 pen), Lea SCHÜLLER (82).
Referee: Yoshimi YAMASHITA (Japan)   Attendance: 17,988.

22.06.2019 Allianz Riviera, Nice: Norway – Australia 1-1 (1-0,1-1) (a.e.t.)
Norway: Ingrid HJELMSETH, Ingrid WOLD (102 Synne Skinnes HANSEN), Maria
THORISDOTTIR, Maren MJELDE, Kristine HEGLAND-MINDE *(YC53)*, Caroline
Graham HANSEN, Vilde Bøe RISA *(YC105+2)*, Karina SÆVIK (72 Frida
LEONHARDSEN MAANUM), Ingrid ENGEN, Isabell HERLOVSEN (77 Lisa-
Marie KARLSENG UTLAND *(YC96)*), Guro REITEN. (Coach: Martin SJÖGREN).
Australia: Lydia WILLIAMS, Stephanie CATLEY, Alanna KENNEDY *(RC104)*,
Ellie CARPENTER (120+2 Amy HARRISON), Elise KELLON-KNIGHT (94 Clare
POLKINGHORNE), Tameka BUTT-YALLOP, Emily VAN EGMOND (116 Karly
ROESTBAKKEN), Chloe LOGARZO, Samantha KERR, Caitlin FOORD, Hayley
RASO (74 Emily GIELNIK). (Coach: Ante MILICIC).
Goals: Isabell HERLOVSEN (31) / Elise KELLON-KNIGHT (83)
Referee: Riem HUSSEIN (GER)   Attendance: 12,229.

Penalties: Caroline Graham HANSEN 1-0, Samantha KERR missed, Guro REITEN
2-0, Emily GIELNIK missed, Maren MJELDE 3-0, Stephanie CATLEY 3-1,
Ingrid ENGEN 4-1.

Norway won after extra time on penalties (4:1).

267

23.06.2019 Stade du Hainaut, Valenciennes: England – Cameroon 3-0 (2-0)
England: Karen BARDSLEY, Steph HOUGHTON, Lucy BRONZE, Alex
GREENWOOD, Millie BRIGHT, Jill SCOTT (78 Lucy STANIFORTH), Keira
WALSH, Ellen WHITE (64 Jodie TAYLOR), Toni DUGGAN, Nikita PARRIS (84
Leah WILLIAMSON), Francesca KIRBY. (Coach: Philip NEVILLE).
Cameroon: Annette NGO NDOM, Yvonne LEUKO *(YC4)*, Estelle JOHNSON,
Aurelle AWONA, Augustine EJANGUE (64 Ysis SONKENG), Raissa FEUDJIO,
Jeannette YANGO, Ajara NCHOUT, Gabrielle ABOUDI ONGUÉNÉ, Gaëlle
ENGANAMOUIT (53 Alexandra TAKOUNDA *(YC90+10)*), Michaela ABAM (68
Ninon ABENA). (Coach: Alain DJEUMFA Defrasne).
Goals: Steph HOUGHTON (14), Ellen WHITE (45+4), Alex GREENWOOD (58).
Referee: QIN Liang (China PR) Attendance: 20,148.

23.06.2019 Stade Océane, Le Havre: France – Brazil 2-1 (0-0,1-1) (a.e.t.)
France: Sarah BOUHADDI, Wendie RENARD *(YC36)*, Marion TORRENT (109 Ève
PERISSET), Griedge MBOCK Bathy, Amandine HENRY, Élise BUSSAGLIA, Amel
MAJRI (118 Sakina KARCHAOUI), Eugénie LE SOMMER, Viviane ASSEYI (81
Gaëtane THINEY), Kadidiatou DIANI, Valérie GAUVIN (90+3 Delphine
CASCARINO). (Coach: Corinne DIACRE).
Brazil: BÁRBARA Micheline do Monte Barbosa, MÔNICA Hickmann Alves,
TAMIRES Cassia Dias Gomes *(YC45+2)*, LETÍCIA SANTOS de Oliveira (89
POLIANA Barbosa Medeiros), KATHELLEN SOUSA Feitoza *(YC101)*, Mirailtes
Maciel Mota "FORMIGA" *(YC70)* (75 Andressa Cavalari Machry
"ANDRESSINHA"), Débora Cristiane de Oliveira "DÉBINHA", Thaysa de Moraes
Rosa Moreno "ISA", MARTA Vieira da Silva, CRISTIANE Rozeira de Souza Silva
(96 GEYSE da Silva Ferreira), LUDMILA da Silva (71 BEATRIZ Zaneratto João
(YC83)). (Coach: Oswaldo Fumeiro Alvarez "VADÃO").
Goals: Valérie GAUVIN (52), Amandine HENRY (107) / Thaysa de Moraes Rosa
Moreno "ISA" (63)
Referee: Marie-Soleil BEAUDOIN (Canada) Attendance: 23,965.

France won after extra time.

24.06.2019 Stade Auguste-Delaune II, Reims: Spain – United States 1-2 (1-1)
Spain: SANDRA PAÑOS García-Villamil, LEILA OUAHABI El Ouahabi, María
Pilar "MAPI" LEÓN Cebrián, IRENE Paredes HERNANDEZ *(YC85)*, María Victoria
"VICKY" LOSADA Gómez (32 NAHIKARI GARCÍA Pérez), ALEXIA PUTELLAS
Segura (79 ANDREA Sánchez FALCÓN), VIRGINIA TORRECILLA Reyes (84
MARIONA Caldentey Oliver), Patricia "PATRI" GUIJARRO Gutiérrez, MARTA
CORREDERA Rueda, JENNIFER HERMOSO Fuentes, LUCÍA GARCÍA Córdoba.
(Coach: JORGE VILDA Rodríguez).
United States: Alyssa NAEHER, Becky SAUERBRUNN, Crystal DUNN, Abby
DAHLKEMPER, Kelley O'HARA, Samantha MEWIS, Julie ERTZ, Rose LAVELLE
(89 Lindsey HORAN), Tobin HEATH, Megan RAPINOE *(YC37)* (90+7 Christen
PRESS), Alex MORGAN (85 Carli LLOYD). (Coach: Jill ELLIS).
Goals: JENNIFER HERMOSO Fuentes (9) / Megan RAPINOE (7 pen, 75 pen).
Refefee: Karalin KULCSÁR (Hungary) Attendance: 19,633.

24.06.2019 Parc des Princes, Paris: Sweden – Canada 1-0 (0-0)
Sweden: Hedvig LINDAHL, Linda SEMBRANT, Nilla FISCHER, Magdalena ERICSSON, Hanna GLAS, Kosovare ASSLANI *(YC68)*, Caroline SEGER, Elin RUBENSSON (79 Nathalie BJÖRN), Sofia JAKOBSSON, Fridolina ROLFÖ *(YC45)* (89 Lina HURTIG), Stina BLACKSTENIUS (90+4 Anna ANVEGÅRD).
(Coach: Peter GERHARDSSON).
Canada: Stephanie LABBÉ, Shelina ZADORSKY, Allysha CHAPMAN (84 Jayde RIVIERE), Kadeisha BUCHANAN *(YC85)*, Sophie SCHMIDT, Ashley LAWRENCE, Desiree SCOTT, Jessie FLEMING, Christine SINCLAIR, Nichelle PRINCE (64 Adriana LEON), Janine BECKIE (84 Rebecca QUINN).
(Coach: Kenneth HEINER-MØLLER).
Goal: Stina BLACKSTENIUS (55).
Referee: Kate JACEWICZ (Australia) Attendance: 38,078.

Janine BECKIE missed a penalty kick (69).

25.06.2019 Stade de la Mosson, Montpellier: Italy – China PR 2-0 (1-0)
Italy: Laura GIULIANI, Sara GAMA, Alia GUAGNI, Elisa BARTOLI, Elena LINARI, Valentina CERNOIA, Manuela GIUGLIANO, Cristiana GIRELLI (39 Aurora GALLI), Barbara BONANSEA (71 Martina ROSUCCI), Valentina GIACINTI, Valentina BERGAMASCHI (63 Ilaria MAURO).
(Coach: Milena BERTOLINI).
China PR: PENG Shimeng, WU Haiyan, LIU Shanshan, LIN Yuping, WANG Shanshan (61 SONG Duan), WANG Yan (62 WEI Yao), ZHANG Rui, WANG Shuang, HAN Peng, GU Yasha (46 YANG Li), LI Ying. (Coach: JIA Xiuquan).
Goals: Valentina GIACINTI (15), Aurora GALLI (49).
Referee: Edina ALVES BATISTA (Brazil) Attendance: 17,492.

25.06.2019 Roazhon Park, Rennes: Netherlands – Japan 2-1 (1-1)
Netherlands: Sari VAN VEENENDAAL, Stefanie VAN DER GRAGT, Merel VAN DONGEN (85 Kika VAN ES), Sherida SPITSE, Daniëlle VAN DE DONK (87 Jill ROORD), Desiree VAN LUNTEREN, Jackie GROENEN, Dominique BLOODWORTH, Shanice VAN DE SANDEN (68 Lineth BEERENSTEYN), Lieke MARTENS, Vivianne MIEDEMA. (Coach: Sarina WIEGMAN).
Japan: Ayaka YAMASHITA, Aya SAMESHIMA, Risa SHIMIZU, Nana ICHISE, Saki KUMAGAI *(YC89)*, Emi NAKAJIMA (72 Yuka MOMIKI), Hina SUGITA, Yui HASEGAWA, Narumi MIURA, Yuika SUGASAWA, Mana IWABUCHI (90+1 Saori TAKARADA). (Coach: Asako TAKAKURA).
Goals: Lieke MARTENS (17, 90 pen) / Yui HASEGAWA (43)
Referee: Melissa Paola BORJAS Pastrana (Honduras) Attendance: 21,076.

269

QUARTER FINALS

27.06.2019   Stade Océane, Le Havre: Norway – England 0-3 (0-2)
Norway: Ingrid HJELMSETH, Ingrid WOLD (85 Synne Skinnes HANSEN), Maria
THORISDOTTIR (YC88), Maren MJELDE, Kristine HEGLAND-MINDE, Caroline
Graham HANSEN, Vilde Bøe RISA, Karina SÆVIK (64 Lisa-Marie KARLSENG
UTLAND), Ingrid ENGEN, Isabell HERLOVSEN, Guro REITEN (74 Amalie Vevle
EIKELAND). (Coach: Martin SJÖGREN).
England: Karen BARDSLEY, Steph HOUGHTON, Demi STOKES, Lucy BRONZE,
Millie BRIGHT, Jill SCOTT, Keira WALSH, Ellen WHITE, Toni DUGGAN (54
Bethany MEAD), Nikita PARRIS (88 Rachel DALY), Francesca KIRBY (74 Georgia
STANWAY). (Coach: Philip NEVILLE).
Goals: Jill SCOTT (3), Ellen WHITE (40), Lucy BRONZE (57).
Referee: Lucila VENEGAS Montes (Mexico)   Attendance: 21,111.

Nikita PARRIS missed a penalty kick (83).

28.06.2019   Parc des Princes, Paris: France – United States 1-2 (0-1)
France: Sarah BOUHADDI, Wendie RENARD, Marion TORRENT, Griedge
MBOCK Bathy (YC4), Amandine HENRY, Élise BUSSAGLIA (YC90+4), Amel
MAJRI, Eugénie LE SOMMER (82 Viviane ASSEYI), Gaëtane THINEY, Kadidiatou
DIANI, Valérie GAUVIN (76 Delphine CASCARINO). (Coach: Corinne DIACRE).
United States: Alyssa NAEHER, Becky SAUERBRUNN, Crystal DUNN, Abby
DAHLKEMPER, Kelley O'HARA, Samantha MEWIS (82 Carli LLOYD), Julie
ERTZ, Rose LAVELLE (63 Lindsey HORAN), Tobin HEATH, Megan RAPINOE
(87 Christen PRESS), Alex MORGAN. (Coach: Jill ELLIS).
Goals: Wendie RENARD (81) / Megan RAPINOE (5, 65).
Referee: Kateryna MONZUL (Ukraine)   Attendance: 45,595.

29.06.2019   Stade du Hainaut, Valenciennes: Italy – Netherlands 0-2 (0-0)
Italy: Laura GIULIANI, Sara GAMA, Alia GUAGNI (YC67), Elisa BARTOLI (46
Lisa BOATTIN), Elena LINARI (YC41), Valentina CERNOIA (YC73), Aurora
GALLI, Manuela GIUGLIANO, Barbara BONANSEA (55 Daniela SABATINO
(YC79)), Valentina GIACINTI, Valentina BERGAMASCHI (75' Annamaria
SERTURINI). (Coach: Milena BERTOLINI).
Netherlands: Sari VAN VEENENDAAL, Stefanie VAN DER GRAGT (87 Anouk
DEKKER), Merel VAN DONGEN, Sherida SPITSE, Daniëlle VAN DE DONK,
Desiree VAN LUNTEREN, Jackie GROENEN, Dominique BLOODWORTH,
Shanice VAN DE SANDEN (56 Lineth BEERENSTEYN), Lieke MARTENS,
Vivianne MIEDEMA (87 Jill ROORD). (Coach: Sarina WIEGMAN).
Goals: Vivianne MIEDEMA (70), Stefanie VAN DER GRAGT (80).
Referee: Claudia Inés UMPIÉRREZ Rodríguez (Uruguay)   Attendance: 22,600.

29.06.2019   Roazhon Park, Rennes: Germany – Sweden 1-2 (1-1)
Germany: Almuth SCHULT, Marina HEGERING, Sara DOORSOUN-KHAJEH,
Carolin SIMON (43 Leonie MAIER), Lina MAGULL, Sara DÄBRITZ, Giulia
GWINN, Svenja HUTH, Alexandra POPP, Linda DALLMANN (46 Dzsenifer
MAROZSÁN), Lea SCHÜLLER (70 Lena OBERDORF).
(Coach: Martina VOSS-TECKLENBURG).
Sweden: Hedvig LINDAHL, Linda SEMBRANT, Nilla FISCHER (66 Amanda
ILESTEDT), Magdalena ERICSSON, Hanna GLAS, Kosovare ASSLANI, Caroline
SEGER, Elin RUBENSSON (86 Nathalie BJÖRN), Sofia JAKOBSSON, Fridolina
ROLFÖ (YC56) (90+5 Lina HURTIG), Stina BLACKSTENIUS. (Coach: Peter
GERHARDSSON).
Goals: Lina MAGULL (16) / Sofia JAKOBSSON (22), Stina BLACKSTENIUS (48).
Referee: Stéphanie FRAPPART (France)   Attendance: 25,301.

SEMI-FINALS

02.07.2019   Groupama Stadium, Décines-Charpieu:
England – United States 1-2 (1-2)
England: Carly TELFORD, Steph HOUGHTON, Demi STOKES, Lucy BRONZE,
Millie BRIGHT (YC40,YC86), Jill SCOTT, Keira WALSH (71 Jade MOORE), Ellen
WHITE, Nikita PARRIS (YC90+5), Bethany MEAD (58 Francesca KIRBY), Rachel
DALY (89 Georgia STANWAY). (Coach: Philip NEVILLE).
United States: Alyssa NAEHER, Becky SAUERBRUNN (YC83), Crystal DUNN,
Abby DAHLKEMPER, Kelley O'HARA (87 Ali KRIEGER), Lindsey HORAN
(YC47), Julie ERTZ, Rose LAVELLE (65 Samantha MEWIS), Tobin HEATH (80
Carli LLOYD), Alex MORGAN, Christen PRESS. (Coach: Jill ELLIS).
Goals: Ellen WHITE (19) / Christen PRESS (10), Alex MORGAN (31).
Referee: Edina ALVES BATISTA (Brazil)   Attendance: 53,512.

Steph HOUGHTON missed a penalty kick (84).

03.07.2019   Groupama Stadium, Décines-Charpieu:
Netherlands – Sweden 1-0 (0-0,0-0) (a.e.t.)
Netherlands: Sari VAN VEENENDAAL, Stefanie VAN DER GRAGT, Merel VAN
DONGEN, Sherida SPITSE (YC85), Daniëlle VAN DE DONK (YC116), Desiree
VAN LUNTEREN, Jackie GROENEN, Dominique BLOODWORTH, Lieke
MARTENS (46 Jill ROORD), Vivianne MIEDEMA, Lineth BEERENSTEYN (71
Shanice VAN DE SANDEN). (Coach: Sarina WIEGMAN).
Sweden: Hedvig LINDAHL, Linda SEMBRANT, Nilla FISCHER, Magdalena
ERICSSON (111 Jonna ANDERSSON), Hanna GLAS, Kosovare ASSLANI,
Caroline SEGER, Elin RUBENSSON (79 Julia ZIGIOTTI-OLME (YC94)), Sofia
JAKOBSSON, Lina HURTIG (79 Madelen JANOGY), Stina BLACKSTENIUS (111
Mimmi LARSSON). (Coach: Peter GERHARDSSON).
Goal: Jackie GROENEN (99).
Referee: Marie-Soleil BEAUDOIN (Canada)   Attendance: 48,452.

Netherlands won after extra time.

THIRD PLACE PLAY-OFF

06.07.2019   Allianz Riviera, Nice: England – Sweden 1-2 (1-2)
England: Carly TELFORD, Steph HOUGHTON, Lucy BRONZE, Alex
GREENWOOD, Abbie McMANUS (83 Rachel DALY), Jill SCOTT, Jade MOORE
(YC90+4), Ellen WHITE, Nikita PARRIS (74 Karen CARNEY), Bethany MEAD (50
Jodie TAYLOR), Francesca KIRBY. (Coach: Philip NEVILLE).
Sweden: Hedvig LINDAHL *(YC85)*, Linda SEMBRANT, Nilla FISCHER,
Magdalena ERICSSON, Hanna GLAS, Nathalie BJÖRN (72 Amanda ILESTEDT),
Kosovare ASSLANI (46 Julia ZIGIOTTI-OLME), Caroline SEGER, Sofia
JAKOBSSON, Fridolina ROLFÖ (27 Lina HURTIG), Stina BLACKSTENIUS.
(Coach: Peter GERHARDSSON).
Goals: Francesca KIRBY (31) / Kosovare ASSLANI (11), Sofia JAKOBSSON (22).
Referee: Anastasia PUSTOVOITOVA (Russia)   Attendance: 20,316.

FINAL

07.07.2019   Groupama Stadium, Décines-Charpieu:
United States – Netherlands 2-0 (0-0)
United States: Alyssa NAEHER, Becky SAUERBRUNN, Crystal DUNN, Abby
DAHLKEMPER *(YC41)*, Kelley O'HARA (46 Ali KRIEGER), Samantha MEWIS,
Julie ERTZ, Rose LAVELLE, Tobin HEATH (87 Carli LLOYD), Megan RAPINOE
(79 Christen PRESS), Alex MORGAN. (Coach: Jill ELLIS).
Netherlands: Sari VAN VEENENDAAL, Stefanie VAN DER GRAGT *(YC60)*,
Anouk DEKKER (73 Shanice VAN DE SANDEN, Sherida SPITSE *(YC10)*, Daniëlle
VAN DE DONK, Desiree VAN LUNTEREN, Jackie GROENEN, Dominique
BLOODWORTH, Lieke MARTENS (70 Jill ROORD), Vivianne MIEDEMA, Lineth
BEERENSTEYN. (Coach: Sarina WIEGMAN).
Goals: Megan RAPINOE (61 pen), Rose LAVELLE (69).
Referee: Stéphanie FRAPPART (France)   Attendance: 57,900.

UNITED STATES BECAME WORLD CHAMPIONS